Fraud and Breach of Warranty: Buyers' Claims and Sellers' Defences

Second Edition

Fraud and Breach of Warranty: Buyers' Claims and Sellers' Defences

Second Edition

Simon Salzedo KC
Barrister, Brick Court Chambers

Andrew McIntyre
Barrister, Brick Court Chambers

Sophie Shaw
Barrister, Brick Court Chambers

Bloomsbury Professional

LONDON • DUBLIN • EDINBURGH • NEW YORK • NEW DELHI • SYDNEY

BLOOMSBURY PROFESSIONAL
Bloomsbury Publishing Plc
50 Bedford Square, London, WC1B 3DP, UK
1385 Broadway, New York, 10018, USA
29 Earlsfort Terrace, Dublin 2, Ireland

BLOOMSBURY and the Diana logo are trademarks of Bloomsbury Publishing Plc

First published in Great Britain 2024

British Library Cataloguing-in-Publication Data

A catalogue record for this book is available from the British Library.

ISBN:	HB:	978 1 52652 902 2
	Epdf:	978 1 52652 904 6
	Epub:	978 1 52652 903 9

Typeset by Evolution Design & Digital (Kent)
Printed and bound by CPI Group (UK) Ltd, Croydon, CR0 4YY

To find out more about our authors and books visit www.bloomsburyprofessional.com. Here you will find extracts, author information, details of forthcoming events and the option to sign up for our newsletters

Preface to second edition

We noted in the Preface to the first edition in 2020 that we had not been sure if there would be sufficient material for such a specialist text, but that new authorities had come thick and fast in the preceding couple of years.

That trend has continued apace. Business sales have given rise to an ever-increasing frequency of judicial decisions. The law on many points appears reasonably settled so that several recent decisions do no more than apply agreed legal principles to findings of fact. We have not mentioned all of them.

However, there remain a few areas that consistently raise more difficult issues. Notification clauses are prominent in the legal issues that require resolution and the regular raising of fraud in the business sale context raises both the temperature of litigation and unresolved points in the law of fraudulent misrepresentation. Perhaps surprisingly, quantum remains an area where parties and courts do not always avoid error.

We are grateful to our publishers for requesting a second edition and we hope that this book will continue to be useful to practitioners in this area.

Simon Salzedo KC
Andrew McIntyre
Sophie Shaw
Brick Chambers, London
March 2024

Preface to first edition

When we learn the common law of warranties and fraud, we begin with old cases and examples which, as often as not, involve the sale of a horse. Horse sales are a fertile source of warranty and fraud issues because of two factors. First, the outcome of the transaction for the buyer is uncertain and depends on the outturn of numerous risks. Some of those risks involve facts that exist at the date of the transaction but are hard to discern: most notably, the health of the horse. Other risks involve post-transaction events that may affect the value of the horse. Second, there is an inherent and unavoidable asymmetry of information between seller and buyer about the first set of risks. The seller may be presumed to know more about the health of the horse than the buyer, but will not be omniscient and the extent of their knowledge may be open to dispute.

Business sales have all the features that made horse sales so interesting to our predecessors. And they have one more feature in addition: the sums of money paid for a business can be very large. This makes the balance of risks between seller and buyer a matter of economic significance to the parties. In short, there is much to argue about if it all goes wrong.

Starting to write this book, we were not sure if there would be sufficient material for such a specialist text. But new authorities have come thick and fast in the last couple of years and we have ended up with more to say than we first expected. We hope that indicates that the book will also be of utility to its readers.

Simon Salzedo QC
Andrew McIntyre
Sophie Shaw
Brick Court Chambers, London
July 2020

Dedication

For our families.

Contents

Table of Cases

C

H

I

J

K

N

O

T

Table of Statutes

Table of Statutory Instruments

Chapter 1

Introduction

WHY THIS BOOK?

1.01 A case could be made that there are no specialist fields of English private civil law apart from the traditional broad divisions into common law and equitable origins, and wrongs relating to contract, torts and fiduciary relationships. However, as time passes, the UK economy grows and decisions of the court are reported ever more frequently, individual areas of those broad divisions are filled in in more detail. Advisers and practitioners come across particular types of case over and again and can benefit from a digest of the detail that has been worked out in that area. Business sale cases now occupy a distinct sub-division of the fields of contract, tort and equitable wrongs and there are enough of them that practitioners may benefit from a specialist digest.

1.02 It is important at the outset to acknowledge that the law of business sale cases merely occupies corners of broader legal fields. If a new problem arises it falls to be answered by the general principles in those fields, not by any special rules for business sale cases. But most problems are not new and it is hoped that this book will assist by describing the relevant corner of the field in sufficient detail to enable a practitioner to identify which paths are well trodden and which require fresh navigational consideration.

1.03 The vast bulk of business sale cases concern allegations of misrepresentation – often fraudulent misrepresentation – and breaches of warranty. Hence the name of this book: Fraud and Breach of Warranty.

THE PARTIES

1.04 Any legal document begins by identifying the parties. For most of this book, there are only two: the seller, or vendor; and the buyer, or purchaser. We have not tried to be prescriptive, or even consistent, in using one or other of the commonest terms for these parties. Either party might be singular or plural and might consist of natural or legal persons. Again, we have not aimed for extreme precision in drawing such distinctions which are not at the heart of the issues that arise in most cases. In Chapter 11 a few minor characters are introduced, who might be important in less run of the mill cases.

1.05 In business sale claims, the allegations are usually, though not always, made by a buyer against a seller. Chapter 10 addresses sellers' claims as a category of their own. For the rest, the claimant will be the buyer, save – naturally – where the context otherwise requires.

THE CONTRACT

1.06 A business sale invariably takes place pursuant to a written contract to which, at least, the buyer and seller are party. Such contracts are, almost as invariably, professionally drawn. They are often called the Share Purchase Agreement ('SPA') or Asset Purchase Agreement ('APA') and these are terms and abbreviations that we use with abandon hereafter. SPAs are more common and we sometimes use 'SPA' as a proxy for both types of agreement. Sometimes, outside this book, 'SPA' stands for 'Sale and Purchase Agreement', which could be either an SPA or an APA.

1.07 Many issues in business sale cases ultimately come down to questions of construction of the SPA or APA. The courts have emphasised over and again that each contract is construed on its own merits and that reference to authority is of limited helpfulness in that process. This fundamental point should be taken as a qualification upon a great deal of what is said in this book about contractual issues. The courts respect party autonomy, meaning, among other things, that the parties will not be assumed to have contracted in the same way as other parties may have done in reported cases if the words of their agreement do not justify that assumption.

1.08 'Party autonomy' is closely related to 'freedom of contract'. The latter term was more commonly used in judgments in earlier times;[1] the former is more frequently referred to now, by way of importation from private international law and the law of arbitration.

1 'Freedom of contract' was described as being 'still fundamental to our commercial law' by Moore-Bick LJ in *Transocean Drilling v Providence Resources* [2016] EWCA Civ 372.

1.09 The essential principles of contractual interpretation have been the subject of surprisingly many recent judgments of the highest courts. Perhaps it is a topic of such general interest and importance that no self-respecting judge can resist the call to place their own stamp on it. In any event, at the time of writing, the happy position has been reached that there is rarely any dispute about what the principles are. They have been established in a series of classic cases in the Supreme Court, culminating in the business sale case of *Wood v Capita*.[1]

1 [2017] UKSC 24. The key earlier cases are *Rainy Sky v Kookmin Bank* [2011] UKSC 50 and *Arnold v Britton* [2015] UKSC 36. For greater detail on the principles of contractual interpretation in English law, the best source is Sir Kim Lewison's *The Interpretation of Contracts,* (Sweet & Maxwell, 2024) in its 8th edition as we write this.

1.10 In short, contractual interpretation of a private contract is the ascertainment of the meaning which the contract would be understood to bear by a reasonable person with all the background knowledge available to all the parties. This is an objective process, which involves reading any disputed term in the context of the entire agreement (including any other agreements entered into as part of the same transaction) and the other background that was available to both parties. The course of negotiations leading up to the contract is excluded from consideration as admissible background, as is evidence of the subjective understanding of the parties. The plethora of authority partly reflects the differing emphasis which is appropriate in different circumstances as between the literal words of the contract and the available background including what has been called 'commercial common sense'.

1.11 Because SPAs are generally professionally drafted and often negotiated in small detail, the emphasis in their interpretation will generally tend to the side of giving effect to the literal words of the agreement rather than straining them to comply with commercial common sense or finding that they are erroneous. The same factors make it unusual to find implied terms in business sale contracts.[1] As with any other contract, rectification is available where the written terms do not accord with the actual common intention of the parties at the time of contracting.[2]

1 A rare case where an implied term was found is *Zedra Trust Company (Jersey) Ltd v Nobahar-Cookson* [2019] EWHC 2191 (Comm).

2 For an SPA case where rectification would have been granted had not the interpretation been decided in line with the parties' intentions, see *Gwynt y Mor Ofto Plc v Gwynt y Mor Offshore Windfarm Ltd* [2020] EWHC 850 (Comm).

1.12 The application of modern principles of contractual interpretation to business sale contracts was summarised by Leggatt LJ (with the agreement of the Chancellor and Longmore LJ) in *Minera Las Bambas v Glencore Queensland Ltd*, as follows:

> 'The principles of English law which the court must apply in interpreting the relevant contractual provisions are not in dispute. They have most recently been summarised by the Supreme Court in *Wood v Capita Insurance Services Ltd* [2017] UKSC 24; [2017] AC 1173 at paras 10–14. In short, the court's task is to ascertain the objective meaning of the relevant contractual language. This requires the court to consider the ordinary meaning of the words used, in the context of the contract as a whole and any relevant factual background. Where there are rival interpretations, the court should also consider their commercial consequences and which interpretation is more consistent with business common sense. The relative weight to be given to these various factors depends on the circumstances. As a general rule, it may be appropriate to place more emphasis on textual analysis when interpreting a detailed and professionally drafted contract

> such as we are concerned with in this case, and to pay more regard to context where the contract is brief, informal and drafted without skilled professional assistance. But even in the case of a detailed and professionally drafted contract, the parties may not for a variety of reasons achieve a clear and coherent text and considerations of context and commercial common sense may assume more importance.'[1]

1 [2019] EWCA Civ 972 at [20].

1.13 Chapters 2 to 6 of this book concern the contractual provisions that feature most prominently in business sale disputes. Foremost among these are warranties and indemnities, which are the subject matter of Chapter 2. Warranties in particular may be the most distinctive feature of SPAs. While other contracts have terms which may be called 'warranties', the word has a special connotation in relation to SPAs. Sellers generally warrant key features of the business they are selling and these are often the first port of call for a disappointed buyer when things go wrong.

1.14 SPAs also regularly contain important limitations on the seller's liability, which are often the subject of dispute. Chapter 3 examines these provisions and the cases that have arisen about them. A specific kind of limitation that is characteristic of SPAs is the qualification of warranties by reference to the knowledge of the seller, or of the buyer, or by reference to disclosures made as part of the sale process. These knowledge and disclosure provisions are considered in Chapter 4.

1.15 A line of authority has grown up in relation to notification provisions which are very characteristic of SPAs. These may be vital, because they generally require certain steps to be taken by a buyer within relatively short timescales (short, in any event, in the context of underlying time bars of six years), failing which the claim will be lost altogether. While the cases in this area, discussed in Chapter 5, always stress that each clause must be interpreted individually rather than by reference to authority, the cases are instructive as to the approach that is likely and, for claimants, cautionary.

1.16 Escrows and earnouts are discussed in Chapter 6. They are also characteristic features of SPAs and can be of tactical importance (escrow provisions) or give rise to claims by sellers (earnouts).

OTHER TOPICS

1.17 The book then moves to the issue of misrepresentation and, especially, fraudulent misrepresentation in Chapter 7. Misrepresentation can vitiate the entire contract or lead to damages assessed on the tortious basis. Claims for misrepresentation are therefore legally very different from claims for breach of warranty, even though the two are often based on the same underlying facts. In litigating such claims it is important to be aware of the differences, especially given the temptation to treat them as similar where the facts are common.

1.18 It is in relation to misrepresentation that it is important to bear in mind another traditional principle of English law, namely 'caveat emptor', or 'buyer beware'. English law traditionally imposes liability for wrongful acts, but far fewer positive obligations to act in particular ways. Sellers are not, in general, obliged to point out the flaws in what they are offering for sale. It is for buyers to make their own inspection, or ask the right questions, in order to elicit the information they require to make their decision whether to buy. This principle can be obscured by the fact that an SPA is often professionally and comprehensively drafted. But it remains there as a kind of bedrock presumption in favour of a seller where there is merely silence.

1.19 Misrepresentation claims overcome the principle of caveat emptor, by demonstrating that the seller was not silent, but took equitable or tortious responsibility for something not in the contract by speaking out with a view to inducing the buyer to purchase. In many, if not most, business sale cases, the claimant will need to demonstrate fraud in order to found a misrepresentation claim that can overcome the limitations in the SPA.

1.20 A number of tricky issues can arise about the remedies for business sale breaches of warranty and fraud. These are sometimes overlooked until the end of a case, but they deserve earlier consideration. The calculation of damages frequently causes confusion as to the proper approach to valuation and the correct counterfactuals to consider. This is the subject of Chapter 8. Other remedies are addressed in Chapter 9 including the question of the juridical nature of rescission and the extent to which it is available where a buyer has taken over the target company and operated it for some time before electing to rescind.

1.21 As already noted above, we look at claims by sellers in Chapter 10 and a host of miscellaneous issues concerning business sale litigation in Chapter 11.

Chapter 2

Warranties and Indemnities and their Breach

2.01 There is no general principle that the terms of a contract must be capable of classification into existing categories.[1] However, the drafting of a business sale agreement often involves drawing on well-known forms of words and types of clause. In particular, many standard forms of warranty and indemnity clause, developed and honed over years of commercial practice, have come before the courts for consideration.

1 *AXA SA v Genworth Financial International Holdings, Inc* [2019] EWHC 3376 (Comm) at [66].

WARRANTIES AND INDEMNITIES GENERALLY

Nature and purpose of warranties and indemnities

2.02 A warranty is a contractual undertaking as to a matter of fact. The party giving the warranty promises, and thereby assumes liability under the contract for, the accuracy of the matters stated. If the warranty is, or becomes, false, then the promisor is, without more, in breach of contract and is obliged to pay damages. As Andrew Baker QC (sitting as a judge of the High Court) put it in *Idemitsu Kosan Co, Ltd v Sumitomo Corporation*:

> 'When a seller, by the terms of the contract under which he sells, "warrants" something about the subject matter sold, he is making a contractual promise. Nothing less. But also I think (and all things being equal) nothing more. That is so just as much for a warranty as to some then present or past matter of fact as it is for a warranty as to the future. By contracting on terms by which he warrants something, the seller is not purporting to impart information; he is not making a statement to his buyer. He is making a promise, to which he will be held as a matter of contract in the sense that any breach of the warranty will be actionable as a breach of contract, subject to any other relevant terms of the contract and to general principles of the law of contract, for example as to remedies.'[1]

1 [2016] EWHC 1909 (Comm) at [14].

2.03 An indemnity is a contractual promise by one party to reimburse the other for losses suffered if a particular set of circumstances arises. An indemnity differs conceptually from a warranty in that it makes no promise about the accuracy of any underlying facts and the occurrence of the circumstances that trigger the indemnity does not give rise a breach on the part of the promisor. Non-payment under the indemnity will be a breach of contract, but the mere occurrence of the circumstances is not.

2.04 Both warranties and indemnities are tools used to allocate risk between the parties to the contract. In the business sale context, they allow the parties to depart from the usual principle of caveat emptor and apportion to the seller certain risks arising from the state or quality of the business or assets being sold. Used in conjunction with (for example) an appropriate exclusion or limitation clause, they may also give the parties a greater measure of certainty and control over the extent of their potential liabilities.

2.05 The process of negotiating and agreeing warranties in a business sale agreement also gives the buyer an additional opportunity to obtain information about the business and to adjust its offer accordingly: as discussed further below, the seller usually gives disclosure against the warranties so as to qualify their scope.[1]

1 See Chapter 4.

2.06 The express warranties and indemnities included in an SPA are likely to be broader in scope than the warranties and indemnities included in an APA, because the purchaser in a share purchase transaction is acquiring the legal entity in its entirety, with all its attendant potential liabilities. The purchaser is therefore likely to require a wider set of contractual assurances from the vendor as to the state of the business. By contrast, an acquisition of assets alone will not necessarily entail the purchaser taking on the liabilities of the business. However, an APA may be subject to warranties implied by statute (for example, under the Sale of Goods Act 1979) that would not apply to an SPA.

2.07 Warranties as to the state of a business or assets being sold will typically be given by the seller, within whose knowledge these matters fall. However, since a warranty is essentially a method of contractual risk allocation rather than a statement by which the warrantor purports to impart information, there is no reason that the warranty cannot be given by some other person or entity, such as the seller's parent company or individual selling shareholders who might also be managers of the company. The buyer too may give warranties as to matters within its knowledge and/or for which it agrees to take responsibility – for example, whether it knows of facts giving rise to a possible claim against the seller.

Warranties, conditions and intermediate terms

2.08 As well as bearing the more general meaning given above, the word 'warranty' is used in a technical sense in contract law to refer to a term of an agreement the breach of which gives rise to a right to claim damages but not a right to treat the agreement as having come to an end. A 'warranty' in this narrow sense is distinguished from a 'condition', the breach of which entitles the innocent party to treat the contract as repudiated; and from an 'intermediate' (or 'innominate') term, which may or may not give rise to a right to treat it as repudiated depending on the nature and consequences of the breach.[1]

1 *Hongkong Fir Shipping Co Ltd v Kawasaki Kisen Kaisha Ltd* [1962] 2 QB 26.

2.09 The fact that a contract term is expressly described in the agreement as a 'warranty' does not inevitably mean that it will be classified as a warranty in the technical sense, such that its breach will only give rise to a right to damages. Whether a term is a warranty in the technical sense will be a question of construction in each case, taking into account matters such as whether the term goes to the root of the parties' bargain and whether damages would be an adequate remedy for breach.[1] However, in business sale contracts, warranties are generally expressly stated to be such and are rarely open to any other construction.[2]

1 *HIH Casualty & General Insurance Ltd v New Hampshire Insurance Co* [2001] EWCA Civ 735. See [**9.67**].
2 See further [**9.66**]–[**9.71**].

Warranties and representations

2.10 The relationship between warranties and representations is considered further in Chapter 7. In summary, a representation is a statement of fact made by or on behalf of one person upon which another person is entitled to rely. A representation made prior to entry into an agreement may be incorporated into the agreement as a warranty, and it does not cease to be a representation merely because it is so incorporated. Moreover, a warranty may be expressly deemed by contracting parties to be a representation for the purposes of a misrepresentation claim. However, despite apparent confusion in a number of first instance decisions, a warranty cannot by itself, in the absence of such provision or some separate pre-contractual statement of fact, give rise to a claim for misrepresentation.

2.11 While liability for misrepresentation can only be established if the representation in question induced the claimant to enter the contract, there is no specific need in a claim for breach of warranty to show that the claimant relied on the warranty that was breached.[1] In *Invertec Ltd v De Mol Holdings BV*,[2] Arnold J considered whether the claimant had relied on certain warranties contained in the SPA; presumably, however, he was referring to the representations that he held to have been made in the same terms as the warranties.

1 *Karim v Wemyss* [2016] EWCA Civ 27 at [26].
2 [2009] EWHC 2471 (Ch) at [365]–[377]. See further Chapter 7 below.

Collateral warranties

2.12 As suggested above, contracts will commonly contain express written warranties, often (but not necessarily) described in terms as warranties, and often adopting familiar forms of words.

2.13 However, in certain circumstances, a claim may also be brought in relation to a warranty that does not form part of the primary contract – for example, because it was given prior to entry into the primary contract, and not repeated in the primary contract; or because it was given orally, when the primary contract was expressed in writing. Such a warranty may be enforceable as a 'collateral' warranty.[1] In *New York Laser Clinic Ltd v Naturastudios Ltd*, Cavanagh J described a collateral warranty as follows:

> 'A collateral warranty is a promise or assertion, with contractual force, which leads to a contract being entered into. If the warranty that is relied upon turns out to be false, the person to whom it is made may have a cause of action against the promisor for breach of contract. It is not necessary that the warranty was made fraudulently, or even negligently.'[2]

1 *De Lassalle v Guildford* [1901] 2 KB 215.
2 [2019] EWHC 2892 (QB) at [34].

2.14 A collateral warranty takes effect as a contract separate from the primary agreement.[1] Accordingly, it will only be enforceable if it was intended to have legal effect and (save where executed as a deed) supported by its own consideration. Consideration for a collateral warranty is usually given by entry into the primary contract. For example, in *Esso Petroleum Co Ltd v Mardon*,[2] an assurance given by the claimant oil company as to the likely throughput of a petrol station was held to give rise to a collateral warranty in circumstances where it had induced the defendant to take on a business lease of the premises.

1 *Heilbut, Symons & Co v Buckleton* [1913] AC 30 at 47 per Lord Moulton.
2 [1976] QB 801.

2.15 If a collateral warranty transpires to be false, the contract breached is the collateral contract consisting of the warranty, not the primary agreement. It follows that a collateral warranty may be given by, and enforced against, a person who is not a party to the primary contract. *New York Laser Clinic* is an example of such a case: there, the defendant gave the claimant certain assurances as to the performance of devices it supplied, which induced the claimant to purchase the devices from hire-purchase companies (who, had in turn, purchased the machines from the defendant). When the assurances turned out to be untrue, the claimant had a cause of action against the defendant for breach of the collateral warranties, notwithstanding that the claimant and defendant had no direct contractual relationship under the primary agreements.

2.16 A collateral warranty may be effective even if inconsistent with the terms of the primary contract.[1]

1 *Brikom Investments Ltd v Carr* [1979] QB 467.

2.17 The doctrine of collateral warranty was conceived and largely developed prior to the enactment of the Misrepresentation Act 1967 and, as Lord Denning MR explained in *Esso v Mardon*,[1] was frequently used to circumvent the rule that an innocent misrepresentation gave no right to damages. Now that damages are recoverable for non-fraudulent misrepresentation in certain circumstances, it may be less likely that a pre-contractual statement of fact will be held to amount to a collateral warranty.[2]

1 [1976] QB 801 at 817.
2 See Chapter 7.

Construction of warranties and indemnities

2.18 Warranties and indemnities are interpreted in accordance with the normal principles of contractual construction.[1] In *Gwynt Y Mör Ofto Plc v Gwynt Y Mör Offshore Wind Farm Ltd*,[2] Phillips LJ (sitting in the High Court) observed, in relation to an indemnity clause, that there was 'no reason to start from the premise that the provisions of the SPA which impose liabilities on the [seller] should be read restrictively'.

1 See Chapter 1.
2 [2020] EWHC 850 (Comm) at [31].

2.19 In *Wood v Sureterm Direct Ltd*, Christopher Clarke LJ, considering the proper construction of an indemnity clause in a SPA, referred to the well-known principles set out in *Arnold v Britton*[1] and *Rainy Sky SA v Kookmin Bank*,[2] but emphasised the need to take care in in using 'business common sense' as a determinant of construction:

> 'What is business common sense may depend on the standpoint from which you ask the question. Further the court will not be aware of the negotiations between the parties. What may appear, at least from one side's point of view, as lacking in business common sense, may be the product of a compromise which was the only means of reaching agreement.
>
> …

> In effect a balance has to be struck between the indications given by the language and the implications of rival constructions. The clearer the language the less appropriate it may be to construe or confine it so as to avoid a result which could be characterised as unbusinesslike. The more unbusinesslike or unreasonable the result of any given interpretation the more the court may favour a possible interpretation which does not produce such a result and the clearer the words must be to lead to that result.'[3]

1 [2015] AC 1619.
2 [2011] 1 WLR 2900.
3 [2015] EWCA Civ 839 at [29]–[31].

2.20 On appeal, the Supreme Court agreed with the Court of Appeal that the indemnity clause in question, which covered losses 'following and arising out of claims or complaints registered with the FSA' relating to mis-selling, did not apply to mis-selling related losses which did not arise from customer claims or complaints.[1] Lord Hodge noted that the SPA may have been a poor deal from the buyer's point of view, but said that 'it is not the function of the court to improve their bargain'.

1 [2017] AC 1173.

Date as of which a warranty is given

2.21 In many business sale cases, there will be a delay between the date on which contracts are signed and exchanged and the date on which the transaction is completed. Where this is so, it will be important for the parties to identify the date as of which the warranties are given, in case material facts relevant to the warranties change in the period between execution and completion. There are various ways of providing for this scenario: for example, the warranties may be expressed to be given as of the date of completion;[1] or they may be given as of the date of execution and be deemed to be repeated as of the date of completion;[2] or they may be given as of the date of execution only, but the vendor may be required to disclose any relevant change of circumstances occurring prior to completion.[3]

1 See, eg, *MAN Nutzfahrzeuge AG v Freightliner Ltd* [2005] EWHC 2347 (Comm) at [62].
2 See, eg, *Equitix EEEF Biomass 2 Ltd v Fox* [2021] EWHC 2531 (TCC) at [183].
3 See further DR Thomson (ed), *Sinclair on Warranties and Indemnities on Share and Asset Sales* (12th edn, Sweet & Maxwell, 2023) at 4.14–4.18. On material adverse change clauses, see [**2.52**]–[**2.56**] and [**9.72**]–[**9.75**].

2.22 Where no specific provision is made in this regard, the starting point is likely to be that the warranties are given as of the moment the agreement is concluded: this was the approach taken in the business sale case of *BSA International SA v Irvine*.[1] It was also the approach taken by agreement of both parties in *The Hut Group v Nobahar-Cookson*.[2]

1 [2010] CSOH 12 at [30]. *BSA v Irvine* was wrongly described as supporting the date of completion in *Lonedale v Scottish Motor Auctions* [2011] CSOH 04 at [183], but in *Lonedale* there was no gap between exchange and completion and the alternative date proposed was rather later.
2 [2014] EWHC 3842 (QB) at [180(1)].

2.23 In *Belfairs Management Ltd v Sutherland*,[1] the warranties in an SPA were said to be 'true and accurate in all respects and not misleading at the date of this Agreement'. The SPA was dated 1 February 2008 and signed by the vendors on the same date, but was not signed by the purchaser until a completion meeting on 11 February 2008. Norris J held that the accuracy of the warranties was to be judged 'as at the 1 February 2008 … or possibly 11 February 2008', though later he observed that it was common ground between the parties that they should be assessed as of 11 February 2008.[2] The Court of Appeal also treated 11 February 2008 as the relevant date.[3] Nothing appeared to turn on this point in *Belfairs*, but the case illustrates the potential for confusion if the contract is at all ambiguous about the relevant date.

1 [2010] EWHC 2276 (Ch) at [6(b)].
2 At [151].
3 [2013] EWCA Civ 185 at [52].

Objective and subjective standards

2.24 There is no reason in principle that a warranty cannot be drafted by reference to a subjective standard, but it is likely that clear words will be required to achieve this.

2.25 In *Belfairs*,[1] the sellers warranted that the target company was not a party to any agreement, arrangement or commitment which could not 'readily be fulfilled or performed by it on time'. At first instance, Norris J held that this required a subjective assessment of future performance by the sellers themselves, and was not 'an absolute warranty relating to outcomes'. However, the Court of Appeal disagreed, noting that the clause said nothing about the sellers or their views as to the achievability of the target company's commitments, or about anyone's opinion being relevant to the inquiry.[2] Rather, on its proper construction, the warranty required an objective assessment as to whether the target company's commitments could readily be fulfilled or performed on time.

1 [2010] EWHC 2276 (Ch) at [166]–[170].
2 [2013] EWCA Civ 185 at [52].

Qualified warranties

2.26 A warranty may be qualified by reference to the knowledge of the party giving it: for example, a seller may warrant that a particular fact is true 'so far as it is aware'. Explicit provision may also be made as to: (a) whose knowledge is to count as that of the warrantor; and (b) what degree of knowledge is necessary to give rise to a breach of warranty. These issues, and the relevance of the parties' knowledge generally, are discussed further in Chapter 4.

2.27 Where there is no specific reference to a party's knowledge or awareness in a warranty, the default position is likely to be that the warranty is not so qualified and that the warrantor 'assumes responsibility for the accuracy of the statement irrespective of his own state of knowledge or belief': *Belfairs*.[1]

1 [2010] EWHC 2276 (Ch) at [154(l)].

Specific features of indemnities

2.28 Indemnities are often thought to offer greater protection to buyers than warranties. In many cases this will be true, but as a rule the scope of an indemnity will depend on the construction of the relevant terms of the contract in question. In *AXA v Genworth*, a claim arising from the sale of an insurance business, Bryan J deprecated an approach that sought first to classify a term as an indemnity and then to identify the consequences of such classification as '*the tail wagging the dog*'. Rather, he said:

> 'I am satisfied that the correct starting point to the construction of Clause 10.8 is not to start with a quest for the precise nature of the clause but rather to construe such clause in accordance with its language, the other terms of the SPA and the admissible factual matrix to the SPA applying well established principles as to contractual construction. Having done so its meaning will be established, and at that stage it will be possible (if appropriate) to express any conclusions as to the nature of the obligation created thereby.'[1]

1 [2019] EWHC 3376 (Comm) at [65].

2.29 Thus, while it has been suggested that parties may generally recover losses under indemnity clauses that would be too remote to be recovered as damages for breach of contract, this will not be true of every indemnity clause.[1] Similarly, an indemnity may allow for recovery of losses without any need to demonstrate causation in the ordinary sense,[2] but there is no universal rule to this effect: in the business sale case of *Al-Hasawi v Nottingham Forest Football Club Ltd*,[3] a party's attempt to rely on an indemnity clause failed because it had not been able to establish causation.

1 *Total Transport Corp v Arcadia Petroleum Ltd* [1998] 1 Lloyd's Rep 351 at 360–361.
2 *Campbell v Conoco (UK) Ltd* [2002] EWCA Civ 704.
3 [2019] EWCA Civ 2242 at [55].

2.30 The decision in *MAN Nutzfahrzeuge AG v Freightliner Ltd* further illustrates that the scope of recovery under an indemnity clause will be a matter of construction in each case. In *MAN Nutzfahrzeuge*,[1] the sellers of a business indemnified the buyers against, inter alia, 'damages suffered … as a result of, in respect of, connected with, or arising out of, under or pursuant to' any breach of warranty or misrepresentation. The sellers argued that this limited the buyers' recovery to the contractual measure of loss. The buyers argued that it included 'reliance' losses. Moore-Bick LJ (sitting in the High Court) held that the clause did indemnify the buyers against reliance losses, but (drawing upon *SAAMCO v York Montague Ltd*[2]) not against 'the entire consequences of entering into the agreement insofar as they could not be said to flow from the inaccuracy of the particular representation'. Without this limitation, he observed, a minor and innocent misrepresentation made honestly and without any want of due care could have exposed the sellers to liability for any and all losses suffered by the buyers as a result of entering into the SPA.

1 [2005] EWHC 2347 (Comm) at [196].
2 [1997] AC 191.

2.31 Where there is a question as to whether or not a particular loss falls within the scope of an indemnity given in an SPA, it may be relevant to examine the scope of any warranties provided in the same agreement. In *Gwynt Y Mör*, Phillips LJ considered the proper construction of a provision in an SPA by which the seller of a business had agreed to indemnify the buyer against damage to certain equipment sustained 'prior to Completion'. The seller had also given a warranty to the effect that no defect or damage had been discovered in the equipment as at the date of the SPA. A dispute arose between the parties as to whether the indemnity covered damage sustained prior to the date of the SPA. Noting the warranty and related provisions on disclosure and limitation of damages, Phillips LJ said:

> '… it would be remarkable, and unlikely to be intended, that a carefully structured and limited warranty was subsumed and rendered largely otiose by an all-embracing indemnity. Further, the Indemnity would remove the suggested incentive to make full disclosure if the defendants would be liable for reinstating the damage in any event. To the extent that there is a question about whether the indemnity covers the warranted matters, the existence of the Warranty is a powerful indication that the indemnity does not so extend.'[1]

Looking at the indemnity in its proper context, he therefore held that it applied only to damage occurring between the execution of the SPA and the date of completion.

1 At [41].

2.32 In at least one case, it has been suggested that a claim under an indemnity is a claim for debt (as opposed to a claim for damages) and is therefore not subject to the usual rules on mitigation of loss.[1] However, in *AXA v Genworth*,[2] Bryan J said (obiter) that 'the weight of authority, and the more orthodox view, is that a claim under a contract of indemnity is a claim in unliquidated damages'. It follows that, in the absence of any specific agreement, it should not be assumed that no duty to mitigate arises in relation to a claim under an indemnity.

1 *Royscot Commercial Leasing Ltd v Ismail* (29 April 1993, unreported, Court of Appeal).
2 At [117], citing *Firma C-Trade SA v Newcastle Protection and Indemnity Association* [1991] 2 AC 1 at 35 per Lord Goff.

PARTICULAR TYPES OF WARRANTY AND INDEMNITY

2.33 The following sections discuss the treatment by the courts of some of the warranties and indemnities most frequently given by vendors in business sale agreements. They are not intended comprehensively to list all of the matters that are commonly warranted or indemnified against in such agreements, but rather to highlight particular areas of interest that have arisen in the authorities, and which may have implications in future cases for buyers' claims or sellers' defences.

Accounts

2.34 The target company's statutory accounts will be a common subject of warranties in an SPA. Frequently, the vendor will warrant that the statutory accounts give a true and fair view of its profits and losses in the relevant accounting period and its state of affairs as at the last day of that period;[1] that they have been prepared in accordance with specified accounting standards;[2] and/or that they comply with relevant legislation.[3]

1 See, eg, *Belfairs* [2010] EWHC 2276 (Ch) at [6(k)].
2 See, eg, *Idemitsu*, appendix to judgment.
3 See, eg, *Bottin International Investments Ltd v Venson Group plc* [2006] EWHC 3112 (Ch) at [81].

2.35 Warranties may also be given in respect of management accounts, which are not subject to specific statutory requirements and are (usually) not audited. For example, it may be warranted that the management accounts have been prepared in good faith;[1] that they have been prepared on a basis consistent with that of the audited accounts;[2] and/or that they fairly present the company's assets, liabilities, profits and losses.[3]

1 See, eg, *Invertec Ltd v De Mol Holdings BV* at [4].
2 See, eg, *Ageas (UK) Ltd v Kwik-Fit (GB) Ltd* [2013] EWHC 3261 (QB) at [8].
3 See, eg, *The Hut Group Ltd v Nobahar-Cookson* at [36].

2.36 It does not follow from the fact that companies have more leeway in preparing management accounts that courts will be less willing to scrutinise them. In *Bottin*, warranties given in an SPA in respect of the accuracy of the target company's management accounts were qualified by reference to the seller's knowledge. Blackburne J held that those warranties had been breached because, amongst other things, there was a huge and unexplained variance between the management accounts prepared in October 1999 (which showed a pre-tax profit of £566,544) and the statutory accounts for 1999 (which showed a loss of £2.226 million). In the premises, it could not be said that the management accounts 'fairly reflect[ed] the trading position of the group' to the best of the seller's information, knowledge and belief at the relevant time.

True and fair view

2.37 The concept of a 'true and fair view' is well-established in company law (appearing, for example, in the Companies Act 2006, s 393), and cases decided under the statutory test are likely to be considered by the courts when construing the meaning of this phrase when used in a contractual warranty. This was the approach taken in *Macquarie Internationale Investments Ltd v Glencore UK Ltd*.[1]

1 [2010] EWCA Civ 697.

2.38 In *Macquarie*, various warranties were given in an SPA in relation to both the audited accounts and the management accounts of the target group. In relation to the audited accounts, it was warranted (inter alia) that these had been prepared in accordance with relevant accounting standards and gave a true and fair view of the group's assets and liabilities. In relation to the management accounts, it was warranted (inter alia) that these had been prepared in accordance with relevant accounting standards; fairly reflected the group's financial position, cash and working capital position; and were not misleading in any material respect. In fact, however, both sets of accounts failed to disclose that the group had incurred a substantial liability to a third party as a result of a billing error which did not come to light until after completion.

2.39 At first instance,[1] Andrew Smith J held that both sets of accounts had been prepared in accordance with the applicable accounting standards: there had not been sufficient evidence of the liability's existence at the relevant time for it properly to be recognised as such in the accounts. He also rejected the purchaser's argument that the audited accounts did not give a true and fair view of the group's liabilities, considering the authorities and noting that, absent exceptional circumstances, compliance with the relevant accounting standards meant that the accounts gave a true and fair view. For largely the same reasons, he held that there was no breach of the less stringent tests imposed by the management accounts warranties.

1 [2009] EWHC 2267 (Comm).

2.40 On appeal, the buyer challenged Andrew Smith J's findings in relation to the management accounts only. Dismissing the appeal, Jackson LJ noted that:

> '… courts have treated compliance with published professional standards as strong evidence that the accounts in question did present a true and fair view … There are no exceptional circumstances in the present case which would have led to the conclusion that the draft audited accounts, despite being prepared in accordance with the relevant accounting standards, did not give a true and fair view of the assets and liabilities.'[1]

In relation to the warranty that the management accounts fairly reflected the group's position, he said:

> '… warranty (a) does not purport to tell the reader anything about unknown or undiscoverable liabilities, whether large or small. It tells the reader that the management accounts fairly reflect those assets and liabilities of the Group which the accounting bases, practices and policies permit or require to be included.'[2]

In respect of the warranty that the management accounts were not misleading in any material respect, he added:

> 'Warranty (c) must be interpreted on the same basis. The phrase "not misleading" does not mean that the management accounts represent the actual position on the ground. Nor does it mean that the management accounts include financial liabilities which are unknown or undiscoverable. The phrase means that the management accounts contain the information which the reader would expect management accounts prepared on the stated basis to contain. The fact that these are management accounts and the reference to their purpose (which the judge found to be internal management) warns the reader that there will be a lesser degree of accuracy than one would expect from audited, statutory accounts.'[3]

In his concurring judgment, Lord Neuberger MR suggested that the narrower warranties given in relation to the management accounts added 'very little' to the overarching warranty that the accounts had been prepared in accordance with relevant accounting standards.[4]

1 [2010] EWCA Civ 697 at [52], [55].
2 At [66].
3 At [67].
4 At [86].

2.41 The Court of Appeal therefore concluded in *Macquarie* that, in circumstances where the undisclosed liability was unknown to and not reasonably discoverable by the vendor at the time of the sale, and its discovery did not require the accounts to be re-stated according to accounting standards, there had been no breach of any of the accounting warranties.

Materiality

2.42 An error or a departure from the strict application of accounting standards will not necessarily mean that the accounts in question do not present a true and fair view of the company's assets and liabilities; it will depend on the materiality of the error or departure. Materiality is an established concept in financial accounting and auditing. In *Sycamore Bidco Ltd v Breslin*, Mann J discussed materiality in the following terms:

> 'The question of materiality is, as the experts accepted, one of subjective judgment on which views of accountants might differ in any given case. In the present case the burden is on the claimants as part of their case to establish the failure of the accounts to portray a full and fair picture and to comply with accounting standards. Since materiality is a subjective concept, and there is room for a difference of views within a range, in order to dismiss the views of one accountant or another I would have to find that that accountant's views were ones that no reasonable accountant could hold. If a reasonable accountant would think that the difference was immaterial, then the claimants would not have fulfilled their burden. That is a heavy burden to fulfil.'[1]

1 [2012] EWHC 3443 (Ch) at [252].

2.43 On the facts of *Sycamore*,[1] it was held that an overstatement of turnover in the target company's accounts by £260,000 (or around 4%) was significant in both absolute and percentage terms; that turnover was a significant item for anyone viewing the accounts; and that the company would have known that its accounts would be seen by potential purchasers. All of these factors pointed towards the conclusion that the overstatement was a material one. The accounts therefore failed to comply with applicable accounting standards and to present a true and fair view of the company's profit and loss, and the vendor was in breach of warranty in relation to the £260,000 overstatement. On the other hand, a separate overstatement of turnover by £43,000 was agreed by the parties' experts not to be material, and Mann J held that this shortcoming was therefore 'not, by itself, sufficient to render the accounts neither true nor fair'.

1 [2012] EWHC 3443 (Ch) at [273].

2.44 However, the characterisation of materiality as a 'subjective concept' in *Sycamore* sits uneasily with the first instance decision in *Macquarie*,[1] in which Andrew Smith J suggested that materiality 'is to be assessed objectively' Rather than asking whether the accountant's views were ones that no reasonable accountant could hold, Andrew Smith J adopted a test of materiality that focused on whether the item in question would have been 'important to the reasonable reader'. On the facts of *Macquarie*, the omission of a liability from the target group's accounts was not material because it would only have made a difference of around 0.5% to the overall figures for turnover and cost of sales in the accounts (or around 1% in the management accounts); and because potential purchasers would primarily be interested in the group's customer base and turnover, rather than the precise amount of its profit or loss (which was, on any view, small).

1 [2009] EWHC 2267 (Comm) at [189].

2.45 In principle, therefore, there remains an element of uncertainty as to the proper approach to materiality in the context of a warranty of true and fair presentation. However, the difference in approach between *Sycamore* and *Macquarie* may be more academic than real. Although he suggested in *Macquarie* that the test of materiality was an objective one, Andrew Smith J also acknowledged that:

> '… it will often be a matter for the judgment of the preparer of the accounts whether or not an item is material and there will often be a margin of discretion in this regard. This could, I think, be of some importance in determining whether there had been breach of a warranty of this kind: it seems to me that [the vendors] have a strong argument that an item would only properly be regarded as material to the financial statements, and so its omission would only give rise to a breach of warranty, if a person signing the accounts could not properly regard it as immaterial.'[1]

This comes very close to the test adopted by Mann J in *Sycamore*. In the Court of Appeal in *Macquarie*, Jackson LJ rejected the buyer's submission that, in effect, 'material' meant 'material to a purchaser', stating that: 'In my view the concept of materiality in warranty (c) must be interpreted by reference to published accounting standards, not by reference to some different or more rigorous test.'[2]

1 [2009] EWHC 2267 (Comm) at [190].
2 [2010] EWCA Civ 697 at [68]. For the submission being rejected see [63].

2.46 Moreover, it is clear from both judgments that similar factors were ultimately taken into account in the assessment of materiality – in particular, the relative significance of the misstatement as a percentage of the overall figures given in the accounts; and the likely importance of the misstated figures to users of the accounts, including prospective buyers. This is consistent withthe statement of Jacob J in *Thomas Witter Ltd v TBP Industries*[1] that '"Material" must be viewed through the eyes of the purchaser: what is "material" to him is what matters.' These also appeared to be the key factors considered to be relevant to the issue of materiality in the more recent business sale case of *Oversea-Chinese Banking Corp Ltd v ING Bank NV*[2] (though no reference was made to either *Macquarie* or *Sycamore* in Moulder J's judgment in that case).

1 [1996] 2 All ER 573 at 605c. This should be understood as referring to what is material to a reasonable purchaser, rather than to the particular purchaser if they happen to have special requirements.
2 [2019] EWHC 676 (Comm) at [96]–[114].

2.47 One other issue that occasionally arises in relation to materiality is the question of aggregation, ie whether a number of separate shortcomings in accounts which are not individually material can be aggregated together to establish a breach of warranty. In *Sycamore*, Mann J suggested, obiter, that they could: 'Imagine this warranty given in relation to accounts in respect of which a £50,000 error would be material, but a £500 one not, and then imagine 100 £500 errors. It would be nonsensical to say that since none of individual errors were individually material the accounts were therefore not materially mis-stated. On those facts, there would be a £50,000 error in the accounts, and the fact that it was made up of a number of small, and otherwise immaterial, items cannot matter.'[1]

1 [2012] EWHC 3443 (Ch) at [353].

2.48 In *Macquarie*,[1] Andrew Smith J expressed a similar view (also obiter), but with the caveat that only items 'of a similar nature' could be aggregated.

1 [2009] EWHC 2267 (Comm) at [216].

Draft accounts

2.49 In *Belfairs*,[1] various specific warranties were given in relation to the target company's audited accounts, but a further general warranty was also given to the effect that 'all written information' supplied to the buyer or its advisers was complete, accurate and not misleading. This warranty was held to apply to a set of draft accounts that had been provided to the buyer in the run-up to the signing of the SPA. As the draft accounts were materially different from the final accounts approved by the company's board, did not present a true and fair view of the company's affairs and misstated certain figures, the seller was held to be in breach of the general warranty as to the completeness and accuracy of 'all written information' given to the buyer.[2]

1 [2010] EWHC 2276 (Ch) at [6(j)].
2 This finding was not challenged on appeal: [2013] EWCA Civ 185.

Events occurring after the end of the last accounting period

2.50 Warranties given as to the accuracy of accounts can provide buyers with a measure of certainty in relation to the target company's financial affairs during the relevant accounting period. However, a substantial period of time may elapse between the end of the previous accounting period and the completion of the sale. Broadly, there are two approaches to protecting the buyer against changes in the interim.

Locked box accounts

2.51 The first option is for the vendor to provide accounts as of a specified date prior to the signing of the SPA, and to give warranties in respect of their accuracy. The specified date may or may not be the date of the last statutory accounts. The parties will agree the consideration for the sale on the basis of these 'locked box' accounts, in principle placing the risk of any decline in value after the date of the accounts on the buyer. However, the parties may seek to temper this risk to the buyer through the use of warranties. For example, the vendor may warrant that it is not aware of any factors likely to have a material adverse impact on its business;[1] or that the company's business will be carried on in the ordinary course and without interruption until completion of the sale.[2]

1 See, eg, *Bottin* at [81(iv)] and [81(vi)].
2 See, eg, *Belfairs* [2010] EWHC 2276 (Ch) at [6(n)].

2.52 The parties may go further still and include a warranty providing that, between the end of the last accounting period and the completion date, there will be no material adverse change in the company's overall financial position. In the event of such a change, the warranty will be breached; thus the risk of material adverse events occurring prior to completion is shifted to the vendor.

2.53 *Levison v Farin*[1] illustrates the last approach. In *Levison*, the defendant vendor warranted that there would be no material adverse change in her business's financial position and net asset value prior to completion, subject to 'normal trade fluctuations'. Five months elapsed between the date of the last accounts and the completion of the sale. In that period, the business's net asset value declined by around 20%. Gibson J held that this change was an adverse and material one; and that, because it was caused by 'the virtual cessation of trade in the companies' as a result of the vendor's illness, it was neither 'normal' nor a 'trade fluctuation'. The vendor was therefore in breach of warranty.

1 [1978] 2 All ER 1149.

2.54 The contracting parties may agree between themselves what will amount to a material adverse change for the purpose of such a clause: for example, in *Kitcatt v MMS UK Holdings Ltd*,[1] 'material adverse impact' was defined as a reduction of at least 20% in the relevant company's operating income or 10% of its revenue. In the absence of advance agreement, however, disputes over the precise threshold of 'materiality' may have to be litigated.

1 [2017] EWHC 675 (Comm) at [196].

2.55 In *Decision Inc Holdings Proprietary Ltd v Garbett*,[1] Mr Simon Gleeson (sitting as a Deputy Judge of the High Court) noted a 'dearth of English authority on material adverse change'. Drawing from cases decided in the context of loan agreements (in which a material adverse change in the financial status of a borrower may constitute a default under the loan), he held that an adverse change would be 'material' in the context of an SPA if 'a reasonable person who had entered into the transaction with the aims and objectives of the buyer would have sought to withdraw from or renegotiate the transaction had he known of the change'.[2] While acknowledging that the accounting profession 'tends to use a ready reckoner of around 5% of profit before tax as its measure of materiality', he held that there was no necessary read-across between the accounting concept of materiality and the use of the term in a contract: in the contractual context, determining materiality 'is a matter of evidence, and cannot be reduced to a mathematical expression'.[3] On the facts, he held that a decline in monthly turnover from historical figures ranging between £314,998 and £515,372 to £269,999 and £283,360 was not so significant as to be a material change.[4]

1 [2023] EWHC 588 (Ch).
2 At [105]–[106].
3 At [112].
4 There was no appeal against this part of the judgment ([2023] EWCA Civ 1284).

2.56 However, in *Finsbury Food Group Plc v Axis Corporate Capital UK Ltd*, Mr Lionel Persey KC (sitting as a judge of the High Court) took a slightly different approach, holding that 'material' referred to a change that was 'substantial' or 'significant' as opposed to *de minimis*.[1] The seller having warranted that there had been no material adverse change in the target company's trading position or turnover in the nine months between the accounts date and the completion date, he went on to hold that only a change of more than 10% in the target company's total group sales would be sufficiently significant or substantial to trigger a breach of warranty. *Decision Inc Holdings* was not referred to in *Finsbury Food Group*, the judgment in the former not having been published at the time of the trial in the latter.

1 [2023] EWHC 1559 (Comm) at [119]–[124].

Completion accounts

2.57 The second option is for the parties to agree the consideration for the sale on the basis of a set of earlier accounts, but to provide for a price adjustment mechanism based on a set of 'completion accounts' to be drawn up as of the date of completion. This effectively shifts the risk of the business declining in value prior to completion onto the vendor.

2.58 In contrast to the preparation of audited accounts, the drawing up of the completion accounts will often be a mutual process, requiring both vendor and purchaser to reach agreement. Disputes may be referred to a third-party expert accountant.[1] Such a process may obviate the need for the vendor to give warranties in respect of the completion accounts. However, warranties may still be given in respect of the accuracy of the interim accounts. In principle, inaccuracies in the interim accounts may give rise to liability for breach of warranty even if corrected in the completion accounts, as O'Farrell J noted in *Triumph Controls UK Ltd v Primus International Holding Co.*[2] However, in practice the vendor's liability for such breach is likely be limited to the extent that the consideration has already been adjusted to reflect the correction, as in *Triumph* itself.[3]

1 See, eg, *O'Brien v TTT Moneycorp Ltd* [2019] EWHC 1491 (Comm).
2 [2019] EWHC 565 (TCC) at [354].
3 See also *Cypher v Bertram* (4 June 2001, unreported, Chancery Division); and see further Chapter 3.

2.59 Where a business sale agreement includes both a price adjustment mechanism based on the completion accounts and a warranty as to the accuracy of the interim accounts, it may not always be clear how the parties are to proceed in the event of a dispute. In *Campbell v Océ (UK) Ltd*,[1] the purchasers of a printing business alleged that, while the sellers had been running the business, they had been overcharging their customers; and the purchasers therefore sought to add a debit item to the completion accounts to reflect the possibility of claims by such customers. The sellers disputed this and sought a declaration from the court that no such adjustments fell to be made. The purchasers counterclaimed for damages, contending that the non-disclosure of the overcharging amounted to a breach of warranty. Laddie J struck out the sellers' claim for declaratory relief, holding that the SPA provided for disputes over the completion accounts to be determined by an independent expert accountant, and – although the overcharging issue also formed the basis of the breach of warranty counterclaim – there was nothing in the SPA to suggest that the expert was to have anything other than exclusive jurisdiction over such disputes. In effect, by proposing an adjustment to the completion accounts, the purchasers had committed the parties to the expert determination process. It is unclear from the judgment whether the converse would have been possible: ie whether the purchasers could have sidestepped the expert determination process by opting not to propose any adjustment to the completion accounts, but instead to pursue a claim for breach of warranty in respect of the interim accounts.

1 [2005] EWHC 458 (Ch).

2.60 A similar issue arose in *General Electric Co v Al Alpine US Bidco Inc*,[1] in which the SPA provided for disputes over the completion statement to be referred to an independent accountant. The sellers contended that a number of disputes raised by the buyers could not properly be resolved through the completion statement process: the completion statement was designed only to 'true-up', as of the date of completion, the financials which had been agreed upon executing the SPA. The completion statement was not, the sellers said, an opportunity for the buyers to revisit the historical accounting treatments and judgments used by the sellers to prepare their earlier accounts. To the extent that any historical accounting treatment had been incorrect, the sellers argued that the appropriate remedy was a claim for breach of the warranties given in respect of those historical accounts, and sought declaratory relief from the court to this effect. On an application by the buyers, however, Miles J stayed the court proceedings in favour of the expert process, noting that the declarations sought by the seller were hypothetical given that: (i) it remained to be seen whether the expert accounting firm would in fact adjudicate on the historical accounting issues; and (ii) even if it did, that adjudication might be in the sellers' favour. It was not therefore necessary for the court to grapple with the underlying question of whether the disputes were properly matters for the completion statement or matters for a breach of warranty claim.

1 [2021] EWHC 45 (Ch).

Projections and forecasts

2.61 In the course of negotiating the sale of a business, the seller may make projections and forecasts as to the business's future performance.

2.62 In contrast to representations, which are not actionable where they amount to assurances about the future, there is no reason why a warranty cannot be given as to the occurrence or non-occurrence of future events. However, to reflect the uncertainty inherent in predicting future performance, a vendor may prefer not to warrant that a particular target will be achieved; rather, it may provide a forecast without warranting its accuracy, instead warranting only that the forecast was prepared or calculated in a particular way. For example, in *Bottin*,[1] the vendor warranted that a forecast of anticipated profits had been 'carefully and diligently prepared' on a basis consistent with that adopted in preparing the statutory accounts.

1 At [81(ii)].

2.63 Where there is ambiguity as to the scope of a warranty about future performance, the courts may construe it in such a way as to limit it to a warranty about the way in which the forecast was prepared. In *Lion Nathan Ltd v CC Bottlers Ltd*, the vendor of a soft drinks business provided a statement of projected revenue which forecast earnings of NZ$2.23 million, and warranted that the statement had been:

> '… calculated in good faith, and on a proper basis having regard for all known matters which are likely to affect EBIT [earnings before interest and tax] for the relevant periods to a material degree and in the opinion of the guarantor as at the date hereof and the forecast results referred to therein are achievable based on current trends and performance.'[1]

The second part of this warranty ('the forecast results … are achievable') was capable of being interpreted in different ways. The Court of Appeal of New

Zealand saw it as a warranty that the company was 'reasonably capable of achieving earnings of $2,223,000 in the period in question'. However, the Privy Council disagreed, holding that it was a warranty that 'reasonable care had been taken in the preparation of the forecast'.[2]

1 [1996] 1 WLR 1438 at 1440.
2 At 1442.

2.64 What, then, will give rise to the breach of such a warranty? In *Lion Nathan*,[1] Lord Hoffmann (giving the judgment of the Privy Council) said that whether reasonable care had been taken in the preparation of forecast was a question of process rather than outcome. Thus, if a profit forecast of NZ$1.25 million was given with a NZ$50,000 margin of error, but a careless mistake led to the forecast being overstated by NZ$25,000, the forecast would not have been made with reasonable care, notwithstanding that the overstatement fell within the given margin of error. On the facts of *Lion Nathan*, it was clear that there had been a failure of process: the vendor had started with the desired result and worked backwards to produce a forecast that would justify its desired purchase price. In doing so it had used overstated and unrealistic figures, double counted certain items and failed to take account of current trends. There had been, as the judge at first instance found and the Privy Council accepted, 'a radical departure from acceptable methods of forecasting'.

1 [1996] 1 WLR 1438 at 1443.

2.65 Two general propositions made by Lord Hoffmann in *Lion Nathan*[1] merit further attention. First, Lord Hoffmann suggested that a projection should generally be based on the 'forecaster's estimate of the most probable outcome, the mean figure within the range of foreseeable deviation'. In straightforward cases such as *Lion Nathan*, this approach is likely to be followed. However, it is less likely to be useful where a particular contingency could have dramatically different outcomes for the company's performance: in such cases, simply taking the average of all possible outcomes might not be methodologically sound.

1 [1996] 1 WLR 1438 at 1445.

2.66 Second, Lord Hoffmann suggested that, when considering what forecast ought reasonably to have been made, a court could 'start with a prima facie assumption that the range of reasonable possible forecasts will be distributed around the figure which was the actual outcome'.[1] Again, while this might be a sensible starting point in the majority of cases, the assumption will no doubt be displaced if the events that led to the forecast becoming inaccurate could not reasonably have been predicted. In such circumstances, the fact that the forecast was significantly out of line with the actual outcome will not necessarily indicate that it was made without reasonable care.

1 [1996] 1 WLR 1438 at 1447.

2.67 The approach to the issue of breach in *Bottin* was broadly similar to the Privy Council's process-focused approach in *Lion Nathan*. In *Bottin*, a profit of £2.5 million had been forecast for the year 2000 but in fact (as the statutory accounts later revealed) the company suffered a loss of £1.34 million. Blackburne J found that the warranty had been breached because, at the time the forecast was made, there had been 'no reasonable basis' for the making of the prediction.

2.68 While claims for breach of warranty might reasonably be expected to be brought where overly optimistic forecasts are made, *Bottin* also illustrates the more unusual possibility that an unduly pessimistic projection may, in the right circumstances, give rise to liability on the part of a seller. In addition to the inflated profit projection of £2.5 million for the year 2000, the vendor in *Bottin* provided the purchaser with certain 'budgeted' figures for 1999. These purported projections for 1999 were included alongside the management accounts for the ten months to 31 October 1999, and, because the 'budgeted' figures were in some respects worse than the actual results shown in the management accounts, they gave the buyer the impression that the company had exceeded its own expectations. However, Blackburne J found that the projections included in the 1999 management accounts had no genuine business purpose and deviated significantly from the projections actually made towards the beginning of 1999. In the premises, he held that, by including the purported projections for 1999, the vendor had breached a warranty to the effect that none of the written information provided to the purchaser was misleading.

Third party contracts and claims

2.69 The purchaser of a business will want to understand, and also typically to protect itself against, any potential liabilities of the business to third parties. Various warranties may therefore be given in relation to the company's relations with third parties: for example, the vendors may warrant that they are not aware of any disputes under contracts with third parties, or any circumstances likely to give rise to such disputes and/or to any default under such contracts.[1]

1 See, eg, *Bottin* at [394].

2.70 The Court of Appeal considered a warranty of this type in *Belfairs*.[1] The vendors had warranted that the target company was 'not a party to any agreement, arrangement or commitment which … cannot readily be fulfilled or performed by it on time'. At the time of completion, the vendors anticipated that the company would enter a framework agreement with the NHS entitling it to bid to supply IT systems. The framework agreement was entered shortly after completion, but the company was ultimately unable to fulfil its obligations under the agreement. The question that arose was whether the NHS's nonbinding offer of the framework agreement as at the date of completion was an 'agreement, arrangement or commitment' for the purposes of the warranty.

1 [2010] EWHC 2276 (Ch) at [168].

2.71 At first instance, Norris J held that it was not: as at the transaction date, the target company had simply been selected as a party to whom an NHS framework agreement would be offered, but it was not at that time subject to any obligation under the framework agreement that had to be 'fulfilled or performed by it on time'.

2.72 On appeal, however, the Court of Appeal held that a reasonable person would interpret 'agreement' as including the NHS contract that both parties expected to be signed promptly after the completion of the SPA. The framework agreement had been at the heart of the parties' deal, and the parties had entered the SPA on the correct common assumption that, immediately afterwards, the company would sign up to the NHS contract. While Norris J's construction was a possible one, the commercially more sensible interpretation was that 'agreement' included the unsigned framework contract.

2.73 A slightly different point in relation to third party contracts arose for consideration in *Triumph Controls*.[1] In *Triumph Controls*, the target company had received complaints and penalty claims from customers as a result of certain operational issues. The buyers contended that the vendors were in breach of warranties to the effect that: (a) so far as they were aware, no matters existed that might give rise to litigation or other proceedings, investigations or enquiries; and (b) the company had not received written notice of, and the vendors were not aware of any circumstances which might result in, any claim with a value in excess of £75,000 in respect of any goods or services supplied by the company.

1 [2019] EWHC 565 (TCC) at [354].

2.74 The vendors argued that there had been no breach of warranty: the customer complaints were part of the ordinary course of business, and ultimately the company had not had to pay any delay damages claims arising out of preacquisition issues. However, O'Farrell J noted that the warranties referred not just to actual liabilities but also to potential liabilities; in that respect, she said, the relevant test was whether the circumstances of the customer complaints gave rise to a real, as opposed to a fanciful, risk of claims, litigation or other proceedings. She cited the decision in *HLB Kidsons v Lloyd's Underwriters*, in which Gloster J had given the following guidance:

> '... a "circumstance ... which may give rise to a loss or claim against" the assured ... requires that the circumstance should be one which, objectively evaluated, creates a reasonable and appreciable possibility that it will give rise to a loss or claim against the assured. It is necessary to emphasise however, that a circumstance may give rise to a loss or

> claim when there is a possibility or perceived possibility that, at some stage in the future, it will do so. There need not be a certainty that it will do so; there need not be a probability or likelihood that it will do so. All that need exist is a state of affairs from which the prospects of a claim (whether good or bad) or loss emerging in the future are "real" as opposed to false, fanciful or imaginary.'[1]

Commenting on this test, O'Farrell J added:

> 'The test is, in part, an objective one, namely, whether the established circumstances could give rise to a claim or proceedings. However, not all such circumstances would be sufficiently serious to engage the warranties; the circumstances must be such that a reasonable person in the position of members of the Knowledge Group [i.e. the representatives of the sellers whose knowledge was deemed relevant for the purposes of the qualified warranties] would recognise them as matters that might give rise to a claim or proceedings.'[2]

1 [2007] EWHC 1951 (Comm) at [73].
2 *Triumph Controls* at [322].

2.75 On the facts of *Triumph Controls*, the above test was satisfied. The fact that the vendors thought that the customer claims could be 'managed' would not eliminate the risk of a claim. The customer complaints and claims were serious, and the company had not disputed that it was responsible for the operational problems that had prompted them. Key customers had made, or threatened to make, claims for damages in respect of those problems. There therefore existed circumstances giving rise to a real risk of claims or proceedings, and the warranties were engaged.

2.76 In *Bell v Singh*, the sellers warranted the accuracy of a questionnaire in which they had stated, inter alia, that they did not know of any circumstances 'likely' to lead to them becoming parties to litigation.[1] Mr Nigel Cooper KC (sitting as a judge of the High Court) construed this as referring only to claims that a reasonable person in the position of the sellers would have thought were 'at least 50% likely' to arise. He rejected the buyers' suggestion that it included claims for breach of warranty or misrepresentation under the agreement itself, as this would be circular: there was no need for such a clause given that the counterparty to the agreement would necessarily have to have a freestanding claim for breach of warranty or misrepresentation in order to trigger a breach by the sellers of the warranty in relation to likely claims.

1 [2022] EWHC 3272 (Comm) at [172]–[173].

Licences, permits and other regulatory approvals

2.77 The profitability of a business may be contingent on its holding certain licences, permits or other regulatory approvals. If so, a vendor may warrant that the relevant licences etc are validly held and that the necessary conditions for their continuation are in place.[1] Not unsurprisingly, it has been held that – in the absence of such a warranty (or representation) – there is no 'common law duty to give full disclosure of all information technology, intellectual property and licensing issues that could materially affect the operation or profitability' of the target business.[2]

1 See, eg, *Liberty Partnership Ltd v Tancred* [2018] EWHC 2707 (Comm) at [38].
2 *Arani v Cordic Group Ltd* [2021] EWHC 829 (Comm) at [165].

2.78 In *Triumph Controls*, O'Farrell J considered the scope of such a warranty in an SPA. The target companies manufactured components for use in the aerospace industry, and (as at the time the sale was completed) were formally accredited for this purpose by the National Aerospace and Defense Contractors Accreditation Program ('NADCAP'). In 2013, shortly after its acquisition by the buyer, one of the companies lost its NADCAP accreditation. Amongst various claims, the buyer brought a claim for breach of a warranty that the company had, and had materially complied with, 'all licences, consents, permits and associated registrations and authorities … necessary to the carrying on of its business in the places and in the manner in which its business is now carried on'.

2.79 The vendors argued that NADCAP accreditation was not a licence, consent, permit or associated registration or authority such as to fall within the scope of the warranty: it was a third-party process accreditation scheme, compliance with which was not required by statute or regulation, and accreditation did not authorise the holder to do something that it would otherwise not be able to do. O'Farrell J rejected this. She held that NADCAP accreditation conferred authority on, or gave permission to, a business to hold itself out as complying with certain standards; it therefore fell within the ordinary and natural meaning of the word 'permit' or 'licence'. Moreover, accreditation was necessary to the carrying on of the target company's business because its major customers required it to hold NADCAP accreditation, either as a matter of policy or through contractual provisions. The warranty was therefore engaged but, on the facts, not breached, because the company had held NADCAP accreditation as at the date of completion and the subsequent loss of accreditation was attributable to the purchaser's own failures.

Insolvency

2.80 The commencement of insolvency procedures in respect of a company is likely to be a major impediment to, or indeed to preclude entirely, any sale of shares or assets. Vendors will often therefore warrant that the target company is not insolvent and has not failed or become unable to pay its debts as they fall due.[1]

1 See, eg, *Belfairs* [2010] EWHC 2276 (Ch) at [6(j)].

2.81 One common form of warranty in this regard is exemplified by *Invertec*.[1] There, the warranty stated that the target company was 'not unable to pay its debts within the meaning of s 123 Insolvency Act 1986'. As Arnold J noted, this language gave rise to a difficulty, because the Insolvency Act 1986, s 123 provided that (save in certain narrow and exceptional circumstances) a company will only be deemed unable to pay its debts if 'it is proved to the satisfaction of the court that the company is unable to pay its debts as they fall due'. In *Invertec* the vendors sought to take advantage of this provision, arguing that the warranty would not be engaged unless it had been proved to the satisfaction of a court that the target company was unable to pay its debts as they fell due. However, Arnold J rejected this as being contrary to commercial sense, noting that it would substantially deprive the warranty of effect.

1 *Invertec Ltd v De Mol Holdings BV* [2009] EWHC 2471 (Ch).

2.82 Further considering the meaning of the warranty, Arnold J added: '… in deciding whether [the company] was able to pay its debts as they fell due as at [the date of the agreement] one must consider not merely those debts which were actually due that date, but also those debts falling due in the future, and in particular those falling due in the near future. This, of course, also entails consideration of the resources which will be, or are reasonably expected to be, available to the company to pay those future debts when they fall due.'[1] He also rejected the vendors' contention that the burden of proving that the company was unable to pay its debts as they fell due necessarily required the purchasers to prepare a profit and loss account and balance sheet as at the date of the agreement: 'Such an analysis might help to prove cash flow insolvency, but I cannot see that it is necessary. I find it particularly hard to see why a balance sheet should be required. A company can easily be cash flow insolvent although it is balance sheet solvent.'[2]

1 [2009] EWHC 2471 (Ch) at [300].
2 At [301].

Tax

2.83 The apportionment of the pre-completion tax liabilities of an acquired business is likely to be the subject of a comprehensive set of indemnities, often set out in a tax covenant rather than in the body of the business sale agreement itself. That being so, the warranties given in respect of pre-completion tax matters may be more limited, focusing on (for example) the target company's proper filing of any required tax returns and its retention of relevant records and documents.[1] However, tax warranties may still be important insofar as they cover matters relevant to the likelihood of post-completion tax liabilities arising, since (depending on the scope of the indemnities) these will ordinarily be the responsibility of the buyer.

1 See, eg, *Teoco UK Ltd v Aircom Jersey 4 Ltd* [2018] EWCA Civ 23 at [5].

2.84 In *Minera Las Bambas SA v Glencore Queensland Ltd*,[1] the Court of Appeal considered a provision requiring the seller to indemnify the buyers in respect of tax 'payable' by the target company in relation to any period before closing. The Peruvian tax authorities raised an assessment and found the company liable to pay certain additional sums, and to return certain VAT refunds for which inadequate documentation had been supplied. The company appealed against the assessment, and the sellers argued that the indemnity was not triggered as the sums had not yet become 'payable'. The Court of Appeal agreed, with Leggatt LJ noting:

> 'If the existence and amount of a debt have been established but the indemnified person has not yet come under an enforceable obligation to pay the debt, it cannot be said that any loss has been suffered which the indemnifier has failed to prevent or to hold the indemnified person harmless against. To treat the Sellers' obligation to pay an amount of money to the Purchasers as triggered in such a situation therefore seems to me to be inconsistent with the general nature and purpose of an indemnity.'[2]

1 [2019] EWCA Civ 972.
2 At [30].

2.85 A separate issue arose in *Minera* in relation to a further indemnity covering the cancellation, loss or unavailability of VAT receivables insofar as this was caused by the sellers' breach of certain warranties. The buyers argued that the indemnity was triggered because there had been a breach of warranty in respect of the documentation required to substantiate the VAT refunds. Specifically, they argued that the company had neither been 'in possession of sufficient information' nor had had 'reasonable access to sufficient information' to enable it to compute its tax liabilities or otherwise meet its legal obligations relating to tax (as was required under the warranties). At first instance, Moulder J rejected this: the company had been in possession of the documents (albeit some of them were held on-site in a remote mountainous location) and had had reasonable access to them in the sense that it could have requested copies from suppliers. Moulder J refused to read into the warranty any requirement that the documents be well-organised, stored in particular places or easy to retrieve. The Court of Appeal agreed: 'Before the Purchasers entered into the SPA they had the opportunity in the course of their due diligence investigations to find out where and how information was held by the Company and, if they thought fit, to seek to negotiate a warranty as to the manner in which documents were stored or as to the ease of retrieval of information. In the absence of any warranty expressly addressing such matters, it is impossible to conjure one out of a bare promise that the Company was "in possession of" information.'[1]

1 At [57] per Leggatt LJ.

Accuracy of information provided

2.86 It is not unknown for the parties to a business sale agreement to include a broadly-worded 'sweeping up' warranty to the effect that all information (or all written information) provided to the buyer is true and accurate.[1] The effect of such a clause will be to transform representations made by the seller (and, indeed, statements that would not necessarily be actionable as representations, for example statements about the future) into contractual warranties.

1 See, eg, *Belfairs* [2010] EWHC 2276 (Ch) at [6(j)].

2.87 In *Karim v Wemyss*,[1] a solicitor selling his practice warranted that 'all other information relating to the Business given by … the Seller to the Buyer' was true, accurate, complete in every respect and not misleading. As a result, the solicitor was deemed to have warranted the truth of representations he had made during negotiations as to turnover and income, even though these were not incorporated into the written SPA as express warranties. The buyer therefore had claims against the solicitor in both misrepresentation and breach of warranty, and was entitled to choose between the tortious and contractual measures of damages.

1 [2016] EWCA Civ 27.

2.88 A widely-drafted warranty referring to 'all information provided' may also override specific, narrower warranties given in relation to particular documents. For example, in *Bottin*, specific warranties were given in relation to a set of management accounts to the effect that they fairly reflected the company's trading position to the best of the vendor's information, knowledge and belief. Separately, the vendor also warranted that 'all written information' provided in the course of negotiations leading up to the SPA was, to the best of its knowledge, 'true and accurate in all respects' and 'not misleading in any respect'. Counsel for the buyer argued that the management accounts were caught not only by the narrower warranty (ie that they 'fairly reflected the company's trading position') but also the wider warranty (ie that they were true, accurate and not misleading in any respect), because they had been provided to the buyer in the course of the negotiations. Blackburne J did not expressly address this argument, but it appears from his judgment that he accepted it, as he held that there was a separate breach of warranty arising from the 'misleading' nature of the management accounts.[1]

1 At [403].

Chapter 3

Excluding or Limiting Liability

3.01 The parties to an SPA will rarely, if ever, seek to exclude all liability for breach of warranty, since to do so would defeat the purpose of including warranties in the contract at all. However, they may, and frequently do, seek to exclude the possibility of liability arising in respect of information provided and statements made other than as contained in the express written warranties; and/or to limit the remedies that will be available in the event of a successful claim for breach of warranty or misrepresentation.

3.02 This is commonly achieved through the inclusion of one or more of the following provisions in the SPA:

(i) an entire agreement clause;

(ii) a clause excluding or restricting liability for misrepresentation; and/or

(iii) a clause limiting the amount or type of damages that will be recoverable in the event of a successful claim.

Each of these types of clause is discussed further below.

GENERAL CONSIDERATIONS

Construction of exclusion and limitation clauses

3.03 The traditional position at common law was that exclusion and limitation clauses were to be construed strictly.[1] In recent years, courts have moved away from this approach and (at least in relation to commercial contracts) shown a greater willingness to acknowledge that parties are entitled to apportion the risk of loss as they see fit.[2] In *Bikam OOD v Adria Cable Sarl*,[3] a case relating to the sale of a majority shareholding in a broadcasting company, Simon J rejected the buyer's submission that exclusion and limitation clauses are to be construed restrictively, and added that '[n]or does any residual hostility apply to clauses which attempt to limit the liability of parties to a fixed financial amount'.

1 *Photo Production Ltd v Securicor Ltd* [1980] AC 827.
2 See, eg, *Tradigrain SA v Intertek Testing Services (ITS) Canada Ltd* [2007] EWCA Civ 154 at [46].
3 [2012] EWHC 621 (Comm) at [35]–[36].

3.04 However, the tide has not turned entirely against the traditional strict approach. In another recent business sale case, *Nobahar-Cookson v The Hut Group Ltd*,[1] the Court of Appeal held that, as a matter of principle, an ambiguity in a limitation clause (in that case, a time limit for warranty claims under an SPA) should be construed *contra preferentem*. It would therefore be unwise to assume that an exclusion or limitation provision in an SPA will invariably be treated in the same way as any other term of the agreement.

1 [2016] EWCA Civ 128. However, see *Persimmon Homes Ltd v Ove Arup and Partners Ltd* [2017] EWCA Civ 373, suggesting that the *contra preferentem* rule has a very limited role to play. *Nobahar-Cookson* was not referred to in *Persimmon*.

Excluding or limiting liability for, or save for, fraud

3.05 It is a well-established rule that, for reasons of public policy, a contracting party cannot exclude liability for its own fraud; fraud is regarded as 'a thing apart'.[1] Although conventionally expressed as a rule against 'excluding' liability for fraud, it is generally understood to apply equally to any attempt to limit liability for fraud.[2]

1 *HIH Casualty and General Insurance Ltd v Chase Manhattan Bank* [2003] UKHL 6 at [15]–[16] per Lord Bingham. See also *S Pearson & Son Ltd v Dublin Corp* [1907] AC 351.

2 See *HIH Casualty* at [63] per Lord Hoffmann, doubting that there was a distinction between exclusion and limitation clauses. See also *Society of Lloyd's v Leighs* [1997] CLC 1398 at 1408, emphasising that a contested clause did not seek to 'exclude or limit' liability for fraud; and *Frans Maas (UK) Ltd v Samsung Electronics (UK) Ltd* [2004] EWHC 1502 (Comm), finding that a limitation of damages clause could not be construed as applying to a party's own fraud.

3.06 However, there remains some uncertainty as to whether a party can exclude or limit liability for the fraud of an agent or employee. The House of Lords left this point undecided in *HIH Casualty*,[1] although Lord Bingham emphasised that, even if it were possible, any such exclusion would have to be 'expressed in clear and unmistakable terms on the face of the contract'.

1 [2003] UKHL 6 at [16].

3.07 The possibility of excluding liability for an employee's dishonesty was revisited in *Frans Maas*.[1] Gross J held that a limitation clause in the standard terms of a bailment contract was effective in limiting a warehouse operator's liability for the dishonest wilful default of its employees, who had been complicit in the theft of a consignment of mobile phones. It has been suggested that, by parity of reasoning, the same approach might be taken to an attempt to exclude liability for an agent's deceit.[2] However, the boundaries of this principle remain to be fully explored. In particular, difficulties are likely to arise where the fraud of an agent or employee is attributable to a company on the normal rules of attribution since, at that point, the fraud of the agent or employee becomes the fraud of the company itself and any attempt to exclude the company's liability would appear to fall foul of the overarching rule that a party cannot exclude liability for its own fraud. (This problem did not arise in *Frans Maas* because the warehouse operator was only vicariously, not directly, liable for the employees' default.[3])

1 [2004] EWHC 1502 (Comm).
2 See, eg, M Jones (ed), *Clerk and Lindsell on Torts* (24th edn, Sweet & Maxwell, 2023) at 17–57.
3 Gross J acknowledged at [151] that the conclusion might have been different had there been personal fraud on the operator's part, as opposed to vicarious liability for wilful default.

3.08 A difficulty of this nature arose in the business sale context in *The Hut Group Ltd v Nobahar-Cookson*.[1] A clause limiting damages was subject to an exception as regards 'any claim insofar as it results from the fraud of the Buyer'. The buyer argued that a fraud perpetrated by its former Group Financial Controller was not attributable to it, and therefore did not fall within the exception to the limitation clause. However, Blair J rejected this, considering the rules on attribution (discussed further in Chapter 4) and noting that the Group Financial Controller was 'heavily involved in the transaction because he was providing the financial information … which was essential for the deal to go ahead'. Looking at the issue as a matter of construction and commercial sense, Blair J held that the fraud was attributable to the buyer, and therefore that the contractual cap on damages did not apply.

1 [2014] EWHC 3842 (QB). The point did not arise on appeal: [2016] EWCA Civ 128.

3.09 The limitation clause considered in *The Hut Group* made an express exception for fraud. It is now tolerably clear that a clause purporting to exclude or limit liability generally will not be ineffective simply because it does not make any such express exception. It is nevertheless common for SPAs to include express carve-outs for fraud.[1] The practice of doing so might be influenced by a concern that the provision should not fall foul of the test of reasonableness. In *Thomas Witter Ltd v TBP Industries Ltd*,[2] Jacob J suggested, obiter, that a clause excluding liability in respect of any misrepresentation (without distinguishing between fraudulent, negligent, or innocent misrepresentation) purported to exclude liability for fraud; and therefore that it failed the test of reasonableness under the Unfair Contract Terms Act 1977 (UCTA 1977), discussed further below.[3] However, following the decision of the House of Lords in *HIH Casualty*, it is now apparent that a widely-drawn exclusion clause should not (despite the lack of any specific carve-out) be taken to exclude liability for fraudulent misrepresentation. It follows that such a clause should not be unreasonable under UCTA 1977 merely because it does not expressly exempt fraud.[4]

1 See, eg, *Invertec Ltd v De Mol Holdings BV* [2009] EWHC 2471 (Ch) at [4]; *Bikam OOD v Adria Cable Sarl* [2012] EWHC 621 (Comm) at [13]; *Idemitsu Kosan Co, Ltd v Sumitomo Corporation* [2016] EWHC 1909 (Comm).
2 [1996] 2 All ER 573.
3 See [**3.58**]–[**3.63**].
4 See further *Government of Zanzibar v British Aerospace (Lancaster House) Ltd* [2000] 1 WLR 2333; *Regus (UK) Ltd v Epcot Solutions Ltd* [2008] EWCA Civ 361 at [34]; *Goodlife Foods Ltd v Hall Fire Protection Ltd* [2017] EWHC 767 (TCC) at [46]–[48] (not challenged on this point on appeal: [2018] EWCA Civ 1371).

3.10 A different (and permissible) approach is to exclude or restrict liability for breach of warranty save where it is fraudulent. Clauses which have this effect can be seen in the cases of *Bell v Singh*[1] and *Next Generation Holdings Ltd v Finch*.[2] In *Arani v Cordic Group Ltd*,[3] clause 6.4.3 disapplied the notice requirement for warranty claims to the extent that the claim arises or is increased or delayed as a result of any fraudulent act, omission or misrepresentation or any wilful misconduct, wilful concealment or wilful misstatement by the vendors. There is the potential for confusion to be caused by the mixing of the concept of a breach of warranty with the concept of fraudulent conduct, since it is theoretically possible and even proper for a party to warrant a fact while lacking any belief in its truth, but the cases so far suggest that such confusion does not cause much difficulty in practice.

1 [2022] EWHC 3272 (Comm). See clause 6.1 at [21].
2 [2023] EWHC 2383 (Ch). See clause 5.5 set out at [115].
3 [2023] EWHC 95 (Comm), discussed in Chapter 5 below.

The Unfair Contract Terms Act 1977

3.11 Exclusion and limitation clauses are in principle subject to the statutory controls set out in UCTA 1977.

3.12 In a business sale case, a provision that excludes or limits liability for breach of warranty is unlikely to fall within the scope of UCTA 1977. UCTA 1977, s 3, which deals with clauses excluding or restricting liability for breach of contract, only applies where one party is dealing on the other's written standard terms of business; this is unlikely to be true of most share or asset purchase agreements.

3.13 Moreover, and in any event, paragraph 1(e) of Schedule 1 provides that s 3 does not extend to any contract 'so far as it relates to' the creation or transfer of securities or of any right or interest in securities (which would include an SPA). On one view, it could be argued that this has no bearing on a clause in an SPA restricting liability for breach of warranty, since such a clause does not directly relate to the creation or transfer of shares. However, the Court of Appeal's decision in *Unchained Growth III Plc v Granby Village (Manchester) Management Co Ltd*[1] suggests that the phrase 'relates to' in Schedule 1 should be given a broad meaning. In that case, a clause requiring tenants to pay a maintenance charge without any deduction or set-off was said to 'relate to' the creation of an interest in land for the purposes of paragraph 1(b) of Schedule 1.

1 [2000] 1 WLR 739.

3.14 A provision that excludes or limits liability for misrepresentation will generally fall within the scope of UCTA 1977, regardless of whether the parties are dealing on standard terms or not, and regardless of whether the agreement involves the creation or transfer of shares. This is the result of the Misrepresentation Act 1967, s 3, which provides:

(1) If a contract contains a term which would exclude or restrict—

(a) any liability to which a party to a contract may be subject by reason of any misrepresentation made by him before the contract was made; or

(b) any remedy available to another party to the contract by reason of such a misrepresentation, that term shall be of no effect except in so far as it satisfies the requirement of reasonableness as stated in section 11(1) of the Unfair Contract Terms Act 1977; and it is for those claiming that the term satisfies that requirement to show that it does.

3.15 The application of the test of reasonableness set out in UCTA 1977 in the context of business sale transactions is considered further below.[1]

1 See [**3.58**]–[**3.63**].

ENTIRE AGREEMENT CLAUSES

3.16 In practice, the parties to an SPA frequently seek to limit their liability for breach of warranty by including a clause specifying that the entirety of their agreement is contained in or constituted by the written terms of the contract. A provision of this nature is commonly referred to as an 'entire agreement' clause.

3.17 As described by Lightman J in *Inntrepreneur Pub Co v East Crown Ltd*,[1] an entire agreement clause ensures that 'any promises or assurances made in the course of the negotiations … shall have no contractual force, save in so far as they are reflected and given effect' in the document or documents specified by the parties. In particular, such a clause prevents either party from claiming that their agreement contains express terms other than those set out in the contractual document(s);[2] or that pre-contractual statements, promises or assurances take effect as collateral warranties.[3] However, in *Rock Advertising Ltd v MWB Business Exchange Centres Ltd*,[4] Lord Sumption suggested (obiter) that 'most standard forms of entire agreement clause' would not prevent the enforcement of a collateral contract capable of operating as an independent agreement and supported by its own consideration, as opposed to a collateral contract relied upon as modifying the main agreement.

1 [2000] 2 Lloyd's Rep 611.

2 *Mileform Ltd v Interserve Security Ltd* [2013] EWHC 3386 (QB).

3 *Deepak Fertilizers and Petrochemical Corpn v Davy McKie (London) Ltd* [1999] 1 All ER (Comm) 69.

4 [2019] AC 119 at [14]. See, to similar effect, the concurring judgment of Longmore LJ in *North Eastern Properties Ltd v Coleman* [2010] EWCA Civ 277 at [83].

3.18 In general, an entire agreement clause will not affect either party's potential liability for misrepresentation, save where clear words are used.[1] In *Al-Hasawi v Nottingham Forest Football Club Ltd*,[2] a clause in an SPA providing that the written agreement 'supersedes and extinguishes all previous discussions, correspondence, negotiations, drafts, agreements, promises, assurances, warranties, representations and understandings' between the parties was not sufficient to exclude the seller's liability for misrepresentation. The same conclusion was reached in respect of a similarly-worded clause in *MDW Holdings Ltd v Norvill*.[3] It is therefore common for an entire agreement clause to be combined with a separate clause aimed at excluding or limiting liability for misrepresentation. Such clauses are considered further below.[4]

1 *Axa Sun Life Services Plc v Campbell Martin Ltd* [2011] EWCA Civ 133.
2 [2018] EWHC 2884 (Ch).
3 [2021] EWHC 1135 (Ch) at [246]–[247]. See also *Capital Green Recycling Ltd v Bird* [2023] EWHC 760 (Comm) at [97].
4 See [**3.23**]–[**3.44**].

3.19 An entire agreement clause that makes no reference to implied terms will not usually prevent the implication of a term into a contract, because the purpose of implication is to elucidate the meaning of the existing written terms.[1] However, it is possible for contracting parties to exclude the possibility of terms being implied by statute, custom or a course of dealing.[2] Clear words will be required to achieve this, particularly where the implied term in question would have given one of the parties a valuable right.[3]

1 *Novoship (UK) Ltd v Mikhaylyuk* [2015] EWHC 992 (Comm) at [32], approving a proposition made in Lewison (ed), *The Interpretation of Contracts* (5th edn, Sweet & Maxwell, 2011) at p 141.
2 *Great Elephant Corp v Trafigura Beheer BV* [2012] EWHC 1745 (Comm) (reversed on other grounds: [2013] EWCA Civ 905); *Exxonmobil Sales and Supply Corporation v Texaco Ltd* [2003] EWHC 1964 (Comm). This assumes that the statute itself permits the parties to exclude the term.
3 *Federal Republic of Nigeria v JP Morgan Chase Bank, NA* [2019] EWHC 347 (Comm) at [37].

3.20 It is less clear whether it is possible for parties to exclude the implication of terms necessary to give business efficacy to the contract. In *Axa Sun Life Services Plc v Campbell Martin Ltd*,[1] Stanley Burnton LJ appeared to suggest, obiter, that it might be possible to do so. However, as Hildyard J pointed out in *J N Hipwell & Son v Szurek*,[2] this would leave the parties with an inefficacious agreement. At the very least, it is therefore likely that courts will strive to avoid a construction of an entire agreement clause that excludes the possibility of a term being implied on grounds of business efficacy.

1 [2011] EWCA Civ 133 at [41].
2 [2018] EWCA Civ 674 at [27].

3.21 An entire agreement clause will not generally preclude the use of extrinsic evidence as an aid to construction of the contract.[1]

1 *NHS Commissioning Board v Vasant* [2019] EWCA Civ 1245; *John v Price Waterhouse* [2002] EWCA Civ 899.

3.22 An entire agreement clause will also not usually limit the parties' ability to vary their agreement subsequently, though in practice entire agreement clauses are often accompanied by separate provisions excluding the possibility of the contract being amended other than in writing (commonly known as 'no oral variation' clauses). In *Rock Advertising Ltd v MWB Business Exchange Centres Ltd*, the Supreme Court upheld the validity of a no oral variation clause in a licence agreement, resolving previous doubts about whether parties could agree to fetter themselves in this way.

CLAUSES EXCLUDING OR RESTRICTING LIABILITY FOR MISREPRESENTATION

3.23 Clauses aimed at excluding or limiting liability for misrepresentation typically take the following forms:

(i) clauses providing that neither party has relied on, or been induced to enter the agreement by, any representations made by the other (commonly known as 'non-reliance' clauses);

(ii) clauses providing that neither party has made any representations to the other (commonly known as 'no representation' clauses);

(iii) clauses excluding liability for misrepresentation; and

(iv) clauses restricting the remedies available for misrepresentation.

Non-reliance and no representation clauses

The effect of non-reliance and no representation clauses

3.24 A non-reliance clause in an SPA estops the parties from asserting that they were induced to enter the agreement by any representation made by the other, save as expressly provided otherwise in the contract.[1] As inducement is an essential element of the tort, this will preclude any claim for misrepresentation.[2] Similarly, a no representation clause prevents the parties from asserting that any actionable representation has been made.[3] Non-reliance and no representation provisions are sometimes combined in the same clause in an SPA.[4]

1 See, eg, *Bottin International Investments Ltd v Venson Group plc* [2006] EWHC 3112 (Ch) at [154]–[155].
2 See Chapter 7.
3 *Springwell Navigation Corporation v JP Morgan Chase Bank* [2010] EWCA Civ 1221.
4 See, eg, *MAN Nutzfahrzeuge AG v Freightliner Ltd* [2005] EWHC 2347 (Comm) at [126].

3.25 Previously, there appeared to be some doubt as to the precise nature of the estoppel to which a non-reliance or no representation provision gives rise. In *E A Grimstead & Son Ltd v McGarrigan*,[1] the seller of a motor vehicle dealership made certain representations as to the financial state of the company. The share sale agreement entered by the parties contained a non-reliance provision specifying that 'the Purchaser acknowledges that it has not been induced to enter into this Agreement by any representation or warranty' (save as set out in a schedule to the agreement). Chadwick LJ suggested (obiter) that this clause was capable of giving rise to an evidential estoppel, but that, because the seller appeared to know at the time of entering the agreement that the acknowledgements of non-reliance did not reflect the true position, the defence of estoppel would have failed.[2]

1 [1999] EWCA Civ 3029.
2 See further on the evidential estoppel point *Watford Electronics Ltd v Sanderson CFL Ltd* [2001] EWCA Civ 317 at [40].

3.26 However, more recent authorities have departed from the suggestion that a non-reliance or no representation clause gives rise to an evidential estoppel or, as sometimes suggested in the alternative, an estoppel by convention.[1] Rather, it is now clear that a non-reliance or no representation provision gives rise to a contractual estoppel.[2] This clarification is important because it means that (contrary to the obiter suggestion in *E A Grimstead*) a non-reliance provision will not be ineffective merely because the party seeking to invoke the clause knew, at the time the contract was entered, that the other party had in fact relied on a representation. It also means there is no requirement for a party invoking a non-reliance or no representation provision to demonstrate that it relied on the provision to its detriment, or that it would be unconscionable to permit the other party to depart from it.[3]

1 On estoppel by convention, see *Springwell Navigation* [2010] EWCA Civ 1221 at [177]–[178].
2 *Peekay Intermark Ltd v Australia & New Zealand Banking Group Ltd* [2006] EWCA Civ 386; *Springwell Navigation*, above.
3 *First Tower Trustees Ltd v CDS (Superstores International) Ltd* [2018] EWCA Civ 1396 at [47]; *Springwell Navigation* at [177]–[178].

3.27 Non-reliance clauses have been considered in a number of other business sale cases.

3.28 In *Bottin*, it was accepted (correctly, said Blackburn J) that a clause in which the buyer acknowledged that it had not relied on any warranty, representation or information in entering into the SPA barred any claim in negligence or non-fraudulent misrepresentation against the other parties to the SPA.[1] Blackburn J added, obiter, that the existence of the clause would also have been relevant to determining whether it was fair, just and reasonable to impose a duty of care in respect of unwarranted matters on an employee of one of the defendants who was not himself a party to the contract but who had made certain representations.[2]

1 *Bottin International Investments Ltd v Venson Group plc* [2006] EWHC 3112 (Ch) at [154].
2 At [155].

3.29 In *Invertec*, the parties to an SPA included a clause acknowledging they had not relied on 'any statement, representation, warranty or understanding … other than as expressly stated in this Agreement as a warranty, representation or undertaking'. The buyer brought claims for fraudulent misrepresentation, negligent misstatement and misrepresentation under the Misrepresentation Act 1967 based on: (a) information supplied by the vendor during negotiations, later warranted in the SPA to be correct; and (b) the warranties themselves, which were alleged to give rise to actionable representations. Arnold J held that the non-reliance clause did not defeat the claims for negligent misstatement or under the Misrepresentation Act 1967, because its language expressly preserved the possibility of the parties relying on representations contained in the SPA, even if those representations were labelled in the SPA as warranties.

3.30 However, the decision in *Invertec* is difficult to reconcile with the later decision in *Idemitsu*. In *Idemitsu*, an SPA included a provision acknowledging that neither party had 'relied on, or been induced to enter into, this Agreement by any representations, warranties or undertakings of any kind other than the Warranties (as modified by the Disclosure Letter)'. The purchaser brought claims for negligent misstatement and misrepresentation under the Misrepresentation Act 1967, based on representations originally said to arise from the contractual warranties in the SPA itself but subsequently said, following amendment of the purchaser's case, to have been made by the vendor offering to sign the execution copy of the SPA. The purchaser argued that the non-reliance clause did not preclude its claims because it preserved the possibility of the parties relying on representations in the same terms as the warranties – essentially the same argument as had succeeded in *Invertec*. However, Andrew Baker QC rejected this and held that the non-reliance clause defeated the purchaser's claims, saying:

> 'Reliance upon a representation the content of which coincides with the content of one of those Warranties is not reliance upon the Warranty in question.'[1]

1 *Idemitsu Kosan Co, Ltd v Sumitomo Corporation* [2016] EWHC 1909 (Comm) at [34].

3.31 *Idemitsu* is therefore at odds with the decision in *Invertec* on this point. *Invertec* was referred to in *Idemitsu*, but not on this specific issue. In reality, the divergence between the cases probably reflects a more fundamental difference in their approach to the question of whether a contractual warranty can also be a representation.[1] In this regard, we suggest that the analysis of Andrew Baker QC in *Idemitsu* is to be preferred. For the reasons discussed in Chapter 7, a warranty is not itself a representation; rather, some separate pre-contractual statement, context or conduct is necessary to found a claim for misrepresentation. It follows that it will not be sufficient for a claimant to demonstrate reliance on the warranty, as opposed to the pre-contractual statement, context or conduct giving rise to the representation, in order to make good its claim. That being so, the fact that a non-reliance clause makes an exception for contractual warranties (as in *Invertec* and *Idemitsu*) should not generally render the clause ineffective against a claim for misrepresentation.

1 See Chapter 7.

Application to fraudulent misrepresentations

3.32 Several first instance decisions, including the business sale case of *Belfairs Management Ltd v Sutherland*,[1] indicate that non-reliance and no representation clauses do not apply to fraudulent misrepresentations.[2] In *Aquila WSA Aviation Opportunities II Ltd v Onur Air Tasimacilik AS* this was said to be 'reflected in a wealth of authority'.[3] In *First Tower Trustees Ltd v CDS (Superstores International) Ltd*,[4] Lewison LJ observed that it 'is plain that no one can exclude liability for his own fraudulent misrepresentation'. If, as discussed further below, most non-reliance and no representation clauses are now properly to be regarded as clauses excluding liability, it would follow that such clauses do not apply to fraudulent misrepresentations.[5]

1 [2010] EWHC (Ch) 2276 (reversed on other grounds: [2013] EWCA Civ 185).
2 *FoodCo LLP v Henry Boot Developments Ltd* [2010] EWHC 358 (Ch) at [166]; *Property Alliance Group Ltd v The Royal Bank of Scotland Plc* [2016] EWHC 3342 (Ch) at [231]; *Ivy v Martin* [2019] EWHC 2510 (Comm) at [14] per Andrew Henshaw QC, suggesting that this would 'probably' be the case but without deciding the issue. The point was conceded by the party alleged to have made the representation in *UBS AG (London Branch) v Kommunale Wasserwerke Leipzig GmbH* [2014] EWHC 3615 (Comm) at [773].
3 [2018] EWHC 519 (Comm) at [112] per Cockerill J.
4 At [74].
5 See [**3.35**]–[**3.38**].

3.33 At first glance, the first instance decision in *The Hut Group* might appear to be inconsistent with this position: in the context of a seller's counterclaim for deceit against the buyer of a sports nutrition business, Blair J considered a non-reliance clause and held that the seller had not relied on the buyer's fraudulent statements. However, it appears from the judgment that this conclusion was not based on the terms of the non-reliance clause per se, but rather on evidence given by the seller at trial which the judge considered was to the effect that it had relied only on the contractual warranties.[1] *The Hut Group* should therefore not be taken to suggest that a non-reliance clause may, by itself, defeat a claim for fraudulent misrepresentation.

1 *Nobahar-Cookson v The Hut Group Ltd* [2014] EWHC 3842 (QB) at [293]–[296].

3.34 In the recent case of *Lawrence v Cowell*, Mr Andrew Lenon KC (sitting as a judge of the High Court) stated that 'clear words are needed to acknowledge non-reliance on fraudulent misrepresentations', thus appearing to leave open the possibility that a non-reliance clause might be drafted in such a way as to defeat a claim for fraudulent misrepresentation.[1] He referred, in particular, to the following remarks of Lewison J in *FoodCo LLP v Henry Boot Development Ltd:*[2]

'Precisely what statements are covered by a non-reliance clause is a question of construction of the clause. But this is subject to the important principles that, as a matter of public policy, a contracting party cannot exclude liability for his own fraud; and that if he wishes to exclude liability for the fraud of his agent he must do so in clear and unmistakable terms on the face of the contract: *HIH Casualty & General Insurance Ltd v Chase Manhattan Bank* [2003] 2 Lloyd's Rep 61. The clause in the present case contains no clear words acknowledging non-reliance on fraudulent misrepresentations.'

However, although the last sentence introduces some doubt, it appears to have been Lewison J's view that it is only liability for fraudulent misrepresentation by an *agent* that can be excluded by clear words; and that, as a matter of public policy, a party cannot exclude liability for his *own* fraudulent misrepresentation, even by the use of clear words. In any event, in both *FoodCo* and *Lawrence v Cowell* the non-reliance clauses in question were found not to exclude claims for fraudulent misrepresentation. It is respectfully suggested that the preponderance of the case law still points against the possibility of using a non-reliance clause to exclude liability for a party's own fraudulent misrepresentation.

1 [2023] EWHC 2644 (Ch) at [146].
2 [2010] EWHC 358 (Ch) at [166].

Application of section 3 of the Misrepresentation Act 1967

3.35 Non-reliance and no representation clauses potentially fall within the scope of the Misrepresentation Act 1967, s 3. Whether a non-reliance or no representation clause is caught by s 3 requires analysis not just of the clause itself but also of the circumstances giving rise to the misrepresentation claim. The starting point is the distinction drawn by Christopher Clarke J in *Raiffeisen Zentralbank Osterreich AG v The Royal Bank of Scotland Plc*:

'… the essential question is whether the clause in question goes to whether the alleged representation was made (or, I would add, was intended to be understood and acted on as a representation), or whether it excludes or restricts liability in respect of representations made, intended to be acted on and in fact acted on; and that question is one of substance not form.'[1]

As Christopher Clarke J explained it:

'… the key question, as it seems to me, is whether the clause attempts to rewrite history or parts company with reality. If sophisticated commercial parties agree, in terms of which they are both aware, to regulate their future relationship by prescribing the basis on which they will be dealing with each other and what representations they

> are or are not making, a suitably drafted clause may properly be regarded as establishing that no representations (or none other than honest belief) are being made or are intended to be relied on. Such parties are capable of distinguishing between statements which are to be treated as representations on which the recipient is entitled to rely, and statements which do not have that character, and should be allowed to agree among themselves into which category any given statement may fall.
>
> Per contra, to tell the man in the street that the car you are selling him is perfect and then agree that the basis of your contract is that no representations have been made or relied on, may be nothing more than an attempt retrospectively to alter the character and effect of what has gone before, and in substance an attempt to exclude or restrict liability.'[2]

1 [2010] EWHC 1392 (Comm) at [310].
2 At [314]–[315].

3.36 In *Welven Ltd v Soar Group Ltd*,[1] the sellers of an engineering business sought to invoke a non-reliance clause in an SPA to defeat a claim for misrepresentation. Citing *Raiffeisen*, Eder J held that the non-reliance clause was not a provision excluding liability for misrepresentation, but rather a provision making clear that no representations were being made in the first place. However, it was significant in *Welven* that the representations alleged by the buyers were not based on separate pre-contractual statements, but on the warranties given in the SPA, which were said by the buyers to amount to representations made immediately prior to signature.[2] The effect of the non-reliance clause was to prevent these contractual warranties being actionable representations. This aspect of the claim (ie the attempt to rely on the warranties themselves as representations) perhaps explains why the non-reliance clause was not characterised as 'rewriting history', and therefore fell outside the scope of the Misrepresentation Act 1967, s 3.

1 [2011] EWHC 3240 (Comm).
2 See Chapter 7.

3.37 Several first instance decisions post-dating *Raiffeisen* suggested a shift away from Christopher Clarke J's 'rewriting history' test and a greater willingness to classify non-reliance clauses as 'basis clauses', defining the terms upon which the parties were contracting, as opposed to clauses excluding liability.[1] However, Christopher Clarke J's approach in *Raiffeisen* was approved by the Court of Appeal in *First Tower Trustees*. In *First Tower Trustees*, Lewison LJ agreed with Christopher Clarke J that a non-reliance or no representation clause will fall within the scope of the Misrepresentation Act 1967, s 3 if, as a matter of fact, one party has made a statement that the other party reasonably understood to be a representation, which was intended to be and was in fact relied on.[2] In his concurring judgment, Leggatt LJ added that, where the non-reliance or no representation clause is contained in the same contract that the alleged misrepresentation is said to have induced, it will fall within s 3 because, *ex hypothesi*, it did not exist as a contract term when the alleged representation was made and relied upon, and 'is therefore not relevant to the question whether the facts necessary to establish liability for misrepresentation have been proved'.[3] Taken together, these propositions strongly suggest that there will be very few cases in which a non-reliance or no representation clause will not be caught by s 3.

1 *Thornbridge Ltd v Barclays Bank Plc* [2015] EWHC 3430 (QB); *Sears v Minco Plc* [2016] EWHC 433 (Ch).
2 At [59], agreeing with Christopher Clarke J's statement in *Raiffeisen* at [308].
3 At [109].

3.38 In theory, a non-reliance or no representation clause contained in a separate contractual document pre-dating the alleged representation might not be subject to s 3, as Christopher Clarke J suggested (obiter) would be the case on the facts of *Raiffeisen*.[1] However, in *First Tower Trustees*, Leggatt LJ said that Christopher Clarke J was wrong on this point.[2] Another possible exception is illustrated by *Welven*, discussed above, though the facts of *Welven* were unusual in that the representations were said to arise from the contractual warranties themselves rather than any separate pre-contractual statements.

1 At [316]–[317].
2 At [108].

3.39 Where a non-reliance or no representation clause falls within the scope of the Misrepresentation Act 1967, s 3, it will not be effective unless it satisfies the requirement of reasonableness in UCTA 1977, s 11(1), discussed below.[1]

1 See [**3.58**]–[**3.63**].

Clauses excluding liability for misrepresentation

3.40 Instead of a non-reliance or no representation clause, the parties to an SPA may include a provision expressly excluding liability for misrepresentation, or waiving their rights in respect of any representations made.[1] Occasionally, such a clause is combined with a non-reliance or no representation clause as part of a 'belt and braces' approach.[2]

1 See, eg, *Bikam OOD v Adria Cable Sarl* [2012] EWHC 621 (Comm) at [13].
2 See, eg, *Welven* [2011] EWHC 3240 (Comm) at [110].

3.41 As such clauses are clearly attempts to exclude or restrict any liability to which a party to a contract may be subject by reason of any misrepresentation, they will fall within the Misrepresentation Act 1967, s 3(1)(a) and will only be effective if they pass the test of reasonableness set out in UCTA 1977.[1] They will also be subject to the general rule that a contracting party cannot exclude liability for its own fraud, discussed above.[2]

1 See [**3.58**]–[**3.63**].
2 See [**3.05**].

Clauses restricting remedies for misrepresentation

3.42 The parties to an SPA may seek to limit their liability in respect of misrepresentation by including a provision restricting the remedies available for such a claim. Claims for misrepresentation may of course be subject to a general limitation of damages clause in the SPA; such clauses are considered further below.[1] However, in relation to misrepresentation specifically, the parties may also agree to exclude the remedy of rescission, which might otherwise be available as an alternative (or in addition) to damages.[2] For example, in *Marplace (Number 512) Ltd v Chaffe Street*,[3] a claim for professional negligence against solicitors instructed in a business sale transaction, the agreement between the buyer and the seller provided that 'save as expressly provided herein [the buyer] has no right to rescind this Agreement either for breach of contract or for negligent or innocent misrepresentation'. A right to rescind might be preserved temporarily in the period between signature of the agreement and completion of the transaction, as in *Marplace*.

1 See [**3.45**]–[**3.57**].
2 See Chapter 9.
3 [2006] EWHC 1919 (Ch).

3.43 It appears that, consistently with the general rule against a contracting party excluding or limiting liability for its own fraud, it will not be possible to exclude the remedy of rescission for fraudulent misrepresentation. In *Welven*, the SPA contained clauses specifying that the purchaser's sole remedy under or in respect of the warranties given would be in damages for breach of contract, and that the purchaser 'shall have no right to rescind this agreement after the date hereof for breach of any of the Warranties or under the provisions of the Misrepresentation Act 1967 or for any reason whatsoever'. Eder J held that these provisions excluded any remedies for innocent or negligent misrepresentation but not fraudulent misrepresentation.

3.44 A clause restricting the availability of rescission as a remedy for misrepresentation will clearly fall within the Misrepresentation Act 1967, s 3(1)(b) and will therefore not be effective unless it passes the test of reasonableness in UCTA 1977.[1]

1 See [**3.58**]–[**3.63**].

LIMITATION OF DAMAGES CLAUSES

Clauses limiting the amount of damages recoverable

3.45 It is common for an SPA to include a clause limiting the amount of damages available, whether in respect of particular claims or in total. For example, the total amount of damages recoverable might be capped at the amount of the purchase price, or at some other maximum figure.[1] Such a clause is often accompanied by a provision identifying a minimum amount below which damages will not be recoverable (the idea behind such a provision being to prevent costly litigation over minor sums).[2]

1 See, eg, *Bikam OOD v Adria Cable Sarl* [2012] EWHC 621 (Comm) at [11].
2 See, eg, *Bottin* [2006] EWHC 3112 (Ch) at [79].

3.46 A limitation of damages clause need not necessarily cap damages at a specified amount. For example, where an SPA includes a mechanism permitting last-minute adjustment of the purchase price based on changes to warranted facts,[1] the recoverable damages for breach of warranty may be limited to the extent that any loss has already been reflected in such adjustment.

1 See [**2.57**]–[**2.60**].

3.47 One such clause was considered by the Court of Appeal in *Dixons Group Plc v Murray-Obodynski*.[1] The SPA contained warranties as to the minimum amount of the company's net assets and gross margin (which were to be calculated based on the completion accounts). The limitation clause also provided that the purchasers would have no claim in respect of any breach 'to the extent that provision or reserve in respect thereof has been made in the Completion Accounts'. The completion accounts made provision for obsolete or returned stock and, as a result, the net asset value and gross margin were less than warranted. The buyer argued that the limitation clause precluded the claimant's claim for breach of the net assets and gross margin warranties, because the provision in the completion accounts for obsolete or returned stock was a provision 'in respect of' those warranties. However, the Court of Appeal rejected this, holding that the provision in the completion accounts for stock might have excluded or limited liability for breach of a warranty as to stock (if there were such a warranty), but not the net assets and gross margin warranties.

1 [2000] 1 BCLC 1.

3.48 The Court of Appeal's very narrow and literal construction of the limitation clause in *Dixons Group* might seem surprising at first, but is perhaps explicable on the facts: because of the way the payment mechanism worked, the claimants would not have recovered anything for the defendants' breach of warranty had the defendants' construction been accepted. However, had the company's net asset value been positive rather than negative, then the Court of Appeal's construction might have led to 'double-counting' of the defendant's liability – in other words, the consideration for the sale would have been reduced *and* the defendant would have had to pay damages for breach of warranty. It is conceivable that a different decision might have been reached had that been the case.

3.49 The interaction between a completion accounts mechanism and a limitation clause was considered again in *Cypher v Bertram*,[1] an application for summary judgment by the defendant vendor in a share purchase transaction. In *Cypher*, two limitation clauses purported to limit claims to the extent that provision had already been made for them in a set of completion accounts. The purchaser brought a claim for breach of warranty based on inaccuracies in the management accounts (which pre-dated the completion accounts). One of the limitation clauses provided that the vendors would not be liable in respect of any claim 'to the extent of any specific provision in respect of the matter to which the claim relates in the Completion Accounts'. Owen J held that specific provision had been made for 'the matter to which the claim relates' – ie the inaccuracies in the management accounts – in the completion accounts; the net asset value had been reduced accordingly, and an adjustment to the consideration had been made to reflect this; and therefore the claim for breach of warranty was excluded in its entirety by the limitation clause. However, a second limitation clause was arguably ineffective, because it only limited claims in respect of any liability or deficiency 'to the extent of any specific provisions *in respect of that liability or deficiency* in the Completion Accounts'.[2] Counsel for the buyer argued that the phrase 'liability or deficiency' referred not to the inaccuracies in the management accounts per se, but rather the losses claimed by the buyer, for which no specific provision had been made in the completion accounts. Owen J accepted that this argument had a real prospect of success.

1 14 June 2001, unreported, Chancery Division.
2 Emphasis added.

3.50 In *Triumph Controls UK Ltd v Primus International Holding Co*,[1] the buyer attempted to circumvent a limitation of damages provision in an SPA (which capped the seller's liability for breach of warranty) by bringing a claim under a separate provision of the SPA requiring the seller to notify the buyer of any breach of the warranties immediately before completion. O'Farrell J held that the definition of 'Claim' in the SPA ('a claim for breach of any of the Warranties') should be read as including a claim for failure to serve a notice of breach, and therefore that the buyer's claim was subject to certain formal notification requirements. As the buyer had not complied with these requirements, the claim failed. It was not necessary to decide, but would seem to follow from O'Farrell J's broad interpretation of the term 'Claim', that the buyer's claim for failure to serve a notice of breach would in any event have been subject to the cap on damages in the limitation clause.

1 [2019] EWHC 565 (TCC).

3.51 By virtue of the Misrepresentation Act 1967, s 3(1)(b), limitation of damages clauses will be subject to the UCTA 1977 reasonableness test insofar as they apply to claims for misrepresentation.[1] As discussed above, they will not apply to clauses limiting the damages available for a breach of warranty unless the parties are dealing on written standard terms (and probably not, in any event, in respect of an SPA).[2]

1 See [**3.58**]–[**3.63**].
2 See [**3.11**]–[**3.12**].

Clauses limiting the type of damages recoverable

3.52 As well as or instead of limiting the amount of damages available, the parties to an SPA may seek to limit the type of damages recoverable. Again, such a clause will generally be subject to the UCTA 1977 reasonableness test insofar as it applies to claims for misrepresentation, pursuant to the Misrepresentation Act 1967, s 3(1)(b);[1] but not insofar as it applies to claims for breach of warranty, unless the parties are dealing on written standard terms and the agreement is not an SPA.[2]

1 See, eg, *Watford Electronics Ltd v Sanderson CFL Ltd*, applying the reasonableness test to a term excluding liability for indirect or consequential loss.
2 See [**3.11**]–[**3.12**].

Exclusion of indirect or consequential loss

3.53 It is common for business sale agreements to exclude liability for 'indirect' and/or 'consequential' loss.[1]

1 See, eg, *Bikam OOD v Adria Cable Sarl* at [11].

3.54 Under the well-known rule in *Hadley v Baxendale*: 'Where two parties have made a contract which one of them has broken, the damages which the other party ought to receive in respect of such a breach of contract should be such as may fairly and reasonably be considered either arising naturally, i.e. according to the usual course of things, from such breach of contract itself, or such as may reasonably be supposed to have been in the contemplation of both parties, at the time they made the contract, as the probable result of the breach of it.'[1]

1 (1854) 9 Ex 341 at 354 per Alderson B.

3.55 This rule is traditionally understood to divide losses into two categories: first, losses flowing naturally from a breach, independently of special circumstances; and second, losses arising because of some supervening event or special circumstances in the parties' contemplation at the time of entering the contract.[1] Where a contract excludes liability for indirect and/or consequential loss, the courts (up to the level of the Court of Appeal) have consistently interpreted this as a reference only to loss in the second category, with no distinction being drawn between the words 'indirect' and 'consequential' in this regard.[2] A provision excluding liability for indirect and/or consequential loss will therefore not exclude a claim for loss of profits if the loss of profits was a direct loss (ie if it flowed naturally from the breach of contract in the usual course of events).[3]

1 See, eg, *Saint Line Ltd v Richardsons Westgarth & Co Ltd* [1940] 2 KB 99.
2 See *Hotel Services Ltd v Hilton International Hotels (UK) Ltd* [2000] 1 All ER (Comm) 750 and cases cited therein.
3 *British Sugar Plc v NEI Power Projects Ltd* (1998) 87 BLR 42.

3.56 While this approach might on the surface seem inconsistent with the general principle that each contract is to be construed on its own terms, it has been rationalised on the basis that 'once a phrase has been authoritatively construed by a court in a very similar context to that which exists in the case in point … a reasonable businessman must more naturally be taken to be having the intention that the phrase should bear the same meaning as construed in the case in point'.[1] However, it appears that, on rare occasions, a different interpretation may be possible: for example, in *Star Polaris LLC v HHIC-Phil Inc*,[2] the court was willing to depart from the normal approach because the contract contained a comprehensive code for the determination of liability.

1 *British Sugar* (1998) 87 BLR 42 at 50 per Waller LJ.
2 [2016] EWHC 2941 (Comm).

Exclusion of lost goodwill

3.57 In *Primus International Holding Company v Triumph Controls UK Ltd*,[1] the Court of Appeal considered the effect of a clause in an SPA excluding liability 'in respect of lost goodwill'. The buyers brought a claim for, inter alia, breach of a warranty that certain financial forecasts had been honestly and carefully prepared. They sought to recover the amount by which they had overpaid for the company as a result of the careless preparation of the forecasts. The sellers tried to invoke the exclusion clause, arguing that the claim was a claim for lost goodwill and relying in this regard on an accounting definition of goodwill as the difference between the price paid for the target company and the fair value of its identifiable net assets. The Court of Appeal rejected this, holding that '"goodwill" in a contract for the sale of a business refers to a type of proprietary right representing the reputation, good name and connections of a business, and is different to the particular or specific meaning attributed to the term by accountants'.[2] The exclusion clause was not designed to exclude a claim such as the buyers'. Rather, as Coulson LJ put it:

> '… the purpose of this exclusion clause was to exclude any claim by Triumph [the buyers] for damages to Triumph's own reputation, good name or business connection arising from a breach of the SPA. Primus [the sellers] were seeking to exclude their liability for any possible damage to Triumph's business reputation which might arise, for example, if – in breach of warranty – the companies had been convicted in the past of money laundering or corruption, but Primus had not disclosed that information to Triumph. If the convictions had become known after the sale, that could have affected Triumph's

> business reputation, because they were by then the sole owners of the discredited companies.'[3]

As Coulson LJ pointed out, if the buyers' interpretation of 'goodwill' were correct, this would have resulted in a very broad exclusion of liability indeed: 'any claim for breach of warranty not relating to existing assets would be covered by the all-encompassing accounting definition of "goodwill" and thus excluded'.[4] That was not, he suggested, a commercially sensible construction of the SPA.

1 [2020] EWCA Civ 1228
2 At [39].
3 At [50].
4 At [52].

THE TEST OF REASONABLENESS IN THE BUSINESS SALE CONTEXT

3.58 UCTA 1977, s 11(1) requires that a contractual provision to which it applies be 'a fair and reasonable one to be included having regard to the circumstances which were, or ought reasonably to have been, known to or in the contemplation of the parties when the contract was made'. The application of this test has been considered in several business sale cases.

3.59 In *E A Grimstead*, Chadwick LJ discussed, obiter, the application of the reasonableness test to a non-reliance clause in a share sale agreement. He said that there were two reasons why courts should uphold such clauses in commercial contracts between experienced parties of equal bargaining power:[1]

> 'First, it is reasonable to assume that the parties desire commercial certainty. They want to order their affairs on the basis that the bargain between them can be found within the document which they have signed. They want to avoid the uncertainty of litigation based on allegations as to the content of oral discussions at pre-contractual meetings. Second, it is reasonable to assume that the price to be paid reflects the commercial risk which each party – or, more usually, the purchaser – is willing to accept. The risk is determined, in part at least, by the warranties which the vendor is prepared to give. The tighter the warranties, the less the risk and (in principle, at least) the greater the price which the vendor will require and which the purchaser will be prepared to pay. It is legitimate, and commercially desirable, that both parties should be able to measure the risk, and agree the price, on the basis of the warranties which have been given and accepted.'

On the facts, Chadwick LJ suggested that the non-reliance clause was reasonable. The purchaser had had the opportunity to investigate the company's books and records, including draft accounts; each party to the agreement was advised by accountants and solicitors; and, for the most part, it would have been clear that the vendor was only prepared to enter into the agreement on the basis that the purchaser relied on its own investigations and judgment.

1 [1999] EWCA Civ 3029.

3.60 The exclusion clause at issue in *Macquarie Internationale Investments Ltd v Glencore (UK) Ltd*[1] was a provision in an SPA precluding the sellers from bringing a claim against the target company or any director, employee, agent or officer thereof in the event that a claim was made by the buyer against the seller. Walker J held that the clause satisfied the requirement of reasonableness under UCTA 1977. He noted, inter alia, that there was no suggestion that the sellers had not understood the clause, and it was part of a carefully calibrated commercial agreement on which they had had expert legal and financial advice. The sellers were not under any particular commercial pressure and indeed had substantially greater resources than the individuals who were protected by the clause.

1 [2008] EWHC 1716 (Comm).

3.61 In *Welven*, Eder J considered, obiter, the reasonableness of a clause in an SPA excluding any remedies for innocent or negligent misrepresentation. He noted that the SPA had been negotiated at arms' length over several months between experienced commercial parties with equal bargaining strength, both of whom knew its terms and were represented by solicitors; that the purchaser had also been advised by accountants; and that the clauses in question did not seek to exclude all liability if a warranty was incorrect, but merely restrict the available remedies to damages for breach of contract. On that basis, he suggested that the term was reasonable.[1]

1 At [114]–[117].

3.62 In *Glossop Cartons and Print Ltd v Contact (Print and Packaging) Ltd*, HHJ Hodge QC (sitting as a judge of the High Court) held that a clause precluding claims for non-fraudulent misrepresentation in a lease sale agreement accompanying an APA was reasonable. He stated:

> '… in my judgment it is entirely reasonable for legally-represented parties engaged in a formal commercial conveyancing process to provide by contract against the elevation of implied and informally expressed representations of this kind into actionable representations. Otherwise … there would be a serious, and unwarranted, departure from the principle of caveat emptor.'[1]

1 [2019] EWHC 2314 (Ch) at [66].

3.63 While these decisions indicate a relatively tolerant approach to exclusion clauses in business sale agreements negotiated between commercial parties of equal bargaining power and with the assistance of advisers, it should be emphasised that each case will turn on its own facts. An exclusion or limitation clause that is materially wider in scope than the provisions discussed above, or that restricts more substantially the remedies available to the parties, may well fail the reasonableness test, even in the context of a business sale transaction entered between commercial parties. The general factors identified by the courts as relevant to the assessment of reasonableness under UCTA 1977 will apply in the business sale context as in any other.[1]

1 See, eg, Potter LJ's helpful summary of the authorities in *Overseas Medical Supplies Ltd v Orient Transport Services Ltd* [1999] 1 All ER (Comm) 981 at [10]; and see further *Goodlife Foods Ltd v Hall Fire Protection Ltd* [2018] EWCA Civ 1371 at [60]–[70].

Chapter 4

Knowledge and Disclosure

RELEVANCE OF THE SELLER'S KNOWLEDGE

4.01 It is not uncommon for a warranty given by a seller in an SPA to be qualified by a reference to the seller's knowledge, awareness or belief. For example, a seller might warrant that a particular state of affairs exists 'to its knowledge'[1] or 'so far as it is aware'.[2]

1 See, eg, *MAN Nutzfahrzeuge AG v Freightliner Ltd* [2005] EWHC 2347 (Comm) at [56].
2 See, eg, *Triumph Controls UK Ltd v Primus International Holding Co* [2019] EWHC 565 (TCC) at [395].

4.02 In principle, a statement by a seller as to its knowledge, awareness or belief may carry with it an implied representation that the seller has reasonable grounds for its belief or has taken steps to investigate the true position.[1] Such a representation is more likely to be implied where the party making the statement is in a better position to know or ascertain the underlying facts than the party to whom the statement is made (as will generally be true of the vendor in a business sale case).[2] However, a contractual warranty qualified by reference to the seller's knowledge, awareness or belief is unlikely by itself to be an actionable representation, because it is not a pre-contractual statement. Some further pre-contractual context, statement or conduct will therefore have to be identified in order to found a claim for misrepresentation.[3]

1 *William Sindall Plc v Cambridgeshire County Council* [1994] 1 WLR 1016.
2 *Brown v Raphael* [1958] Ch 636.
3 See Chapter 7.

4.03 Where the scope of a seller's warranty is qualified by a reference to its knowledge, awareness or belief, questions may arise as to precisely whose knowledge etc counts as that of the seller. If the seller is a company, and the contract does not make explicit provision, there is not always a straightforward answer to this question. In *Meridian Global Funds Management Asia Ltd v Securities Commission*,[1] Lord Hoffmann (giving the judgment of the Privy Council) held that the attribution of knowledge to a company would be determined by application of: (a) the primary rules of attribution found in the company's constitutional documents and/or implied as a matter of company law; and (b) the general rules of attribution found in the law of agency. In exceptional cases where the first two categories of rules do not provide an answer, it would be necessary to consider the specific purpose of the proposed attribution and to ask: 'whose act (or knowledge, or state of mind) was for this purpose intended to count as the act etc of the company?'. More recent authorities have emphasised the need to consider the context and purpose for which the attribution is relevant even in cases that are not 'exceptional' in the sense in which the term was used in *Meridian*.[2]

1 [1995] 2 AC 500 at 506–507.
2 *Bilta (UK) Ltd (In Liquidation) v Nazir* [2015] UKSC 23 at [191] per Lord Toulson and Lord Hodge at [191]; *Singularis Holdings Ltd (In Liquidation) v Daiwa Capital Markets Europe Ltd* [2019] UKSC 50 at [34] per Baroness Hale.

4.04 *Meridian* was a case involving liability under a statute. In *Jafari-Fini v Skillglass Ltd*, Moore-Bick LJ described the application of *Meridian* in a contractual context as follows:

> 'In the context of an obligation which arises under a contract the task of identifying the natural persons whose knowledge or state of mind is to be attributed to the company for the purpose of that obligation can easily be identified as one of construing the contract. It is therefore necessary to ask who among [the company's] directors, employees and agents did the parties intend should be regarded as the company for the purposes of [the relevant obligation] ….'[1]

1 [2007] EWCA Civ 261 at [97].

4.05 While the courts' approach to attribution of knowledge is therefore reasonably clear as a matter of principle, it may be difficult to predict in any individual case whether (for example) the knowledge of a junior employee, or a senior employee not consulted or involved in the business sale transaction, will be treated as that of the company. The most that can be said is that this will be determined in light of the parties' intent, assessed objectively and against the background of the relevant factual matrix in accordance with the ordinary principles of interpretation.

4.06 Questions may also arise as to the level of knowledge required on the part of the seller in order to give rise to liability for breach of a warranty qualified by a reference to its knowledge, awareness or belief. In *BSA International SA v Irvine*,[1] the vendors warranted that, 'so far as the Warrantors are aware', there were no subsisting circumstances that might give rise to any notice being received from competition authorities in relation to the business of the target company. Following the conclusion of the SPA, the target company was served with a notice by the Office of Fair Trading in relation to suspected price-fixing activities. Lord Glennie held that, on the proper construction of the SPA, it would not be sufficient to found a claim for breach of warranty that the warrantors had been aware of the underlying facts giving rise to the service of the notice; it would also be necessary to show that they had been (or ought reasonably to have been) aware that those facts might lead to the notice being served. In this regard, Lord Glennie drew a distinction between 'awareness' and 'mere knowledge', noting that awareness 'suggests a measure of understanding'.[2]

1 [2010] CSOH 12.
2 At [38].

4.07 In order to put these matters beyond doubt, a warranty qualified by reference to the seller's knowledge may expressly identify: (a) the scope of any investigation that has been conducted by the seller; and/or (b) the individuals whose knowledge is relevant for the purposes of the warranty. For example, in *MAN Nutzfahrzeuge*,[1] the SPA included a provision specifying that any representation or warranty qualified by reference to the knowledge of a party would be deemed to refer to 'the actual knowledge (without further enquiry)' of certain named individuals, listed separately.

1 *MAN Nutzfahrzeuge AG v Freightliner Ltd* [2005] EWHC 2347 (Comm) at [60].

4.08 Similarly, in *Triumph Controls*, several of the seller's warranties were qualified by the phrase 'so far as the Sellers are aware'. Clause 8.2 provided that this phrase referred to:

> 'the actual knowledge of the Sellers after they have made all reasonable enquiries of [five named individuals], who shall themselves have made due and careful enquiries in respect of the aspects of the business of the Target Companies for which they are respectively responsible.'

O'Farrell J described the meaning of this term as follows:

> 'The effect of this provision is that Primus is deemed to have knowledge of the matters covered by the warranties if reasonable enquiries of and by the named individuals … would have disclosed such matters. The test is an objective one. The nature and level of enquiries made by Primus is immaterial. Any lack of knowledge or lack of understanding by Primus as to the operational failings is immaterial. The deeming provision is concerned with what was known or should have been known to Primus from the reasonable enquiries stipulated in clause 8.2.'[1]

1 *Triumph Controls UK Ltd v Primus International Holding Co* [2019] EWHC 565 (TCC) at [316].

RELEVANCE OF THE BUYER'S KNOWLEDGE

Effect of the buyer's knowledge

4.09 It is common practice for the parties to an SPA to limit the scope of the seller's warranties through the mechanism of disclosure. Typically, the terms of an SPA will expressly preclude the buyer from bringing a claim for breach of warranty in respect of matters properly disclosed to it by the seller. This may be achieved by a provision in the SPA stating that the warranties are given subject to matters properly disclosed;[1] a term providing that the buyer waives its right to bring a claim for breach of warranty in respect of matters disclosed by the seller;[2] or some other provision. The effect of the buyer's knowledge will depend on the terms of the contract in question.[3]

1 See, eg, *New Hearts Ltd v Cosmopolitan Investments Ltd* [1997] 2 BCLC 249 at 258.
2 See, eg, *Eurocopy v Teesdale* [1992] BCLC 1067 at 1069.
3 *Prentice v Scottish Power plc* [1997] BCC 269 at 274.

4.10 In the absence of any specific contractual provision, it is unlikely that a buyer will be precluded from bringing a claim for breach of a warranty merely because it knew the warranty to be false at the time of entering the contract. In *Infiniteland Ltd v Artisan Contracting Ltd*,[1] Park J rejected the existence of any such general rule of law, preferring the suggestion that it was a matter of construction of the particular contract in each case. However, such a claim may face practical obstacles. In particular, a buyer may have difficulty proving that it has suffered loss in circumstances where the purchase price it agreed with the seller was (presumably) informed by its knowledge of the warranty's falsity.[2] Moreover, if the buyer has given a warranty of its own as to (for example) its knowledge of matters giving rise to any claims against the seller, any claim that it subsequently brings against the seller for breach of warranty may be vitiated by the buyer's own breach.[3]

1 [2004] EWHC 955 (Ch) at [113]–[115]. The point did not arise on appeal ([2005] EWCA Civ 758).
2 *Eurocopy v Teesdale* [1992] BCLC 1067 at 1070. See Chapter 8.
3 For an example of such a clause, see *Lonedale Ltd v Scottish Motor Auctions (Holdings) Ltd* [2011] CSOH 04 at [10].

Standard of disclosure

4.11 It is open to the parties to an SPA to agree the form and extent of any disclosure that will be deemed to be adequate against the warranties.[1] In practice, disclosure is often required to be given in the form of a disclosure letter, typically accompanied by a disclosure bundle (whether in hard copy or electronic form) containing copies of any separate documents being disclosed or a (usually virtual) data room.

1 *Triumph Controls UK Ltd v Primus International Holding Co* [2019] EWHC 565 (TCC) at [335(v)].

4.12 It is common practice for parties to an SPA to include an express requirement in their agreement that disclosure be 'fair'.[1] There is some support in the case law for the suggestion that disclosure must be fair even in the absence of an express reference to fairness in the contract,[2] but this will be a question of construction in each case.[3] Whether disclosure is fair must be tested objectively.[4] A duty of fairness is not necessarily satisfied by compliance with the formal requirements of disclosure set out in the contract itself.[5]

1 See, eg, *Sycamore Bidco Ltd v Breslin* [2012] EWHC 3443 (Ch) at [208].
2 *Prentice v Scottish Power plc* [1997] BCC 269 at 275.
3 See [**4.19**].
4 *Infiniteland Ltd v Artisan Contracting Ltd* [2005] EWCA Civ 758 at [72].
5 *Curtis v Lockheed Martin UK Holdings Ltd* [2008] EWHC (Comm) 2691 at [79].

4.13 A number of authorities suggest that, in order to preclude a claim for breach of warranty, the seller must disclose the relevant matters with sufficient precision. For example, in *Levison v Farin*, the seller of a dress-making business disclosed the fact that the business was trading at a loss due to her illness, but did not disclose the precise amount of the losses. The net asset value of the business declined between the date of the last accounts and the date of completion, and the buyer sued for breach of a warranty that there would be no material change in the net asset value in that period. The seller's disclosure was not sufficient to defeat the buyer's claim. Gibson J noted that:

> '… a protection by disclosure will not normally be achieved by merely making known the means of knowledge which may or do enable the other party to work out certain facts and conclusions.'[1]

1 [1978] 2 All ER 1149 at 1157.

4.14 In *Daniel Reeds Ltd v EM ESS Chemists Ltd*, the Court of Appeal held that the omission of a particular pharmaceutical licence from a disclosure letter that listed and identified other licences did not amount to fair disclosure of the fact that said licence had expired. As Beldam LJ put it:

> '… fair disclosure requires some positive statement of the true position and not just a fortuitous omission from which the buyer may be expected to infer matters of significance.'[1]

1 [1995] CLC 1405.

4.15 *Levison v Farin* was cited and applied by the Court of Session in *New Hearts Ltd v Cosmopolitan Investments Ltd*, another business sale case, in which the parties had agreed that the warranties were given 'subject to matters fairly disclosed (with sufficient details to identify the nature and scope of the matter disclosed) in the Disclosure Letter'. The disclosure letter incorporated by reference, and purported to disclose the content and terms of, a list of documents, including the last accounts and the management accounts of the target company. Lord Penrose held that this was insufficient to defeat the buyer's claim for breach of warranty based on the over-valuation of the target group's principal asset, noting that:

> 'Mere reference to a source of information, which is in itself a complex document, within which the diligent enquirer might find relevant information will not satisfy the requirements of a clause providing for fair disclosure with sufficient details to identify the nature and scope of the matter disclosed.'[1]

1 At 259. See further *Curtis v Lockheed Martin UK Holdings Ltd* [2008] EWHC (Comm) 2691 at [78] per Simon J, citing *New Hearts*: 'The context of the disclosure is important: disclosure without an appropriate context, even if not deceitful, may be unfair ….'

4.16 In *MAN Nutzfahrzeuge*,[1] the relevant disclosure provision in an SPA stated that 'any matter which is or should be revealed by inspection of the statutory registers and books and minutes of each of the [target companies] which would have been revealed by the making of such inspection as would have been made by a prudent purchaser and its professional advisers' was deemed to have been disclosed to the buyer. Moore-Bick LJ rejected the submission that the seller's disclosure necessarily encompassed not only the information contained in those documents, but also inferences to be drawn from it – specifically, the inference that VAT fraud had occurred. Rather, he stated, the natural meaning of the clause was that 'only matters that can be directly ascertained from an inspection of the relevant documents are to be treated as having been disclosed'.

1 *MAN Nutzfahrzeuge AG v Freightliner Ltd* [2005] EWHC 2347 (Comm) at [334].

4.17 In *Kitcatt v MMS UK Holdings Ltd*,[1] Males J considered a disclosure clause which (like the clause in issue in *New Hearts*) required the seller to give disclosure 'in sufficient detail to enable a reasonable buyer to identify the likely nature and scope of' the matter disclosed. Males J said that this meant that the disclosure 'had to be sufficient to enable a reasonable buyer to understand its significance. A passing reference to some problem would not be good enough.'

1 [2017] EWHC 675 (Comm) at [25].

4.18 More recently, partial disclosures of matters giving rise to broader or repeated breaches of warranty were held to be insufficient in *MDW Holdings Ltd v Norvill*[1] and *Equitix EEEF Biomass 2 Ltd v Fox*.[2]

1 [2021] EWHC 1135 (Ch) at [222]–[226].
2 [2021] EWHC 2531 (TCC) at [292]–[315].

4.19 It should not be assumed, however, that as a matter of general principle courts will always seek to construe contractual disclosure requirements in a very burdensome way for sellers. Some authorities, including *MAN Nutzfahrzeuge*,[1] have emphasised the need to approach each contract on its own terms. In *Infiniteland Ltd v Artisan Contracting Ltd*,[2] the Court of Appeal noted that Lord Penrose's remark in *New Hearts*, set out above, had been made against the background of a contractual provision expressly requiring the disclosure letter to give 'sufficient details to identify the nature and scope of the matter disclosed'. By contrast, the parties to the share sale agreement in *Infiniteland* had agreed no such requirement. Rather, the seller had warranted that 'the contents of the Disclosure Letter and of all accompanying documents ... fully, clearly and accurately disclosed every matter to which they related', and the disclosure letter had stated that matters previously disclosed to the buyer's accountants and in the disclosure bundle were deemed to be disclosed. In the circumstances, the Court held that the seller's disclosure obligation had been satisfied in relation to such matters as might fairly be expected to come to the knowledge of the buyer's accountants from an examination of the documents and written information supplied to them. Chadwick LJ cautioned that:

> 'The adequacy of the disclosure in the present case must be measured against the requirements of the share sale agreement into which these parties have entered; not against the requirements of a different agreement in another case.'[3]

1 *MAN Nutzfahrzeuge AG v Freightliner Ltd* [2005] EWHC 2347 (Comm) at [178].
2 [2005] EWCA Civ 758.
3 See further *Cypher Holdings v Bertram* Owen J, 14 June 2001, unreported, Chancery Division, distinguishing *New Hearts* and holding (at [24]–[25]) that a statement in a due diligence report in the disclosure bundle to the effect that certain figures were provisional estimates amounted to fair and proper disclosure of the fact that the management accounts did not in all respects reflect the assets and liabilities of the company.

4.20 *Triumph Controls*[1] further illustrates the need to consider the terms of each contract in their proper context in order to ascertain the required standard of disclosure. After providing a useful summary of the principles to be derived from the previous authorities, O'Farrell J examined the disclosure clause in the parties' SPA. She noted that:

(i) the clause permitted disclosure to be given 'in or under' the disclosure letter, and did not require every breach to be set out expressly in the letter;

(ii) the parties had agreed in principle that disclosure could be given by the provision of access to documents in an electronic data room; and

(iii) the clause required a relevant matter to be 'fairly and clearly disclosed ... with sufficient detail to identify the nature of the matter disclosed' but did not require details of the extent, or scope, of the matter to be set out.[2]

In the premises, O'Farrell J held that the seller had adequately disclosed certain delivery and quality failings by making a series of specific disclosures in the disclosure letter that cross-referred to correspondence with major customers and internal strategic documents, all of which were available in the electronic data room.

1 At [335].
2 Contrast *New Hearts*, above, in which the seller was required to provide 'sufficient details to identify the nature *and scope* of the matter disclosed' (emphasis added).

Matters not disclosed but within the buyer's knowledge

4.21 In a business sale transaction, the buyer may well have come across information that is relevant to the warranties given by the seller (for example, during the due diligence process), but which for one reason or another is not formally disclosed by the seller in accordance with the contractually agreed disclosure mechanism. As discussed above, there is no clear authority for any general rule of law that a buyer is precluded from bringing a claim for breach of a warranty in respect of matters previously known to it.[1] The better view is that the consequences of such knowledge will be a matter of construction of the particular contract in each case.

1 See [**4.10**].

4.22 The parties to an SPA may therefore seek to make express provision for the possibility of the buyer having acquired knowledge of matters relevant to the warranties other than through the disclosure mechanism. For example, they may agree that the buyer shall have no claim for breach of warranty in respect of matters of which it has 'actual knowledge' at the time of entering into the SPA.[1] The buyer may also warrant that it is not aware of any fact or matter giving rise to a breach of warranty (thus giving rise to a potential counterclaim by the seller in the event that the buyer tries to bring a claim in respect of a breach of which it had prior knowledge).[2] Conversely, the agreement might provide that the buyer's remedies against the seller shall not be limited or prejudiced by any information obtained by the buyer save through the disclosure mechanism (such a clause sometimes being described as a 'knowledge saving provision').

1 See, eg, *Lonedale Ltd v Scottish Motor Auctions (Holdings) Ltd* [2011] CSOH 04 at [10].
2 See, eg, *Equitix EEEF Biomass 2 Ltd v Fox* [2021] EWHC 2531 (TCC) at [271].

4.23 Some doubt has been cast on the efficacy of the last type of clause by the Court of Appeal's decision in *Eurocopy v Teesdale*.[1] In *Eurocopy*, an SPA included two clauses (3.3 and 4.1) providing, in summary, that the seller's warranties were given subject to matters set out in the disclosure letter, but that 'no other information relating to the Company of which the Purchaser has knowledge (actual constructive or imputed)' would preclude or affect any claim by the purchaser for breach of warranty. The purchaser brought a claim for breach of warranty based on matters that had not been disclosed to it in the disclosure letter, but that it allegedly knew from other sources prior to entering the SPA. The seller sought to defend the claim on the basis of the purchaser's actual knowledge. The purchaser's application to strike out the defence was dismissed. On appeal, the Court of Appeal upheld the lower court's decision that – notwithstanding clauses 3.3 and 4.1 of the SPA – the purchaser's actual knowledge gave rise to an arguable defence to the claim for breach of warranty. In respect of the buyer's reliance on clauses 3.3. and 4.1, Nourse LJ held:

> 'That is certainly an argument – it may be a strong one – which will enable the plaintiff to contend at trial that whatever view a valuer might take as to the relevance of the purchaser's knowledge of material circumstances in making his bid, the defendants are nevertheless precluded from relying on that matter by the terms of the contract. However I am far from satisfied that that point is so plainly and obviously against them that the defendants should be prevented from taking it at this stage.'[2]

1 *Eurocopy v Teesdale* [1992] BCLC 1067.
2 At 1073.

4.24 Reference was made to *Eurocopy* by the Court of Appeal in *Infiniteland.*[1] However, the contractual provision at issue in *Infiniteland* was materially different from that in *Eurocopy*, as it did not purport to preserve the purchaser's right to bring a claim for breach of warranty in circumstances where the purchaser had actual knowledge of the relevant facts.[2] Rather, it provided that the purchaser's rights and remedies in respect of any breach of warranty would not be affected 'by any investigation made by it or on its behalf into the affairs of any Group Company … except to the extent that such investigation gives the Purchaser actual knowledge of the relevant facts or circumstances'. As Chadwick LJ observed, this put beyond argument the point raised in *Eurocopy* and made clear that the purchaser could not rely on the saving provision if it had actual knowledge.

1 *Infiniteland Ltd v Artisan Contracting Ltd* [2004] EWHC 955 (Ch).
2 See *Infiniteland Ltd* at [81].

4.25 The doubt created by *Eurocopy* therefore persists, and a note of caution has rightly been sounded in other texts as to the effectiveness of provisions that purport to preserve the buyer's right to claim for breach of warranty in the face of actual knowledge of the warranty's falsity.[1] However, in the apparent absence of any general rule of law precluding such claims, it is difficult to see why such a clause should not be effective.[2] *Eurocopy* was an appeal against a decision made on a strike-out application, and the seller's defence was being tested against a low threshold.[3] *Eurocopy* should be read in that context, and should not be treated as authority for any broader principle of law.

1 See, eg, DR Thomson (ed), *Sinclair on Warranties and Indemnities on Share and Asset Sales* (12th edn, Sweet & Maxwell, 2023) at 4-25.
2 See the judgment of Park J in *Infiniteland Ltd v Artisan Contracting Ltd* [2004] EWHC 955 (Ch) at [113]–[115].
3 Nourse LJ's conclusion (at 1073) was that the point was not 'plainly and obviously against 'the seller. He also said that 'the mere fact that any judge has said that a defence is arguable is something which should cause this court to act with very great caution before taking a different view', suggesting that the standard of review the Court of Appeal was applying was not a strict one.

4.26 Even where an SPA includes a knowledge saving provision, it does not necessarily follow that the buyer's knowledge will be irrelevant for all purposes. In *Campbell v Océ (UK) Ltd*,[1] Laddie J held that – notwithstanding the inclusion of such a provision – the claimant sellers were entitled to rely upon the buyers' knowledge: (i) to defeat the allegation that the equitable remedy of specific performance was unavailable because the sellers had come to court with 'unclean hands'; and (ii) in relation to damages, to argue that the buyers had not in fact overpaid for the target company because they had known in advance of the matters alleged to have reduced the company's value.

1 [2005] EWHC 458 (Ch).

Attribution of knowledge to the buyer

4.27 Whether the knowledge of an employee or agent can be attributed to the buyer will be determined in line with the ordinary principles of attribution of knowledge, discussed above in the context of the seller's knowledge.[1] However, two further points may be made in relation specifically to buyers.

1 See [**4.03**]–[**4.04**].

4.28 First, where a buyer instructs agents (for example, accountants or auditors) in the course of the due diligence exercise, it remains unclear whether the knowledge of those agents can be treated as the buyer's 'actual knowledge' for the purpose of a knowledge saving provision. This point was considered, obiter, by the Court of Appeal in *Infiniteland*.[1] The majority (Chadwick LJ and Carnwath LJ) considered that the reference in the saving provision to the purchaser's 'actual knowledge' did not include knowledge obtained by its accountants; had this been intended, the parties would have expressly included 'imputed knowledge' in the saving provision, the distinction between actual and imputed knowledge being well known. However, Pill LJ disagreed: he noted that the accountants, who had been retained by and were acting on behalf of the purchaser, were under a duty to disclose relevant information to the purchaser, and that it was unlikely that the parties to the SPA had intended that the consequences of the accountants failing in their duty to the purchaser should rest with the vendor.

1 *Infiniteland Ltd v Artisan Contracting Ltd* [2004] EWHC 955 (Ch).

4.29 Second, it is not unusual in a business sale for directors of the target company to become directors of the purchasing company. For practical reasons, this may occur prior to the date of the SPA and/or the date of completion. *Sycamore Bidco Ltd v Breslin*[1] suggests that the knowledge of such directors acquired in their capacity as directors of the target company will not be attributed to the purchaser so as to preclude a claim by the purchaser for breach of warranty.

1 [2012] EWHC 3443 (Ch) at [382]–[389].

Chapter 5

Notification of Claims Clauses

INTRODUCTION TO NOTIFICATION CLAUSES

Purpose of notification clauses

5.01 The purpose of a notification clause is to make clear in sufficiently formal terms that a claim is being made against the vendor. A notification requirement provides a vendor with a degree of certainty by ensuring that it knows either that it will not face any claims, or the basis on which claims will be pursued, within a specified time frame. This enables vendors to make financial provision as necessary for any claims brought against them.[1]

1 *Ipsos SA v Dentsu Aegis Network Ltd* [2015] EWHC 1171 (Comm) at [19].

5.02 As Stuart-Smith LJ explained in *Senate Electrical Wholesalers Ltd v Alcatel Submarine Networks Ltd*:[1]

> 'The clear commercial purpose of the clause includes that the vendors should know … in sufficiently formal written terms that a particularised claim for breach of warranty is to be made so that they may take such steps as are available to them to deal with it …. The commercial purpose may not be sensibly served if an uninformed and uninformative notice is given ….'[2]

1 [1999] 2 Lloyd's Rep 423.
2 See also *Stobart Group Ltd v William Stobart and William Tinkler* [2019] EWCA Civ 1376, at [36].

5.03 The courts have recognised the value of such certainty. Serious consideration is given to an assertion by a vendor that a notification clause has not been complied with, and such claims are not dismissed as merely technical.[1]

1 *Laminates Acquisition Co v BTR Australia Ltd* [2003] EWHC 2540 (Comm), at [29]; *Senate v Alcatel* at [91]

Effect of non-compliance with a notification clause on breach of warranty claims

5.04 The consequences of non-compliance with a notification clause are severe. A purchaser's claim for breach of warranty against a vendor will fail, and the purchaser will therefore be denied a remedy regardless of the substantive merits of its claim. This will be the case even where the court has found that there has in fact been a breach of warranty.[1]

1 See, eg, *Curtis and Ranger v Lockheed Martin UK Holdings Ltd* [2008] EWHC 2691 (Comm), in particular at [106]–[109]. Simon J held that there had been a breach of warranty but that the sellers were not liable given the buyer's non-compliance with the notification requirements.

5.05 As explained by Richard Millett QC sitting as a Deputy High Court Judge in *Teoco UK Ltd v Aircom Jersey 4 Ltd*, discussing a notification requirement:

> '33 … It was intended as a gateway to liability on the part of the Seller. The parties agreed that in respect of Claims which did not comply, the Seller would have no liability. It was, as Cooke J said in *Laminates* (at [29]), an important delineation of the Seller's liability. The parties placed on the Purchaser the onus of compliance and allocated the risk of non-compliance to the Purchaser.'[1]

1 [2016] 4 WLUK 527.

5.06 Given that a purchaser's non-compliance with a notification clause may provide a complete answer to a breach of warranty claim, it may often be appropriate for the issue of compliance to be considered as a preliminary issue or by way of a strike out application. The early consideration of notification defences in this manner can avoid the incurrence of costs in bringing and defending claims that are fatally flawed from the outset.

5.07 Examples of cases where claims were foreclosed by findings against a claimant on a preliminary issue regarding notification include *ROK Plc v S Harrison Group Ltd*[1] and *Ener-G Holdings v Hormell*.[2] In *ROK*, it was held that only one of the claimant's two claims had been properly notified and in *Ener-G*, the decision of Burton J that the claim had not been notified in accordance with the relevant clause was upheld by a majority on appeal.

1 [2011] EWHC 270 (Comm).
2 [2012] EWCA Civ 1059.

5.08 Examples of strike out decisions on notification include *Zayo Group International Ltd v Ainger*[1] and *Ipsos SA v Dentsu Aegis Network Ltd*.[2]

1 [2017] EWHC 2542 (Comm).
2 [2015] EWHC 1171 (Comm).

CONSTRUCTION OF NOTIFICATION CLAUSES AND NOTICES – GENERAL PRINCIPLES

5.09 In light of the stringent consequences of non-compliance with notification clauses, the proper construction of both the notification clause and the notice are of critical importance. The vast majority of notification disputes concern issues of construction, with a defendant vendor arguing for a restrictive interpretation and the purchaser submitting that a broader construction should be adopted.

5.10 In practice, the construction of the notification clause and of the purported notice are considered together as a single question: does the notice satisfy the contractual requirement? It is therefore unsurprising that there is a considerable degree of overlap in the principles applicable. The principles of construction are outlined below, and a number of the key themes that can be drawn from the cases are addressed in the following section.

Construction of notification clauses

Ordinary principles of contractual construction applicable

5.11 The notification clause itself must be construed in accordance with the ordinary principles of contractual construction. These are considered briefly in Chapter 1 above.

Each clause turns on its own wording

5.12 A number of decisions make clear that the construction of each notification clause turns on its own wording. Gloster J provided a clear statement to that effect in *RWE v Nukem Ltd v AEA Technology plc*.[1] This statement has been endorsed in many subsequent decisions. By way of example, David Richards LJ held in *Hopkinson v Towergate Financial (Group) Ltd* that:

> 'On both grounds of appeal, Ms Smith referred us to a number of authorities on claims notice provisions in share sale agreements. Like the Judge, I have not found them to be of any assistance in the construction of this particular provision, and like the Judge and Ward LJ in *Forrest v Glasser* [2006] EWCA Civ 1086; [2006] 2 Lloyd's Rep 392 at [24], I would simply repeat the observation of Gloster J in *RWE v Nukem Ltd v AEA Technology plc* [2005] EWHC 78 that "Every notification clause turns on its own individual wording."'[2]

1 [2005] EWHC 73 at [10].
2 [2018] EWCA Civ 2744 at [52].

5.13 That is not to say, however, that earlier decisions construing notification clauses are of no relevance to the question of construction in a future case. Principles guiding construction can be drawn from earlier cases and relied upon. For example, in *Teoco*,[1] Newey LJ reiterated the general principle that the construction of each notification clause turns on its own wording before observing that '[r]eference to previous decisions can still, however, be of some assistance'. Newey LJ went on to consider a number of earlier decisions, drawing guiding principles of construction from them, such as the importance of certainty (from the *Senate v Alcatel* case) and issues concerning specificity (considered further below) from the *RWE Nukem* case. Similarly, in *Zayo Group International Ltd v Ainger*, Mr Simon Bryan QC sitting as a Deputy High Court Judge held:

> 'In this regard, the observations that Simon J identifies in *Ipsos* [making a similar statement to Gloster J in *RWE Nukem*] have not restrained judges from making observations and identifying propositions that they derive from the authorities. There is nothing inappropriate in doing so provided that sight is maintained of the context in which any observations or propositions are made (and their applicability or otherwise to the clause under consideration), and the particular clause under consideration is construed having regard to its own language, and with regard to its surrounding factual matrix and the terms of the contract as a whole.'[2]

1 [2018] EWCA Civ 23 at [21].
2 [2017] EWHC 2542 (Comm) at [44].

Contra proferentem?

5.14 A notification clause is, in essence, an exclusion clause, as it can restrict a purchaser from pursuing an otherwise valid claim. The consequence of this is that such clauses should be construed *contra proferentem* if necessary to resolve any ambiguity in construction.[1] A buyer may therefore seek to rely on the principle to argue for a less restrictive reading of a notification clause.

1 See [**3.03**]–[**3.04**].

5.15 The application of the *contra proferentem* principle was considered most fully by Briggs LJ in *Nobahar-Cookson v The Hut Group Ltd.*[1] At first instance, Blair J had concluded that the *contra proferentem* principle did not apply in that case because both parties were subject to time bars in similar terms. He had held at that:

> 'THG submitted that since the clause was capable of operating harshly, the time-bar provision should be construed *contra proferentem.* However, in this contract both parties were subject to time-bars in similar terms, so that each was subject to the same limitation (see eg Lewison, *The Interpretation of Contracts* (5th ed, 2011) p 619–620). There is no reason to apply such a canon of construction to mutual rights and limitations.'[2]

1 [2016] EWCA Civ 128.
2 [2014] EWHC 3842 (QB) at [79(1)].

5.16 Briggs LJ, however, reached a different conclusion. He held that recent decisions about exclusion clauses have continued to affirm the utility of the principle that, if necessary to resolve ambiguity, exclusion clauses should be construed narrowly, including in relation to commercial contracts. For example, in *Laminates*,[1] Cooke J had been required to construe a contractual time limit for giving notice of a claim and had treated it as axiomatic that he should apply 'the usual principles which apply to the construction of exclusion clauses'.

1 *Laminates Acquisition Co v BTR Australia Ltd* [2003] EWHC 2540 (Comm) at [16]–[17], referring also to *Association of British Travel Agents Ltd v British Airways Plc* [2000] Lloyd's Rep 209.

5.17 Briggs LJ continued:

> '[18]. In my judgment the underlying rationale for the principle that, if necessary to resolve ambiguity, exclusion clauses should be narrowly construed has nothing to do with the identification of the *proferens*, either of the document as a whole or of the clause in question. Nor is it a principle derived from an identification of the person seeking to rely upon it. Ambiguity in an exclusion clause may have to be resolved by a narrow construction because an exclusion clause cuts down or detracts from the ambit of some important obligation in a contract, or a remedy conferred by the general law such as (in the present case) an obligation to give effect to a contractual warranty by paying compensation for breach of it. The parties are not lightly to be taken to have intended to cut down the remedies which the law provides for breach of important contractual obligations without using clear words having that effect: see *Gilbert-Ash (Northern) Ltd v Modern Engineering (Bristol) Ltd* [1974] AC 689 per Lord Diplock at 717H, applied in *Seadrill Management Services Ltd v OAO Gazprom* [2010] EWCA Civ 691, by Moore-Bick LJ at para 29.
>
> [19]. This approach to exclusion clauses is not now regarded as a presumption, still less as a special rule justifying the giving of a strained meaning to a provision merely because it is an exclusion clause. Commercial parties are entitled to allocate between them the risks of something going wrong in their contractual relationship in any way they choose. Nor is it simply to be mechanistically applied wherever an ambiguity is identified in an exclusion clause. The court must still use all its tools of linguistic, contextual, purposive and common-sense analysis to discern what the clause really means. In the *Seadrill Management* case Moore-Bick described the principle as:
>
>> "essentially one of common sense; parties do not normally give up valuable rights without making it clear that they intend to do so".

> [20]. In the present case the Buyer challenged by respondent's notice the judge's conclusion that clause 5.1 should not be construed *contra proferentem* because both sides gave warranties to each other, subject in each case to exclusion clauses. In my judgment that challenge to the judge's analysis is well made. I can see no reason to disapply the principle that resolves ambiguities in a particular exclusion clause by a narrow construction, merely because the same contract contains an exclusion clause limiting the extent of contractual warranties given by the other party. The same principle may be used where necessary to resolve ambiguities (if there are any) in either of them.
>
> [21]. For those legal reasons I approach the issue as to the construction of clause 5.1 upon the basis that there remains a principle that an ambiguity in its meaning may have to be resolved by a preference for the narrower construction, if linguistic, contextual and purposive analysis do not disclose an answer to the question with sufficient clarity.'

5.18 It is therefore the case that a purchaser may seek to rely on the *contra proferentem* principle in arguing for a less restrictive reading of a notification clause. In *The Hut Group*, Briggs J held at [29] that '[t]he natural meaning of the language is by no means so clear as to preclude serious consideration of the commerciality or otherwise of rival interpretations or, for that matter, to preclude recourse to the principle that ambiguous exclusion clauses should be construed narrowly'. He went on to hold that:

> '[39]. I have been considerably assisted by my perception that the undoubted ambiguities in this exclusion clause are properly to be resolved by having recourse to the narrower of the two available interpretations …
>
> [40]. In conclusion, therefore, I consider that a purposive interpretation of clause 5.1 on a fairly narrow balance favours the judge's conclusion, but that is significantly reinforced by being the narrower of the available interpretations of a seriously ambiguous exclusion clause. In this perhaps unusual case, a thoroughly modern recourse to purposive construction happily marches hand in hand with a perhaps more old-fashioned recourse to rules or canons of construction, which continue to assist the court where all else fails.'

5.19 It should be noted, however, that in a number of subsequent decisions, an appeal to the *contra proferentem* principle has not aided claimants as the courts have found the relevant clause to be sufficiently clear. In *Teoco*,[1] Newey LJ held that recourse to the *contra proferentem* principle 'did not lend any real support' to the appellant purchaser's contentions that the requirements of the notification clause had been satisfied. Similarly, the claimant purchaser in *ROK*[2] submitted that any ambiguity should be resolved *contra proferentem*, but the judge did not have recourse to the principle in determining the preliminary issue. Nonetheless, it is a principle to be borne in mind. Both sides are likely to contend that the meaning of a clause is clear but if a judge does not agree, the principle may operate to tip the balance in favour of a claimant.

1 *Teoco UK Ltd v Aircom Jersey 4 Ltd* [2018] EWCA Civ 23 at [28]. For a similar conclusion, see *Zayo Group International Ltd v Ainger* [2017] EWHC 2542 (Comm) at [93].
2 *ROK Plc v S Harrison Group Ltd* [2011] EWHC 270 (Comm) at [46].

Construction of notices

Objective construction taking into account relevant context

5.20 The starting point for construing a unilateral notice is the speech of Lord Steyn in *Mannai Investment Co Ltd v Eagle Star Life Assurance Co Ltd.* At page 767G, Lord Steyn explained:

> 'The question is not how the landlord understood the notices. The construction of the notices must be approached objectively. The issue is how a reasonable recipient would have understood the notices. And in considering this question the notices must be construed taking into account the relevant objective contextual scene.'[1]

1 [1997] AC 749. The *Mannai* case concerned the interpretation of a clause concerning a tenant's notice required to exercise a break clause in a lease.

5.21 Lord Hoffmann further endorsed the objective approach, stating at page 775E that:

> 'When therefore, lawyers say that they are concerned, not with the subjective meaning but with the meaning of the language which the speaker has used, what they mean is that they are concerned with what he would objectively be understood to mean.'

5.22 In considering the contextual scene, Lord Steyn explained at page 768B: 'The real question is what evidence of surrounding circumstances may ultimately be allowed to influence the question of interpretation. That depends on what meanings the language read against the objective contextual scene will let in.'

5.23 The *Mannai* decision was applied in the context of breach of warranty claims by Cooke J in *Laminates Acquisition v BTR Australia Ltd*,[1] who held that 'The question is how this notice would be understood by a reasonable recipient with knowledge of the context in which it was sent.'

1 [2004] 1 All ER (Comm) 737.

Principles applicable to contractual construction are relevant

5.24 The principles applicable to the construction of a notice are therefore similar to the ordinary principles of contractual construction, as set out above, albeit that the court is construing words used by only one party and not agreed words. Accordingly, the courts do draw on the principles of contractual interpretation to assist with construing notices.

5.25 For example, in *Stobart Group Ltd v William Stobart and William Tinkler*, drew on the decision in *Wood v Capita*[1] in holding that the order in which a judge considers the factual context and the wording of the relevant notice was immaterial. Simon LJ held that:

> 'It is clear from Lord Hodge's judgment in *Wood v Capita* (above) at [12] that the order in which the analysis is carried out is immaterial:
>
> > "To my mind once one has read the language in dispute and the relevant parts of the contract that provide the context, it does not matter whether the more detailed analysis commences with the factual background section and the implication of the rival constructions or a close examination of the relevant language in the contract, so long as the court balances the indications given by each."[2]

1 [2017] AC 1173.
2 At [30].

CONSTRUCTION OF NOTIFICATION CLAUSES AND NOTICES – SPECIFIC ISSUES

Specificity

Range of options

5.26 In drafting the sale agreement, the parties can choose the degree of specificity that a notification clause requires a purchaser to give a seller when notifying it of a potential claim. In practice, the clauses range from setting a very low threshold through to requiring the provision of a highly detailed document. The level of precision required by the notification clause may also be based upon the degree of detail known to the seller at the relevant time.

5.27 The following section considers a range of notification clauses and the degree of specificity that they have been held by the courts to require. When considering how much information must be specified in a notice, although each clause must be construed on its own facts and in its own context, it is likely to be instructive to consider cases in which the construction of similarly worded clauses has fallen to be determined. To the extent there is any doubt as to the degree of specificity required, a buyer would be well-advised to err on the side of caution.

Practical examples

5.28 In the *Senate v Alcatel* case,[1] the sale agreement contained the following notification clause:

> 'Notwithstanding any other provisions of the Agreement, the Vendor shall not be liable under this Agreement in respect of any breach of the warranties … unless notice of it is given by the Purchaser to the Vendor *setting out such particulars of the grounds on which such claim is based as are thenknown to the Purchaser* … promptly and in any event … within eighteen months of the completion date' (emphasis added).

1 *Senate Electrical Wholesalers Ltd v Alcatel Submarine Networks Ltd* [1999] 2 Lloyd's Rep 423.

5.29 The Purchaser had sent a first letter to the seller on 26 December 1991 which stated that 'It is now clear that the Management Accounts were manifestly inaccurate … The purpose of this letter is to notify you for the purpose of Clause 11.5.1 of the Agreement … that a substantial claim is likely to be made against STC for breach of warranties contained in the Agreement. We shall provide you with further details of the ground of this claim and of quantum in the near future.' A further letter was sent on 22 June 1992 (well within 18 months of the completion date), which contained further particulars and grounds for the claim.

5.30 At first instance, the judge held that the further letter could not be relied upon as it had not been sent promptly (on which point there was no appeal), but that the earlier letter had satisfied the notice requirement. His conclusion was driven by the fact that the Purchaser had given 'particulars of the grounds on which such Claim is based as are then known to the Purchaser' at two meetings in November and December 1991.

5.31 The Court of Appeal disagreed. Stuart-Smith LJ held that the judge had been wrong to hold that the Purchaser had complied with the notification clause. The letter of 26 December 1991 had not intended to incorporate what had passed at the meetings, and even if it had purported to do so, this would not have constituted compliance with the notification clause: 'in our view it is plain that the clause requires the grounds known to the purchaser shall themselves be set out in writing'. Stuart-Smith LJ went on to explain that this would allow incorporation of another document but not merely a 'bald reference to an earlier oral exchange'.

5.32 When considered against the purpose of notification provisions – providing certainty – this is an unsurprising result. While the purchaser may consider that it has made the position clear orally, requiring a written record ensures that there is no dispute as to the matters of which the seller has been informed.

5.33 On the subject of specificity, Stuart-Smith LJ held:

> 'Certainty is only achieved when the vendor is left in no reasonable doubt not only that a claim may be brought but of the particulars of the ground upon which the claim is to be based. The clause contemplates that the notice will be couched in terms which are sufficiently clear and unambiguous as to leave no such doubt and to leave no room for argument about the particulars of the complaint.'[1]

1 [1999] 2 Lloyd's Rep 423 at [91].

5.34 In *Bottin (International) Investments Ltd v Venson Group Plc*, the share purchase agreement contained the following notification clause:

> '(o) No claim under the Warranties shall be deemed to have been made unless notice of such claim was made in writing to the Warrantors specifying such detail of the event or circumstances giving rise to such claim as are available to the Investor and an estimate (if capable of preparation by the Investor) of the total amount of the Warrantors' liabilities therefore claimed.'[1]

1 [2004] EWCA Civ 1368

5.35 In considering what details were required, Peter Gibson LJ started by focusing closely on the words of the clause, noting that only 'such detail or the event or circumstances *giving rise to the claim*' (emphasis added) needed to be given. This meant that only details of what had happened to cause the claim, not details of or in respect of the claim itself. For example, particulars did not have to be provided of any allegation of knowledge on the part of the warrantors.[1]

1 For a further example of the court rejecting submissions that details of the seller's alleged knowledge be included in a notification letter, see *TP Icap Ltd v Nex Group Ltd* [2022] EWHC 2700 (Comm) at [33]–[36]. In particular, as regards the identification of the individuals who were said to have had the relevant knowledge, it was noted that it would have been open to the buyer simply to have stated the names of each of the eight individuals whose knowledge was relevant for the purposes of the warranties as alternatives in the notification letter.

5.36 Peter Gibson LJ also contrasted the case with that of *Senate v Alcatel*. He noted the statement of Stuart-Smith LJ that '[c]ertainty is only achieved when the vendor is left in no reasonable doubt not only that a claim may be brought but the particulars of the ground on which the claim is to be based', but considered that this statement was clearly tied to the terms of the particular clause in question in *Senate v Alcatel*,[1] and was made against the background of a 'wholly uninformative notice'.

1 [2004] EWCA Civ 1368 at [52].

5.37 Peter Gibson LJ continued by considering each alleged breach of warranty in turn. The buyers had, in each case, set out the circumstances giving rise to the claim. For example, in one instance, they had done so by reference to a significant discrepancy between the profits that had been shown in management accounts and the large loss that had actually been incurred.[1] Further, the buyer had provided a total estimate of the warrantor's liability, and the notification clause did not require evidence in support of an estimate nor evidence of a valuation exercise.[2]

1 [2004] EWCA Civ 1368 at [56].
2 [2004] EWCA Civ 1368 at [61]–[62].

5.38 In *Curtis and Ranger v Lockheed Martin UK Holdings Ltd*,[1] the relevant notification clause stated that:

> '[n]one of [the relevant individuals] shall be liable for any General Warranty Claim … unless [they] shall have received from [LM] written notice containing details of the General Warranty Claim … (setting out in reasonable detail the specific matter or claim in respect of which such General Warranty Claim is made so far as then known to [LM]) including the amount of such General Warranty Claim … on or before the second anniversary of Completion in the case of a General Warranty Claim …'.

1 *Curtis and Ranger v Lockheed Martin UK Holdings Ltd* [2008] EWHC 2691 (Comm).

5.39 The only breach of warranty that had been established was a failure fully and fairly to disclose an agreement known as the 'Exploitation Agreement'. The Exploitation Agreement was a contract between Stasys (the entity of which the entire share capital had been sold to the claimant) and a number of other parties who collectively contributed to an EU project referred to as Pubcys, which was to develop a computerised system to track magazine stocks, including their disposal and recycling. The Exploitation Agreement was held not to have been disclosed, and was a crucial document in Italian proceedings (of which the buyers were aware).

5.40 The notification letter sent was, however, very thin. It contained statements such as 'an issue has arisen in relation to certain costs potentially to be incurred by the Company …', failed to identify the Exploitation Agreement as the agreement which was alleged in the Italian proceedings to have been breached and did not attempt to link the limited details about the Italian proceedings to the warranties that it asserted had been breached. As Simon J held, 'even a reasonable recipient who was aware of the relevant background would not have been informed by the terms of the letter …'.[1]

1 [2008] EWHC 2691 (Comm) at [106].

5.41 It was therefore perhaps unsurprising that Simon J held that the notification requirements had not been complied with and that the sellers were accordingly not liable in respect of the warranty claim. Not only was the letter uninformative but the notification clause was also relatively onerous, requiring the specific matters in respect of which a warranty claim was made as known by the buyers at that time to be set out.

5.42 In *Teoco UK Ltd v Aircom Jersey 4 Ltd*, the notification clause provided that:

> 'No seller shall be liable for any Claim unless the Purchaser has given notice to the Seller of such Claim setting out reasonable details of the Claim (including the grounds on which it is based and the Purchaser's good faith estimate of the amount of the Claim (detailing the Purchaser's causation of the loss, liability or damage alleged to have been suffered or incurred)).'[1]

1 [2018] EWCA Civ 23.

5.43 At first instance, Richard Millett QC, sitting as a Deputy High Court Judge, concluded that the relevant letters said to have constituted notifications for the purpose of the notification requirements did not set out the grounds on which the claims were based because they did not identify the warranties said to have been breached.[1]

1 [2016] 4 WLUK 527 at [35(iii)], [46], [50], [56].

5.44 The Court of Appeal agreed that the notification clause had not been complied with because the letters did not identify the particular warranties on which the claims were based. Newey LJ considered a number of other authorities before concluding at [27] that:

> 'I accept [counsel's] submission that the "setting out" of the "grounds" of a claim that paragraph 4 called for meant that the legal basis of the claim had to be identified. It is not inconceivable that, exceptionally, that could have been achieved without mentioning a warranty or other provision in terms (if, say, recitation of the relevant facts had unequivocally indicated a specific warranty). Having regard to the decision of the House of Lords in *Mannai Investment Co Ltd v Eagle Star Life Assurance Co Ltd* [1997] AC 749, it is also possible to imagine circumstances in which reference to the wrong warranty would not have invalidated a notice (if a reasonable recipient would not have been misled by the error and would have understood which warranty the Purchaser was intending to rely on).

In general, however, it seems to me that "setting out" the "grounds" of a claim required explicit reference to particular warranties or other provisions. Moreover, the present case was not one in which either the Purchaser erroneously referred to the wrong warranty or the facts unequivocally pointed to a specific warranty … As the Judge said, the "omnibus reference to Warranty Claims or Tax Claims" was not good enough. The phrase will have included the relevant warranties and other provisions, but, since it also encompassed a multitude of other possibilities, it did not serve to identify the "grounds" of the claims.'

5.45 If the parties have agreed that notification of the 'grounds' of the claim must be given, a putative claimant must therefore ensure that adequate details of each aspect of the claim are set out. As can be seen from *Teoco*, a claimant attempting to keep its options open by using widely-framed terms must be alive to the risk that it may be held that no claims have been properly notified all.

5.46 In *ROK*,[1] the notification clause provided:

'The Vendor is not liable for a Claim or a claim under the Tax Undertaking or the Indemnities unless the Purchaser has given the Vendor notice in writing of the Claim or the claim under the Tax Undertaking or the Indemnities, specifying in reasonable detail the nature of the Claim or claim under the Tax Undertaking or the Indemnities and the amount claimed (based in each case on the information then available to the Purchaser) … .'

1 *ROK Plc v S Harrison Group Ltd* [2011] EWHC 270 (Comm).

5.47 Richard Siberry QC, sitting as a Deputy High Court Judge, agreed with the claimant's submission that this was a 'relatively "low threshold" notice clause in comparison with some of the notice clauses that have been before the Courts'. He continued:

'It requires written notice of the Claim which specifies, in reasonable detail, the nature of the Claim and the amount claimed. But it does not require details (or particulars) to be given of the grounds on which the Claim is based (as in *Senate Electrical)*, or of the matter (*Laminates*) or event or circumstances (*Bottin)* which have given rise to the Claim, or of the specific matter(s) in respect of which the claim is made (*RWE Nukem, Curtis*). The parties have not provided for that degree of specificity (cf Ward LJ's comments in para 23 of his judgment in *Forrest v Glasser*). They have chosen an expression, "the nature of the Claim", which is more general and less prescriptive, as was recognised by Dyson J in *Odebrecht*, in contrasting the phrase "*nature of such breach*" with the detail of the breach.'[1]

1 [2011] EWHC 270 (Comm) at [61].

5.48 The wording of the clause in this case was taken together with the fact that a further clause required that, if any claim notified was to be pursued, proceedings were to be issued and served within six months, and detailed particulars would have to be given in those proceedings. The intention of the notification clause was to ensure that the warrantors were aware of any claims, and the nature and potential quantum of any such claims, within the specified period, so that they would know that the security given in respect of the warranties had to be maintained.

5.49 Nonetheless, the judge held that the stipulation that 'the nature of the claim' be specified 'in reasonable detail' required, as a minimum, that the notice should identify the contractual provision under which the claim was said to arise. He held:

> 'In my judgment the stipulation that "the nature of the Claim" be specified "in reasonable detail" requires, as a minimum, that the notice should identify the contractual provision under which the Claim is said to arise. It would not, in my judgment, have been sufficient for a notice to state simply, "ROK hereby notifies you that it has a Claim for breach (or breaches) of Warranty (estimated at £x)". Nor would it be sufficient for it to assert facts without identifying the Warranty relied on as giving rise to a Claim in respect of those facts. As clause 6.4 of the SPA expressly provides, the Warranties are "separate and independent" warranties, and each separate Claim under a Warranty must therefore be notified.
>
> Thus I reject ROK's submission that the Letter, which did not mention the Profit Forecast Warranty, constituted sufficient notice of its pleaded Claim for breach of that Warranty. The fact that the grounds now relied on in the Letter as supporting the Claim under the CVR Warranty are in substance the same as those relied on as supporting the Claim under the Profit Forecast Warranty is not enough. The letter gave no indication to SHG that there might also be a claim under the Profit Forecast Warranty, and so did not satisfy the commercial purpose of notifying SHG of the nature of one of the Claims now pleaded against it.'[1]

1 [2011] EWHC 270 (Comm) at [63]–[64].

5.50 Considering the effect of the words 'based in each case on the information then available to the Purchaser', the judge held:

> 'I accept ROK's submission that the words in parentheses, "based in each case on the information then available to the Purchaser", did not expand the requirement to give "reasonable detail": they merely excuse inaccuracies or other deficiencies in the notice resulting from limited information available to the Purchaser at the time any notice

> was served. The structure of the Notice Clause, and in particular the fact that these words appear in parentheses at the end of the first paragraph, after the statement of what is to be specified "in reasonable detail", militate against any construction which would treat those words as requiring more detail than would have been the case if those words had been absent.'[1]

1 [2011] EWHC 270 (Comm) at [66].

5.51 The judge then considered the words 'in reasonable detail', holding that:

> 'The words "in reasonable detail" were presumably intended to add something to a requirement to specify the nature of the Claim and the amount claimed. It is impossible to define, in abstract terms, what would, or would not, constitute reasonable detail – though it is clear, as ROK submitted, that these words did not require ROK to give as much detail as possible in the light of available information. What constitutes reasonable detail will depend on the nature of the Claim, bearing in mind also that it is unlikely to have been the parties intention, at the time of contracting, that the details to be provided should be as extensive as those that would be required, doubtless after further investigation, in the legal proceedings to be issued and served within six months of the notice.'[1]

1 [2011] EWHC 270 (Comm) at [67].

5.52 Turning to the notification letter, the judge described it as 'in comparison with some of the notice letters that have been before the Courts, an informative letter'. In setting out the details given by the notice letter, the judge gave helpful guidance to parties drafting notice letters in cases involving similar notification clauses. He held at [72]:

> 'In my judgment, this informative Letter (with its accompanying schedules) did provide reasonable detail of the nature of ROK's Claim for breach of the CVR Warranty, and the amount of that Claim (and in doing so satisfied the commercial purposes identified in para. 62 above). SHG was thereby notified, not only of ROK's allegation of breach of the CVR Warranty, but also of the alleged factual basis for that Claim, of the global figure then claimed, and of the likely maximum amounts that would be claimed in respect of individual packages. The fact that the Claim has since been refined, with the particularisation of individual packages and alleged shortfalls in CVR allowances (and the recognition of the limitation to SHG's maximum liability), does not detract from the validity of the Letter, which I find comfortably satisfied the requirements of the Notice Clause with respect to ROK's Claim for breach of the CVR Warranty.'

5.53 The notifiation clause in *Hut Group v Nobahar-Cookson*[1] was framed in very similar terms to the relevant clause in *ROK*. Blair J adopted the reasoning set out above, simply noting at paragraph 101:

> 'Clause 5.1 of Schedule 5 of the SPA required the notice of the Claim on the Sellers to specify "... in reasonable detail the nature of the Claim and, so far as practicable, the amount claimed in respect of it ...". As to this type of provision, see *ROK Plc v S Harrison Group* (ibid) at [61] and following.'[2]

1 [2014] EWHC 3842 (QB).
2 There was no appeal from this aspect of the decision.

5.54 Blair J held at [108] that '[a]t this stage, not much was contractually required in my view, and details would quite likely follow'. Despite this statement, and the decision that the notice letter in *ROK* 'comfortably' satisfied the notification requirements, those drafting notification letters to satisfy similarly worded notification clauses should have regard to the *ROK* decision for guidance.

5.55 The requirement for 'reasonable detail' to be given in respect of certain matters was considered in *Dodika Ltd v United Luck Group Holdings Ltd*.[1] The notification clause provided that: 'any Indemnity Claim or Claim under the Tax Covenant shall be enforceable if the Buyer gives written notice to the Warrantors stating in reasonable detail the matter which gives rise to such Claim, the nature of such Claim and (so far as reasonably practical) the amount claimed in respect thereof on or before the Second Claims Escrow Release Date'.[2]

1 [2020] EWHC 2101 (Comm).
2 See [93].

5.56 It was common ground that the relevant letter provided reasonable detail of the nature of the claim, but the 'key battleground' was whether the letter gave reasonable detail concerning the 'matter which gives rise to the claim'. Whether it was 'reasonably practical' to quantify the claim was held to be a triable issue not suitable for summary determination.[1]

1 [2020] EWHC 2101 (Comm) at [102]–[107].

5.57 Having carried out a review of the authorities, the judge held that the exercise to be conducted was 'merely a matter of interpreting the language of the notification on an objective basis and asking simply whether or not reasonable detail of the factors required to be notified have been notified'.[1]

The judge continued:

> 'the "matter giving rise to the Claim" refers to the facts, events or circumstances on which the Claim is based (ie the factual basis of

> the Claim). In other words, the notification must provide sufficient or reasonable detail of the circumstances on which the Defendant relies in support of or to make good its Claim …
>
> The requirement of "reasonable detail" translates into an obligation of the notifying party to provide sufficient information so that the receiving party, acting reasonably, knows what matter (facts, events or circumstances) gives rise to the Claim being made or contingently made (as well as the nature of the Claim and, if reasonably practical, the amount of the Claim) ….'[2]

1 [2020] EWHC 2101 (Comm) at [111].
2 At [112]–[114].

5.58 On the facts, the judge held at [115] that the notification letter did not provide 'reasonable detail' of the matters giving rise to the claim. Reference to a tax investigation did not constitute notification of the matters giving rise to the claim as no details were given as to the facts on the basis of which a claim under the relevant tax covenant was or could be made. Unless the facts emerging from the tax investigation in question were identified, the sellers were not in a position to assess 'even in a general sense' the prospects of liability for a breach of the relevant tax covenant.

5.59 The judge's decision was, however, overturned on appeal.[1] While Nugee LJ held that the judge had been correct that the 'matter which gives rise to the claim' was the underlying events, facts or circumstances' and not the fact of the tax investigation, he held that the notification letter had provided 'reasonable detail' as required.[2] Nugee LJ held that:

> '*Mannai* shows that the information conveyed by a unilateral notice to the reasonable recipient is in principle capable of being affected by the background context, and that includes the knowledge that the actual recipient has; and such knowledge seems to me to be in principle capable of being relevant not only to the question of construction but to the question of compliance.'[3]

1 [2021] EWCA Civ 638.
2 At [21]–[40].
3 At [34].

5.60 Nugee LJ held that the SPA had not stated precisely what information the notice needed to contain, and what constituted 'reasonable detail' must depend on all the circumstances, including what was already known to the recipient of the notice. In circumstances where the relevant matters were already known 'exactly', Nugee LJ considered a requirement to state particular details '… seems to me to elevate the requirement to state matters in reasonable detail into empty formalism'. While Nugee LJ was clear that he had found it a difficult decision,[1] against that background he held (in agreement with the

Vice Chancellor and Popplewell LJ) that the notification letter did state the matters giving rise to the claim in reasonable detail. While this judgment may therefore assist parties looking to rely on a notification letter which does not contain certain matters that are known to the other party,[2] it remains advisable for as much detail as possible to be included to avoid the risk of being held not to have complied with the notification requirements.[3]

1 Popplewell LJ did not find it such a difficult decision on the basis that: (i) the further level of detail available but not included was still at a high level of generality; (ii) the additional detail was known to the respondents; and (iii) it would have served no commercial purpose to have set out the further level of detail in light of (i) and (ii): see [2021] EWCA Civ 638 at [44]–[46]. The Vice Chancellor agreed the he was also less hesitant for the reasons given by Popplewell LJ: see [47].

2 In *TP Icap Ltd v Nex Group Ltd* [2022] EWHC 2700 (Comm), the court drew on *Dodika* in rejecting a submission that a notification clause required a notification letter mechanically to carry across language from the warranties even though such language would 'have advanced any of the commercial purposes for giving notice'. See [45]–[49].

3 See *Drax Smart Generation HoldCo Ltd v Scottish Power Retail Holdings Ltd* [2024] EWCA Civ 477 for a further decision considering *Dodika*, with a warning at [50] that: 'Notice of claim clauses should not become a technical minefield to be navigated, divorced from the underlying merits of a buyer's claim. While a seller's interest will always be to knock the claim out if it can on the technical ground that the notice is insufficient, courts should not interpret such clauses as imposing requirements which serve no real commercial purpose unless compelled to do so by the language of the clause.' In applying this at [54] to [59], Males LJ allowed a claim to proceed which calculated the damages claimed on a different basis to that suggested in the notification letter.

5.61 As a further note of caution, a party giving notice of multiple potential claims must consider whether it should include a calculation of its total loss claimed or a loss figure for each claim. This issue arose in *Decision Inc Holdings Proprietary Ltd v Garbett*.[1] The notification clause in the SPA in that case provided that:

> 'The sellers shall not be liable for a Claim unless notice is given in writing summarising the nature of the Claim (in so far as it is known to the Buyer) and, as far as is reasonably practicable, the amount claimed has been given by or on behalf of the Buyer to the Sellers… [within certain time periods depending on the type of claim].'

1 [2023] EWCA Civ 1284. The discussion of the notice requirements begins at [66]. See also the first instance decision at [2023] EWHC 588 (Ch).

5.62 The judge at first instance had held that the notification clause did not require loss estimates to be given for each individual breach of warranty allegation. While noting that appellate courts should be slow to interfere with such findings on appeal, the Court of Appeal disagreed. Newey LJ held that it was 'not reasonably open' to the judge to have found that it was not possible or reasonably practicable to give an amount claimed for a breach of the specific warranty in question, noting that the judge had in fact undertaken such an exercise himself. Newey LJ determined that the correct interpretation of the notification clause did require the claimants to state the amount claimed in respect of each breach of warranty alleged, and not just to give an 'omnibus figure'. As the claimants had not done so, the defendants could not be held liable for any such breach.

Matters already known to the seller

5.63 Another issue that may arise relates to whether a notice must address matters already known to the seller.

5.64 In *Senate v Alcatel*,[1] the Court of Appeal had concluded that the notification requirements had not been complied with. The final argument that the claimant raised was that the notification clause had imposed no obligation to give written notice of facts and matters which were already known to the vendors.

1 *Senate Electrical Wholesalers Ltd v Alcatel Submarine Networks Ltd* [1999] 2 Lloyd's Rep 423.

5.65 The court considered authorities from a number of fields including insurance and shipping law, amongst them the judgment of Lord Denning MR in *Barrett Bros (Taxis) Ltd v Davies Lickiss and Milestone Motor Policies at Lloyd's, Third Parties*.[1] Lord Denning MR had noted that '[t]he law never compels a person to do that which is useless and unnecessary', and that if the insurer was already aware of the relevant matters, it was not prejudiced by the non-compliance and so could not rely on the condition to defeat the claim.

1 [1966] 2 Lloyd's Rep 1.

5.66 Stuart-Smith LJ held that:

> 'We share the reservations expressed about Lord Denning's broad proposition but, whatever the correctness of *Barratt Bros*, the question whether or not the appellants had been prejudiced and whether or not it is futile to require strict compliance with cl 11.5 of the agreement must depend upon the construction to be placed upon that clause and the commercial purpose it was intended to serve.'[1]

1 [1999] 2 Lloyd's Rep 423 at [90].

5.67 Upholding the first instance decision, Stuart-Smith LJ continued:

> '… Certainty is a crucial foundation for commercial activity. Certainty is only achieved when the vendor is left in no reasonable doubt not only that a claim may be brought but of the particulars of the ground upon which the claim is to be based. The clause contemplates that the notice will be couched in terms which are sufficiently clear and unambiguous as to leave no such doubt and to leave no room for argument about the particulars of the complaint. Notice in writing is required in order to

constitute the record which dispels the need for further argument and creates the certainty. Thus there is merit in certainty and accordingly, in our judgment the point taken by the appellants is not a matter of mere technicality and it is not without merit.'[1]

1 [1999] 2 Lloyd's Rep 423 at [91].

5.68 The construction of the clause will therefore determine the relevance of the seller's knowledge. It is clear following the Court of Appeal's decision in *Dodika* that the knowledge of the seller may have a bearing on what constitutes 'reasonable detail' where the notification clause imposes such a requirement,[1] but a party issuing a notice would be well advised to err on the side of caution.

1 *Dodika Ltd v United Luck Group Holdings Ltd* [2020] EWHC 2101 (Comm) at [21]–[40].

5.69 While compliance with notification requirements is necessarily a question of construction in every case, it is unlikely that (in the absence of an express provision to the contrary) any notification clause would be construed as not requiring the buyer to give notice of matters already known to the sellers. Given that the purpose of a notification clause is to provide certainty to sellers about the possibility of claims being brought against them, the mere fact that the seller knows of matters that may form the basis of a claim is not sufficient to inform it whether such a claim will in fact be pursued. The better view is therefore that notices may not generally exclude reference to material matters on the basis that the same information is already known by the seller.

Time periods

5.70 A notification clause in an SPA will specify a time period within which the relevant notification must be provided. The most common formulation is for the date to be set by reference to the completion of the transaction. For example, in *Senate v Alcatel*,[1] the notice was to be provided 'promptly and in any event … within eighteen months of the completion date'. In *Bottin*, the notice was to be provided 'prior to the third anniversary of Completion'.

1 *Senate Electrical Wholesalers Ltd v Alcatel Submarine Networks Ltd* [1999] 2 Lloyd's Rep 423.

5.71 Whether a notice has been supplied 'promptly' will be a question of fact for the judge to assess. In *Senate v Alcatel*, the judge at first instance had determined that a letter sent in June 1992 giving further particulars of the claim could not be relied upon because it had not been sent promptly, whereas the letter sent in December 1991 had been sent promptly, following meetings at which the claimant had given oral particulars of its complaints in November 1991. Neither of these findings was challenged on appeal. It is notable that the agreement in *Senate v Alcatel* was dated 19 April 1991, and the letter sent in June 1992 was therefore well within the 18-month longstop.

5.72 The more recent decision in *Towergate Financial (Group) Ltd v Hopkinson*[1] confirms that claimants must not overlook a requirement for notification to be provided 'as soon as possible' or 'promptly' regardless of whether there is a cut-off date provided for in the future.

1 [2020] EWHC 984 (Comm).

5.73 The claimants were seeking a declaration that they were entitled to be indemnified against certain liabilities for professional negligence pursuant to an indemnity provision in the SPA. A preliminary issue hearing was held on the narrow question of whether it was correct to construe the indemnity provisions as requiring any claim to be notified 'as soon as possible', as contended for by the defendants; and, if it was correct, what circumstances triggered the commencement of the period encompassed by the phrase 'as soon as possible' and how soon thereafter notice had to be given.

5.74 The relevant notification clause provided as follows:

> 'The Purchaser shall not make any Claims against the Warrantors nor shall the Warrantors have any liability in respect of any matter or thing unless notice in writing of the relevant matter or thing (specifying the details and circumstances giving rise to the Claim or Claims and an estimate in good faith of the total amount of such Claim or Claims) is given to all the Warrantors as soon as possible and in any event prior to:
>
> 6.7.1 the seventh anniversary of the date of this Agreement in the case of any Claim solely in relation to the Taxation Covenant;
>
> 6.7.2 the date two years from the Completion Date in the case of any other Claim; and
>
> 6.7.3 in relation to a claim under the indemnity in clause 5.9 on or before the seventh anniversary of the date of this Agreement.'

5.75 Notice had been given in July 2015, shortly before the seventh anniversary of the SPA.

5.76 Construing the clause, Cockerill J held that the notification clause established a dual condition precedent requiring notice to be served as soon as possible, and in any event within seven years. As to the trigger for the running of time, referring to decisions made at earlier stages of the case, considered below, she endorsed the decisions of Leggatt J and the Court of Appeal. Leggatt J had held:

> 'However, whilst there may well be scope for argument about the exact point at which a notice may be given under clause 6.7, it seems to me that the clause can sensibly be interpreted as requiring notice as

a precondition of making a claim once there is an identifiable matter or thing which may give rise to a claim under the indemnity provision.

Once one accepts that the relevant matter or thing is not an actual claim under the indemnity, it seems to me that the best interpretation of the clause is that it is intended to denote a matter or thing which may give rise to such a claim.'[1]

1 [2017] EWHC 2330 (Comm) at [40]–[41].

5.77 On the facts, Cockerill J had no difficulty in finding that the claim had not been notified as soon as possible. She was guided particularly by the earlier notification of possible liability by the claimants to their insurers.

5.78 At an earlier stage in the same case, a different timing question had arisen concerning the giving of notice by the claimants in circumstances where it was anticipated that a relevant claim would arise under an indemnity but no indemnity claim could in fact be made at the time the notice was given.[1]

1 [2017] EWHC 2330 (Comm).

5.79 Leggatt J considered the same notification clause alongside the relevant indemnity, which provided that:

'The vendors and their respective spouses undertake to indemnify the purchaser and/or the Group in full against all losses, liabilities, costs and expenses which the Group or the purchaser may suffer as a result of, or in connection with, any claim or claims for professional negligence including, but not limited to, claims or complaints arising from misselling.'[1]

1 As set out at [2017] EWHC 2330 (Comm) at [4].

5.80 Two Skilled Persons Reviews were being carried out by the FCA into sales made both before and after the SPA had been entered into. One concerned advice given in respect of 'enhanced transfer value schemes', which had resulted in clients transferring their benefits out of defined benefit pension schemes, and the other concerned the promotion and sale of unregulated collective investment schemes and other unregulated schemes.

5.81 The defendants had argued that: (i) the '*matter or thing*' of which notice had to be given was notice of a claim under the indemnity; and (ii) no claim under the indemnity could be made in that case until a claim was actually made against the purchaser by a third party.

5.82 This argument was rejected by Leggatt J, who held that:

'… I see nothing in the language of the agreement which requires that a claim must be made by a third party against the claimants before notice can be given under clause 6.7.

> It seems to me that, as a matter of general principle, no liability can arise under clause 5.9 to indemnify the purchaser unless and until not only has a claim for professional negligence of the relevant kind been made against the Group or the claimants, but such a claim has resulted in an ascertained liability or loss for which a liability to indemnify can arise.
>
> It is not suggested by the defendants that a loss must actually have been incurred before notice of a claim under the indemnity in clause 5.9 can be given under clause 6.7. It is accepted by them that notice can be given at a time when there is only a potential liability – at least in the sense that no loss has actually been incurred for which an indemnity can be claimed.
>
> That seems to me to be a realistic concession. It would make no sense, and indeed would seem highly unreasonable, to prevent the purchaser from giving notice of a claim under clause 6.7, and hence potentially of being able to make a claim under the indemnity provision, in circumstances where, for example, proceedings had been brought against it by a third party but no judgment had yet been given in those proceedings at the time when the seven year period expired.
>
> However, once one accepts that it is not necessary in order to give a valid notice under clause 6.7 that a loss which gives rise to a right to be indemnified under clause 5.9 has been incurred, I cannot see anything in the language of clause 5.9 or otherwise which necessitates the conclusion that no notice can be given under clause 6.7 unless and until a claim for professional negligence has actually been made by a third party against the purchaser. Indeed, it seems to me that that can potentially introduce equally arbitrary results where, for example, a letter before claim might have been written on behalf of the third party which clearly intimated the intention to make a claim, but no claim had actually been made.'[1]

1 [2017] EWHC 2330 (Comm) at [34]–[38].

5.83 Leggatt J rejected the defendants' suggestion that this rendered the notification clause entirely open-ended such that, on the day after the share purchase agreement was completed, the purchaser could make a very vague notification that they intended to claim in relation to any liabilities which they might incur as a result of unspecified claims for professional negligence. Such an open-ended notice would fall outside the reasonable interpretation of the notification clause in terms of the specificity required. He concluded at [40] that 'it seems to me that the clause can sensibly be interpreted as requiring notice as a precondition of making a claim once there is an identifiable matter or thing which may give rise to a claim under the indemnity provision.' He therefore held that it could not be concluded on a summary judgment application that the notice given in this case was premature.

5.84 The defendants in *Towergate* were arguing in this reverse summary judgment application that the notice was premature despite having been made very shortly before any breach of warranty claim would have become contractually time-barred. This was a particularly unattractive position given that the effect of the construction contended for by the defendants would likely have been that notice could not properly have been given before the contractual limitation period expired. The decision was upheld on appeal.[1]

1 [2018] EWCA Civ 2744 at [48]–[52].

5.85 A time-bar provision for breach of warranty claims may also be formulated by reference to the time at which the putative claimant became aware of relevant matters. In *Nobahar-Cookson*,[1] the notification clause required the buyer to give notice of any claim 'as soon as reasonably practicable and in any event within 20 Business Days after becoming aware of the matter'.

1 *Nobahar-Cookson v The Hut Group Ltd* [2016] EWCA Civ 128.

5.86 Notice had been served by the buyer on 6 February 2012 and it was therefore common ground that, if the sellers could show that the buyer had become 'aware of the matter' by 9 January 2012, then its warranty claim would be contractually time-barred. There was also no appeal from the first instance judge's factual finding that the buyer had become aware of the facts sufficient to prove its breach of warranty claim before 9 January 2012, but that the buyer was not aware of the claim identified in the notice until after that date because it only became so aware upon receipt of advice to that effect from its forensic accountants.

5.87 The Court of Appeal was required to choose between three alternative constructions of the phrase 'aware of the matter': (i) aware of the facts giving rise to the claim (even if unaware that those facts did give rise to a claim); (ii) aware that there might be a claim under the warranties; and (iii) aware of the claim in the sense of awareness that there was a proper basis for the claim. At first instance, Blair J had held construction (iii) to be the true construction.

5.88 Briggs LJ, upholding the first instance decision, found that construction (ii) was so uncommercial that it ought to be rejected, and that a purposive construction aided by the *contra proferentem* principle led to the conclusion that construction (iii) was the proper meaning of the clause.[1] Moylan J and Hallett LJ also endorsed the first instance decision but noted that they would have placed greater emphasis on commerciality or commercial sense.[2]

1 [2016] EWCA Civ 128 at [37]–[38].
2 At [40]–[41].

5.89 While every notification or contractual limitation clause must be construed on its own terms, the reasoning in the *Nobahar-Cookson* decision provides helpful guidance on the commerciality of different constructions of clauses based on the potential claimant's awareness of certain matters.

Fraud exception

5.90 A notification clause may carve out an exception for claims arising out of fraud or wilful misconduct. An example of this can be seen in *Arani v Cordic Group Ltd.*[1] The sellers issued a claim for the release of retained sums forming part of the sale price that were to be held in escrow before being released to the sellers 16 months following completion unless a claim had been notified in accordance with the relevant notification provisions, as follows:

> '6.3 Limitations: Notwithstanding any other provision of this Agreement, but subject to clause 6.4, the Vendors will not be liable:
>
> 6.3.1 Time:
>
> (i) For any Warranty Claim unless notice of the Warranty Claim is given in writing by the Purchaser to the Vendors setting out full particulars of the grounds on which the Warranty Claim under this Agreement is based within the 16 months following Completion, except that for a Warranty Claim relating to Tax or a claim under the Tax Deed, the time limit is seven years from the end of the accounting period in which the corporation tax return relating to the accounting period of the Company current at Completion is due to be filed. …
>
> 6.4 Non-applicability of Limitations: The limitations and exclusions contained in this Agreement will not apply to any claim under this Agreement to the extent that it:
>
> …
>
> 6.4.3 arises (in whole or in part), or is increased or delayed,as a result of any fraudulent act, omission or misrepresentation or any wilful misconduct, wilful concealment, or wilful misstatement by the Vendors…'

1 [2021] EWHC 829 (Comm) and a further judgment of Bright J at [2023] EWHC 95 (Comm).

5.91 The buyers defended the claim for release of the sums on the basis that the sellers were not entitled to the sums due to breaches of warranty. A counterclaim was also brought relating to the same breaches of warranty as well as raising a number of additional matters. The sellers brought a summary judgment and strike out application, seeking to have the claim summarily dismissed and the defence struck out on the basis that the allegations of breach of warranty had not been notified in accordance with the notification requirments in the SPA. The letters that were sent had been sent one day after the end of the 16 month period. The buyers then sought permission to amend the defence and counterclaim, including to reflect the discovery of documents which showed that the sellers had known that the facts stated in the warranties were untrue and had deliberately covered them up.

5.92 Andrew Hochhauser KC sitting as a Deputy High Court Judge granted the sellers' application for summary judgment and ordered that the retained sums be paid over.[1] This was on the basis that the notification letters had been sent outside of the notification period, and in any event had not complied with the substantive provisions of the clause which required 'full particulars' of the claim being made and an estimate of the sum claimed to be given. Clause 6.4.3 which provided the exception to the notification requirements for fraud claims did not, under the structure of the SPA, provide a basis for the retained sums to continue to be held in escrow beyond the release date 16 months after completion. Permission was, however, granted for the buyers to amend the counterclaim given the parties agreed that the notification provisions did permit a claim for fraudulent breach of warranty to be brought after the notification period, and such claims were held to have a real prospect of success.[2] The counterclaim was ultimately successful following a further trial.[3]

1 [2021] EWHC 829 (Comm) at [152]–[154].
2 [2021] EWHC 829 (Comm) at [164].
3 [2023] EWHC 95 (Comm) at [117]–[118].

Service of notice

5.93 A further requirement often found in notification or contractual limitation clauses is that the relevant notice or proceedings be served on the warrantor or seller in a particular manner.

5.94 While the mechanism for service described in the relevant clause may be clear, a number of issues have arisen around a contractual requirement for 'personal' service. In *Bottin*,[1] the Court of Appeal considered the question of personal service on a company. Clause 19 of the agreement had provided (emphasis added):

> 'Any notice, request instruction or other document to be given under this Agreement to any of the Parties by any of the others shall be in writing and *delivered personally or sent by prepaid recorded delivery post to their addresses set out in this agreement*. Any Party may change the address to which notices are to be sent to it by giving written notice of the change of address to the other Parties in the manner provided for in this clause for giving notice. Any notice delivered personally shall be deemed to be received when delivered and any notice sent by prepaid recorded delivery post shall be deemed received 5 business days after posting.'

1 *Bottin (International) Investments Ltd v Venson Group Plc* [2004] EWCA Civ 1368.

5.95 On the facts of *Bottin*, the notice had been handed to a receptionist at the registered offices of the defendant company. The first instance judge had held that this method of delivery had satisfied clause 19, and the Court of Appeal agreed.

5.96 Peter Gibson LJ started his consideration of this point by agreeing with the first instance judge that the requirement in clause 19 of delivery 'personally' 'did not mean that Bottin personally had to effect the delivery but that the adverb "personally" qualified the delivery to the recipient of the notice'. He also agreed with the first instance judge that neither Civil Procedure Rules (CPR) 6.4(4) nor the Companies Act 1948, s 725 could provide assistance as neither had been incorporated into the agreement.

5.97 He disagreed, however, with the judge's finding that 'personal' delivery to a company would have been satisfied merely by leaving the notice at the registered office, with no need to consider into whose hands, if any, it was delivered. First, he rejected the suggestion that 'personal' delivery on a company connoted delivery to the registered office:

> 'There is nothing in cl 19 to require that the personal delivery to a party which is a company has to be at the company's registered office, still less anything to suggest that personal delivery can be effected merely by leaving the document in question somewhere in the building which is the registered office. That gives no meaning to "personally".'[1]

1 [2004] EWCA Civ 1368 at [46].

5.98 Turning to the facts of the case, he held that:

> 'The judge went on to say that service at the registered office by leaving it with the receptionist was sufficient. Apart from the superfluous reference to the registered office, on the particular facts that conclusion is in my judgment correct. I agree with Mr Glick when he says that personal delivery of a notice to a company is effected by delivering the notice to somebody authorised to receive it. I disagree with him when he says that the only person to have such authority is somebody in a senior position in the company. The function of a receptionist ordinarily is to receive people visiting, and letters or parcels being delivered to, the employer of the receptionist. In the present case there was in evidence the witness statement of the process server, Mr Greenman, who delivered the December notice to the receptionist; that was accepted on the receptionist's express assurance that it would come to the attention of a director. As the judge pointed out, the Defendants did not adduce any evidence as to what happened to the December notice after it was left with the receptionist. It is to be inferred that it did come to the attention of a director. In my judgment, the December notice was delivered personally to Venson.'[1]

1 [2004] EWCA Civ 1368 at [47].

5.99 It therefore appears to be the case that 'personal' delivery to a company will require delivery to somebody authorised to receive it, but that does not necessarily need to be a senior individual.

5.100 The question of 'personal' delivery of a notice to an individual was considered in *Ener-G Holdings v Hormell*.[1] In that case, the agreement provided as follows:

> '13.2 Service
>
> Any such notice may be served by delivering it personally or by sending it pre-paid recorded delivery post to each party (in the case of the Buyer, marked 'for the attention of directors') at or to the address referred to in the Agreement or any other address in England and Wales which he or it may from time to time notify in writing to the other party.
>
> 13.3 Deemed service
>
> Any notice delivered personally shall be deemed to be received when delivered (or if delivered otherwise than between 9.00am and 5.00pm on a Business Day, at 9.00am on the next Business Day), any notice sent by pre-paid recorded delivery post shall be deemed to be received two Business Days after posting and in proving the time of despatch it shall be sufficient to show that the envelope containing such notice was properly addressed, stamped and posted.'

1 [2012] EWCA Civ 1059.

5.101 The claimant had arranged for its notice to be served on the defendant in two ways. First, a process server was instructed to deliver a notice in an envelope addressed to the defendant to his home address (which was the address specified in the agreement). No-one answered when the process server rung the bell at this address, and so the process server left the envelope in the front porch on a table. The defendant found the envelope that afternoon and read the notice. Second, an identical copy of the notice was sent the same day by recorded delivery to the same address. This was deemed by clause 13.3 to have been received two business days after posting.

5.102 The claimant's position was that the notice left in the defendant's porch had been 'personally' delivered, whereas the defendant contended that it had not been because it had not been handed to the defendant himself.

5.103 Lord Neuberger MR upheld the decision of the first instance judge that the notice left in the defendant's porch had not been delivered to him 'personally'. First, Lord Neuberger MR dismissed the claimant's contention that the notice had been 'delivered personally' because it was left at the defendant's residence by a person, namely the process server. Drawing on the decision in *Bottin*, he held that:

> 'where parties are concerned to prescribe how a notice may be served or delivered, the identity of the server of the notice is rarely, if ever, important, whereas the identity of the recipient is, at least normally, of central importance. The law and common sense both support the notion that if "personal" service or delivery of a document is required, it should be handed to the intended recipient personally.'[1]

1 [2012] EWCA Civ 1059 at [18].

5.104 He also rejected the claimant's attempt to distinguish *Bottin* on the grounds that the relevant clause in that case had not contained the qualification that was found in *Ener-G* that the personal delivery was to be effected at a specified location, holding that:

> 'I see the force of that, but it is not a powerful point, because it is far from absurd, or even capricious, for the parties to have so limited the locations where personal service could be effected. Such a restriction merely renders it easier for the intended recipient to avoid personal service. But the recorded delivery process was an obvious alternative.'[1]

1 [2012] EWCA Civ 1059 at [22].

5.105 Lord Neuberger MR therefore held that the notice left in the porch had not been 'delivered personally'.

5.106 A further issue in *Ener-G*, was, however, whether the means of service in clause 13.2 were exhaustive. Lord Neuberger MR held that the means of service in clause 13.2 were permissive only, and that leaving the notice in the porch after which it had been read by the defendant was sufficient.[1]

1 Unusually, on this point the claimant was arguing that clause 13.2 was exhaustive and the defendant was arguing that it was not exhaustive.

5.107 First, he considered the language of clause 13.2:

> '[27] The notion that cl 13.2 was intended to be permissive rather than exclusive, receives obvious support from the fourth word of the clause, 'may', particularly when it is contrasted with the mandatory word 'shall' in the immediately preceding cl 13.1. The force of the point is only slightly diluted by the fact that cl 13.2 envisages two alternative means of delivery: the word 'shall' would have been quite appropriate if it had been intended to be exhaustive.
>
> [28] I consider that some support for this conclusion is to be found in cl 1.5.7, with its statement that '[u]nless expressly stated to the contrary … "in writing" or "written" includes faxes'. There is nothing in cl 13.2 which appears to exclude cl 1.5.7, and, if delivery by fax is permitted, it would seem to be inconsistent with the notion that the

two prescribed methods of delivery in cl 13.2 were exclusive. I accept that it can be said that, if cl 13.2 does permit delivery only by the two specified methods, then delivery by fax is 'expressly' precluded, but it seems to me that, if one is looking to find the intention of the parties, cl 1.5.7 does provide mild assistance to Mr Hormell's case.'

5.108 Second, he considered the purpose of the clause and commercial common sense:

'[29] The argument that it would have been pointless to spell out two methods of service in cl 13.2, unless they were intended to be exclusive, has some initial attraction. However, in my view, on closer analysis, the argument has no force. The purpose of a provision such as cl 13.2, if it is not exclusive, is to shift any risk from the server to the intended recipient: see *Blunden's* case [2002] 2 EGLR 29 at 32 per Robert Walker LJ. Thus, if a document is served in accordance with cl 13.2, it is treated as served, or delivered, even if it does not come to the attention of, or even if it is not received by, the intended recipient (see the cases cited at [23], above). But if a document is served or delivered in any other way (eg by ordinary post or by being left at the intended recipient's premises rather than being handed personally to him), there is no such presumption.

[30] That argument works perfectly well for the provision for sending by recorded delivery. However, at least at first sight, it is unnecessary for personal service: there would appear to have been no need for any presumption in such a case, as personal service, once established as a matter of fact, will always be effective. I consider that the answer to that point lies in the fact that personal delivery of a document on Ener-G might involve the document not coming to the attention of the directors, as it would encompass delivery on a non-director who had actual or ostensible authority to accept service (see the *Bottin (International) Investments* case [2004] All ER (D) 322 (Oct) at [47] per Peter Gibson LJ, cited at [21], above). If a document was personally delivered to such a person, who then failed to pass on the document to a director, cl 13.2 would make it clear that service had been effected.

[31] In my judgment, commercial common sense also assists Mr Hormell's argument. If Ener-G had not sent the second notice by recorded delivery, it would have been very unattractive for Mr Hormell to argue that Ener-G's right to claim on the warranties was lost by virtue of no notice having been delivered within the two-year period prescribed by cl 6.3.3(b). The purpose of providing for the notice was to ensure that Mr Hormell was notified within the two-year period of a warranty claim, so that he would know that he was free of any such claim if he received no such notice within the two-year

period. As he saw the first notice within the two-year period, that aim would have been achieved even without the second notice.'

5.109 Lord Neuberger MR continued by holding that 'clear words would normally be required before one could ascribe to the parties an intention that a recipient who actually receives a notice in time should nonetheless be treated as not having received the notice at all'.[1]

1 [2012] EWCA Civ 1059 at [32].

5.110 He also drew support for his conclusion from the decision of the Court of Appeal in *Yates Building Co Ltd v RJ Pulleyn & Sons (York) Ltd*,[1] in which a notice exercising an option sent by ordinary post was valid even though the relevant contractual provision had specified registered or recorded delivery.

1 [1976] 1 EGLR 157.

5.111 It is clear that the Court of Appeal did not find the question of the exclusivity of the modes of service straightforward. Gross LJ gave a reasoned judgment concurring with Lord Neuberger MR, but Longmore LJ dissented on this point.

5.112 Longmore LJ considered it counter-intuitive to conclude that the parties intended alternative methods of service to be permissible when trouble had been taken to spell out two specific methods. He also drew on the fact that the service clause of the agreement relating to the service of legal proceedings expressly permitted service in accordance with the agreement or 'any other manner allowed by law'. He further noted the oddity of a noncontractual method of service in effect becoming a contractual notice when it came to the attention of the defendant, thus starting the running of time for the claimant to commence legal proceedings, and distinguished the giving of notice from a communication that relates to the making of a contract.

5.113 Whether a clause concerning modes of service is prescriptive or permissive will be a question of construction in each case. As Gross LJ noted, 'the court will of course give effect to exclusivity – notwithstanding the consequences – if indeed that is the bargain the parties have made'. Clear language will, however, be required. Gross LJ concluded:

> 'As illustrated by the judge (at [16]), treating cl 13.2 as exclusive would facilitate a party asserting that the initial cl 6.3.3(b) notice was out of time despite actual receipt of the document and full knowledge of its contents. For reasons I have already sought to adumbrate, a construction which reduces the risk of such an outcome has much to be said for it. In my view, absent clear wording providing for exclusivity, this consideration strongly favours a permissive construction of cl 13.2 – and, especially when considered together with the very considerable

significance of the use of the word "may" in cl 13.2, it serves to tilt the balance in favour of the respondent's case on the appeal.'[1]

1 [2012] EWCA Civ 1059 at [65].

5.114 A further question may arise as to the meaning of clauses concerning the 'service' of legal process. For example, in *Ageas (UK) Ltd v Kwik-Fit (GB) Ltd*, Green J considered the following clause:

> 'Any claim for breach of Warranties other than the Tax Warranties which is made within the relevant time limit specified above shall, unless previously satisfied, settled or withdrawn, be deemed to be withdrawn and no longer enforceable unless legal proceedings in respect thereof are (i) commenced by validly issuing and serving legal process within six months of the making of such claim and (ii) being pursued with reasonable diligence.'[1]

1 As set out at [2013] EWHC 3261 (QB) at [21].

5.115 The agreement did not set out any particular mechanism by which legal proceedings were to be served on the defendant, although provisions were included concerning mechanisms by which notices could be delivered.

5.116 The relevant facts were uncontroversial. There was no dispute that the notice was valid and had been properly served, and that the period of six months following the deemed delivery date of the notice ended on Saturday 28 January 2012, such that the claimant had to commence and serve legal proceedings by that date. Solicitors had confirmed that they were instructed to accept service of proceedings on the defendant's behalf. The claim form was issued on 18 January 2012, and was sent to the relevant solicitors by fax, email and DX on Thursday 26 January 2012. The defendant became aware of the claim against it the same day.

5.117 The defendant sought to argue that the concept of 'serving' a document had to be understood in accordance with domestic procedural law. It was argued that CPR 6.14 had the effect that service of the claim form was only completed on 30 January 2012, taking into account the deemed two-day extension and the exclusion of weekends. The result of this construction would have been that the claim form was served after the contractual limitation period.

5.118 Green J rejected this construction. He started his analysis by making clear that 'the perspective from which the provision must be interpreted is that of the parties, not the reasonable lawyer'. He continued that '[t]his has some significance in the present case because whilst the word "serving" … refers broadly to legal concepts the draftsmen has neither defined those terms in the SPA nor linked them to any specific procedural rule save to say that English law governs'.[1] He went on to note that a phrase such as 'serving' can bear a wide range of (sometimes conflicting) meanings.

1 [2013] EWHC 3261 (QB) at [53].

5.119 He concluded that valid service had taken place on 26 January 2012, within the contractual limitation period. There were four steps in the reasoning. First, the purpose of the clause was to bring the existence of a warranty claim to the actual attention of the vendor within a relatively abbreviated period of time such that once the time limits had passed, the vendor would know for all relevant commercial purposes that it was free from the risk of proceedings (or, as a corollary, to make the vendor aware that there were claims that it was not free of the risk of litigation). The date upon which the vendor in this case had the relevant knowledge was 26 January 2012.

5.120 Second, there were no clear words ascribing to the parties an intention to treat a person who had actually been served as being deemed not to have been served at all (endorsing the decision in *Ener-G* considered above).

5.121 Third, the conclusion reached by Green J created greater certainty:

> 'On the Defendant's construction what *prima facie* is a straightforward clause becomes a trap for the unwary. Without any express language to put the parties on notice the word "serving" imports a concealed extension and an exclusion. It is only possible to determine that a document (the claim) delivered and received towards the end of a working week is in fact to be treated as having been served after the weekend by drawing inferences from surrounding terms such as "validly", "legal proceedings" and "legal process". From these broad and unspecific terms, and from the fact that the contract is subject to English law and jurisdiction, it is argued that the parties are to be presumed to have intended that they should then go searching in the CPR for r.6.14 for a gloss on Schedule 4(3). But this is very far from apparent from its wording.'[1]

1 [2013] EWHC 3261 (QB) at [60].

5.122 Fourth, in the context of the agreement as a whole, the parties, and a reasonable person, considering the word 'serving' in Schedule 4(3) in the context of the SPA as a whole would treat that phrase as meaning actual delivery.

5.123 A similar clause was considered in *T&L Sugars Ltd v Tate & Lyle Industries Ltd*.[1] Flaux J reached the same result as Green J had in *Ageas*, although he disagreed with Green J's reasoning.

1 [2014] EWHC 1066 (Comm).

5.124 The relevant clause provided as follows:

> '11.3 Commencement of Proceedings
>
> Any claim notified pursuant to Clause 11.2 shall (if it has not been previously satisfied, settled or withdrawn) be deemed to be irrevocably withdrawn 12 months after the notice is given pursuant to Clause 11.2 ... unless at such time legal proceedings in respect of the relevant claim have been commenced by being both issued and served.'

5.125 The factual background was again uncontroversial. Notice has been validly given such that the period for issuing and serving proceedings ended on 30 March 2013. Solicitors had been instructed to accept service of proceedings. The claim form had been issued on 27 March 2013 and a copy of the claim form and particulars of claim had been delivered to the relevant solicitors the same day. 27 March 2013 was, however, the Wednesday before Easter.

5.126 The defendant contended that all of the claimant's claims were contractually deemed to have been withdrawn because they were not issued and served in time within the meaning of clause 11.3.

5.127 Flaux J considered Green J's decision in *Ageas* but because he disagreed with Green J's reasoning, he did not follow it. Instead, he held that the word 'served' in clause 11.3 meant 'served in accordance with the CPR'.

5.128 First, he held that 'issued' must have been intended to mean 'in accordance with English procedural rules' given the presence of an exclusive jurisdiction clause. He continued:

> '"Issued" in that context cannot have some ordinary, non-legal meaning, for example the sending of a draft claim form and Particulars of Claim, as sometimes occurs to facilitate settlement before proceedings are formally issued. That would not amount to proceedings being "issued". On the basis that "issued" in this context means issued in accordance with the CPR, it would be very odd if "served" in the same phrase did not also connote served in accordance with the CPR, but had some ordinary non-legal meaning, whatever that entails. So far as I can tell, the significance of the word "issuing" in the provision Green J was considering does not seem to have been discussed in that case.'[1]

1 [2014] EWHC 1066 (Comm) at [15].

5.129 Second, Flaux J considered that the natural meaning of the word 'served' in context was 'served in accordance with the procedural rules in force in England at the relevant time':

> 'I am afraid that I do not find the contrary reasoning of Green J in *Ageas* that the parties as reasonable businessmen would have intended "served" to have some ordinary meaning of delivered and received at all compelling. It seems to me that, if the parties had intended to convey that it should be sufficient that the defendant had notice of the proceedings within the twelve month period by receipt of the claim form even though actual service under the CPR had not occurred, they would more naturally have used words such as "the buyer has delivered the claim form" or "the seller has received notice of proceedings" within 12 months in clause 11.3.'[1]

1 [2014] EWHC 1066 (Comm) at [16].

5.130 Flaux J also took into account the fact that the agreement was drafted in a manner that showed the parties were alive to the service of legal process being something distinct from the giving or receipt of a contractual notice and that the service of legal process should operate by a different set of rules.[1] He also disagreed with Green J's reliance on the *Ener-G* decision in requiring clear words to ascribe to the parties an intention that the party that has actually received a claim form has not been served, noting that there was a distinction between the service of contractual notice and the service of legal proceedings.

1 For example, a clause appointing a process agent to accept service in legal action or proceedings.

5.131 While Green J had held that importing the CPR into the meaning of the phrase 'issued and served' led to further uncertainty because it was unclear whether CPR 6.14 or CPR 7.5 applied, Flaux J considered that the CPR was clear as to the applicable provisions as to when proceedings have actually been served. CPR 7.5 and CPR 6.14 draw a clear distinction between the date when service is actually effected (when the step to be carried out has been completed) and the date when service is deemed to take place for the purpose of the further steps required under the CPR. He explained:

> 'If one asks oneself why that distinction is there, it is not as [counsel] suggests because service does not actually occur until the deemed day, but because, whereas CPR 7.5 is looking at when actual service takes place, so that a claimant who takes the requisite step, depending upon which method of service he employs, can be sure that he has served within the four months of validity of the claim form (thereby avoiding, if relevant, any limitation issues), CPR 6.14 is looking at when service will be deemed to have taken place for the purpose of other steps in the proceedings thereafter, beginning with the filing of an acknowledgment of service.'[1]

1 [2014] EWHC 1066 (Comm) at [31]. Green J had considered this point obiter in *Ageas* and reached the same conclusion.

5.132 Applying his reasoning to the facts, Flaux J held:

> 'In other words, by virtue of CPR 7.5 because the "step required" was delivering the claim form to Linklaters' offices, actual service was effected on 27 March 2013. The date of actual service was not extended or suspended until the date of deemed service on 2 April 2013 under CPR 6.14. The combined effect of the two rules is that whilst the defendant was actually served on 27 March 2013, the fourteen days for acknowledgment of service under CPR 58.6 ran from 2 April 2013 and expired on 16 April 2013. The claimant could not have entered judgment in default until after that date, even though actual service had been effected 20 days prior to that date.'[1]

1 [2014] EWHC 1066 (Comm) at [39].

5.133 Flaux J accordingly held in favour of the claimant that service was in time because it had been completed under CPR 7.5 within the time required by the contract, even though it had not been deemed complete under CPR 6.14. Green J in *Ageas* made the same finding, obiter, as an alternative route to his own conclusion in favour of the claimant. Although the point was conceded in the other direction by counsel for the claimant in *Ener-G*, there are now two first instance decisions to the effect that if the CPR applies, then it is the CPR 7.5 date that is relevant for compliance with a provision in this form.

5.134 A party seeking to comply with a clause requiring legal proceedings to be 'issued and served' by a certain date would therefore be well advised to ensure that its service is effected in time both in accordance with at least CPR 7.5 (and ideally, with CPR 6.14 as well) and in a manner that ensures that it is 'actually delivered' by the relevant date. In practice, the date of service will often be the same whichever test is applied, although in the case of posting, service will be considered to have been effected under the CPR earlier than the date of 'actual delivery'.

5.135 Two scenarios may warrant further consideration of the competing approaches of Green J and Flaux J by the Court of Appeal. The first is a situation where the proceedings have been served under the CPR by posting on the deadline day but not received until a day later. The second is where proceedings have been served in accordance with the CPR but not received by the defendant.

Multiple warrantors

5.136 In *Zayo Group International Ltd v Ainger*,[1] Mr Simon Bryan QC (sitting as a Deputy High Court Judge) considered a strike out application brought on the grounds that a breach of warranty claim had not been properly notified. There were a number of 'Management Vendors' named in the SPA, who had severally given the 'Management Warranties'. The SPA provided as follows in Schedule 6:

> '3. The liability of the Management Vendors in respect of any claim for any breach of the Management Warranties shall be several. No Management Warranty Claim shall be made against any Management Vendor in respect of facts or circumstances unless a claim is made against all Management Vendors who are liable in respect of the same facts or circumstances. For the avoidance of doubt, the liability of a Management Vendor in respect of any Management Warranty Claim may be release or satisfied only if the liability of all the Management Vendors who are liable in respect of the same facts or circumstances is released or satisfied on the same terms.
>
> ...
>
> 3.2 No Management Vendor shall have any liability for a Management Warranty Claim except in circumstances where the Purchaser gives notice to the Management Vendors before the date that is eighteen months of Completion. The notice must be in writing and state in reasonable detail the nature of the Management Warranty Claim (to the extent the Purchaser is aware of such detail) and a reasonable estimate of the amount claimed, with reasonably sufficient details in order to allow the Management Vendors the ability to exercise their other rights under this Schedule 6.
>
> 3.3 The liability of each of the Management Vendors in respect of any Management Warranty Claim shall terminate if proceedings in respect of it shall not have been commenced by being both properly issued and validly served on the relevant Management Vendor within the period of nine months from the date on which the Purchaser gives notice of such Management Warranty Claim to the relevant Management Vendor.'

1 [2017] EWHC 2542 (Comm).

5.137 The defendants argued that one of the Management Vendors (the fifth defendant) had not been given notice in accordance with Schedule 6, paragraph 3.2 and accordingly none of the defendants had any liability (relying on various limbs of Schedule 6, paragraph 3). It was common ground that if the fifth defendant had not been properly notified, the claim against her would fail, but the claimants disputed the effect of any non-notification of the fifth defendant on the claims brought against the other defendants.

5.138 As to service on the fifth defendant, there was no dispute as to the facts. A courier had taken a copy of the notice to the address that had been given for the fifth defendant on the final afternoon of the period in which notice could be given. The fifth defendant had in fact moved to New Zealand but had not provided a new address as permitted under the SPA. On being told that the fifth defendant no longer resided at the address, the courier did not leave the notice but delivered it to the address of the first defendant instead.

5.139 Clause 12 of the SPA had specified the manner in which notices were to be provided, either by hand delivery or sending by registered post. In the case of hand delivery (including by courier), the notice was deemed to be received at the time of delivery. Mr Bryan QC held that 'Delivery is effected, and a valid notice is given, where the notice is left at the property.' He rejected a range of submissions by the claimant arguing that the fifth defendant's failure to update her address in the SPA altered the claimant's obligations under Schedule 6, paragraph 3.2 and held that the notice had not been validly served on the fifth defendant, such that the claims against her were dismissed.

5.140 Turning then to the consequences of non-service on the fifth defendant, Simon Bryan QC held:

> 'In the above circumstances I am satisfied, and find as a matter of construction, that the ordinary and natural meaning of the first sentence of paragraph 3.2 is that contended for by the Defendants, namely that no Management Vendor shall have any liability for a management Warranty Claim except in circumstances where the purchaser gives notice to the Management Vendors plural (namely the seven named persons in Schedule 1 to the SPA). Accordingly, as Ms Jaggard was not validly served no Management Vendor (ie none of the Defendants) is under any liability to Zayo. Consequent upon such finding the claim against each of the Defendants is dismissed.'[1]

1 [2017] EWHC 2542 (Comm) at [101].

5.141 This decision is a cautionary tale for claimants who must serve notices on a number of warrantors pursuant to an SPA. While clauses may be drafted differently, such that it will not always be the case that every warrantor must be served, if there is any doubt as to the clause's construction the risk of not serving one of the warrantors may be very great indeed.

BURDEN OF PROOF OF COMPLIANCE WITH NOTIFICATION REQUIREMENTS

5.142 Given that a notification clause generally operates as a condition precedent to liability, it is for the party bringing a claim to demonstrate that it has complied with the notification requirement.

5.143 In *Laminates Acquisition Co v BTR Australia Ltd*, Cooke J held at that:

> 'The starting point here must be, regardless of the proviso dealing with the need for legal proceedings within a specific time, that the terms of the notice provision are clear in debarring claims which

> have not been notified within the required period. Thus the clause begins "No claim … shall be brought … unless …". A compliant notice is therefore a matter of importance. Secondly, since the clause provides for conditions precedent to the liability of BTR under the Agreed Assurances, it is for Laminates to establish, as a matter of fact, compliance with those conditions precedent, although, because this is an exclusion clause, the usual principles which apply to construction of exclusion clauses apply when interpreting the clause itself.'[1]

1 [2004] 1 All ER (Comm) 737 at [31].

APPLICATION TO MISREPRESENTATION CLAIMS

5.144 Where warranties may be treated as representations, a buyer cannot seek to circumvent the notification requirements purely because they refer only to 'warranties' or 'warranty claims'.

5.145 In *Bottin*, Peter Gibson LJ rejected an argument that a notification clause referring solely to warranties should be construed strictly such that a breach of the notification requirements would not prove a bar to misrepresentation claims. He held that:

> 'To my mind it makes no commercial sense for the Agreement to impose conditions as to the giving of notice of a breach of warranty and to the commencement of proceedings for such breach and limiting the maximum liability if Bottin was intended to be left free of the conditions and those time limits and the limits on liabilities by treating the same warranties as representations … the obvious commercial purpose in the conditions and limits was to enable the Warrantors to know that they would not be sued on the warranties if no notice was served in time and proceedings were not brought in time and that, if they were sued, there was a quantified limit to their liability.'[1]

1 *Bottin (International) Investments Ltd v Venson Group Plc*, at [64]–[65].

5.146 Although it is ultimately a further question of construction, and it may be possible to draft a clause reaching a different result, it is hard to imagine a reason why contracting parties would seek to differentiate between misrepresentation and breach of warranty claims when drafting notification requirements.

5.147 The same approach arises in respect of contractual time-bar provisions. Endorsing the decision in *Bottin*, the Court of Session in *BSA v Irvine* held that '[t]he paramount consideration, in my opinion, is the fact that the parties could not have intended to allow one party to circumvent the carefully drawn timebar provisions by formulating their claim as one for misrepresentation rather than for breach of warranty ....'[1]

1 [2009] CSOH 77.

5.148 Contractual time-bars are commonly, however, subject to an exclusion for fraud. For example, the time-bar in *MAN v Freightliner* was subject to the following carve-out:

> 'For the avoidance of doubt the time limits referred to in this Section 12.3 shall not apply to any claim (whether made by way of representation, warranty or indemnity) in respect of fraud or fraudulent misrepresentation.'[1]

1 [2005] EWHC 2347 (Comm). See further [**3.05**]–[**3.09**].

5.149 The exclusion may also be expressed more broadly. An example can be seen in *Liberty Partnership Ltd v Tancred*, where the contractual time-bar was subject to the following qualification

> 'Nothing in clause [8.5] applies to a Claim … that arises or is delayed as a result of dishonesty, fraud or wilful concealment.'[1]

1 [2018] EWHC 2707 (Comm).

5.150 In *Liberty Partnership*, the primary contractual limitation period had expired. The claimant alleged that the claims had been delayed as a result of wilful concealment, and there was a preliminary issue as to whether there had in fact been wilful concealment such that the claims should be allowed to proceed to trial. The Court allowed a number of claims to proceed but held that those which had not been the subject of wilful concealment could not be pursued.

5.151 A further matter that may concern a potential claimant who seeks to claim rescission for misrepresentation as well as bringing claims for breach of warranty is whether serving notice in accordance with the SPA could be considered an affirmation of the contract that the party claims has been rescinded.[1] This scenario is unlikely to arise frequently given that the more common claim is for damages.

1 See further [**9.39**].

5.152 In *Bottin*,[1] the buyer claimed to have exercised its right to rescind when it served its draft amended particulars of claim, and to have confirmed its election through its solicitors shortly thereafter. It had not, however, sought rescission at the time of serving its notice. The seller argued that rescission should be refused because the buyer had affirmed the continued existence of the SPA. Once the buyer believed the seller to be in breach of various obligations to provide information, it sought to enforce its rights by seeking the appointment, pursuant to the SPA, of an independent consultant to obtain information. The seller refused consent to the appointment, denying that it was in breach of the SPA, which ultimately led to the commencement of the proceedings.

1 First instance decision of Blackburne J [2006] EWHC 3112 (Ch).

5.153 Blackburne J held at [407] that the relevant question was 'whether at a time when [the buyer] had sufficient knowledge of the underlying facts to make its claim in deceit it nevertheless affirmed the existence of the contract'. On the facts, he held that the buyer had not had sufficient knowledge to conclude that it had been a victim of fraud until shortly before it served its amended particulars based on disclosure that had been ordered by the court. No acts that could constitute affirmation had been taken after that time.

5.154 In a case where the potential claimant is aware that it has been the victim of deceit before it has served a notice concerning breaches of warranty claims, the claimant should confirm its election to rescind in advance of, or alongside, serving its notification letter. The letter should make clear that it is served without prejudice to the primary position that the SPA has been rescinded. This should not invalidate the notice, as (where there has been an election to rescind) the question whether rescission has or has not been validly effected is a question of past fact: if it has, then the notice falls away; if it has not, then the notice takes effect.

Chapter 6

Escrow and Earnout Provisions

INTRODUCTION TO ESCROW AND EARNOUT PROVISIONS

6.01 It is commonplace for SPAs to include so-called 'escrow' provisions to provide the buyer with some security against possible claims. An escrow arrangement ordinarily provides that a proportion of the purchase price will be paid to a third party and held 'in escrow', meaning that it can only be released when certain conditions are met or certain processes followed.

6.02 'Earnout' provisions are also common, their basic purpose being to compromise different views of the prospects of the business. In the negotiation, it is normal for the seller to talk up the prospects and the buyer to be sceptical: an earnout arrangement effectively means that the initial purchase price reflects the buyer's scepticism (at least in part), but if the seller's more optimistic view turns out to be right, then the buyer pays more after the profits have materialised. An earnout arrangement generally provides that, in addition to the purchase price paid at completion for a company, further consideration will be given by the buyer to the seller if certain (usually financial) metrics are met by the acquired company within a set period following completion.

ESCROW PROVISIONS

6.03 The usual escrow arrangement provides for a part of the purchase price to be paid into an account held by a third-party bank or institution in accordance with the SPA. Payments out of the escrow account will be made in the circumstances specified in the SPA and only on the basis of joint instructions from both (or all) parties. These will usually be either that there has been no indemnity or breach of warranty claim notified within the relevant period, or alternatively that the claims have been resolved and payments out shall follow the determination or settlement accordingly.

The purpose of escrow provisions

6.04 The main reason that a buyer might insist on the inclusion of an escrow arrangement is to ensure that some form of security is in place as regards the seller's potential liability in respect of warranty or indemnity claims brought by the buyer post-completion.

6.05 Particular concerns may arise on the part of a buyer where it suspects that the proceeds of the sale are to be distributed to the seller's shareholders before the expiry of any contractual limitation period, as is fairly common in business sale transactions. The buyer may also have reason to believe that the seller is in financial difficulties, or may simply prefer to have access to a specified fund against which it can recover without the risk of enforcement proving difficult for any reason.

The terms of escrow arrangements

6.06 There are a number of different aspects of an escrow arrangement that can be tailored to the specific transaction. These include: (i) the length of time the funds are to be held in escrow, which will usually match the contractual notification period unless there is a dispute; (ii) the proportion of the purchase price that is to be held in escrow; (iii) whether the funds are to be paid into escrow on completion or at a later date if there is a dispute; (iv) which party should receive any interest earned on the sum in escrow; (v) who is to hold the funds (for example a firm of solicitors, a bank or a different financial institution); and (vi) what process should be followed if entitlement to the sums retained in escrow is disputed.

6.07 Examples of escrow arrangements can be seen in a number of cases, although the escrow arrangements themselves usually form part of the background to the case rather than being in dispute. For example, *Chalabi v Jaffar*[1] was a dispute involving back to back agreements where the claimants sold shares to the defendants and the defendants then sold shares and assets on to a third party (TSYS) on the same day. US$8 million of the sum paid by TSYS to the defendants was retained in escrow for two years in respect of potential warranty claims, and the defendants bore the risk of the loss of this US$8 million.[2] Similarly in *Demco Investment and Commercial SA v InterAmerican Life Assurance (International) Limited*,[3] £700,000 was paid on completion and £300,000 was paid into an escrow account to be paid 14 months later subject to any adjustments to reflect the liabilities of the seller under the warranties (which was capped at one third of the total purchase price).[4] Disputes about the return of sums held in escrow (and earnout provisions) may be brought by buyers alleging breaches of warranty.[5]

1 [2011] EWHC 203 (Comm).
2 See [5] and [34].
3 [2012] EWHC 2053 (Comm).
4 See [6].
5 See for example *Scott v Singh* [2020] EWHC 1714 (Comm).

6.08 *Teoco UK Limited v Aircom Jersey 4 Ltd* provides an example of an escrow arrangement that required the party seeking the ongoing retention of the funds in escrow pending resolution of a dispute (usually the purchaser) to obtain a written opinion from a commercial barrister stating that it has a '*more likely than not*' prospect of succeeding in its claims. In that case, the SPA allowed the purchaser to retain £4.1 million of the purchase price (which was the maximum aggregate liability of the sellers) until one month before the contractual time limit. At this point, it was obliged to pay an amount equal to the estimated value of any disputed claims into an escrow account. In the case of a claim estimated to be worth more than £250,000, the purchaser was to:

> 'obtain a written opinion, from a commercial barrister …, that … the Purchaser has a more than likely chance of success and … provide a copy of such opinion to the Sellers together with the Purchaser's estimate'.[1]

1 [2018] EWCA Civ 23.

6.09 In determining whether the SPA should provide for an opinion to be provided by counsel if funds are to be held in escrow pending full resolution of a dispute, the parties should consider the process by which the opinion is to be provided. If witness statements and submissions are given by each party, the process may itself prove to be an expensive and time-consuming exercise even before legal proceedings have been commenced. The process may, however, focus minds on the merits of the dispute.

6.10 The importance of agreeing appropriate mechanisms for the release of funds in escrow can be seen in the decision in *Bir Holdings Limited v Mehta*. £250,000 of the total purchase price was paid into a 'Retention Account', held by the buyer's solicitors, by the buyer on completion. As explained by HHJ Cooke, pursuant to the agreement:

> '2 … If the Retention Agent was notified of a "Relevant Claim" as defined in the contract (broadly, a claim under the warranties or indemnities) before 23 December 2011 they were to pay the amount of that claim to the defendants [buyers]. Any balance at that date was to be paid to the claimants as sellers.
>
> 3. The effect was that any amount stated to be due by the defendants would be paid to them without enquiry as to the merits or any opportunity for the claimants to object. Disputes over claims of this sort would of course be very likely to arise but, crucially for the purpose of this claim, the contract did not provide any mechanism for determination of any such disputes or what would happen if it turned out that the claims made by the defendants were unfounded.'[1]

1 [2014] EWHC 3903 (Ch).

6.11 On 4 July 2011, the defendants' solicitors put forward six claims under the contract, quantified at £293,159. The defendants gave notice declaring these to be 'Relevant Claims' on 13 September 2011 (which it was common ground that they were entitled to do). On 16 September 2011, the defendants' solicitors paid out the entire balance held the in the Retention Account to their clients, plus accrued interest.

6.12 The sellers argued that only £21,000 of the claims advanced was justified and sought the repayment of the remainder from the buyers either in restitution or by way of an implied term in the SPA that 'any Relevant Claim would be accurately calculated and based on factual substance'.

6.13 HHJ Cooke held that the term alleged could not be implied into the contract:

> '[26]. I agree with [counsel] that the term pleaded could not be implied. Although the process of implication of terms is now said to be simply another aspect of interpretation of the contract, where that interpretation involves putting into the contract wording, or even a whole clause, which it did not originally contain, it is still in my view appropriate to approach the question by asking whether an objective observer would conclude that the parties must have intended that wording to be included in order for the contract to make commercial sense. The wording to be added is the minimum necessary to make the contract commercially sensible, since the court has no power to improve the bargain the parties actually made, or to decide what it would have been reasonable for them to agree in the circumstances.
>
> [27]. In this case, the structure of the provisions relating to the Retention Account was plainly intended to be favourable to the buyers by permitting them to deduct amounts alleged by them to be due without being required to justify the deduction to the claimants in advance, still less obtain the claimants' consent. It would be inconsistent with that commercially advantageous position to imply an obligation on the defendants to prove that the claims they put forward were accurately calculated and supported by the facts. It is no doubt right that other formulations might have been put forward which would not have had that inconsistency; for instance an obligation to repay any amount to the extent that the claim to it was later agreed or determined not to be justified, but no such alternative formulation was pleaded, and no application was made to amend.'

6.14 HHJ Cooke recognised, however, that the plea of unjust enrichment was appropriate to deal with the circumstances of the case. He held:

> '[28]. The alternative plea of unjust enrichment is however entirely appropriate to deal with the circumstances of the case. It

is necessary for the claimant to show the essential elements of the claim before the court will order restitution on equitable grounds, namely (a) that a benefit has been conferred on the defendant (b) at the expense of the claimant and (c) that it would be unjust in the circumstances for the defendant to retain it. The first two elements are incontestable; the provisions of the contract have enabled the defendants by putting forward Relevant Claims effectively to pay to themselves money from the Retention Account that would otherwise have been paid to the claimants.

[29]. As to whether retention would be unjust, the claimants in my judgment may show this if, in relation to any of the claims made, either (a) the claimants show that that claim is unjustified, or (b) the defendant withdraws or abandons that claim.

[30]. The onus of proof in the first of these alternatives is on the claimant, which properly reflects the commercial advantage that the contract confers on the defendants. Thus, to the extent the defendants continue to rely on the claims put forward to justify the payment of money to them from the Retention Account, the claimant must prove that such claims are either not properly made (eg that there was no breach of the warranty alleged) or are excessive in amount …

[31]. To the extent however that the defendants have withdrawn or abandoned such claims, the justification for having received the money taken in reliance on such claims falls away and retention of that money is unjust unless some alternative ground can be established which entitles them to payment. It will be for the defendants to establish any such alternative ground, and the defendants accordingly have the burden of proof in doing so. This in my judgment is the case both where a head of claim is abandoned entirely and where it is conceded that the amount originally claimed under a particular head is not justified under that head.'

6.15 While it was ultimately possible for the sellers to challenge the buyers' entitlement to the sums they had obtained from the Retention Account, the case provides a cautionary tale for sellers, showing the danger of agreeing escrow arrangements which make it possible for one party to seek unilaterally the withdrawal of funds from escrow.

Alternatives to escrow arrangements

6.16 It may not in all cases be possible for the parties to reach agreement on the appropriate terms of an escrow arrangement when negotiating the SPA. There are, however, other ways in which a buyer can seek security in respect of any potential warranty claims, and the circumstances of a transaction will determine which (if any) method is agreeable to both parties.

6.17 For example, one alternative may be for a buyer to obtain warranty and indemnity insurance, although this will require an insurer to accept the risk. A further alternative would be for the buyer to require a guarantee or indemnity either from a parent company of the seller or a bank.

EARNOUT PROVISIONS

6.18 An earnout arrangement provides that, in addition to the price paid at completion for a company, a further part of the purchase price will be calculated by reference to the performance of the company after completion.

Purpose of an earnout agreement

6.19 There are a number of reasons why parties negotiating an SPA may agree to include an earnout provision in respect of part of the consideration to be paid by the buyer.

6.20 If the parties disagree on the value of the company to such an extent that no absolute price can be agreed, an earnout arrangement allows the parties to let actual future performance provide a bridge between their positions. This may be particularly useful if the target business is either rapidly growing and the seller considers that the value should reflect an ongoing upwards trajectory, or the target business is in difficulty and the buyer does not want to risk overpaying if it is unable to turn the business around. Both the buyer and the seller are protected, at least to a certain degree, from under or over-valuation of the business at completion.

6.21 An earnout arrangement may also assist a buyer seeking to reduce borrowing costs in respect of its purchase, as it reduces the price payable at completion and defers payment to a later date (and only then if the business proves to be successful).

6.22 A seller may also benefit from an earnout arrangement, as the arrangement may enable the seller to share in some benefit of future value which the buyer is able to add to the business which was not achievable by the seller, perhaps due to the connections or reputation of the buyer or the buyer's ability to realise synergies with part of a broader corporate group.

6.23 There are a number of potential downsides associated with earnout agreements that should also be considered. First, the ongoing interest of the seller in the continuing performance of the business means that the seller must remain alive to its operation (if it not otherwise involved on an ongoing basis) and the buyer is likely to be restricted in its dealings with the business during the earnout period. Second, there are real risks of disputes arising. These can be minimised by detailed negotiation in advance of completion (and a number of the matters that should be considered closely are discussed below), but the risks cannot be ruled out entirely.

6.24 The tax consequences of an earnout arrangement are outside the scope of this text but should also be considered. Whether an earnout arrangement is tax efficient or inefficient will depend on the particular circumstances of the transaction and the parties.

Terms of an earnout arrangement

6.25 Earnout arrangements are capable of being, and are usually, tailored very closely to the transaction in question.

6.26 Aspects of the arrangement that can be customised include: (i) the particular metric against which the seller's entitlement to an earnout payment is to be assessed, the level of performance required to trigger the seller's entitlement to an earnout payment and the details of how that metric is to be assessed or calculated; (ii) the length of the earnout period and the timing of any earnout payments; (iii) the rights the seller has to access information about the target company's performance and/or to control the management of the target company during the earnout period; (iv) any limits on the rights of the buyer with regard to the target company's operations during the earnout period; (v) whether the buyer must provide any security in respect of its potential future liability to make an earnout payment; and (vi) whether the right to an earnout payment is expressly subject to a right of set-off against any warranty or indemnity claims brought by the buyer.

6.27 It is crucial that the SPA provides a very clear definition of the financial metrics that will govern whether an earnout payment is to be made and the procedure by which that metric is to be assessed. The process agreed must then be followed closely and will be upheld by the courts.[1]

1 Where the issue between the parties as regards an earnout claim is a short point of construction of the SPA, summary judgment or strike out applications may be an appropriate way of resolving matters more speedily than requiring a full trial. See for example *Clearcourse Partnership Acqireco Ltd v Jethwa* [2023] EWHC 1122 (Ch) at [118]–[138].

6.28 In *Barratt v Treatt plc*, the SPA had defined the earnout as:

> '… the amount which is the average of the aggregate pre-tax profit or loss of the Earthoil Plantations Group and of the Earthoil Kenya Group as shown in the audited accounts of the Earthoil Plantations Group and of the Earthoil Kenya Group for the two calendar years ending 31 December 2011 (and adding back the aggregate value of (i) all or any claims, expenses, liabilities paid by the Companies to any of the Sellers arising directly in connection with the unfair or

> wrongful dismissal of such Sellers prior to 31 December 2011 which is determined by an employment tribunal or at a court of competent jurisdiction and (ii) all professional or other fees and expenses incurred by the Companies in connection therewith, to the extent that such payments affect the Earn-out) multiplied by 11, divided by two PROVIDED THAT all profits and/or losses generated pursuant to transactions between Group Companies shall be disregarded in determining the aggregate pre-tax profit or loss; PROVIDED FURTHER THAT the value of the Earn-out shall not be less than zero'.[1]

1 [2013] EWHC 3561 (Ch).

6.29 The SPA had provided for the following mechanism for settling the earnout payment required:

> '3.2 At any time during the five months prior to 31 May 2012 [the buyer] shall deliver to [the seller] an Earn-out Notice. The Earn-out Notice shall specify the Earn-out and, setting out in reasonable detail, the basis on which the Earn-out has been calculated.
>
> 3.3 If [the buyer] has not delivered the Earn-out Notice to [the seller] by close of business on 31 May 2012, the Earn-out Notice will be deemed to have been served on that date and the matter shall be deemed to be a dispute and referred to accountants in accordance with clause 3.5 and the following provisions shall apply.
>
> 3.4 In the absence of referral of any dispute to accountants in accordance with clause 3.5 within 30 Business Days after delivery to [the seller] of the Earn-out Notice, the amount of the Earn-out shall be as specified in the Earn-out Notice and [the buyer] shall pay the Earn-out to [the seller] in accordance with clause 3.7.
>
> 3.5 If, within 30 Business Days after delivery to [the seller] of the Earn-out Notice, there remains an outstanding dispute in respect of the audited accounts of the Earthoil Plantations group or the Earthoil Kenya Group or the calculation of the Earn-out, the dispute may be referred by either [the buyer] or [the seller] (acting together) to a firm of chartered accountants, nominated jointly by the parties or (failing nomination within 10 Business Days after request by either party) nominated at the request of either party by the president of the Institute of Chartered Accountants in England and Wales.'

6.30 Following completion, the buyer had altered the financial year-end of the 'Plantations Group' and the 'Kenya Group' to 30 September to bring them into line with the buyer's own accounting periods. It had not prepared additional audited accounts for December year-ends, and the result was that no audited accounts were available for the two calendar years ending 31 December 2010 and 2011 as required by the SPA for the purposes of calculating the earnout payment due.

6.31 The buyer had prepared the notice by reference to what it considered to be the 'best alternative available', which were the consolidated audited accounts for the years ending 30 September 2010 and 2011 and the December management accounts for the three-month periods ending in December 2009, 2010 and 2011. The calculations in the notice sought to extrapolate from these figures. There was no dispute that although this was a departure from the SPA by the buyer, it had acted in good faith in the mistaken belief that the process conformed with the SPA requirements.

6.32 Briggs LJ made clear that the requirement for the earnout to be calculated using audited accounts was a form of protection to the sellers. It was of real importance and this was not merely a technical breach of contract. He held:

> '[12]. This was, in my view, no mere technical breach of contract. The obligation to go first in calculating the Earn-out was placed by clause 3 of the SPA squarely on the shoulders of the Buyer. Where a corporate business is sold through a share-sale for a price payable later by reference to its performance following sale, in circumstances where the buyer is in complete control, the protection afforded to the seller by a requirement that the performance-related Earn-out be calculated by reference to audited rather than management accounts is plain. First, it provides an important measure of objectivity in the preparation of the underlying accounts, and in the application for that purpose of appropriate accounting policies and standards. Secondly, audited accounts provide, in their notes, independent professionally verified explanation of the basis upon which the important parts of those accounts have been prepared, all of which would be available to the Sellers for the purpose of forming their own views about whether, and if so to what extent, to challenge the accounts pursuant to any procedure (such as that set out in clause 3.5 of the SPA) for disputing the Earn-out derived from those accounts.
>
> [13]. By contrast, a calculation and determination of Earn-out based only on management accounts, or upon consolidated audited accounts of a different group, such as the Buyer's group, would provide no such protection. To the extent that they were based upon management accounts, the Sellers would be exposed to the Buyer's own uncontrolled decision-making as to how they should be compiled, and to the temptation upon the Buyer to compile them on a basis likely to reduce, rather than increase, the amount of the Earn-out. Similarly, management accounts contain no notes explaining the basis upon which important items have been compiled, still less notes prepared or verified by independent professionals.

> [14]. It is, for present purposes, nothing to the point that the management accounts upon which the Buyer in fact relied in preparing the Notice may have been models of even-handed objectivity. The point is simply that the requirement that the Earn-out be calculated upon the basis of the relevant audited accounts was a form of contractual protection to the Sellers of real importance, rather than a mere formality.'

6.33 The Court of Appeal therefore upheld Morgan J's decision that the earnout notice based other than on audited accounts for the financial period ending 31 December 2010 and 2011 was invalid. In doing so, Briggs LJ dismissed an argument that the fallback process required an independent accountant to calculate the earnout payment in any event:

> '[22]. I recognise in that context that where, due for example to the absence of requisite audited accounts, the Buyer either serves no purported Earn-out Notice at all, or a notice which is invalid because it is not based upon such accounts, then clause 3 of the SPA contemplates nonetheless that the amount of the Earn-out will still have to be determined by the independent accountant, notwithstanding those difficulties. In my judgment however, the true construction of a commercial contract (where issues arise as to the practicability of alternative constructions) is to be addressed primarily by reference to an analysis of how the contract works when the parties comply with it, rather than when they ignore it, as the Buyer did in the present case. From that viewpoint, the plain contemplation of the parties was that the Earn-out specified in an Earn-out Notice would be based upon the relevant audited accounts, that the reasonable details of the calculation would also be based upon those accounts, and that outstanding disputes would be both identified and resolved by reference to those accounts, albeit that the expert would not in every respect be bound by them.'

6.34 A further important consideration for parties considering an earnout arrangement is whether the terms being negotiated will ensure that the party operating the business after completion will conduct the business in such a way that will not adversely impact the earnout provisions. This is likely to be the subject of much negotiation given that a buyer will usually be reluctant to agree to constraints on the operation of the business.

6.35 Common formulations may require the buyer to carry on the target business in the ordinary manner, not to sell the business and/or not to alter the accounting policies. By way of example, the SPA under consideration in *Barratt* had provided, inter alia, for the following restrictions on the buyer's control of the business:

> '6 Earn-out Protections
>
> 6.1 Subject to clause 6.2, the Buyer undertakes with the Sellers that, during the period prior to the Earn-out Notice being served, it will

(save with the consent in writing of all the Sellers such consent not to be unreasonably withheld or delayed):

(a) ensure that the business of the Group Companies shall be carried on in the ordinary course;

(b) not sell the Company or otherwise transfer or otherwise dispose of the whole or any substantial part of the business, undertaking and assets of the Organic Product Business whether by a single transaction or by a series of related transactions, or cease carrying on a significant part of the business of the Organic Product Business;

...

(d) procure that the Group Companies keep separate books of account from those of the Buyer and the Buyer's Group and therein makes true and complete entries of all its dealings and transactions of and in relation to its business;

...

(h) save in respect of the accounting reference dates (or equivalent) of the Group Companies not change the accounting policies, principles, bases and practices as applied by the Group Companies prior to the date hereof other than where such policies principles, bases and practices are inconsistent with those of the Buyer in which case the policies of the Buyer shall be applied;

...

(j) carry on the business of the Group Companies through the Group Companies and not divert any such business from the Group Companies and not divert from the Buyer's Group to the Group Companies any order which the Buyer ought to know are or may become a loss making order; and

...

(l) will not deliberately take any actions with the intention of artificially reducing the amount of the Earn-out;

...

and

(n) procure that the Company prepares monthly unaudited management accounts in a form suitable for presentation to the Boards and provides a copy of such management accounts to the Sellers not later than the end of the calendar month following the month to which the accounts relate.'[1]

1 See first instance decision at [2013] EWHC 3561 (Ch) at [11].

6.36 Whether a buyer has in fact complied with its obligations can lead to hard fought litigation if the earnout payment is not earned or the target business fails. An example of this is provided by *Porton Capital Technology Funds v 3M UK Holdings Ltd.*[1]

1 [2011] EWHC 2895 (Comm).

6.37 The first defendant had bought the entire share capital of a business known as Acolyte from the vendors, some of whom were the claimants. The consideration for the shares was a cash sum and an earnout payment based on net sales for the calendar year 2009. The business was ultimately not successful and was terminated in late 2008. The claimants alleged that the failure and termination of the business involved breaches of contract on the part of the first defendant, and that the wrongful termination had been induced by the second defendant. The defendants' position was that they had always acted in good faith and in accordance with the SPA. The first defendant was, it said, entitled to terminate the business in circumstances where it had sought consent and offered compensation and the vendors had acted unreasonably. The reason no earnout had become payable was because of the failings of the sole product of the business and the fact that the market had moved against that product.

6.38 The decision of Hamblen J gives a lengthy examination of the facts, which were necessarily central to establishing whether the first defendant had breached its obligations under the SPA. He concluded that the defendant had breached its obligations: (i) diligently to seek regulatory approval; and (ii) actively to market the product.[1] He also concluded that the vendors' consent to terminate the business was not unreasonably withheld,[2] and that the termination of the business was a repudiatory breach of the SPA.

1 [2011] EWHC 2895 (Comm) at [166] and [218].
2 At [234].

6.39 Hamblen J was then required to consider what the net sales of Acolyte would have been if the defendant had performed its obligations under the SPA. In doing so, he rejected the claimants' assertion that he should apply the principle in *Armory v Delamirie* that where the actions of the defendant had made the quantification of damages more difficult, the court should resolve any uncertainties in favour of the claimant. He held:

> 'This is not a case concerning the value of goods which the defendant has refused to produce or of the suppression of evidence, as in *Armory v Delamirie*. Nor is it a case involving the loss of the chance of success in legal proceedings, as in *Browning v Brachers*. It is a claim for lost profits for breach of contract. There is factual and expert evidence before the court relating to that claim. There is documentation before the court relevant to the claim. The evidential playing field is a level one. Whilst it is correct that the claim involves a degree of conjecture,

that is the case in relation to very many contractual damages claims and in all such cases it can be said that it is the defendant's breach of contract which has made that conjecture necessary. As a matter of authority there is no requirement to apply the principle of *Armory v Delamirie* to a case such as the present, and as a matter of principle I consider that there is good reason not to do so and that the application of the principle should not be extended further than is necessary.'[1]

1 (1722) 1 Strange 505.

6.40 In *Porton*, Hamblen J went on to evaluate the evidence, ultimately awarding damages of US$1,299,808. There may, however, be circumstances in which the principle in *Armory v Delamirie* should be applied, and it should be borne in mind by sellers seeking compensation from particularly unscrupulous buyers. The most recent authority at the highest level, consistently with the approach of Hamblen J, characterises that principle more narrowly than it has been treated in some earlier cases: in *Morris-Garner v One Step* Lord Reed referred to *Armory* as an example of the principle that 'In so far as the defendant may have destroyed or wrongfully prevented or impeded the claimant from adducing relevant evidence, the court can make presumptions in favour of the claimant.'[1]

1 [2019] AC 649 at [38].

6.41 Further protection for sellers in transactions structured by way of an upfront payment plus an earnout may be found in warranties given by the buyer. These can be of particular utility in transactions where the target business is to be merged with another business owned by the buyer, the prospects of which are likely to have a material impact on whether earn-out thresholds are met.

6.42 An example of the protection that can be provided by warranties given by the buyer can be seen in *Kitcatt v MMS UK Holdings Ltd*.[1] The claimants sold an advertising agency to the first defendant, which was a subsidiary of the second defendant. The SPA provided for the merger of the claimants' advertising agency with another agency (Digitas) in the second defendant's group to form a new agency, to be known as KND. KND was to be managed by the claimants. The consideration for the sale took the form of an initial payment plus deferred consideration to be calculated according to the earnings of KND in 2012 and 2013.

1 [2017] EWHC 675 (Comm).

6.43 In order to protect the claimants, the SPA contained 'buyer warranties' provided by the first defendant. These included a warranty that MMS and three named individuals who were members of the senior management of Digitas and its parent company were not 'aware of any facts or circumstances that could reasonably be expected to have a material adverse impact upon the Operating Income and/or Revenue in 2012 or 2013 (being a reduction of at least 20% in the case of Operating Income and 10% in the case of Revenue) including … the resignation or expected loss of any client of Digitas'.[1]

1 [2017] EWHC 675 (Comm) at [26].

6.44 The sole remedy for a breach of this warranty was stated to be 'an adjustment to Revenue and/or Operating Income for the purposes of calculating the Deferred Consideration if and to the extent that the Deferred Consideration is adversely affected by a matter that gives rise to a breach of the Buyer Warranties'.

6.45 At the time of the sale, more than half of Digitas' earnings came from work on four major brands for one client, P&G. In an unusual structure, Digitas and then KND were dependent on other companies (known as 'brand agency leaders') subcontracting the P&G work to them. In the year after the SPA was signed, however, work on three of the four P&G brands was taken away from KND and moved in-house by the brand agency leaders. The fourth P&G brand was lost for unrelated reasons. This had such an impact on KND's revenue that nothing was payable to the claimants by way of deferred consideration.

6.46 The claimants complained to the senior management of the group and had understood that agreement had been reached that adjustments would need to be made for the purpose of determining their entitlement to deferred consideration. Following the blocking of a payment of deferred consideration, however, the claimants started proceedings alleging breach of the buyer warranty set out above. The defendants argued that the warranty was unenforceable because it was meaningless given there was no baseline from which to calculate the 10% or 20% reduction, and further denied that there had been any breach of the warranty by either defendant.

6.47 Addressing the buyer warranty, Males J held:

'(1) The warranty is given by "the Buyer", that is to say by MMS, not by any of the three Named Individuals, although it is a warranty by MMS as to the state of its own awareness and that of the Named Individuals.

(2) The warranty in para (a) is not a guarantee of future performance. Rather it is a clause providing for an allocation of risk.

(3) In broad terms, the risk in question is the existence of facts or circumstances that could reasonably be expected to have a material adverse impact on Operating Income (ie profitability) or Revenue during the years which are relevant for the purpose of calculating the Deferred Consideration. Two examples are given of facts or circumstances which could have such an impact, one of which is the expected loss of a client.

(4) It is obvious that the loss of a major client is capable of having – and could reasonably be expected to have – an adverse impact on

future performance. In theory, no doubt, it is always possible that if one client is lost, another may be gained, with no net loss overall. However, to suppose that because of this theoretical possibility the loss of a major client would be viewed without concern is unrealistic.

(5) The way in which the risk is allocated is that MMS bears the risk of facts or circumstances of which any of the Named Individuals or MMS itself is aware which have not been disclosed to the claimants, but the claimants bear all other risks, including for example that major clients may be lost in any other circumstance.'[1]

1 [2017] EWHC 675 (Comm) at [197].

6.48 He went on to reject the suggestion that the warranty was unenforceable, construing the warranty by reference to the ordinary principles of construction.

> 'In these circumstances there is in my judgment no difficulty in construing the clause, which is directly concerned with the reasonable expectations of the parties, as providing for a comparison between what would reasonably be expected on the basis of the information in fact provided and what would reasonably be expected if the facts and circumstances in question had been disclosed. That is the natural meaning of the clause which gives effect to its overall purpose and accords with commercial common sense.
>
> ...
>
> I would be reluctant to conclude that a clause which was obviously intended to provide an important protection to one party and which underpinned the whole structure of the deal (including the allocation of Initial and Deferred Consideration) was meaningless and therefore unenforceable. That would in my view be a last resort (cf the cases cited by Leggatt J in *Astor Management AG v Atalaya Mining plc* [2017] EWHC *a* 425 (Comm), [2017] 2 BCLC 119 at [64] and [65]) ....'[1]

1 [2017] EWHC 675 (Comm) at [206], [212].

6.49 He also held that there had been a breach of warranty, as the significant changes to the operation of the brand agency leader model within the group were known by the named individuals at the time the SPA was signed and had not been disclosed. The matters of which the named individuals were aware could also reasonably have been expected to have a material adverse impact. He rejected, however, any suggestion of a breach of warranty by the second defendant, which had not been a party to the SPA.

6.50 On the facts, Males J also agreed with the claimants that a binding agreement had been entered into with the second defendant which settled the breach of warranty claim on the basis that certain adjustments would be made to the calculation of the deferred consideration for both relevant years. Having calculated the relevant adjustments, he held that a deferred consideration payment of £2.6 million was due to the claimants.

6.51 In *Asher v Jaywing PLC*,[1] the court considered an alleged oral agreement said to supersede the earnout provisions that had been included in the SPA 18 months previously. The SPA had provided for three possible earnout payments to be made depending on the performance of the target company. The first payment was made in full but the buyer's position was that the conditions relating to the second and third potential earnout payments had not been satisfied. The sellers contended that they were entitled to these payments under the terms of the further oral agreement, or alternatively that the buyer was: (i) estopped from relying on the strict terms of the SPA; or (ii) the buyer was in breach of the terms of the SPA and the sellers were entitled to damages in the same amount as the potential earnout sums.

1 [2022] EWHC 893 (Ch).

6.52 The judge carried out a thorough review of the evidence surrounding the meeting in question, with a particular focus on the documentary evidence available, and concluded that he was not satisfied that any binding agreement had been reached, let alone an agreement which the parties intended to be legally binding, incorporating the terms alleged by the sellers.[1] He noted the difference between what 'a commercial person may consider to be an agreement' and a 'legally binding agreement'.[2] This conclusion meant the judge did not need to consider in detail the 'no oral modification' clause in the SPA, or issues of: (i) whether there was an intention to create legal relations, certainty and valid consideration; (ii) authority to enter into any variation to the SPA; and (iii) estoppel.[3]

1 [2022] EWHC 893 (Ch), see this conclusion at [129], with the reasons at [133]–[188].
2 [2022] EWHC 893 (Ch) at [130]–[132].
3 Although he did do so in short order: [2022] EWHC 893 (Ch) at [190]–[227].

6.53 The judge did, however, find that the buyer had breached the SPA in failing to comply with the contractual provisions govering the production of 'Reference Accounts' and an 'Earn-out Statement' as regards the second and third potential earnout payments.[1] In assessing whether damages were payable as a result, the judge held that this was a case where assessing whether there was in fact any entitlement to earnout payments was 'a relatively straightforward exercise' and this was the approach he took, drawing on expert evidence from both parties.[2] Having considered the various stages of the analysis, he concluded that no earnout payments were due.

1 [2022] EWHC 893 (Ch) at [228]–[244].
2 Distinguishing *One Step (Support) Ltd v Morris-Garner* [2018] UKSC 20 and *Glossop Cartons and Print Ltd v Contact (Print and Packaging) Ltd* [2021] EWCA Civ 639 on the basis that those cases were authority for the proposition that if an assessment of loss or damage

on a conventional basis is too complex, a judge is free to adopt a more broad brush approach but that was not the case on these facts. See [2022] EWHC 893 (Ch) at [248]–[250].

6.54 The cautionary words of the judge in his conclusion should be borne in mind by any party considering a variation to the terms of an SPA as regards the earnout provisions or otherwise:

> 'It will be apparent from what I have said that the Claimants' claim must be dismissed in its entirety. It is impossible not to have some sympathy for the position they found themselves in as it is clear that Mr Craven believed that Jaywing were onboard with a plan which would allow them to hit their earn-out target. There was however no agreement. The clear lesson, as in so many cases, is that, if a legally binding agreement is the intended outcome, it should always in some way be clearly recorded in writing.'[1]

1 [2022] EWHC 893 (Ch) at [335].

Chapter 7

Misrepresentation and Fraud

VARIETIES OF MISREPRESENTATION

7.01 There are three main varieties of misrepresentation which need to be distinguished:

(i) misrepresentation in breach of a duty of care at common law, often called 'negligent misstatement' and analysed as an instance of the tort of negligence;

(ii) fraudulent misrepresentation amounting to the tort of deceit; and

(iii) 'innocent' misrepresentation inducing a contract as defined in the Misrepresentation Act 1967.

7.02 The above tri-partite classification is a simplification. Other texts divide misrepresentation by reference to the different remedies available for it. While this might seem topsy-turvy, it has an historical basis in the different origins of: (a) the equitable remedy of rescission for misrepresentation (whether fraudulent or innocent); and (b) common law actions for damages for deceit and for negligent misstatement. When *Derry v Peek*[1] was decided in 1889, these remedies were the outcomes of clearly separate causes of action. These different origins are still relevant to the interpretation of the 1967 Act and to a few other issues. But in recent decades, there has been a gradual assimilation of the requisite elements of misrepresentation and misstatement, regardless of the remedy claimed, and, for the most part, it is now more convenient to treat misrepresentation under the three varieties set out here.[2]

1 (1889) 14 App Cas 337 per Lord Herschell at 359: 'The principles which govern the two actions differ widely.'

2 For a view that emphasises the importance of the separate origins of the claims for rescission and damages, see J Cartwright (ed) *Misrepresentation, Mistake and Non-Disclosure* (6th edn, Sweet & Maxwell, 2022) Ch 2.

7.03 Business purchase claims can involve any or all of the varieties of misrepresentation. Even though there might be a common factual core to each cause of action in a given case, the three varieties of misrepresentation have different origins, elements and consequences.

NEGLIGENT MISSTATEMENT

Misrepresentation and fraud

7.04 Since the House of Lords' seminal decision in *Hedley Byrne v Heller*,[1] it has been clear that where the defendant owes a relevant duty of care to the claimant, a claim may be made for damages for negligence if the claimant suffers damage caused by the defendant's misstatement. Since the Court of Appeal's decision in *Esso v Mardon*,[2] it has been settled that where one party to pre-contractual negotiations represents to the other a fact of which the representor has specialist knowledge, there will be a *Hedley Byrne* duty of care in negligence, notwithstanding the contractual surroundings. *Esso v Mardon* was itself akin to a business sale case as the contract was for a business tenancy agreement for a garage, and the misrepresentation was as to the landlord's estimate of likely throughput of petrol sales.

1 [1964] AC 465.
2 [1976] QB 801.

7.05 The authority of *Esso v Mardon* on this point was confirmed by the Supreme Court in *Cramaso v Ogilvie-Grant*. Lord Toulson referred to *Esso* in his short concurring judgment. Lord Reed gave the leading judgment in which he noted that:

> 'The law does not impose a general duty of care in the conduct of contractual negotiations, reflecting that each party is entitled, within the limits set by the law, to pursue its own interests.'

But also that:

> '... it has long been accepted that the relationship between the parties to contractual negotiations may give rise to such a duty in respect of representations which the representor can reasonably foresee are likely to induce the other party to enter into the contract, unless circumstances negativing the existence of such a duty, such as those mentioned in para 38, are present.'

The circumstances which he mentioned in paragraph 38 were:

> '... for example, where the representation was accompanied by an effective disclaimer of responsibility, or where the representation was subject to a time limit which had lapsed, or where reliance on the representation was not reasonably foreseeable, or where the parties by their contract effectively excluded liability for negligent pre-contractual representations, or where the contract itself governs the subject matter of the representation.'[1]

1 [2014] AC 1093.

7.06 *Cramaso*, like *Esso v Mardon*, was not quite a business sale case, but was analogous to one: the representation concerned the population of grouse on a commercial grouse moor in the context of a negotiation for the representee to take a lease from the representor. The main issue in *Cramaso* was whether there was a duty of care owed by the vendors to the eventual tenant, which was a company which was not brought into existence until after the representation had been made to its promotors. The Supreme Court analysed the situation as being one where the representation had continuing effect until the contract was entered into, so that the representee assumed responsibility to the tenant company, not just to its promotor who had been the original representee. Lord Reed held that the promotor became the agent for the company and continued to rely on the representation in that capacity.

7.07 The principle has been applied in the business sale cases of *Abu Dhabi Investment Company v H Clarkson & Company*[1] and *Invertec v de Mol Holding BV*.[2] *Invertec* illustrates a further general point concerning duties of care in negligence. In the tort of negligence (by contrast to deceit), an individual who makes a misstatement in the course of acting for a corporate seller is unlikely to assume a personal duty of care to the buyer, following *Williams v Natural Life Health Foods*.[3] In *Williams*, the claimant was a franchisee who had been misled by a misstatement made by the franchisor company. The company had been dissolved and the claimant sued the individual who was the principal shareholder and managing director of the company. The claimant had had no direct dealings with the individual and was therefore not owed a duty of care by him. As *Invertec* shows, the same approach may be taken even when the individual is the representor where the proper analysis is that the individual did not assume a personal responsibility over and above the responsibility of the vendor company.

1 [2008] EWCA Civ 699.
2 [2009] EWHC 2471 (Ch) per Arnold J at [389]. On the other hand, we respectfully doubt whether HHJ Eyre QC was correct in *Scott v Singh* [2020] EWHC 1714 (Comm) at [41] to strike out an allegation that a seller owed a duty of care in relation to representations concerning financial projections, on the basis that the special expertise found in *Esso v Mardon* was not present even though the defendant seller was apparently the sole controller of the company.
3 [1998] 1 WLR 830.

7.08 In *Invertec*, the individual representor was a director and sole beneficial owner of the vendor company, so it was a simple matter for the court to hold that the company itself owed a duty of care in respect of the statements. The individual was the person whose misstatements counted as those of the company.[1] However, if the duty of care is assumed by an individual on the vendor side and there is a dispute as to whether their negligent misstatement binds the vendor itself, then there is Court of Appeal authority for the (controversial) proposition that the issue is one of vicarious liability, ie, whether the act of the employee was so closely connected to acts that employee was authorised to do that it may fairly and properly be regarded as having been done in the course of employment.[2] In the case of a merely negligent, as opposed to fraudulent, misstatement made by an employee of the vendor in the course of a business sale, it is highly likely that that test will be satisfied.

1 See *MAN v Freightliner* [2005] EWHC 2347 (Comm) at [154].
2 *So v HSBC* [2009] 1 CLC 503, criticised in *Bowstead & Reynolds on Agency* (23rd edn, Sweet & Maxwell, 2024) at 8-180, the authors of which take the view that the test should be the authority test that has been held to apply in cases of deceit, as to which see the discussion below in relation to vicarious liability for deceit. The definitive statement of the test is now contained in *WM Morrison Supermarkets v Various Claimants* [2020] UKSC 12, [2020] AC 989.

7.09 There are relatively few examples of the detailed consideration of negligent misstatement claims in the business sale context. That is because in most cases a claim for breach of warranty or misrepresentation will either be easier to establish or will lead to more favourable damages, for example because of contractual limitations on what may be recovered without proof of fraud.

7.10 In *Esso v Mardon*, even though the case was decided by the Court of Appeal in 1976, the facts occurred in 1963 and 1964, so the Misrepresentation Act 1967 did not apply. The Court of Appeal was willing to fashion a remedy in collateral warranty which might not be adopted today, and which had been rejected by Lawson J at first instance. At the time, the remedy in negligent misstatement seemed just as problematic: Ormrod LJ suggested at 827F that:

> 'it is an attractive argument that, when a contract results, the rights of the parties should be governed by the terms agreed, subject of course, to the right to sue for damages for fraud or under the Misrepresentation Act 1967. In fact, since this Act was passed there may be virtually no room for an action in negligence in such cases.'

However, Shaw LJ's approach was different, stating at 832H:

> 'It is difficult to see why, in principle, a right to claim damages for negligent misrepresentation which has arisen in favour of a party to a negotiation should not survive the event of the making of a contract as the outcome of that negotiation. It may, of course, be that the contract ultimately made shows either expressly or by implication that, once it has been entered into, the rights and liabilities of the parties are to be those and only those which have their origin in the contract itself.'[1]

1 The first instance decision is reported at [1975] QB 819.

7.11 Viewed from the present day, the approach of Shaw LJ is clearly to be preferred to that of Ormrod LJ. It is now clear that the negligent misstatement claim was a more orthodox way than collateral warranty for the Court to find for the tenant as to liability and remains so even after the passage of the 1967 Act.

DECEIT

7.12 In contrast to negligent misstatement, deceit or fraudulent misrepresentation is regularly the subject of consideration in business sale disputes. It is therefore treated in a little more detail here, though general texts on the law of tort, contract and misrepresentation cover similar ground.

7.13 In business sale cases, the purchaser often needs to prove fraud to make full recovery because of contractual time bars, limitations of damages provisions and non-reliance clauses.[1] A fraud claim can also open the door to recovery of capital put into the business post-acquisition, or other consequential losses, which may not be available on a warranty measure of loss.[2] In some cases, a claim under the Misrepresentation Act 1967 may not be available because the representor is not party to the contract.[3] Another advantage is the beneficial approach to causation and inducement that accompanies a finding of fraud and yet another is that contributory fault (including unreasonable reliance on the representation) is no answer to fraud.[4]

1 See, eg, *Belfairs v Sutherland* [2010] EWHC 2276 (Ch) at [8]; *Welven v Soar Group* [2011] EWHC 3240 (Comm) at [113], [114]; *Al-Hasawi v Nottingham Forest* [2018] EWHC 2884 (Ch) at [7]. See further Chapter 3.

2 See, eg, *Glossop Cartons v Contact (Print and Packaging)* [2019] EWHC 2314 (Ch) at [1].

3 See, eg, *Glossop Cartons v Contact (Print and Packaging)* at [58].

4 Eg, *Bottin v Venson* [2006] EWHC 3112 (Ch) at [301]; *Belfairs v Sutherland* at [19], citing *Redgrave v Hurd* (1881) 20 ChD 1 at 13–14.

7.14 In business sale cases, as in others, 'fraud must be precisely alleged and strictly proved'.[1] If fraud is alleged, it must be alleged distinctly against individuals considered separately.[2] 'Liability … depends on the conjunction of a false statement and dishonest state of mind.'[3] Fraud cannot be found by aggregation of the states of mind of different individuals, though it suffices if the dishonest state of mind is found in a natural person who directed the representor to make the statement or who allowed it to be made.[4] Courts generally expect that an allegation of fraud should be made promptly once the facts have been revealed to the claimant.[5] However, there is ultimately only one standard of proof, the civil standard of the balance of probabilities, which is applied to all the evidence against the background of the inherent probabilities.[6]

1 *Bradford v Borders* [1941] 2 All ER 205 per Lord Wright at 218H; *Belfairs v Sutherland* [2010] EWHC 2276 (Ch) at [121]; the same phrase was used by the Privy Council in *Crawford v Financial Institutions Services* [2005] UKPC 40 at [13]. And cf *Invertec* at [13]. For an application of this approach to proof see *Bottin v Venson* at [280].

2 *Belfairs v Sutherland* [2010] EWHC 2276 (Ch) at [13].

3 Per Moore-Bick LJ in *MAN v Freightliner* [2005] EWHC 2347 (Comm) at [156].

4 Ibid.

5 A failure to do so influenced the trial judge against the claim in the classic case, discussed below, of *Derry v Peek*. The point is referred to by Arnold J in *Invertec* [2009] EWHC 2471 (Ch) at [251]–[252].

6 *Belfairs v Sutherland* [2010] EWHC 2276 (Ch) at [8]. Earlier suggestions that especially cogent evidence is required for fraud should no longer be followed: *Re B* [2009] 1 AC 11; *Re S-B* [2010] 1 AC 678; *Vald. Nielsen v Baldorino* [2019] EWHC 1926 (Comm) at [149].

7.15 In outline, what is required for a claim in deceit is: (i) the defendant made a representation of fact; (ii) which was false; (iii) without an honest belief that it was true; (iv) intending it to induce the claimant to act; (v) which did induce the claimant to act; (vi) suffering loss and damage as a result.[1] The claimant bears the burden of proof in respect of each element. The elements of a claim in deceit are considered in more detail immediately below in an account which largely follows the lines of the comprehensive summary given in a business sale case by Jacobs J in *Vald. Nielsen v Baldorino* ('*Vald. Nielsen*').[2]

1 For an authoritative statement in four rather than six points, see *Bradford Building Society v Borders* [1941] 2 All ER 205 at 211 per Viscount Maugham; *The Kriti Palm* [2007] 1 Lloyd's Rep 555 at [251] per Rix LJ.

2 At [130]–[158]. As noted at [130], Jacobs J's summary was given with cognisance of the Court of Appeal's decision a few weeks earlier in *Nederlandse v Rembrandt Enterprises* [2020] QB 551. Further detailed summaries have been given in business sale cases by: Miles J in *European Real Estate Debt Fund (Cayman) Ltd v Treon* [2021] EWHC 2866 (Ch) at [340]–[378]; Henshaw J in *Ivy Technology v Martin* [2022] EWHC 1218 (Comm) at [338] ff; Nigel Cooper KC in *Bell v Singh* [2022] EWHC 3272 (Comm) at [152]–[158]; and Butcher J in *Goyal v BGF Investment Management* [2023] EWHC 1180 (Comm) at [38]–[63].

Elements of deceit: (i) a representation of fact

The principles

7.16 A representation is a statement of fact made by or on behalf of one person upon which another person is entitled to rely.[1] That definition makes clear that for a statement to be a representation it must have the character of a statement upon which the representee is entitled to rely. That character is judged against the entire relevant context.[2] A statement is not an actionable misrepresentation if it is a mere 'gratis dictum', or 'sales talk' or one which a reasonable representee would take with a pinch of salt.[3]

1 Per Christopher Clarke J in *Raiffeisen Zentralbank v RBS* [2011] 1 Lloyd's Rep 123 at [81].

2 This point is also explained in *Raiffeisen* at [86], adopted in *Vald. Nielsen v Baldorino* [2019] EWHC 1926 (Comm) at [138].

3 These terms and their origins are referenced by Teare J in *Nederlandse Industrie (NIVE) v Rembrandt* [2019] 1 All ER (Comm) 543 at [89]–[91].

7.17 It is important in a claim for deceit to identify precisely the representation(s) which are alleged.[1] If a representation is made expressly in writing, the words should be easy to state (assuming the document is still extant). If the representation is made expressly in speech then in principle its words are capable of being identified, though there may be evidential issues. Even if the precise words can be established, it is sometimes also important for a claimant to identify the sense in which the statement was intended by the representor to be, and was by the representee, understood. Sometimes, there can be a thin line between construing an express representation and finding that the words used in their context implied additional representations. If this is the effect of the claimant's case as to the meaning of an express representation, then the implied representations should also be clearly identified and formulated as part of, or alternative to, that case. In business sale cases, representations about accounting figures can often be subject to multiple possible understandings, for example, as to whether they relate to net or gross, fixed or current assets, long term or current liabilities, cash or accruals, or whether they reflect the figures from the past, or expectations for the current or future periods.[2] These are matters which a claimant should consider carefully before formulating the claim.

1 Eg, *Vald. Nielsen v Baldorino* [2019] EWHC 1926 (Comm) at [132].
2 Eg, in *EA Grimstead v McGarrigan* [1999] EWCA Civ 302, a trial finding of misrepresentation was overturned by the Court of Appeal on the basis of a difference as to whether or not representations about assets did or did not include stock and whether a statement about liabilities did or did not include accrued interest.

7.18 In principle, the sense or meaning of an express representation is determined objectively by assessing how it would have been understood by a reasonable representee in the position, and with the known characteristics, of the actual representee, against the context in which it was made including the characteristics of the representor.[1] However, if the tribunal can establish a single meaning or sense which was both the one intended by the representor and the one understood by the representee, then this may be used as a short cut. Thus in *EA Grimstead v McGarrigan*, Chadwick LJ said:

> 'It is, of course, possible to reach the conclusion that a representation was intended by the representor to mean one thing; and understood by the representee to mean another. In such a case it will be necessary to go on to consider whether the meaning as understood by the representee was one which the representation could properly bear in the circumstances in which it was made. But that enquiry will not arise if representor and representee made and understood the representation in the same sense – whatever that sense may be.'[2]

1 *Raiffeisen* at [81]; *Moto Mabanga v Ophir Energy* [2012] EWHC 1589 (QB) at [25]–[26], which is often cited for a helpful summary of the principles as to when a representation (especially an implied representation) is made.
2 [1999] EWCA Civ 302.

7.19 There is authority to suggest that if a statement is implied then it is necessary that the representor understands themself to make the representation in the same sense in which it was understood by the claimant.[1] Similarly, it has been said that if a representation is ambiguous then it must be demonstrated to have been intended by the representor in the relevant sense and understood by the representee in the same sense,or that the representee deliberately used ambiguous language in order to mislead.[2] These points are necessary to satisfy the requirements of dishonesty (the representor lacked belief in the statement in the sense in which it was false), intention to induce (the representor intended the statement to be understood in the relevant sense) and inducement (the representee understood it in the same sense). But at this initial stage of analysis, the question is what statement, objectively, was made. If a statement is truly ambiguous, even after considering its context, then it may constitute two (or more) representations. Both (or all) representations would be made, but only the one intended by the representor is capable of being dishonestly made and only the one understood by the representee is capable of being relied upon. It is only if these coincide that a claim for deceit can be sustained.

1 *Vald. Nielsen v Baldorino* [2019] EWHC 1926 (Comm) at [137] citing *Goose v Wilson Sandford* [2001] Lloyd's Rep PN 189 at [41].

2 *Vald. Nielsen* at [141] citing *The Kriti Palm* [2007] 1 All ER (Comm) 667 at [253]. And see KR Handley (ed) *Spencer Bower & Handley Actionable Misrepresentation* (5th edn, LexisNexis, 2014) at 4.14 and J Cartwright (ed) *Misrepresentation, Mistake and Non-Disclosure* (6th edn, Sweet & Maxwell, 2022) at 3-06.

7.20 A representation which was not stated in express terms by the defendant can be found to have been made by the defendant by implication from other statements or from the defendant's conduct,[1] or from a combination of the two, which is usually analysed as an implication from the express statements against a context or background which includes the defendant's conduct. In determining whether, and if so what, implied representation has been made, the fundamental question is the same as that involved in construing an express representation: namely, what would a reasonable person in the position of the representee have understood the representor to be stating by the representee's words and conduct in their context.[2] In undertaking this exercise, a 'helpful test' was formulated by Colman J in *Geest plc v Fyffes plc*[3] as being 'whether having regard to the [representor's] conduct in such circumstances, a reasonable [representee] would naturally assume that the true state of facts did not exist and that, had it existed, he would in all the circumstances necessarily have been informed of it'. The Court of Appeal has approved this as indeed a 'helpful test', while confirming that it 'is not to water down the requirement that there must be clear words or clear conduct of the representor from which the relevant representation can be implied'.[4] It follows from that statement that no actionable misrepresentation can be implied from mere silence 'by itself';[5] some words or deeds of the representor must be the foundation of the inference.

1 Eg, ordering a meal at a restaurant or taking delivery of goods generally implies a representation of ability and willingness to pay: *Property Alliance Group v Royal Bank of Scotland* [2018] 1 WLR 3529 at [126].

2 This paraphrases the test expressed by Toulson J in *IFE Fund v Goldman Sachs* [2007] 1 Lloyd's Rep 264 at [50], which has been approved in several authorities.

3 [1999] 1 All ER (Comm) 672 at 683B.

4 *Property Alliance Group v Royal Bank of Scotland* at [132].

5 *Raiffeisen* at [84]; *Vald. Nielsen v Baldorino* [2019] EWHC 1926 (Comm) at [135]. The matter is put in this particular way because there is authority that where there is a duty to speak, mere silence may amount to a clear and unequivocal representation sufficient to found an estoppel (as opposed to a claim in misrepresentation): *Greenwood v Martins Bank* [1933] AC 51; *Geniki Investments v Ellis Stockbrokers* [2008] EWHC 549 (QB) at [45]. It would be desirable for a single approach to be arrived at for ascertaining whether or not a representation has been made for these two purposes, but the law has not yet achieved that unity.

7.21 The claimant has to identify a representation as to existing (including past) fact, as opposed to mere opinion, or even a promise about the future (which may be contractual, but cannot of itself be a representation). Issues can arise as to the correct analysis of statements which on their face are opinions, statements about the future or statements about the law, but which imply representations of fact.[1] In general, however, the key point is that a statement of any sort implies a representation that it is honestly believed by the representor.[2] Thus, a statement that a business will make a profit next year is, literally, a statement about the future or an opinion, but it invariably implies a representation that the speaker *honestly believes* that the business will make a profit next year. If that implied representation is false, then it will generally also be dishonest by its very nature.

1 *Vald. Nielsen v Baldorino* [2019] EWHC 1926 (Comm) at [133]. The famous statement that 'The state of a man's mind is as much a fact as the state of his digestion' was applied to a statement of the purpose of a debenture, which was analysed as including a statement of present fact that the issuer intended to use the loan for those purposes: *Edgington v Fizmaurice* (1885) 29 Ch D 459. For more detailed discussions of this principle see KR Handley (ed) *Spencer Bower & Handley Actionable Misrepresentation* (5th edn, LexisNexis, 2014) Ch 2 and J Cartwright (ed) *Misrepresentation, Mistake and Non-Disclosure* (6th edn, Sweet & Maxwell, 2022) at 3.14–3.50, and see also Cartwright's view that in fraud, it should not matter whether the statement is of fact or otherwise, discussed in the same work at 3.48, 4.26 and 5.08.
2 *Belfairs v Sutherland* [2010] EWHC 2276 (Ch) at [13], [95]; *Vald. Nielsen* at [176].

Express and implied representations in the business sale context

7.22 In most business sale transactions, the vendor will make formal disclosures to the purchaser, either in the form of a disclosure letter and enclosures, or the contents of a data room.[1] Unless the contract provides otherwise, these will normally constitute express representations and in principle, if false, will be capable of founding a claim in misrepresentation.[2]

1 See Chapter 5.
2 See, eg, *Bottin v Venson* at [157] and *Al-Hasawi v Nottingham Forest FC* [2018] EWHC 2884 (Ch).

7.23 A statement of opinion, such as a forecast of future performance, as well as invariably implying a representation that the opinion is honestly held,[1] will usually, though not invariably, also imply a representation that the representor has formed that opinion on the basis of reasonable grounds. In other words, the representor believes that such reasonable grounds exist and, if the representor is in a position to know, there may be an implied representation that such reasonable grounds do in fact exist.[2] Whether such an implication arises depends on the context. Another way of approaching the issue is to argue that the absence of reasonable grounds is evidence of a lack of honest belief in the opinion stated.[3] If so, then that supports the inference of a representation of reasonable grounds, since the representee is entitled to assume that the representor is honest. The classic dictum is Bowen LJ's from *Smith v Land and House Property Corporation*:[4] 'if the facts are not equally known to both sides, then a statement of opinion by one who knows the facts best involves very often a statement of a material fact, for he impliedly states that he knows facts which justify his opinion'.

1 *Ivy Technology v Martin* [2022] EWHC 1218 (Comm) at [345].
2 *Ivy Technology v Martin* at [346].
3 *Belfairs v Sutherland* at [2010] EWHC 2276 (Ch) [101].
4 (1884) 28 Ch D 7. See also *Brown v Raphael* [1958] Ch 636 and *Vald. Nielsen* at [134].

7.24 For example, in *Barings plc (In Liquidation) v Coopers & Lybrand*,[1] Evans-Lombe J applied this approach, finding that the finance director of Barings had a far more detailed understanding of his company's financial statements than its auditors could possibly have acquired after two to three weeks of investigation. The Court held that the finance director's representations included the implied representation that he had reasonable grounds for making the statements he did. An example in a business sale case is *Bottin International Ltd v Venson Group plc*,[2] where Blackburne J held at that, in putting forward certain profit forecasts and management accounts to a prospective investor, the Chairman/CEO, Deputy CEO and Finance Director of a company represented that they believed that the management accounts were correct; that they genuinely held the opinion that the forecasts would be achieved; and that there were reasonable grounds for that opinion.

1 [2002] EWHC (Ch) 461 at [51].
2 At [264].

7.25 In business sale cases, an implied representation which is commonly made is that the accounting or other information provided by a vendor to a purchaser is believed by the representor to be honestly compiled or, at least, is not known by the representor to be false, or dishonestly drawn. Thus, in *Bottin*, by providing management accounts, the individuals concerned represented that 'to the best of their information knowledge and belief (and save as expressly disclosed) those accounts fairly reflected Venson's trading position for the ten months to which they related'. Similarly, in *MAN v Freightliner*,[1] Moore-Bick LJ held that a financial controller who answered questions about the target company's accounting records thereby implicitly stated that: 'as far as he was aware, the books of account had been honestly maintained and the financial statements based upon them had been honestly drawn and that therefore they could be relied upon to provide a true and fair picture of ERF's financial position', or 'that those accounts had been prepared honestly and that he was not aware of anything that prevented them from giving a true and fair view of the group's financial position', or 'the accounts of ERF on which those discussions were based had been honestly drawn and that as far as he knew they gave a true and fair view of ERF's financial position at the various times to which they related'. A succinct way of expressing these implicit statements would be to say that the financial information which is presented is presented in good faith.

1 [2005] EWHC 2347 (Comm) at [78]–[83]. Note also at [114] that Moore-Bick LJ held that an alternative case of dishonest concealment was 'little more than a reflection of' the implied misrepresentations he found to have been made.

7.26 A related implied representation is that accounts are based on honest business practices and thus not liable to be undermined if and when impropriety is uncovered (as far as the representor is aware). This appears to have been the nature of the misrepresentation in *Briess v Woolley*:[1] 'It is admitted by the respondents that throughout these negotiations, which culminated in the sale of all the shares in the company to the plaintiffs, the defendant Rosher never disclosed that the accounts of the company, though based upon figures which were accurate in themselves, were to his knowledge the result of fraudulent and dishonest trading.' The existence of the representation in this form was not an issue in the reported appeals.

1 [1954] AC 333, per Lord Oaksey at 340.

7.27 The form of implied representations was directly in issue in *Mellor v Partridge*, where the alleged representations included: (i) statements that the target company had high standing and reputation, 'thereby implicitly representing that that reputation was justified, without revealing that it was liable to be undermined or destroyed if certain alleged systematic fraudulent trading practices … were to come to light' (the 'Reputation Representation'); and (ii) encouragement to rely on financial information which did not enable the discovery that the target 'might be vulnerable to claims from dissatisfied customers alleging that [it] had sold them fakes' (the 'Balance Sheet Representation'). At first instance, the judge refused to strike out the Reputation Representation, but did strike out the Balance Sheet Representation on the basis that there was no obligation to provide for contingent liabilities in the absence of the target company believing that such claims would materialise. On appeal, the Court of Appeal agreed with the judge that the Reputation Representation was a sustainable allegation, even though what was stated was literally true. Lewison LJ said:

> 'First, a representation which is literally true may nevertheless be a misrepresentation if relevant facts are concealed. Second, allied to this proposition is the proposition that a representation may be implicit. Often the two will overlap. A half truth may amount to deceit if it is suggestive of a falsehood and intended so to be. … What the court must consider is what a reasonable person would have inferred was being implicitly represented by the representor's words and conduct in their context. These are fact sensitive questions which, in my judgment, can only be fairly determined at trial. Third, in *Gordon v Selico Co Ltd* [1986] 1 EGLR 71, 77H Slade LJ, giving the judgment of the Court of Appeal, said that the principle "buyer beware" "has no application where a purchaser has been induced to enter the contract of purchase by fraud."'[1]

1 [2013] EWCA Civ 477 at [17].

7.28 The Court of Appeal partially reinstated the Balance Sheet Representation on the basis that certain contingent liabilities arguably should have been provided for in the relevant accounts.[1] *Briess v Woolley* does not appear to have been cited and no consideration is given in the judgment to the question whether the Balance Sheet Representation could have been justified in pleading terms on the broader basis that it is implicit in putting forward accounting information that the representor does not know that information to be based on fraudulent trading which would undermine the figures if discovered (by leading to the need to allow for liabilities arising from the fraudulent activity). It is submitted that this broader basis could and should have been considered in *Mellor v Partridge*.

1 At [19].

Are SPA warranties also representations?

7.29 An important question in several business sale cases has been whether the statements made by the warranties in the agreement also constitute representations made by the vendor. In some agreements, it is expressly provided that the warranties may be treated as representations inducing the purchaser to enter into the agreement.[1] But in several other cases, there has been dispute about whether the warranties in the SPA can be relied on as representations. This matter has arisen at first instance on several occasions and it is ripe for appellate consideration. We examine below the cases on this in chronological order.

1 See, eg, *Bottin v Venson* [2004] EWCA Civ 1368 at [11] (Sch 3, cl 3(a)); *MAN v Freightliner* [2005] EWHC 2347 (Comm) at [56] (Art 4.1); *Bikam v Adria Cable* [2012] EWHC 621 (Comm) at [9] and [41].

7.30 In *Club Travel 2000 Holdings Ltd v Murfin*,[1] there was a warranty that the target's losses in the period between the last accounting date and the completion date 'shall not exceed £1.1 million'. HHJ Pelling QC (sitting as a judge of the High Court) found that the losses did exceed the warranted figure. However, there were no damages for breach of warranty, because warranty claims fell to be set off against certain loan notes issued by the purchaser which were not, in the events which had happened, repaid. That meant that the claim in deceit, based on the same warranty, was critical. The purchaser (Holdings) pleaded a claim in deceit solely based on the warranty itself being a representation. There was a provision in the SPA which acknowledged that the purchaser entered into the SPA 'in reliance upon the warranties' and, as HHJ Pelling QC pointed out, reliance is only relevant to a tortious claim. HHJ Pelling QC concluded 'with a degree of hesitation' that the deceit claim could be maintained on the basis that the warranties were also representations.[2] He gave two further reasons for permitting the claim. The first reason was that very clear words are required to exclude claims in fraud and the second was that fraud claims were expressly preserved in the SPA. But neither of these reasons went to the key question, which is whether a representation was made by the giving of a warranty. In the event, the judge was not persuaded that the defendant had been dishonest in relation to the representation he found to have been made and dismissed the deceit claim.

1 [2008] EWHC 2729 (Ch).
2 See at [48]. The defendant appeared in person at the trial.

7.31 In *Invertec*,[1] Arnold J held that claims in fraudulent misrepresentation based on warranties in the SPA were admissible (and ultimately succeeded) on two bases. The first basis was that certain of the claims were pleaded on the basis of information supplied by the vendor during negotiations, irrespective of the fact that the same information's correctness was then warranted in the SPA. There was a separate question considered later in the judgment whether the entire agreement clause barred such claims.[2] The second basis, described by Arnold J as more fundamental, was that the warranties were also representations of fact about the state of the target which the purchaser knew prior to signing would be contained in the SPA. Although not spelled out in the judgment, the reasoning here seems to be that at the moment immediately before the SPA was entered into, the vendor represented – by its conduct in agreeing to execute the SPA – that the warranties were true as an inducement to the purchaser to enter into the SPA.

1 [2009] EWHC 2471 (Ch) at [362]–[364].
2 See Chapter 3.

7.32 The issue of overlap was also considered in *Belfairs v Sutherland*,[1] where Norris J first considered the claims in fraudulent misrepresentation, which he dismissed and then turned to breach of warranty. There was an entire agreement and non-reliance clause which provided that the parties had not relied on any prior statements or representations, but this did not apply to fraud.[2] Norris J held that clause governed the relationship between representation and warranty and since it did not apply to fraud, it did not affect a claim in fraudulent misepresentation. Although the same matters were warranted as had been represented, the statements relied upon in the claim for fraudulent misrepresentation were not the warranties themselves, but earlier statements that preceded the agreement of the SPA. However, as in *Club Travel 2000*, the fraud claims were dismissed on their merits.

1 [2010] EWHC 2276 (Ch) at [149].
2 See Chapter 3.

7.33 In *Welven v Soar Group*,[1] Eder J confronted the same issue. In this case, claims for misrepresentation were put squarely on the basis of the warranties contained in the SPA being representations made immediately prior to signature.[2] Eder J held that the non-reliance clause made it clear that no representations were made. The clause stated that the purchaser had not been induced to enter the agreement by any representation etc save for those contained in the agreement. Eder J said that the relevant schedule 'does not contain any representations. Schedule 4 contains only contractual warranties. That was the basis on which the parties were contracting i.e. that these matters were contractually warranted and were not pre-contractual representations.'[3] That reasoning defeated any claim for negligent or innocent misrepresentation, but Eder J also recorded his agreement with the concession made on behalf of the vendors that the non-reliance clause could not be relied on to avoid a claim based on fraud. However, Eder J went on to consider, and reject, the claim of fraud on the basis that the warranties were representations for the purpose of a claim in fraudulent misrepresentation.

1 [2011] EWHC 3240 (Comm).
2 See at [108] for the pleaded allegations of misrepresentation.
3 See at [110]–[113].

7.34 The same issue arose again in *Sycamore Bidco v Breslin*,[1] where Mann J held that warranties were not representations, for the purpose of claims in negligent misrepresentation and under the Misrepresentation Act 1967. In *Sycamore Bidco* the relevant claims were not made in fraud. Mann J held that the warranties in the SPA were warranties as distinct from representations and there was nothing to suggest that they were intended to have a dual character. Mann J also relied on the 'conceptual problem' that if a representation was only made in a contract, then it could not have induced the making of the contract, noting that counsel for the claimant 'expressly disclaimed the relevant representations being made at any earlier time'. Counsel relied on the decision of Arnold J in *Invertec* (see **7.31** above). Mann J held that while the wording of the contracts in the two cases was different, there was no material distinction between the two, but he disagreed with Arnold J. In doing so, he rejected the idea that it made a difference that the parties knew in advance what would be contained in the agreement, since they also knew that they would be expressed only as warranties.

1 [2012] EWHC 3443 (Ch) at [200]–[211].

7.35 The issue came up in converse form in *Hut Group v Nobahar-Cookson*[1] where Blair J accepted a submission that pre-contractual statements about profit were not actionable representations on the ground that by the time they were made, it was known that if the deal went through then the numbers would be warranted in the SPA. His decision on this point is something of a makeweight since he also found that there was no dishonesty in that regard.

1 [2014] EWHC 3842 (QB) at [291].

7.36 Yet again, the question whether warranties were also representations was raised in *Idemitsu Kosan v Sumitomo* before Andrew Baker QC sitting as a Deputy High Court Judge. As in *Sycamore Bidco*, the misrepresentation claims were made only in negligent misstatement and under the Misrepresentation Act 1967, but not in fraud. The defendant applied for summary judgment on the basis that the warranties were not also representations. Following argument, the claimant amended its case to make clear that it alleged that representations were made by offering to sign the execution copy of the SPA, thereby making representations in terms of the statements contained in the warranties schedule of the SPA. Mr Baker QC set out the nature of a warranty thus:

> 'When a seller, by the terms of the contract under which he sells, "warrants" something about the subject matter sold, he is making a contractual promise. Nothing less. But also I think (and all things being equal) nothing more. That is so just as much for a warranty as to some then present or past matter of fact as it is for a warranty as to the future. By contracting on terms by which he warrants something, the seller is not purporting to impart information; he is not making a statement to his buyer. He is making a promise, to which he will be held as a matter of contract in the sense that any breach of the warranty will be actionable as a breach of contract, subject to any other relevant terms of the contract and to general principles of the law of contract, for example as to remedies.'[1]

1 [2016] EWHC 1909 (Comm).

7.37 Mr Baker QC held that Mann J in *Sycamore Bidco* was right, and Arnold J in *Invertec* was wrong. Arnold J's error was in confusing a finding that a relevant statement was factual in nature and so capable of becoming a representation with a finding that it was represented to be the case. He therefore held that 'if a contractual provision states only that a party gives a warranty, that party does not by concluding the contract make any statement to the counterparty that might found a misrepresentation claim'.

7.38 Mr Baker QC accepted that it was right in principle that language found in pre-contractual negotiating materials, including draft contractual wording, might form the content of a pre-contractual representation. However, in a case where the only fact relied on was the providing and offering to sign the draft contract, the only statement made was that the vendor was willing to give certain warranties.

7.39 We seek now to explain this run of first instance authorities. First, it is almost common ground amongst the judgments that pre-contractual representations do not cease to be actionable merely because they are later incorporated into warranties.[1] Second, it will normally be the case, especially where there is an entire agreement clause in ordinary terms, that a claim in negligent misrepresentation or under the 1967 Act cannot be based on the warranties, because it will be clear that they have not been relied upon. Third, a series of first instance judges (each apparently unaware of the earlier cases) has held that SPA warranties can be treated as representations for the purpose of a claim in fraud, even if the terms of the SPA exclude reliance upon them for the purpose of non-fraud claims. In *Sycamore Bidco* Mann J held that this was not the correct approach, disagreeing with one of the earlier cases, *Invertec*. In *Idemitsu*, Andrew Baker QC agreed with Mann J on this point.

1 There is an arguable exception in *Hut Group v Nobahar-Cookson* [2014] EWHC 3842 (QB) at [291] but there is little reasoning and the approach on this issue is questionable. At best, it must turn on the particular facts of the case.

7.40 In terms of authority, the position is unsatisfactory for two reasons: first, the earlier decisions were not cited in the later ones (other than the trilogy of *Invertec*, *Sycamore Bidco* and *Idemitsu*); second, *Sycamore Bidco* and *Idemitsu* did not involve fraud claims, so they are arguably obiter so far as concerns their disapproval of the earlier approach. It is therefore necessary to consider the position in principle.

7.41 The better analysis is that a warranty does not, without more, imply any representation, because a vendor might quite properly agree to compensate the purchaser if losses exceed a given figure without representing that they will not do so. As explained most clearly by Andrew Baker QC in *Idemitsu*, parties may agree that a matter (for example an accounting quantity) is warranted so that the vendor will compensate the purchaser for any difference between the true figure and the warranty, without the vendor necessarily representing that it is true. A warranty itself cannot be a representation, because it is not pre-contractual, but given at the moment of contracting. A promise to enter into a warranty is also not a representation because it is a mere promise. The real issue that arises in these cases is whether there is any other context, statement or conduct that transforms the promise to enter into a warranty into a representation that the subject matter of the warranty is true. That may be the position, but equally it may not, and it certainly does not follow from the mere willingness of the vendor to give the warranty. If this is the correct analysis, then the consequence is that even a fraud claim cannot be based on a promise to enter into a warranty, nor on a warranty once given, without some further fact to turn that promise into a representation.

7.42 As to the earlier cases: in *Club Travel 2000*, *Belfairs*, and *Welven*, while the reasoning on this issue was unsatisfactory, the fraud claims were dismissed, so the erroneous identification of representations as being inherent in the warranties was obiter dicta. In *Invertec*, the fraud claims were upheld, but the first basis given for this – pre-contractual representations as opposed to those identified in the warranties – was legally sound,[1] so the result of the case is defensible. Accordingly, there is no real obstacle to first instance courts accepting the reasoning of Mann J and Andrew Baker QC in *Sycamore Bidco* and *Idemitsu* which is correct in principle. Indeed it has been held that a first instance court is required to follow the more recent decisions in preference to *Invertec*.[2]

1 As it was put by Adrian Beltrami QC in *Panasonic Europe v Core Communication Investments* [2019] EWHC 2520 (Comm) at [35], such is 'an entirely different claim'.

2 *Arani v Cordic Group Ltd* [2021] EWHC 829 (Comm) at [162(3)] per Andrew Hochhauser QC.

7.43 The position may be summarised as follows. A pre-contractual representation must be identified. Some contracts provide that the warranties in the contract are relied on as pre-contractual representations and such provisions bind the parties. However, unless the contract makes such provision, statements in the contract itself will not be pre-contractual, so they cannot be actionable representations. In particular, contractual warranties are not representations merely by virtue of their status as warranties. Nor can they be converted into pre-contractual representations by reference merely to their inclusion in a signature version of the draft contract. That is because the contractual effect of a warranty is that the warrantor takes responsibility if it turns out not to be true, but that does not require or imply that the warrantor represents that the subject matter of the warranty is true. On the other hand, if a statement has been represented in the run up to the contract, it does not cease to be a representation merely because it is also incorporated into the contract as a warranty. The overriding principle is that in every case there must be a factual inquiry as to whether a particular statement has been represented pre-contract as being true, and that inquiry is not concluded (in either direction) by the fact that a similar or identical statement has been warranted in the contract.

Elements of deceit: (ii) falsity

7.44 To be actionable as a misrepresentation, the statement that is represented must be false. This is an objective matter: even if it is clear the representor believed the statement to be false, it must still be demonstrated that it was in fact false.[1] As to what counts as falsity, authority suggests several tests. In *With v O'Flanagan*,[2] Lord Wright MR said 'A representation is not like a warranty; it is not necessary it should be strictly construed or strictly complied with; it is enough if it is substantially true; it is enough if it is substantially complied with.' In *Bottin v Venson*,[3] it was common ground that a representation is false in law 'if it is substantially false' or 'if the general impression created by the statement is false'. A fuller explanation is:

> 'It is not necessary for what was said to be entirely correct, provided it is substantially correct, and the difference between what is represented and what is actually correct would not have been likely to induce a reasonable person in the position of the claimant to enter into the contract. The claimant must show that the difference between what was represented and the truth would have been likely to induce a reasonable person in its position to enter into the contract.'[4]

This is potentially a confusing test bearing in mind that in fraud there is a presumption of inducement. It may be equally apt to say that in determining truth or falsity, the maxim *de minimis non curat lex* is applied, so that a claimant cannot succeed by pointing to minor or immaterial falsehoods. What is material is that which would influence a reasonable person in deciding whether or not to enter into the contract at all, or without any amendments.

1 KR Handley (ed) *Spencer Bower & Handley Actionable* Misrepresentation (5th edn, LexisNexis, 2014) at 4.02.
2 [1936] Ch 575 at 581.
3 At [385].
4 Per Christopher Clarke J in *Raiffeissen v RBS* [2011] 1 Lloyd's Rep 123 at [149], adopting the approach approved in the context of insurance by Rix J in *Avon Insurance v Swire* [2000] Lloyd's Rep IR 535 at [17], which was also adopted by Jacobs J in *Vald. Nielsen v Baldorino* [2019] EWHC 1926 (Comm) at [144].

7.45 Truth or falsity is determined as at the time when the claimant relies upon the representation.[1] In this connection, it is important to bear in mind that a representation, once made, is normally deemed to have continuing effect, meaning that it is treated as being made, and re-made, at every moment in time until the claimant relies upon it, unless it is withdrawn or varied by the representor.[2] This approach is strictly applied, so that a representation can be true when uttered, but false at the relevant moment, when it is relied upon, or vice versa.[3] This principle has been applied to a representation as to the representor's present intention, rejecting the argument that a change in the intention after the representation was made would not falsify such a statement,[4] but accepting that some such representations depending on their precise nature may be treated as ephemeral.[5] The effect is to impose a duty to speak on a representor who discovers that what he said earlier was or has become false.

1 *Briess v Woolley* [1954] AC 333 at 353–354. If a claimant relies more than once, then falsity is reconsidered on each occasion of reliance.
2 *With v O'Flanagan* [1936] Ch 575; *Briess v Woolley*; *Belfairs v Sutherland* [2010] EWHC 2276 (Ch) at [11] (general principle), [131] (provision of accounts is a continuing representation about the state of affairs on the accounting date), [91], [136] (examples of withdrawal before reliance); *Cramaso*; *Karim v Wemyss* [2016] EWCA Civ 27 at [36] (representation that business was 'on course' for particular turnover and profit was a continuing representation that it remained on that course until completion.).
3 See, eg, *Erlson Precision Holdings v Hampson Industries* [2011] EWHC 1137 (Comm), where rescission was granted on the basis that a forecast was true when made but had become false before the SPA was signed.
4 *Goyal v BGF Investment Management Ltd* [2023] EWHC 1180 (Comm) at [67].
5 Ibid at [68].

Elements of deceit: (iii) absence of honest belief

7.46 In the context of misrepresentation and deceit, the mental element of dishonesty can be simply summarised as an absence of honest belief in the statement made. The classic statements of this principle remain those of Lord Herschell in *Derry v Peek*. *Derry v Peek* was a claim by a shareholder in a company which was authorised by special Act of Parliament to build certain tramways. The plaintiff shareholder had purchased shares in reliance on a prospectus issued by the defendant company directors which included this statement:

> 'One great feature of this undertaking, to which considerable importance should be attached, is, that by the special Act of Parliament obtained, the company has the right to use steam or mechanical motive power, instead of horses, and it is fully expected that by means of this a considerable saving will result in the working expenses of the line as compared with other tramways worked by horses.'[1]

1 (1889) 14 App Cas 337.

7.47 In truth, the special Act of Parliament authorised the use of steam power only with the consent of the Board of Trade. That consent was withheld for significant parts of the tramways and the company was wound up causing loss to the shareholders. At trial, Stirling J held that the statement was false and noted that there were 'circumstances of great suspicion with regard to these directors' because they had accepted money from the promoters of the company (which they later returned). Even so, after hearing them give evidence, Stirling J concluded that the directors did each believe that the statement in the prospectus was substantially true. His judgment is not completely clear on the state of mind of the directors with respect to the legal position represented in the prospectus, but he did find in terms that they believed that there was no practical danger that the Board of Trade would refuse consent. On that basis, they were not 'so reckless or careless that they ought to be fixed with the consequences of deceit'.[1] Stirling J also held that the plaintiff, Sir Henry Peek, would have taken the shares even if the relevant section of the statute had been set out fully in the prospectus, so inducement was not established. At trial, then, the claim failed as to both fraud and inducement.

1 (1887) 37 Ch D 541 at 558.

7.48 In the Court of Appeal, Cotton LJ stated the law as to dishonesty in this way (emphasis added):

> 'What, in my opinion, is a correct statement of the law is this – that where a man makes a statement to be acted upon by others which is false, and which is known by him to be false, or is made by him recklessly, or without care whether it is true or false – *that is, without any reasonable ground for believing it to be true* – he is liable in an action of deceit at the suit of any one to whom it was addressed and who was materially induced by the misstatement to do an act to his prejudice.'[1]

Cotton LJ went on to make clear that in his opinion a representor who made a statement without reasonable ground for believing it breached a duty to the representee and was liable in deceit. He held that on the facts found by Stirling J, the defendants had no reasonable ground for believing that the company had been given the right to use steam or mechanical motive power and they were therefore in breach of the duty as he held it to be. Cotton LJ also overturned the judge's finding on inducement on the basis that to sustain an action in deceit the misrepresentation did not have to be decisive but only 'a material inducement'. Sir James Hannen and Lopes LJ gave concurring judgments to similar effect. Lopes LJ set out in clear terms that deceit required one of four degrees of state of mind on the part of the defendant: (i) knowing the statement is false; (ii) not believing it to be true; (iii) recklessness as to its truth; and (iv) believing it to be true, but without any reasonable grounds for such belief.[2]

1 (1887) 37 Ch D 541 at 566.
2 (1887) 37 Ch D 541 at 585. In the House of Lords, Lord Herschell pointed out that the third of these degrees is an instance of the second rather than a distinct type.

7.49 In the House of Lords, the judgment of Stirling J dismissing the action was restored. Having recited above the views of the Court of Appeal, the point can be shortly stated, as it was by Lord Watson thus:

> '... they seem to have held that a man who makes a representation with the view of its being acted upon, in the honest belief that it is true, commits a fraud in the eye of the law, if the court or a jury shall be of opinion that he had not reasonable grounds for his belief. I have no hesitation in rejecting that doctrine, for which I can find no warrant in the law of England.'[1]

1 (1889) 14 App Cas 337 at 345.

7.50 However, as already stated, the leading judgment was given by Lord Herschell, whose statements of the law on this subject remain definitive. Having quoted Cotton LJ's statement of the law (see **7.48** above), Lord Herschell drew the following key distinction:[1] 'To make a statement careless whether it be true or false, and therefore without any real belief in its truth, appears to me to be an essentially different thing from making, through want of care, a false statement, which is nevertheless honestly believed to be true.' He then stated that he would demonstrate from authority that 'without proof of fraud no action of deceit is maintainable.'[2]

1 (1889) 14 App Cas 337 at 361.
2 Ibid at 362.

7.51 In relation to a dictum in one of the earlier cases, Lord Herschell made the following important point about the relationship between fraud and reasonable grounds:

> 'I think there is here some confusion between that which is evidence of fraud, and that which constitutes it. A consideration of the grounds of belief is no doubt an important aid in ascertaining whether the belief was really entertained. A man's mere assertion that he believed the statement he made to be true is not accepted as conclusive proof that he did so. There may be such an absence of reasonable ground for

> his belief as, in spite of his assertion, to carry conviction to the mind that he had not really the belief which he alleges. If the learned Lord intended to go further, as apparently he did, and to say that though the belief was really entertained, yet if there were no reasonable grounds for it, the person making the statement was guilty of fraud in the same way as if he had known what he stated to be false, I say, with all respect, that the previous authorities afford no warrant for the view that an action of deceit would lie under such circumstances. A man who forms his belief carelessly, or is unreasonably credulous, may be blameworthy when he makes a representation on which another is to act, but he is not, in my opinion, fraudulent in the sense in which that word was used in all the cases … [T]here has always been present, and regarded as an essential element, that the deception was wilful either because the untrue statement was known to be untrue, or because belief in it was asserted without such belief existing.'[1]

1 (1889) 14 App Cas 337 at 369.

7.52 After a full survey of authority, Lord Herschell summarised the law in the following way, which has survived intact ever since:

> 'I think the authorities establish the following propositions: First, in order to sustain an action of deceit, there must be proof of fraud, and nothing short of that will suffice. Secondly, fraud is proved when it is shewn that a false representation has been made (1) knowingly, or (2) without belief in its truth, or (3) recklessly, careless whether it be true or false. Although I have treated the second and third as distinct cases, I think the third is but an instance of the second, for one who makes a statement under such circumstances can have no real belief in the truth of what he states. To prevent a false statement being fraudulent, there must, I think, always be an honest belief in its truth. And this probably covers the whole ground, for one who knowingly alleges that which is false, has obviously no such honest belief. Thirdly, if fraud be proved, the motive of the person guilty of it is immaterial. It matters not that there was no intention to cheat or injure the person to whom the statement was made.'[1]

1 (1889) 14 App Cas 337 at 374.

7.53 Lord Herschell reiterated more succinctly the relationship between reasonable grounds and fraud in the following dictum:

> 'At the same time I desire to say distinctly that when a false statement has been made the questions whether there were reasonable grounds for believing it, and what were the means of knowledge in the possession of the person making it, are most weighty matters for consideration. The ground upon which an alleged belief was founded is a most important test of its reality. I can conceive many cases

where the fact that an alleged belief was destitute of all reasonable foundation would suffice of itself to convince the Court that it was not really entertained, and that the representation was a fraudulent one.'[1]

1 (1889) 14 App Cas 337 at [375]–[376]. For its application to modern business sale cases, see per Blackburne J in *Bottin v Venson* at [266] where he held that 'the absence of any reasonable ground for the forecast was so glaring that Mr Frost cannot genuinely have held the opinion that such profit would be made', and by contrast per Norris J in *Belfairs v Sutherland* [2010] EWHC 2276 (Ch) at [101], and at [108], where he made the point that 'illogicality is not dishonesty'.

7.54 Lord Herschell held that there was no reason to overturn Stirling J's finding that the evidence of the defendant directors was truthful. Examining their evidence, Lord Herschell concluded that the effect of it was that they each believed the consent of the Board of Trade was as a matter of course following the passage of the Act. On that basis, he held that they honestly believed that the statement in the prospectus was 'substantially true'. Accordingly, on the law as he had held it to be, they were not liable in deceit. It may be noted that this case is also an example of the principle that falsity and corresponding dishonesty is established only in respect of a material difference between the statement made and the true position, because even on the view of the matter that Lord Herschell accepted was believed by the defendants, the statement in the prospectus was not quite accurate.

7.55 For a recent business sale example of this principle, see *Hut Group v Nobahar-Cookson*,[1] where the finance director sent statutory accounts to the purchaser stating: 'this has run through our PwC audit process and therefore reflects any items for adjustment – there are no more adjustments other than wording and narrative'. Blair J found that the draft accounts 'were on any view some way from being signed off by the auditors' and it was 'a matter of surprise that Mr Rajanah felt able to express himself in the email in the way he did.' Nevertheless, Blair J found there was no fraud on the basis of Mr Rajanah's evidence that 'he believed that in substance the audit process was "pretty much" finalised' and that the adjustments which were made afterwards did not affect EBITDA. While this is perhaps reminiscent of the position in *Derry v Peek*, in modern conditions, the exoneration of this statement is perhaps a little surprising and certainly close to the borderline.

1 [2014] EWHC 3842 (QB) at [298]–[301].

7.56 In assessing honesty of belief, the statement against which the representee's state of mind is measured is only the statement that the representee understood themself to be making. It was put as follows by Lord Jenkins speaking for the Privy Council in *Akerhielm v de la Mare*:[1] 'The question is not whether the defendant in any given case honestly believed the representation to be true in the sense assigned to it by the court on an objective consideration of its truth or falsity, but whether he honestly believed the representation to be true in the sense in which he understood it albeit erroneously when it was made.'[2]

1 [1959] AC 789 at 805.
2 This dictum could be taken as indicating that the first inquiry should be what the defendant intended by the statement, before dishonesty can be addressed. However, it is submitted that the prior question is what representation(s) were made, judged objectively as explained above. After that it is necessary to consider whether any representation that was made was one in respect of which the defendant had the required dishonest state of mind and then whether it was also the subject of the claimant's reliance. Only if all requirements are satisfied is deceit proved.

7.57 In this respect, the same principle (representor must understand the representation in the relevant sense) has sometimes been put as an element of the dishonesty requirement of the tort, and sometimes as an element of the intention requirement. We therefore refer to it here and return to it below in considering intention to induce. Thus, in *The Kriti Palm*, Rix LJ combined them stating (emphasis added):

> '*Because dishonesty is the essence of deceit* it is possible to be fraudulent even by means of an ambiguous statement, but in such a case *it is essential that the representor should have intended the statement to be understood in the sense* in which it is understood by the claimant (and of course a sense in which it is untrue) or should have deliberately used the ambiguity for the purpose of deceiving him and succeeded in doing so'.[1]

The same point was pithily expressed by Christopher Clarke J in *Raiffeisen*, also combining understanding and intention (emphasis added):

> 'it is necessary for the claimant to identify the representation made and to show that the representor knew that that was what he was saying. It is not sufficient that the representation was false in a sense which the representor did not *understand or intend* it to bear.'[2]

1 *AIC Ltd v ITS Testing Services: the Kriti Palm* [2007] 1 Lloyd's Rep 555 at [253].
2 At [339].

7.58 In general, there is now a single test for dishonesty in criminal and most civil law contexts, as determined by the Supreme Court in *Ivey v Genting Casinos*[1] and applied to the equitable wrong of dishonest assistance in breach of trust by the Court of Appeal in *Group Seven v Nasir*.[2] This test is whether the defendant's conduct was honest by the standards of ordinary people in the light of all that the defendant knew or believed. Whether this has any relevance to a claim in fraudulent misrepresentation is controversial. In *Erlson Precision Holdings v Hampson Industries*,[3] Field J held that if an individual like a CEO of a listed company 'knows that a forecast has been falsified by events to which he is privy but remains silent intending that the forecast should be relied on by persons to whom the forecast is directly communicated, dishonesty on the part of that individual will have been proved without it being necessary distinctly and separately to show a conscious awareness of a duty to correct the statement'. In *PAG v RBS*,[4] the Court of Appeal raised, but did not answer, the question whether the new single test might make it possible for a person who impliedly represents X without realising that he does so to be held to be dishonest. In *Vald. Nielsen*[5] Jacob J said 'It is not necessary that the maker of the statement was "dishonest" as that word is used in the criminal law.'.

1 [2018] AC 391. This test was based on the earlier authority of the Privy Council in *Royal Brunei v Tan* [1995] 2 AC 378 and in *Barlow Clowes v Eurotrust* [2006] 1 WLR 1476.
2 [2019] 3 WLR 1011.
3 [2011] EWHC 1137 (Comm) at [43].
4 [2018] 1 WLR 3529 at [158].
5 At [147].

7.59 However, it could be said that the existing test in the context of deceit is consistent with the broader principle from *Ivey* on the basis that ordinary people consider it to be dishonest knowingly to make a representation in which the representor lacks honest belief. It might be objected that this is circular, as the term 'honest belief' itself assumes a concept of honesty. On that basis, it may be suggested that the question whether a particular individual had an 'honest belief' is to be assessed in the light of the *Ivey* test: given all that the representor in fact knew and believed, was any belief they may have had in the subject matter of the representation one that an ordinary honest person could have held? In practice, such fine analysis does not often arise; though it might become relevant if a representor was found to have persuaded themself of a proposition which an honest person would have rejected on the basis of the other facts known or believed by the representor. That could lead to the conclusion that the representor believed the statement they made, but did not do so honestly. In that rather narrow scenario (which it is important to restrict to one in which it is neither reason nor reasonableness, but only honesty, that would lead the hypothetical ordinary person to reject the belief)[1] a real question could be raised as to whether relevant dishonesty was or was not established for the purposes of deceit.

1 Recalling here that 'illogicality is not dishonesty' per Norris J in *Belfairs v Sutherland* [2010] EWHC 2276 (Ch) at [108].

7.60 To summarise, to establish deceit, it is necessary to show that the representor did not have an honest belief in the truth of the statement as they themself understood it. That is not the end of the mental elements required to establish a cause of action in deceit, as the next requirement also relates to the mind of the representor.

Elements of deceit: (iv) intending it to induce the claimant

7.61 To establish liability in deceit, it is necessary to show that the representor was dishonest in the sense discussed immediately above of lacking an honest belief in the truth of what was represented. But a further mental element is required in addition, which is normally described as intention. It is usually formulated as being that the representor must intend the representation to induce the claimant, or to be relied on by (or on behalf of)[1] the claimant. That brings in the requirements that the representor intends that the statement they make: (i) is one on which persons like the claimant should be induced by (or rely) in the manner of their actual inducement (or reliance); and (ii) should be understood by such persons in the same sense or meaning as that in which it is in fact relied upon. Putting these points negatively, there is no liability for deceit by: (i) a person who utters a falsehood without any intention that it should be relied on by persons like the claimant sharing similar purposes; or (ii) a person who utters a falsehood without intending it should be understood in the sense in which the claimant understands and is induced by it.

1 Inducement is the underlying concept: it can be achieved, and can be intended to be achieved, through indirect means. In a business sale context, this would include making a representation to the purchaser's due diligence advisers or to employees below the decision-making level. This is discussed above in relation to the negligent misstatement case of *Cramaso v Olgivie-Grant* and below by reference to *MAN v Freightliner* [2005] EWHC 2347 (Comm). For approval of the concept of intending indirect reliance and citation of earlier authorities, see *Abu Dhabi Investment Company v H Clarkson* [2008] EWCA Civ 699 at [33], and for its application to a due diligence process in which the ultimate buyers had not been incorporated at the time the representations were made, see ibid at [38].

7.62 The language in which this principle is expressed refers to what the representor 'intends' should happen. That language could produce a temptation to overstate the requirement. Such language is one reason why the cases and texts are concerned to maintain the consistency of this principle with Lord Herschell's rejection of the relevance of the representor's motive. It would be closer to the sense of modern English to refer to what the representor knows or realises might occur, rather than to what they intend should occur.[1] This has been encapsulated in the concept of knowingness: the representor must knowingly make a dishonest and false representation. That language has fallen out of use in this context,[2] but it would eliminate any temptation to consider motive and gives a proper sense of the true principle. For example, a representor who makes a fraudulent misrepresentation realising that it might be relied upon, but hoping that it will not, will be liable, even though in ordinary English they would not be said to have 'intended' reliance. For the use of 'knowing' in this context, see per Lindley LJ in *Angus v Clifford*:

> 'If it is fraud, it is actionable, if it is not fraud, but merely carelessness – it is not. The passages [in Lord Herschell's speech in *Derry v Peek*] about knowledge – knowingly making it, and making a statement without believing its truth, are based upon the supposition that the matter was really before the mind of the person making the statement, and, if the evidence is that he never really intended to mislead, that he did not see the effect, or dream that the effect of what he was saying

could mislead, and that that particular part of what he was saying was not present to his mind at all, that I should say is proof of carelessness rather than of fraud.'[3]

1 For example, in *Ansbacher v Binks Stern* [1998] PNLR 221 the Court of Appeal applied the test of whether the representor intended to convey, or 'at least was willing to give the impression' of the relevant meaning.
2 It has not fallen entirely out of use. See, eg, the passage quoted above from *Raiffeisen* at [339]: 'it is necessary for the claimant to identify the representation made and to show that the *representor knew that that was what he was saying*'.
3 [1891] 2 Ch 449 at 466.

7.63 The classic example of the first limb of this principle is *Peek v Gurney*[1] in which the House of Lords held that a false statement in a prospectus was only intended to induce subscriptions to the new share issue and not to be relied upon by aftermarket purchasers. However, more recent authority has tended to emphasise that, where fraud is otherwise demonstrated, the determination of who constitutes persons like the claimant and what reliance constitutes the kind of reliance foreseen is made on a broad basis, not an excessively narrow one. In *Goose v Wilson Sandford*,[2] the Court of Appeal stated that the intention required is only that the representee should act upon the representation; not that the intention must be for any particular type of act of reliance. In *Mead v Babington*[3] this was adopted but said to be 'subject to the rules on remoteness of damage'. In the business sale context, these issues are unlikely to create much difficulty. If a fraudulent misrepresentation is made in circumstances where it is likely to find its way to an intended purchaser or their advisers, then it would take rather special facts for the representor to avoid a finding that their 'intention' was for the purchaser to rely on the representation in deciding whether to enter into the transaction.

1 (1873) LR 6 HL 377. Note that this case is no longer authoritative on its facts, both because: (i) in modern conditions it is arguable that reliance by aftermarket purchaser is foreseeable: *Possfund v Diamond* [1996] 1 WLR 1351; and (ii) liability for statements in a prospectus was put on a statutory footing in the Directors Liability Act 1890 and is now contained in the Financial Services and Markets Act 2000, s 90.
2 At [48].
3 [2007] EWCA Civ 518 at [17].

7.64 The second limb of this principle is that the representor must 'intend' the representation to be understood in the sense in which it was false and was relied upon.[1] Thus if D makes a certain representation, X, without belief that X is true, but D does not (subjectively) realise that X was the representation that was (objectively) made by their words or conduct, then D will not be liable for deceit, because D does not intend the representation to be understood in the relevant sense. As noted above, this requirement is sometimes treated as part of the requirement of dishonesty and sometimes as part of the requirement of intention, but it has the same origins in the early cases and is the same principle. We suggest, adopting Lindley LJ's language, that it is best understood as part of a requirement of 'knowingness' – nobody is liable for fraud who does not know that they are making a statement capable of bearing the meaning alleged by, and relied on by, the claimant.[2]

1 *Barton v County NatWest* [1999] Lloyd's Rep Bank 408 at [32]; *Goose v Sandford* at [41]; *Cassa di Risparmio della Repubblica di San Marino SpA v Barclays Bank Ltd* [2011] 1 CLC 701 at [215]; *Vald. Nielsen v Baldorino* [2019] EWHC 1926 (Comm) at [137]; *Glossop Cartons v Contact (Print & Packaging)* at [65]; *Marme Inversiones v Natwest Markets* [2019] EWHC (Comm) 366 at [117].

2 This formulation covers the case of deliberate ambiguity, but excludes the case where the relevant sense of the statement does not occur to the representor.

7.65 The classic source of this limb of the intention principle is *Smith v Chadwick*, where Lord Blackburn set out several points. First, motive is irrelevant: if the defendants trick the claimant into investing, it is no defence to the claim of fraud that they believed the investment to be good. Second, 'if with intent to lead the plaintiff to act upon it, they put forth a statement which they know may bear two meanings, one of which is false to their knowledge, and thereby the plaintiff putting that meaning on it is misled, I do not think they can escape by saying he ought to have put the other'. Third:

> 'There is a third possible case, that a man may make a statement which he intended to mean one thing only, but which negligently and stupidly he sends out in such a shape as to bear another meaning, and the plaintiff acts upon that meaning. On that I need only say that the defendant, in such a case, would have great difficulty in establishing that it was only honest blundering; but if he did, as for instance, by shewing that his manuscript sent to the printer, contained the word "not," which by some printer's error was omitted in the published prospectus, or that 10,000 was by a printer's error printed 100,000, which escaped notice in revising the proofs, I should say it was not a fraud, though perhaps gross negligence.'[1]

1 (1884) 9 App Cas 187 at 201. This is the source referenced by Viscount Maugham in *Bradford v Borders* [1941] 2 All ER at 211.

7.66 The theme was taken up by Bowen LJ in *Angus v Clifford*, referring to *Smith v Chadwick* in support of this point:

> 'A man ought to have a belief that what he is saying is true; but a man may believe what he is saying – the expression which he uses – to be true, because he is honestly using the words in a sense of his own, which, however inappropriate, however stupid, however grossly careless, if you will, is the special sense in which he means to use the words, without any consciousness being present to his mind that they would convey to other reasonable persons a different sense from that in which he is using them – a man may believe a statement in that sense of his own, and yet the use of the language may be wholly improper, that is to say, in respect of want of caution in the use of it. It does not follow because a man uses language that he is conscious

of the way in which it will be understood by those who read it. Unless he is conscious that it will be understood in a different manner from that in which he is honestly though blunderingly using it, he is not fraudulent, he is not dishonest. An honest blunder in the use of language is not dishonest.'[1]

1 [1891] 2 Ch 449 at 472.

7.67 As noted above, the principle that it is essential that the representor understands the representation in the relevant sense was applied by the Privy Council in *Akerhielm v de Mare*, where it was treated as part of the requirement of dishonesty rather than as an aspect of the representor's intention to defraud. In *Goose v Wilson Sandford*, also referred to above, the Court of Appeal, though relying on *Akerhielm*, made clear that it was the intention part of the test that was under consideration rather than the dishonesty part. It is submitted that it is not important whether the principle is treated as part of the dishonesty requirement or the intention to induce requirement, but it should not be overlooked that there is here only one principle, not two. We suggest that the preferable way to analyse it is that it is part of showing that the fraudulent representation was made knowingly, or with the intention of deceiving and inducing the claimant.

7.68 In his judgment in *Raiffeisen*, Christopher Clarke J said:

> 'The rule [that a representation must be made with the intention of inducing the claimant to act] is less easy to apply in respect of implied rather than express statements because the representor may not appreciate what a court later holds to be the implications of what he said. Nevertheless if he intended what he said to be relied on by the representee in deciding whether to contract he must be taken to have intended that the representee should rely on the objective meaning of what he said.'[1]

1 *Raiffeisen Zentralbank v RBS* [2011] 1 Lloyd's Rep 123 at [222]. Adopted by Picken J in *Marme Inversiones 2007 v Natwest Markets* [2019] EWHC 366 at [261]–[262].

7.69 On this view, if D makes an implied representation which is held (objectively) to mean X, which is false and not believed by D, but without realising that X was what he stated, then this could be a misrepresentation meeting the intention to induce requirement, even though it will not be held to be dishonest and therefore cannot complete a cause of action for damages for deceit. However, there are problems with this distinction. As a matter of authority, despite the otherwise comprehensive citation of authority in *Raiffeisen*, *Goose v Wilson Sandford* does not appear to have been cited, and in *Goose*,[1] the principle was applied to an implied representation in respect of which it was held 'it is incumbent on the representee to show that the representor intended his statement to be understood by the representee in the sense in which it is false'. In principle too, it is not easy to see why it should be easier to establish an implicit fraudulent misrepresentation than an express one.

1 At [41].

Elements of deceit: (v) the inducement of the claimant

7.70 As with most tortious causes of action, a claimant must show causation running from the defendant's breach of duty to the claimant's loss. Causation in the law generally requires two elements. The first element is factual (or 'but for' or 'necessary') causation: the breach of duty must have been a factual cause of the loss in the sense that, without the breach of duty, the loss would not have been sustained. Factual causation is determined by a purely factual (though hypothetical) inquiry. However, caution is required in relation to deceit, because this requirement may be relaxed where fraud is established, as discussed below.[1] The second element is legal (or 'substantive' or 'proximate') causation: the breach must be a legal cause of the loss, meaning that it is one of the substantive causes of the loss, not just an accidental, adventitious or merely necessary cause.

1 It is settled that in cases of innocent or negligent misrepresentation it must be shown that the claimant would not have entered into the contract had the representation not been made: *Nederlandse Industrie v Rembrandt Enterprises* at [15].

7.71 Torts like deceit are sometimes called 'reliance based', reflecting the fact that in deceit (as in negligent misstatement), causation is not established unless the causal chain from breach to loss includes reliance by or on behalf of the claimant on the statement made by or on behalf of the defendant. As Cartwright points out, although the language of reliance often replaces the language of causation when discussing reliance based torts, the concept of reliance focusses on only one part of the causal chain, namely the influence of the representation upon the claimant's own actions.[1] Thus, the question as laid down in *Edgington v Fitzmaurice*[2] is whether the misrepresentation so influenced the claimant as to be one of the causes of the claimant's relevant act of reliance. As in other causation questions, it is generally sufficient to found the claim if the defendant's wrong is one of several causes of the damage. In relation to deceit, this was confirmed by the Supreme Court in *Zurich v Hayward*.[3] In business sale cases, vendors sometimes claim that causative effect of a misrepresentation was eclipsed by the purchaser's positive reasons to buy, its professional advice or its reliance on contractual representations and warranties, but this argument rarely succeeds if a material fraud is demonstrated.[4]

1 J Cartwright (ed) *Misrepresentation, Mistake and Non-Disclosure* (6th edn, Sweet & Maxwell, 2022) at 3-53.

2 (1885) 29 ChD 459.

3 [2017] AC 142 at [33].
4 See, eg, *MAN v Freightliner* [2005] EWHC 2347 (Comm) at [121]–[124], *Invertec* at [367]. On the other hand, where the allegations of fraud are rejected, it is not unusual for the defendant's inducement argument to succeed as well: see, eg, *Welven v Soar* at [156].

7.72 In *Zurich v Hayward*,[1] Lord Toulson remarked that the relevant criterion is inducement rather than reliance. Although inducement is a broader concept than reliance, in most cases the difference between the two is imperceptible because reliance is the way in which a statement induces the claimant to transact or take some course of action. *Zurich* was exceptional because the claimant had not believed the representation to be true. In such an exceptional case, the precise nature of the inquiry is more important and is illuminated by bearing in mind the distinction between inducement, which is the relevant question, and reliance, which is the usual vehicle for inducement to be established. A somewhat more practical reason to focus on inducement rather than reliance is that it explains why the chain from representation to the claimant's act does not have to be direct: a purchaser's representation may influence an adviser, executive or other intermediary, upon whose report the ultimate decision maker of the purchaser will rely.[2]

1 At [70].
2 See, eg, *MAN v Freightliner* [2005] EWHC 2347 (Comm) at [120]–[121].

7.73 Accordingly, to make good a cause of action in deceit, it must be demonstrated that the claimant was induced by the fraudulent misrepresentation (usually by relying upon it, directly or indirectly), having understood it in the relevant sense.[1] In other words, if there is more than one possible sense or meaning of the statement made, then the claimant must be induced by the statement in the sense or meaning which it is found to bear. In combination with the requirement discussed above that the defendant must intend that same meaning, there has to be a correspondence between the representor's state of mind in intending their statement to be understood as meaning X and the representee's state of mind in actually understanding it as meaning X.

1 *Raiffeisen Zentralbank v RBS* [2011] 1 Lloyd's Rep 123 at [87].

7.74 What exactly is inducement? In *Zurich v Hayward*, where the question for the Supreme Court was whether inducement was possible if the claimant did not believe the representation to be true, the leading judgment of Lord Clarke is notably reluctant to provide any kind of definition. Lord Clarke agreed with the statement that 'The claimant must have been influenced by the misrepresentation' and cited a passage from Bowen LJ in *Edgington v Fitzmaurice* and concluded:

> 'Mr Hayward relies upon the references in the textbooks and, indeed, in cases like *Edgington v Fitzmaurice* to the requirement that the representation must have impacted upon the representee's mind.

> To my mind that simply means that the representee must have been induced to act as he did in reliance upon the representation.'[1]

1 [2017] AC 142 at [25]–[27].

7.75 In establishing inducement, the claimant is assisted by an evidential presumption of fact that infers inducement from the facts that a material misrepresentation (that is, one that is likely to induce a reasonable person to enter the contract) was made and the claimant did enter the contract.[1] If the misrepresentation is made fraudulently, then the presumption is 'very difficult to rebut'.[2] This is important in business sale cases because it is often difficult for a purchaser to demonstrate exactly what they would have done if circumstances had varied from the actual course of events. An approach that has been taken is to view the misrepresentations themselves as an 'evidentiary weapon' fashioned by the defendants against themselves. In other words, the existence of the misrepresentation provides evidence of causation on the basis that the defendant was 'not prepared to risk the consequences of telling the truth'.[3] This approach can be understood as an explanation for, or expression of, the presumption of inducement.

1 At 196; *Pan Atlantic v Pine Top* [1995] 1 AC 501 at 542A; *Barton v County NatWest* [1999] Lloyd's Rep Bank 408; *Marme v Natwest Markets* [2019] EWHC 366 (Comm) at [291]–[292].

2 *Zurich v Hayward* [2017] AC 142 at [37]; *Nederlandse Industrie v Rembrandt Enterprises* at [43], and cf at [25].

3 Per Jacobs J in *Vald. Neilson* at [503]–[504], cf also ibid at [511], adopted by HHJ Hodge QC in *Glossop Cartons v Contact (Print and Packaging)* [2019] EWHC 2314 (Ch) at [56].

7.76 The business sale case of *Downs v Chappell* concerned a claim by a purchaser for damages for deceit. The purchaser of a bookshop asked to see accounts to confirm the stated turnover and profit figures. They required independent verification of the figures provided and were not prepared to proceed without this. The vendor gave figures which he knew were false, which his accountants carelessly verified to the purchaser.[1] Although the trial judge found that the purchaser would not have contracted without verification of the figures, he also found that they would still have proceeded if the true figures had been provided. On this basis, he held that causation was not established and the claim failed. The Court of Appeal reversed the judge, holding that the judge found that the representations induced the purchaser to contract and that is all that had to be established by way of causation:

> 'The Judge was wrong to ask how they would have acted if they had been told the truth. They were never told the truth. They were told lies in order to induce them to enter into the contract. The lies were material and successful; they induced the plaintiffs to act to their detriment and contract with Mr. Chappell.'[2]

1 There was also a claim against the accountants, but that is not our concern here.

2 *Downs v Chappell* [1997] 1 WLR 426 at 433E.

7.77 This passage has been treated as authoritative. It was applied in the business sale cases of *Man v Freightliner* and *Bottin v Venson*.[1] It was cited without disapproval by Lord Clarke in *Zurich v Hayward*[2] and applied by the Court of Appeal in *Nederlandse Industrie v Rembrandt*.[3] Thus, one point that is clear is that the question whether the claimant was induced by the fraudulent misrepresentation does not depend on, or even involve consideration of, how the claimant would have reacted to knowing the truth. It therefore seems that if any counterfactual question is relevant to causation, it can only be the question what would have happened if the representation had not been made at all. In a case like *Downs v Chappell* this approach benefits the claimant, because the claimant demonstrated that they insisted upon a statement being made (and verified) about turnover and profit, which of itself confirmed inducement. But in a different case, a vendor might make a misrepresentation which has not been sought by the purchaser. In that case the question could still be raised: would the purchaser have proceeded in any event if the representation had not been made at all? In other words, is 'but for' causation established between breach and loss?

1 *Man v Freightliner* [2005] EWHC 2347 (Comm) at [123]; *Bottin v Venson* at [301].
2 *Zurich v Hayward* [2017] AC 142 at [38].
3 At [47].

7.78 Whether the question of 'but for' causation is relevant was left expressly open in *Zurich v Hayward*, Lord Clarke saying:

> 'As to … rebutting the presumption of inducement, the authorities are not entirely consistent as to what is required to rebut the presumption.
>
> However, it is not strictly necessary to address those differences in this case because, however precisely the test is worded – whether what must be proved is that the misrepresentation played "no part at all" or that it did not play a "determinative part", or that it did not play a "real and substantial part" – I would accept the submission made on behalf of Zurich that the presumption is not rebutted on the facts as found in this case.'[1]

1 [2017] AC 142 at [36]. The issue was also left open by the Court of Appeal in *Nederlandse v Rembrandt Enterprises* at [44], whilst noting first instance authority in *Raiffeisen* and *Cassa di Risparmio v Barclays* [2011] 1 CLC 701 tending to support the lesser requirement to satisfy inducement. The decisive reasoning in *Nederlandse* at [49] is consistent with either view.

7.79 There is authority to the effect that if a fraudulent misrepresentation is any one of the factors that influenced the representee in deciding to enter a contract, then it will be presumed to be sufficient to satisfy the test of inducement and, thus of both factual and legal causation of whatever loss may accrue to the claimant from the transaction. In other words, the only way for the defendant to rebut the presumption is to show that the misrepresentation played no part, or no significant part, in the claimant's decision making process.[1] On the other hand, after a lengthy though obiter analysis in *Marme Inversiones v Natwest Markets*,[2] Picken J opined that there was much to be said for the view that 'but for' causation should be required in all cases of misrepresentation. The issue was raised in *Vegesentials Ltd v The Shanghai Commercial & Savings Bank Ltd*,[3] where HHJ Jarman KC held that:

> 'the better approach in this particular case is to ask whether in common sense terms there was a sufficient causal connection between the Letter and the claimed losses, although it may well be that the same result would flow on these particular facts from an application of the "but for" test.'

1 *Zurich v Hayward* [2017] AC 142 at [36]–[38]; *Vald. Nielsen v Baldorino* [2019] EWHC 1926 (Comm) at [157]; *MAN v Freightliner* [2005] EWHC 2347 (Comm) at [121] and [124].

2 [2019] EWHC 366 (Comm) at [317]. It might also be noted that Eder J appeared to apply a 'but for' analysis in finding no inducement in *Welven v Soar* at [126].

3 [2024] EWHC 7 (Ch) at [54]–[57].

7.80 This is an issue where the differing origins of the equitable claim to rescind and the common law claim to damages could well lead to different approaches. Thus *Chitty on Contracts*[1] has a section heading '"*But for" causation not required for rescission for fraud*' under which the authorities for that view are summarised and it is said 'The rule applies only to fraud, and only when the remedy sought is rescission. The victim of fraud cannot recover damages unless the loss for which damages are claimed would not have been suffered but for the fraud.' This approach makes perfect sense in principle and historically. However, damages at common law are compensatory and that very fundamental principle incorporates the assumption that 'but for' causation has been established between breach and loss. Several recent business sale decisions confirm that 'but for' causation between the misrepresentation being made and the claimant's act of reliance is a requirement of a claim for damages in deceit.[2] On the other hand, for rescission in equity, the question should be whether it is unconscionable for the defendant to hold the claimant to the contractual bargain,[3] and it is easy to see why in the case of a material fraudulent misrepresentation a positive answer to that question may be given without proof of factual causation. Pragmatically, however, there is something to be said for arriving at a policy view that recognises one test, whichever it is to be, for satisfying causation in a claim of fraudulent misrepresentation. It remains to be seen in which direction the higher courts will go when a decision is necessary.

1 *Chitty on Contracts* (35th edn, Sweet & Maxwell, 2023) at 10-048.

2 Eg, *Ivy Technology v Martin* [2022] EWHC 1218 (Comm) at [370], citing *European Real Estate Debt Fund (Cayman) Ltd v Treon* [2021] EWHC 2866 (Ch) at [374], in turn citing *Vald. Nielsen v Baldorino* [2019] EWHC 1926 (Comm) at [159], where the proposition had been common ground.

3 See, eg, per Romer LJ in *With v O'Flanagan* [1936] Ch 575 at 586.

Elements of deceit: (vi) loss and damage

7.81 Damage is required to complete a cause of action in deceit, as confirmed by Lord Blackburn in *Smith v Chadwick* in a passage that was re-affirmed by the Supreme Court in *Zurich v Hayward*.[1] The measure of loss is considered separately in the next chapter.

1 [2017] AC 142 at [66], quoting *Smith v Chadwick* at 195.

Authority, aggregation, corporate and vicarious liability for deceit

7.82 As Moore-Bick LJ explained in *MAN v Freightliner*,[1] the essence of fraudulent misrepresentation is making a statement without honest belief intending the claimant to rely on it, from which it follows that 'liability depends on the conjunction of a false statement and dishonest state of mind'. In this dictum, the phrase 'dishonest state of mind' encompasses both the absence of honest belief in the truth of the statement and intention that the claimant should be induced. For that reason, fraud is only established if one individual has both responsibility for the statement and the relevant dishonest state of mind. The paradigm case is where a single individual both makes the statement and has all the elements required for a dishonest state of mind. In that case, the individual representor will be liable for deceit and a further question may arise whether other defendants may also be liable for the representor's tort.

1 [2005] EWHC 2347 (Comm) at [156].

7.83 A defendant who is a knowing and active party to a scheme to defraud or is complicit in the commission of a deceit as part of a common design is liable in deceit as a joint tortfeasor, even if the representation was actually made by another.[1] A defendant may also be liable for representations made by another if the defendant manifestly approves and adopts those representations; in other words the defendant's approval or agreement to the statement is manifested and – perhaps – communicated to the claimant.[2]

1 *Clerk & Lindsell on Torts* (24th edn) at [4-04] and [17-11].
2 *Ivy Technology v Martin* [2022] EWHC 1218 (Comm) at [351]–[354].

7.84 In *Marme v Natwest Markets*,[1] Picken J gave extensive obiter consideration to submissions that, at least in the case of an implied representation, if the representor intends the statement to be relied upon, but does not realise what it means or that it is false, and if another individual is aware that the statement is made and is false, then the employer of both individuals is liable in deceit. To the extent that this reasoning depends on the adoption of the suggestion from *Raiffeisen* at [222] that a representor may be dishonest without knowing what the representation means, we respectfully disagree.[2] However, subject to that point, this reasoning seems to take a longer way round the issue than is needed. If an individual is sufficiently responsible for a representation that they can be said to permit it to be made and is aware that it is in fact made and that same individual understands its meaning and lacks an honest belief in its truth, then deceit is established against that individual.

That involves no aggregation and is an orthodox approach. It does leave over the question whether the employer of the individual is also liable, but it is hard to see any principled basis on which aggregation of states of mind or conduct of several individuals could make any difference to that question.[3]

1 At [256]–[265].
2 See above at [**7.68**].
3 'Where someone commits a tortious act, he at least will be liable for the consequences; whether others are liable depends on the circumstances' per Lord Rodger in *Standard Chartered Bank v Pakistan Shipping* [2003] 1 AC 959 at [40].

7.85 In business sale cases, a representation may be made by an individual who is actually the vendor in which case it may be that no question arises about other persons' liability. The next case is where the individual who makes the representation is acting on behalf of another individual who is the vendor. In that case, the vendor will be liable as primary tortfeasor if they have both responsibility for the representation in the sense of knowing it is being made and also a dishonest state of mind. If the vendor in that scenario is not personally dishonest (and even does not know that the representation is being made), they may still be liable vicariously for the deceit of the representor on the principles of vicarious liability discussed further below.

7.86 If the vendor is a corporation, the same principles apply. If an individual who is liable for deceit is a person whose statements count as the company's statements for the purpose of the relevant transaction (applying the approach set out in *Meridian Global Funds v Securities Commission*[1]), then the company will be liable as primary tortfeasor, along with the individual.[2] On the other hand, if the individual against whom deceit is established is not the person whose acts count as those of the company, then it will be necessary to consider whether the company is vicariously liable for their tort.

1 [1995] 2 AC 500.
2 The individual is liable in deceit even if he was acting only as servant or agent; in this case, the approach in *Williams v Natural Life* does not apply: *Standard Chartered Bank v Pakistan Shipping* [22]–[23], applied in a business sale case in *Hemsley v Graham* [2013] EWHC 2232 (Ch) at [413].

7.87 As to the test of vicarious liability, this is another area where as a matter of first principles, it might be expected that a different approach would apply based on the differing origins of the equitable remedy of rescission for misrepresentation from the common law claim for damages for deceit. In relation to the equitable remedy, the question is whether the principal who contracts through an agent should be fixed with the consequences of the agent's misrepresentation. That question turns on whether the agent's conduct was within the scope of their authority as agent. On the other hand in a common law claim for damages, the question ought to be whether the employer is responsible for the damage caused by their employee. That question turns on whether the tort was committed within the course of employment.

7.88 However, the principled approach seems to have given way to a pragmatic assimilation of tests so that in any case of fraudulent misrepresentation vicarious liability turns on whether the representation was made within the scope of the representor's authority from the defendant. This is generally thought to have been decided by the House of Lords in *Armagas v Mundogas*[1] and has certainly been confirmed by the Court of Appeal in *Hockley Mint v Ramsden.*[2] It remains to be seen how this will be reconciled with the application of the course of employment test for other torts, including negligent misstatement.[3] However, in the light of the tightening of the course of employment test by the Supreme Court in *WM Morrison v Various Claimants*,[4] the difference may be less likely to be critical in future cases.

1 *The Ocean Frost* [1986] 1 AC 717. But cf the analysis of Evans-Lombe J in *Barings Bank v Coopers & Lybrand (No 7)* [2003] PNLR 34 at [700]–[702].
2 [2019] 1 WLR 1617.
3 *So v HSBC* [2009] 1 CLC 503.
4 [2020] UKSC 12.

7.89 In *Briess v Woolley*[1] the plaintiffs bought all the shares of a company after negotiations with its managing director, one Rosher, who was also one of the shareholders. Rosher knew, but did not disclose, that the accounts of the company were based on fraudulent and dishonest trading. He was held at trial to be liable to the plaintiffs in deceit. The issue on appeal was whether one of the other shareholders, Sir Charles McRea, was also liable. There was no suggestion that Sir Charles had any knowledge of Rosher's fraud. The first question, as stated by Lord Reid, was 'the extent of the authority conferred on Mr Rosher by the shareholders'. That authority was stated in a meeting minute which recorded that 'it was agreed that Mr Rosher who had already been in negotiation with [the purchaser] should take the matter up further with that company with a view to completing the transaction on the above basis.' The House of Lords, disagreeing with the Court of Appeal on this point of construction, held that this gave Rosher authority to 'make such further statements and representations and to give such answers to any questions by the company and do such other things as he should think desirable or necessary to achieve a sale.'[2] The second issue that arose was that there was no clear finding of any misrepresentation being made after the date of the meeting when Rosher was authorised to act for the shareholders. However, the House of Lords held that the earlier misrepresentations were continuing misrepresentations which were relied upon by the plaintiffs when they made the contract, which was after Rosher had become the agent of the other shareholders.

1 [1954] AC 333.
2 Per Lord Reid at 347–348.

7.90 Thus *Briess v Woolley*[1] is authority for two important propositions. First, a fraudulent misrepresentation is generally treated as being of continuing effect until it is relied upon. This proposition is not in doubt, though it does of course depend on the interpretation of the representation.[2] Second, where a person authorises another to negotiate a transaction generally, the actual authority so conferred includes authority to make such statements and representations as the agent considers desirable to conclude the transaction. If the agent does so fraudulently, then the principal will be liable. This second proposition requires closer examination. In *Philipp v Barclays Bank UK Ltd*[3], the Supreme Court approved the view expressed in *Bowstead & Reynolds on Agency* (22nd edn) at Article 23: 'Authority to act as agent includes only authority to act honestly in pursuit of the interests of the principal.' The two cases can be reconciled only if a distinction is drawn between carrying out a fraud against the principal (outside the scope of authority) and carrying out a fraud from which the principal would benefit if it succeeds (within the scope). It seems that that must be the right approach. For a detailed discussion of the issue concluding that for the principal's liability 'It is sufficient for the fraudulent misrepresentation to have been made in the course of a negotiation which the agent had the principal's actual or ostensible authority to carry out', see *Ivy Technology v Martin*.[4] *Briess v Woolley* and *Ivy Technology v Martin* are both accepted on this point in *Bowstead & Reynolds on Agency* (23rd edn).[5]

1 [1954] AC 333.
2 *Ivy Technology v Martin* at [356].
3 [2023] UKSC 25.
4 [2022] EWHC 1218 (Comm) at [373]–[428]. For a further example, see *MDW Holdings Ltd v Norvill* [2021] EWHC 1135 (Ch) at [262]. The appeal at [2022] EWCA Civ 883 did not concern this issue.
5 See [8-183] and [8-196].

7.91 In *MAN v Freightliner*[1] only one individual, Mr Ellis, knew of the fraud. Mr Ellis was the financial controller of the target company and the question was whether the target's parent company was liable for his fraud. Moore-Bick LJ formulated 'the critical question' as being 'whether [parent company] put him forward to speak about the accounts and financial position of [target company] in such a way as to hold him out as having authority to speak about such matters on its behalf'. This question was very fact sensitive since all involved knew that Mr Ellis was employed by the target. However, Moore-Bick LJ found that he was brought to negotiating meetings where he was invited to answer questions about the target's finances on behalf of the vendor parent company.[2] By doing so without disclosing his knowledge that the accounts were false, Mr Ellis made fraudulent misrepresentations for which the parent company was liable. By contrast, when Mr Ellis was answering questions as part of the due diligence exercise, he was acting in his capacity as employee of the target and not the parent vendor.[3] This case thus neatly illustrates the factual nature of the inquiry into vicarious liability in a business sale context.

1 [2005] EWHC 2347 (Comm) at [91].
2 Ibid at [92]–[109].
3 Ibid at [110]–[113].

7.92 Moore-Bick LJ also stated in *MAN v Freightliner* that a company could be responsible for a misrepresentation if a person (such as a director) representing the company directs or allows a statement known by that person to be false to be made by another.[1] Even though the individual making the representation may be honest, the company will be liable in deceit if it (acting by the director) directs or allows the statement to be made. An example of the application of this principle is *Erlson Precision Holdings v Hampson Industries*,[2] where a chief executive officer was aware that false forecasts had been made by others who did not know they were false. Field J held:

> 'Pursuant to the approach adopted by Moore-Bick LJ in *Man v Freightliner* [2005] 2347 (Comm), paragraph 156, it follows, in my opinion, that to establish its case the claimant must prove that Mr Ward was aware that the forecasts were being communicated to potential buyers and that knowing that they were false and/or misleading he decided not to reveal Cummins's intention to terminate its relationship with HPA with the intention that the forecasts should continue to be relied on.'[3]

1 [2005] EWHC 2347 (Comm) at [156].
2 [2011] EWHC 1137 (Comm).
3 [2011] EWHC 1137 (Comm) at [42].

THE MISREPRESENTATION ACT 1967

7.93 The Misrepresentation Act 1967 has three principal sections: 1, 2 and 3. Section 1 provides that it is no bar to rescission for misrepresentation that the misrepresentation has become a term of the contract or the contract has been performed. Section 2 provides for damages claims for non-fraudulent misrepresentation and thus creates a statutory tort. Section 3 provides that a term excluding or restricting liability for misrepresentation is not effective unless it satisfies the requirement of reasonableness under the Unfair Contract Terms Act 1977.

7.94 It is necessary to look more closely at s 2 before going onto to the issues that may arise in business sale cases. Breaking it into stages, s 2(1) applies to a representee who: (i) has entered into a contract; (ii) after a misrepresentation has been made to him; (iii) by another party thereto; and (iv) as a result has suffered loss. If the representor would have been liable to damages had the misrepresentation been made fraudulently, then the representor shall be 'so liable' notwithstanding that the misrepresentation was not made fraudulently.[1] A statutory defence is provided if the representee 'proves that he had reasonable ground to believe and did believe up to the time the contract was made that the facts represented were true'.

1 Lord Reed called this 'a complex provision which has the effect of dispensing with the need to establish a duty of care in English law where a person has entered into a contract after a misrepresentation has been made to him by another party to the contract': *Cramaso v Ogilivie-Grant* at [37]. The gap had previously been filled by a judicial willingness to find collateral contracts as in *Esso v Mardon*: per Cavanagh J in *New York Laser Clinic v Naturastudios* [2019] EWHC 2892 (QB) at [35].

7.95 Section 2(2) gives the court a discretion in the case of a non-fraudulent misrepresentation, where the representee is entitled to claim rescission, to declare that the contract subsists and award damages in lieu of rescission. Any damages awarded under s 2(2) are to be taken into account in assessing any liability under s 2(1).

7.96 Business sale cases often involve claims under the 1967 Act either as an alternative to a fraud claim or as the principal claim if fraud is not alleged. The principles involved in ascertaining whether a misrepresentation has been made and if so what it is are the same under the 1967 Act as they are in the tort of deceit.[1] They include the requirement that the representor intends the representation to be acted on by the other party.[2] The common principles also include the presumption that if a misrepresentation is made with the intention of inducement, then the other party did indeed rely upon it.[3]

1 *Moto Mabanga v Ophir Energy* [2012] EWHC 1589 (QB) at [24].
2 *Banque Keyser v Skandia* at [1990] 1 QB 665 at 790C.
3 *Gosling v Anderson* (1972) 223 EG 1743.

7.97 The requirement in s 2(1) that the misrepresentation must have been made by a party to the contract into which the claimant was induced can be restrictive, especially in situations with several linked contracts and parties.[1] However, the restriction is not quite as severe as first appears, since the 1967 Act covers representations made by an agent of the contracting representor.[2] Moreover, it has been held that a representation is made *to* the claimant wherever there exists 'a connection between the maker and the recipient of a kind that enables the court to be satisfied that the maker was intending the recipient to rely on the document in a particular way'.[3]

1 As explained at *Taberna v Selskabet* [2017] QB 633 at [43]–[49]; and see *Glossop Cartons v Contact (Print and Packaging)* [2019] EWHC 2314 (Ch) at [58].
2 Damages under the 1967 Act were awarded for a misrepresentation made by the agent of a vendor of land in *Gosling v Anderson* (1972) 223 EG 1743.
3 *Taberna v Selskabet* [2017] QB 633 at [11], applied to the facts at [12].

7.98 Claims under the 1967 Act often raise issues as to remedies, including the measure of damages and these are considered separately in Chapter 8. But at this stage, it is appropriate to mention that, unlike fraud, in a claim under the 1967 Act, contributory fault seems likely to be an available defence.[1]

1 This was the considered, but obiter, view of Moore-Bick LJ in *Taberna v Selskabet* [2017] QB 633 at [52].

OTHER TORT CLAIMS BASED ON MISREPRESENTATION

7.99 Misrepresentation can be the basis of other tort claims, which can help a claimant to widen out the net of defendants beyond those who make representations.[1] In *Ivy Technology v Martin*,[2] Mr Andrew Henshaw QC as a deputy judge of the High Court considered the arguability of such claims in the context of an application for a freezing order. The claimant was the purchaser under an SPA. It made claims against Mr Bell, who was a non-party to the SPA but who held significant ultimate beneficial interests in the target companies. The purchaser alleged that Mr Bell conspired with the vendor for the vendor to make misrepresentations and to breach a non-competition covenant in the SPA. The judge held that it was arguable that unlawful means for the purpose of conspiracy could include making fraudulent misrepresentations and misrepresentations under the 1967 Act, even though the latter had some conceptual difficulty. He also held, following earlier authority, that it was arguable that breach of contract could be an unlawful means. At trial, the same judge held that both breach of contract and deceit were unlawful means.[3] In *Vald. Nielsen*,[4] a conspiracy claim based on fraudulent misrepresentation succeeded at trial, though it added nothing to the deceit claim itself.

1 For the possibility of claims against a person as an accessory to a deceiver, see J Cartwright (ed) *Misrepresentation, Mistake and Non-Disclosure* (6th edn, Sweet & Maxwell, 2022) at 5-22.

2 [2019] EWHC 2510 (Comm).

3 *Ivy Technology v Martin* at [590].

4 [2019] EWHC 1926 (Comm) at [387]. See similarly *Hemsley v Graham* [2013] EWHC 2232 (Ch) at [419].

Chapter 8

Damages

GENERAL POINTS ABOUT DAMAGES

8.01 Although damages are generally said to be compensatory, 'damages in contract serve a different remedial purpose from damages in tort'. As a result, of this difference in purpose, there is a difference in the principles. 'Damages in tort are generally intended to place the claimant as nearly as possible in the same position as he would have been in if the tort had not been committed.' On the other hand, 'damages in contract are … intended to place the claimant in the same position as he would have been if the contract had been performed'.[1]

1 *One-Step (Support) v Morris-Garner* [2019] AC 649 at [31]. For extensive citations of authoritative statements of this principle, see *Classic Maritime v Limbungan Makmur* [2019] EWCA Civ 1102 at [66]–[88], where the point being made was that the reason for the breach is irrelevant to the assessment of damages.

8.02 This difference between the two measures is exemplified by the case of a standard SPA claim for breach of warranty and an equivalent claim in misrepresentation for the same underlying factual matter. The damages for breach of warranty will, prima facie, be the difference between (Warranty True) the value of the shares or business if the warranty had been complied with (what the claimant would have obtained if the contract had been performed) and (Warranty False) the value of the shares or business as it in fact was (what the claimant in fact obtained), at the date of the breach.[1] This measure isolates the difference made to value by the breach of warranty.[2] On the other hand, the starting point for a claim for misrepresentation will be the difference between (P) the price paid for the business (what the claimant paid out in reliance upon the representation) and the true value of the business (what the claimant obtained) plus any recoverable consequential losses between the date of the transaction and the trial.[3] These two measures will generally differ because of consequential losses, which may be very significant if the company does badly after the transaction completes. They can also differ if the bargain is shown to have been bad or good, in the sense that (Warranty True) does not equal (P), in other words, if the price paid was not equal to the value of the business as warranted.

1 As to the precise date, see above at [**2.21**]–[**2.23**].

2 In *Arani v Cordic Group* [2023] EWHC 95 Bright J assessed loss by estimating the impairment to value caused by the breach of warranty and cross-checking that the impairment did not exceed the Warranty True value. Mathematically, this approach is unobjectionable, but caution

should be exercised as not all impairments can realistically be measured in isolation from a full valuation.

3 *Wemyss v Karim* [2016] EWCA Civ 27 at [23].

8.03 In a case where the same facts amount to a breach of warranty and an actionable misrepresentation, the claimant is entitled to claim damages on whichever basis is most favourable.[1] As an illustration of the significance of the different measures of loss, one can take the facts of *Sycamore Bidco v Breslin*.[2] There, the purchase price was £16.75 million. The breach of warranty claim was said by the claimants to be worth about £6 million and quantified by the judge at approximately £4.75 million. However, if the misrepresentation claim based on exactly the same breaches had not failed (it failed on the basis that the warranties were not also representations), the claimants said that the true value of the company by the date of trial was nil and so their claim would have exceeded £16 million.

1 *Wemyss v Karim* at [40].

2 [2012] EWHC 3443 (Ch) at [201].

8.04 The English law of contract recognises as a general principle freedom of contract, meaning that the law does not take a general jurisdiction to save parties from bad bargains or re-write contracts with the benefit of hindsight or second thoughts. An aspect of that general principle which is always in the background in business sale cases is the doctrine 'caveat emptor' (buyer beware).[1] The meaning of this is that a vendor (or more broadly any contracting party) is not obliged to make full disclosure to the purchaser (or other party) unless a specific legal duty to do so arises. Duties to disclose arise under contractual provisions and can also arise from circumstances which make non-disclosure equivalent to an implied misrepresentation. The point to bear in mind is that remedies will only be awarded for the breach of an obligation, either contractual or tortious; the law does not protect the buyer (or any other contractual party) from making a bad bargain.

1 *Bell v Lever Brothers* [1932] AC 161 per Lord Atkin at 221 and 227.

8.05 An important principle is that a judge should assess damages even if it is difficult to do so with precision or certainty. Even though the claimant has the burden of proving its loss, once the claimant has established on a balance of probabilities that it has suffered a loss caused by the defendant's wrong, the court should move to assessment of that loss. Assessment is a different process which does not require anything further to be proved on the balance of probabilities. In assessment of loss, the court does the best it can on the evidence available. The leading statement of this principle is from *Parabola Investments v Browallia Cal Ltd* where Toulson LJ said:

> '... Some claims for consequential loss are capable of being established with precision (for example, expenses incurred prior to the date of trial). Other forms of consequential loss are not capable

> of similarly precise calculation because they involve the attempted measurement of things which would or might have happened (or might not have happened) but for the defendant's wrongful conduct, as distinct from things which have happened. In such a situation the law does not require a claimant to perform the impossible, nor does it apply the balance of probability test to the measurement of the loss. The claimant has first to establish an actionable head of loss.
>
> This may in some circumstances consist of the loss of a chance, …, but we are not concerned with that situation in the present case, … . The next task is to quantify the loss. Where that involves a hypothetical exercise, the court does not apply the same balance of probability approach as it would to the proof of past facts. Rather, it estimates the loss by making the best attempt it can to evaluate the chances, great or small (unless those chances amount to no more than remote speculation), taking all significant factors into account: [citations omitted].'[1]

1 [2011] QB 477 at [22]–[23]. Part of this statement was expressly approved by the Supreme Court in *One Step (Support) v Morris-Garner* [2019] AC 649 at [37].

8.06 This approach is regularly applied in business sale cases where the evidence may not permit the court to be confident about the valuations that are relevant to quantum. Even in such cases, the court does not say that the claimant has failed to prove its case, but instead does the best it can.[1] That said, this approach is subject to the ordinary rules of procedural fairness and the court must not adopt an approach which the defendant has not had a fair opportunity to address. If the difficulty arises because of the way that the claimant has put their case, for example, by 'deliberately [adopting] a high risk policy of aiming at jackpot damages', then a court should not attempt 'to rescue the plaintiff's case'.[2]

1 *Wemyss v Karim* [2016] EWCA Civ 27 at [40]–[49]; *Cardamom v McAllister* [2019] EWHC 1200 (Comm) at [77]–[83].

2 *Senate v Alcatel* [1999] 2 Lloyd's Rep 423 at [54].

8.07 On the other hand, in some cases it may be permissible to assess damages on the basis of giving the claimant a 'fair wind' because it is the defendant's misconduct which has resulted in the need for the court to conjecture.[1] Authority has not always spoken with a single voice about the width of application of this principle, which derives from the very old case of *Armory v Delamirie*,[2] but recent cases have adopted an approach like of that of Hamblen J in *Porton v 3M*, who reviewed the authorities and said:

> 'This is not a case concerning the value of goods which the defendant has refused to produce or of the suppression of evidence, as in *Armory v Delamirie*. Nor is it a case involving the loss of the chance of success in legal proceedings, as in *Browning v Brachers*. It is a claim for lost

> profits for breach of contract. There is factual and expert evidence before the court relating to that claim. There is documentation before the court relevant to the claim. The evidential playing field is a level one. Whilst it is correct that the claim involves a degree of conjecture, that is the case in relation to very many contractual damages claims and in all such cases it can be said that it is the defendant's breach of contract which has made that conjecture necessary. As a matter of authority there is no requirement to apply the principle of *Armory v Delamirie* to a case such as the present, and as a matter of principle I consider that there is good reason not to do so and that the application of the principle should not be extended further than is necessary.'[3]

1 The term 'fair wind' is from the loss of a chance case of *Browning v Brachers* [2005] EWCA Civ 753.
2 (1722) 1 Strange 505.
3 *Porton v 3M* [2011] EWHC 2895 (Comm) at [244].

8.08 The present position in relation to the issues discussed in the previous paragraph was summarised by Lord Reed in *One Step v Morris-Garner*, in terms that confirm that the *Armory* principle is to be applied narrowly and, as Hamblen J said 'not … extended further than is necessary':

> 'Evidential difficulties in establishing the measure of loss are reflected in the degree of certainty with which the law requires damages to be proved. As is stated in Chitty, para 26-015:
>
> > "Where it is clear that the claimant has suffered substantial loss, but the evidence does not enable it to be precisely quantified, the court will assess damages as best it can on the available evidence."
>
> In so far as the defendant may have destroyed or wrongfully prevented or impeded the claimant from adducing relevant evidence, the court can make presumptions in favour of the claimant … .'[1]

1 At [38].

8.09 Having quantified the damages that were caused by the breach of duty in question, they may fall to be reduced if the defendant shows that: (i) part of the loss was avoided; (ii) part of the loss was caused by the claimant's own unreasonable failure to mitigate loss; or (iii) credit should be given for benefits obtained by the claimant in consequence of the same breach of duty. None of these matters typically arise in relation to breach of warranty claims, because the clear focus on the difference in value at the date of the transaction will usually defeat any such argument by a defendant, but they may well do so in tortious claims including for fraudulent misrepresentation, so they will be considered below under that heading.

8.10 The effect of taxation on damages is a potentially complex area, for which reference may be made to *McGregor on Damages*[1]. As always, express contractual terms can be relevant. For example, in *Sycamore Bidco v Breslin*,[2] there was a stipulation that claims could be grossed up if they would be subject to tax. Mann J made no finding about how that worked on the basis of his findings in the case, and taxation has not often featured in business sale cases. Taxation seems unlikely to play a major role in most cases under current tax law and practice. The reason for this is HMRC Extra Statutory Concession D33, which came into force to ameliorate the effect of the decision in *Zim Properties v Proctor*.[3] ESC D33 provides in short that compensation or damages or a settlement sum received in respect of a chose in action in connection with property which is an asset for chargeable gains purposes may be treated as a sum derived from that asset, so that any gain is calculated with the benefit of the base cost of the asset, rather than a base cost of zero as would apply to the chose in action.

1 J Edelman et al (ed) *McGregor on Damages* (22nd edn, Sweet & Maxwell, 2024), ch 19.
2 At [468].
3 (1984) 58 TC 371.

8.11 For an exception, see *Levison v Farin* (which pre-dates ESC D33). In that case, damages were awarded for breach of warranty on the basis of a reduction in the company's net assets from what was warranted. Gibson J said the following, and held that the tax benefit should be deducted from the damages:

> '… the defendants, by reason of the breach of warranty, received the shares of the company with the net asset value of that company less by £8,500 than it should have been if the warranty had been performed. Over a period of three or four years thereafter, because of the losses in the company, which produced the reduction in net asset value, and hence the breach of warranty, the defendants have paid a smaller sum in tax than otherwise they would have paid, in the amount of £2,940.'[1]

It may be noted that this form of deduction was applicable as a result of the assessment of damages on the basis of net asset values. If (as is more normal these days) damages are assessed on the basis of the capital value of the business as a whole, then this should take into account taxation within the valuation model.

1 [1978] 2 All ER 1149 at 1159c.

8.12 A further example where taxation was considered can be found in *4 Eng v Harper*,[1] where David Richards J ordered damages relating to lost income to be grossed up for tax on the basis of an undertaking by the claimant to refund the additional sum if a favourable ruling was obtained from the tax authorities.

1 [2009] Ch 91 at [105].

DAMAGES FOR BREACH OF WARRANTY

Nature of a warranty as it impacts on damages

8.13 The word 'warranty' has different meanings, even within the confines of contract law. In particular, in an insurance contract, 'warranty' has a special meaning distinct from its more common legal usage. In a business sale contract, 'warranty' is used in its more general contractual law sense, but with particular connotations. 'Warranty' in its general contractual meaning is best understood in contradistinction to other concepts, in particular conditions and representations.

8.14 The distinction between warranties and conditions was redefined or clarified by the Sale of Goods Act 1893.[1] After this, a warranty was a contractual undertaking 'the breach of which may give rise to a claim for damages but not to a right to reject the goods and treat the contract as repudiated'.[2] This is different from a condition, the breach of which would give rise to a right to treat the contract as repudiated. So the first point about a warranty is that its breach sounds only in damages, not in a right to treat the contract as repudiated.

1 For detail of the history before 1893 and the difference made by the Act, see R Goode (ed) *Goode on Commercial Law* (5th edn, Penguin Books Ltd, 2017) at 11.04–11.10.

2 Sale of Goods Act 1893, s 11(1)(b).

8.15 The second key concept to distinguish from a warranty is a 'mere' representation. In the law of contract (leaving tort to one side) a representation is a statement intended to induce a contract. If the representation is false then it is a misrepresentation and in equity it may found a claim to rescind the contract (regardless of fault on the part of the representor). A warranty differs from a representation: (a) in point of time: a warranty is given as part of the contract (or a collateral contract); whereas a representation is made prior to contracting; and (b) in point of remedy: breach of warranty sounds in damages; whereas misrepresentation (in this sense) founds an equitable claim to rescind the contract.

8.16 Both of these distinctions have a common thread: a warranty is not something that must be true for the contract to be carried out; the parties' consent to the contract is not vitiated if the warranty proves to be false. What then, positively, is a warranty? It is a contractual undertaking by the warrantor. If a warranty proves to be false, that fact constitutes a breach of contract on the part of the warrantor, because the warrantor has contractually undertaken that it is true. The established approach to breach of warranty can seem counter-intuitive, because the breach of contract is not the result of anything that the warrantor does or fails to do: it is simply the result of the facts not corresponding to the warranty. But this is the essential nature of a warranty as a contractual undertaking: giving and accepting a warranty involves expressly agreeing that any falsity in the warranty will be treated as a breach of contract sounding in damages.

8.17 Because a warranty sounds in damages, if there is a breach, then the warrantor will pay damages for the financial difference made by the breach. In the context of a business sale contract, the core warranties are those given by the seller to the buyer and are generally set out expressly in a schedule. In grammatical form, these seller's warranties generally look like statements about the target company: its accounts are accurate, certain management accounts have been prepared on a consistent basis, its business will be carried out in the usual course between exchange and completion, and the like. However, because warranties sound *only* in damages, they are not in general understood as representations which the warrantor asserts to be true in order to induce the other party to believe them to be true and act accordingly, but as statements for which the warrantor undertakes financial responsibility, whether true or false.

8.18 Some agreements specify a measure of damages or other remedies payable for breach of warranty. For example:

(a) In *New Hearts v Cosmopolitan Investments*,[1] the SPA provided for a measure of damages which was based on the difference in asset value attributable to the breach of warranty, but which was badly drafted so as to make it highly uncertain what were the relevant bases and dates of valuation that were warranted or on which compensation was to be based. It is possible that the drafter of the agreement in *New Hearts* was trying to reflect the position at common law; if so, it was an ill-advised effort.

(b) In *MAN v Freightliner*,[2] the SPA included a provision at Article 12.1 that the seller would indemnify and hold harmless the buyer against any 'Damages' arising out of 'any breach or inaccuracy of any representation or warranty … contained in this Agreement'. 'Damages' were defined as 'any loss, liability, claim, damage (including incidental and consequential damage) or expense (whether or not involving a third party claim) including legal expenses'. Moore-Bick LJ held that this wording 'allows the injured party to recover wide-ranging consequential losses even in the case of breach of warranty'.

(c) In *Welven v Soar*[3] the SPA provided that if any of the warranties were breached, 'then the measure of damages shall be determined by the Courts under normal contractual principles of loss of bargain arising from the breach'. Since no claim for breach of warranty reached trial, this clause was never tested, but it was at best otiose and at worst, confusing.

(d) In *Bir Holdings v Mehta*[4] the SPA provided that in the event of breach, without restricting the rights of the buyer to claim damages on any basis, the seller would pay any shortfall in assets or additional liability as compared to the warranties.

1 [1997] 2 BCLC 249.
2 [2005] EWHC 2347 (Comm) at [59], [61] and [190].
3 [2011] EWHC 3240 (Comm) at [7].
4 [2014] EWHC 3909 (Ch) at [7].

8.19 Assuming that there is no contractual provision otherwise, the measure of loss for breach of warranty is the difference between the value of the shares or business as warranted (Warranty True) and the true value of the shares or business (Warranty False) at the date of the breach.[1] That basic measure is the result of applying the fundamental principle that the claimant is entitled to be put in the position it would have been in had the defendant performed the contract in accordance with its terms. A breach of warranty is a breach of contract and damages are on the basis that if the contract had been carried out, then the warranty would have been true.

1 Whether the date of the breach equates to the date of exchange of contracts or the date of completion where the two differ is addressed above at [**2.21**]–[**2.23**].

8.20 It has occasionally been argued that the date for the assessment of damages for breach of warranty should be varied from the date of the breach to take into account later information. The argument was considered in detail by Popplewell J in *Ageas v Kwik-Fit*, where he held that:

> 'The *Bwllfa* approach, as applied in *The Golden Victory* [2007] 2 AC 353, supports the proposition that when assessing damages for breach of contract by reference to the value of a company or other property at the date of breach, whose value depends upon a future contingency, account can be taken of what is subsequently known about the outcome of the contingency as a result of events subsequent to the valuation date where that is necessary in order to give effect to the compensatory principle. In an appropriate case, the valuation can be made with the benefit of hindsight, taking account of what is known of the outcome of the contingency at the time that the assessment falls to be made by the court.
>
> …
>
> I would, however, sound a note of caution. There are, in my view, two qualifications to the adoption of such an approach. The first is that it can only be justified where it is necessary to give effect to the overriding compensatory principle. The prima facie rule, from which departure must be justified, is that damages are to be assessed at the date of breach and that only events which have occurred at that date can be taken into account.
>
> Secondly, it is important to keep firmly in mind any contractual allocation of risk made by the parties. Party autonomy dictates that an award of damages should not confound the allocation of risk inherent in the parties' bargain. It is not therefore sufficient merely that there is a

future contingency which plays a part in the assessment. It is necessary to examine whether the eventuation of that contingency represents a risk which has been allocated by the parties as one which should fall on one or other of them. If the benefit or detriment of the contingency eventuating is a risk which has been allocated to the buyer, it is not appropriate to deprive him of any benefit which in fact ensues: it is inherent in the bargain that the buyer should receive such benefit.'[1]

1 [2014] Bus LR 1338 at [35], [37], [38]. Paragraph [36] contains an example concerning the sale of a horse which is controversial: Christopher Clarke LJ considered it but did not reach a conclusion in *OMV Petrom v Glencore International* [2016] 2 Lloyd's Rep 432 at [56].

8.21 In the outcome, Popplewell J held that it had not been demonstrated either that the conventional approach based on the breach date rule would offend against the compensatory principle or that any relevant risks were not conferred on the buyer.

8.22 As luck would have it, Popplewell J's treatment of the breach date rule in the context of breach of warranty, which he handed down on 4 July 2014, was considered in two further business sale cases decided on consecutive days in November 2014. First, in *The Hut Group v Nobahar-Cookson*, Blair J set out the principles in a form agreed by counsel before him, but with that judge's express approval too:

> 'In the case of the quantification of damages for breach of warranty in an agreement for the sale of shares (1) The proper measure of damages is a comparison between the value of shares as warranted and their actual value, that is, "warranty true" vs. "warranty false". (2) The normal rule is to make that comparison as at the date of the breach, which is the date of the contract, taking account only of events up to that date. (3) Where value depends on the outcome of a future contingency, the known outcome of that contingency may sometimes be taken into account. (4) However that will only be done where "necessary to give effect to the overriding compensatory principle". (5) The prima facie rule from which departure must be justified is that damages are to be assessed at the date of breach without hindsight. (6) Hindsight cannot be used to confound the allocation of risk under the bargain. It is inappropriate for the court to deprive a buyer of the benefit of a contingency from which, under the contract, he is intended or entitled to benefit. (7) In a share purchase agreement involving a once and for all exchange of consideration, the party which receives the business or a shareholding in the business assumes the risks, or the rewards, of its subsequent performance or failure to perform. For these principles see *Ageas (UK) Limited v Kwik-Fit (GB) Limited* [2014] EWHC 2178 (QB) where Popplewell J reviews the authorities, and as to the general exclusion of hindsight see *Joiner v George* [2002] EWCA Civ 160 at [74], Sir Christopher Slade.

For the avoidance of doubt, it is not suggested that the mere fact that shares sold in breach of warranty later recover their value because the business in fact does well has any effect on quantum assessed as at the date of breach. Any such argument would be insupportable, not least because the buyer is entitled to the benefit of the upside, having taken the risk of the downside.'[1]

1 [2014] EWHC 3842 (QB) at [184]–[185]. The argument for a later date of assessment to take into account improvements in the target's position since the transaction was rejected at [212]–[219].

8.23 Second, on the following day, HHJ David Cooke (sitting as a judge of the Chancery Division) handed down judgment in *Bir Holdings v Mehta*. HHJ Cooke made the point that:

> 'In a breach of warranty case such as this an assessment of the value of an income earning asset is required. There is a conceptual difference between assessing the loss to a claimant by reduction in an income stream he receives directly (such as charter income [as in *The Golden Victory*]) and the reduction in the capital value of an asset which itself earns an income stream.'[1]

HHJ Cooke then considered *Ageas* and described it as 'the high water mark' of the *Bwllfa* principle at least in this context. He then dismissed the argument based on *Bwllfa* and *The Golden Victory* on the basis of several grounds including that the issue is the value of the company and 'It is of no assistance to say that this [a risk which should have been disclosed to satisfy a warranty] might or might not have resulted in future loss of income; in that wide sense almost all factors affecting the value of a business could be said to involve the outcome of future events.'

1 [2014] EWHC 3909 (Ch) at [61]–[81].

8.24 It is perhaps not entirely fair to describe *Ageas* as the 'high water mark' of a principle of measuring loss at a later date. The analysis in *Ageas* was in fact followed by both Blair J and HHJ Cooke. While it may be fair to say that Popplewell J appeared to treat the argument for later assessment with a degree of respect, he did reject it in terms that will apply to more or less any ordinary breach of warranty in a business sale contract. The short point is that in a business sale context, the various risks of the business are allocated to the buyer save that the seller takes the risk that the warranty is false at the date it is given. On that basis, it is hard to conceive of a case where it will be right to assess damages at any other date. However, it may remain arguable that an exception should be made if a court concludes that the conventional assessment would result in a windfall for the buyer, as is perhaps hinted at in Kerr J's obiter discussion of these cases in *Equitix Eeef Biomas 2 Ltd v Michael Fox*.[1]

1 [2021] EWHC 2531 (TCC) at [423]–[427].

8.25 These principles were confirmed by the Court of Appeal following detailed consideration in *MDW Holdings Ltd v Norvill.*[1] The principles to be extracted from the earlier authorities were set out at [49]. It was held that the majority in *The Golden Victory*[2] had applied the *Bwllfa* principle to take account of subsequent events in quantifying damages for breach of contract only because the breach in that case was an anticipatory repudiatory breach, which resulted in a different valuation exercise. That approach does not apply where the defendant has committed an actual, not anticipatory, breach of contract:

> 'There is a strong case for saying that, in general at least, the position should be similar in relation to warranties given on a share sale.'

However:

> 'If, none the less, there can be cases in which account can be taken of what happened subsequently as regards a contingency which existed on the date of assessment when determining what, if any, damages are payable for breach of warranty on a share sale, they must be rare. They would doubtless involve situations in which the buyer might otherwise be said to have gained a "windfall", but the mere fact that the valuation of the relevant shares has increased since the date of assessment cannot demonstrate such a "windfall": it is inherent in the selection of a date of assessment that subsequent changes in value can fall to be disregarded. Still less could it be appropriate to categorise a post-assessment rise in value as a "windfall" if it were attributable to steps that the purchaser had itself taken since the transaction. Further, as Popplewell LJ said in *Ageas*, it would be "important to keep firmly in mind any contractual allocation of risk made by the parties".'

1 [2022] EWCA Civ 883.
2 [2007] 2 AC 353.

8.26 A further corollary of the measure of loss for breach of warranty is that a purchaser is not entitled to claim damages which represent an indemnity against payments that may have to be made following the purchase, as that is not a measure of the difference in value at the transaction date. Arguments to the contrary were rejected by Simon Bryan QC in *Zayo v Ainger*[1] and by Moulder J in *Oversea-Chinese Banking Corporation Ltd v ING Bank NV*, who reviewed the authorities and summarised them in the following way:

> 'Accordingly, it seems to me that neither the authorities nor the textbooks, support the proposition advanced by OCBC that on a claim for breach of warranty of quality on a share sale, the measure of damages claim could be a hypothetical indemnity and the amount which could have been claimed under that hypothetical indemnity. As stated above, it seems to me that in determining the "loss of bargain" it may be necessary to adjust the valuation methodology but neither

the authorities nor the textbooks support an entirely different measure of damages for breach of a warranty as to quality on a share sale other than the diminution of the value of the asset.'[2]

1 [2017] EWHC 2542 (Comm) at [117].
2 [2019] EWHC 676 (Comm) at [39].

Warranties of quality and warranties of process

8.27 In some cases, the loss caused by a breach of warranty is a pure question of valuation: what was the value of the business had certain figures been as warranted, against its true value. However, not all cases are this straightforward. The main distinction that arises in business sale cases is between warranties of quality and warranties of process. The underlying principle that gives rise to this distinction was stated by Lord Reed: 'What is crucial is first to identify the loss: the difference between the claimant's actual situation and the situation in which he would have been if the primary contractual obligation had been performed. Once the loss has been identified, the court then has to quantify it in monetary terms.'[1]

1 *One-Step (Support) v Morris-Garner* [2019] AC 649 at [31].

8.28 In a business sale case, many warranties are in the form, or to the effect, that certain figures are correct – earnings before interest, taxes, and amortisation (EBITDA) in year N was (at least) £X, there are no liabilities in addition to those provided for in the accounts, etc. These are called 'warranties of quality', meaning that they define the quality of the business being sold. That term is a little inapt in the business context, but easier to understand in a more basic sale of goods context from which it derives. Where a warranty of quality has been breached, the identification of 'the difference between the claimant's actual situation and the situation in which he would have been if the primary contractual obligation had been performed' (per Lord Reed cited above) is straightforward. In such a case, the claimant's actual situation is that it obtains the shares or business as they actually are and the comparable counterfactual is that the claimant would have obtained the shares or business as they would have been had the warranty of quality been true. In other words, the question is simply what is the difference in value of the business attributable to EBITDA in year N being £X-D instead of £X, or to the amount of liabilities exceeding those provided for by £Y.

8.29 Warranties of quality may be seen as absolute obligations: the seller undertakes that EBITDA was £X and it is nothing to the point if the reason that EBITDA was lower was no fault of the seller, unknown to the seller, etc. The obligation is absolute and the liability is strict. Although the valuation issues thrown up by such questions are not always simple, and are discussed further below, nevertheless the legal principle applicable in such cases is clear and straightforward.

8.30 It is important to note that if a breach of warranty of quality is established, then it does not avail a vendor to argue that the purchaser would have paid the same even if the correct information had been given in the warranty.[1] That argument confuses the tort and contract measures of loss. A warranty does not amount to an inducement to purchase, but only a contractual undertaking that if matters are not as warranted, damages will be paid. The enforcement of damages is a matter of enforcing the secondary obligation to pay damages for the breach of the contractual undertaking, not a matter of compensating for reliance on a misstatement. In many circumstances, a tort claim is more beneficial for a claimant, but this is one respect in which breach of warranty is a superior claim: the claimant does not need to establish anything about its own conduct in a hypothetical world. If a purchaser buys and the warranty is breached, then damages are the difference between what the vendor promised and what the vendor delivered.[2]

1 This argument was attempted, and rightly rejected, in *Sycamore BidCo v Breslin* at [393]–[397].
2 This sentence was approved by Kerr J in *Equitix Eeef Biomas 2 Ltd v Michael Fox* [2021] EWHC 2531 (TCC) at [389].

8.31 Because the SPA normally involves an allocation of risk between buyer and seller, the outcome of subsequent events will not normally be relevant to this difference in value: *Equitix Eeef Biomas 2 Ltd v Michael Fox*;[1] *MDW Holdings Ltd v Norvill*.[2] The same point means that a defendant vendor is unlikely to be able to get any argument of failure to mitigate off the ground: the purchaser has no opportunity to mitigate the loss because the loss is defined as the receipt of a business worth less than the one that was promised.[3] By the same token, an argument that loss from breach of warranty should be reduced for successful mitigation should not generally succeed. Such an argument was accepted as common ground in *Millbrook Healthcare BidCo Ltd v Croll*,[4] but it does not appear to have been correct as a matter of principle.

1 [2021] EWHC 2531 (TCC).
2 [2022] EWCA Civ 883 at [49].
3 This sentence was approved by Kerr J in *Equitix Eeef Biomas 2 Ltd v Michael Fox* at [402] and [429].
4 [2023] EWHC 290 (Comm) at [191].

Warranties of process: *Lion Nathan*

8.32 The position is more complex where there is a breach of a warranty of process. For example: the management accounts have been carefully prepared; the budget has been diligently prepared after due inquiry of certain individuals; these are warranties of process. That is to say, the vendor undertakes that it has carried out a particular process to a particular standard. It is theoretically possible for that standard to be defined at any level. But English law does not generally recognise distinctions finer than: (i) absolute obligation; (ii) honest or good faith conduct (for example in giving a forecast); and (iii) the exercise of reasonable care and skill, the exact equivalent of avoiding negligence. Contracts could refer to other standards (eg gross negligence) but these are not well defined in the law and are likely to end up being treated as equivalent to one of the three standards in this paragraph. For example, due or reasonable diligence is generally no different from reasonable care and skill. The most common form of obligation in business sale warranties of process is the obligation to prepare particular accounts or projections with reasonable care.

8.33 The leading, but controversial, case illustrating the approach to a warranty of process in a business sale case is the decision of the Privy Council in *Lion Nathan v C-C Bottlers*. The relevant warranty related to a 'projected revenue statement' which forecast the target company's EBIT during the two months that remained of the financial year after the transaction. This was the vendor's projection of the likely profits during the first two months of the purchaser's ownership of the business. The warranty of this projection was:

> 'The projected revenue statement has been calculated in good faith, and on a proper basis having regard for all known matters which are likely to affect E.B.I.T. for the relevant periods to a material degree and in the opinion of the guarantor as at the date hereof *and* the forecast results referred to therein are achievable based on current trends and performance.'[1]

It should be noted that the warranty fell to be read in two parts, divided at the 'and' which has been highlighted above (though not highlighted in the original).

1 [1996] 1 WLR 1438.

8.34 The projected revenue statement forecast earnings to be NZ$2,223,000 and they turned out to be NZ$1,233,000. The judge and the Court of Appeal of New Zealand held that the forecast had not been calculated on a proper basis and the results were not 'achievable', so both parts of the warranty were breached. The judge held that the 'achievable' requirement was concerned with picking what the forecaster believes to be the most probable outcome and that it 'meant that it was more likely than not that the actual profit would be around about the forecast figure'. Expert evidence was that a proper forecast would have been around NZ$1.2 million and the judge added 1/3 of that figure as a reasonable tolerance, to arrive a 'highest tolerable forecast' of NZ$1.6 million. He applied a contract-based multiplier of 20 to the difference between NZ$1.6 million and the warranted figure of NZ$2.223 million (after adjusting for tax) to arrive at the damages for this breach of warranty.

8.35 In relation to the first part of the warranty, the Court of Appeal of New Zealand agreed that the multiplier of 20 was an appropriate way of valuing the company on the facts, but held that the 1/3 tolerance applied by the judge was too generous to the vendors and replaced it with a tolerance of 10% on either side. However, the Court of Appeal also accepted the argument that the tolerance should be applied on both sides of the appropriate forecast, so that the damages would be based on the difference between the actual forecast (NZ$2.223 million) and the most appropriate forecast (NZ$1.2 million). In respect of the second part of the warranty, the Court of Appeal held that 'the comparison is between the value of the company as acquired in fact, and the value it would have had if the forecast was achievable'. On the Court of Appeal's view this was less than the figure for the breach of the first part of the warranty, so it did not feed into the final outcome.

8.36 In the Privy Council, the advice was given by Lord Hoffmann on behalf of the Board. He noted that the Court of Appeal's judgment amounted to a finding that the second part of the warranty 'was the equivalent of a warranty as to quality': namely, a warranty that the target 'was a company reasonably capable of achieving earnings of NZ$2,223,000 in the period in question'. Lord Hoffmann then set out the key distinction:

> 'In the case of a warranty as to the quality of the goods, the purchaser is prima facie entitled to the difference between what the goods as warranted would have been worth and what they were actually worth. … On the other hand, if one construes paragraph 32 as a warranty that reasonable care has been taken in the preparation of the forecast, there is no analogy with a warranty of quality. The forecast, though prepared with reasonable care, may on account of unknown or unforeseeable factors turn out to be substantially inaccurate. It therefore does not warrant that the company has any particular quality. The prima facie rule for breach of a warranty of quality of goods cannot be applied. One must therefore return to the general principle of which that rule is only one example, namely that damages for breach of contract are intended to put the plaintiff in the position in which he would have been if the defendant had complied with the terms of the contract.'[1]

1 [1996] 1 WLR 1438 at 1441F and 1442A–B.

8.37 Lord Hoffmann then said that:

> '… the judge was also right in construing the second half as having the same meaning as the first, namely that reasonable care had been taken in the preparation of the forecast. The construction given to the second half by the Court of Appeal amounts in substance to a warranty that for the purposes of calculating the value of the company, it could be assumed that the forecast would be correct. Their Lordships think that this is exactly the form of warranty which the vendor did not wish to give. They therefore agree with the judge that the crucial question in this case is the ascertainment of what a properly prepared forecast would have been.'[1]

1 [1996] 1 WLR 1438 at 1442D–E.

8.38 Thus the difference between the Privy Council and the Court of Appeal of New Zealand turned on a point of construction of the warranty. The Privy Council construed the warranty as a single statement with a single meaning: that reasonable care had been taken in the preparation of the forecast. This is a vivid illustration of the point made at **8.32** above that the law tends to assimilate contractual standards to one of the three recognised standards: absolute, honest or reasonably careful. The words of the warranty did not mention 'reasonable care' or negligence or any other recognised synonym of the standard of reasonable care. Nonetheless, the Privy Council held that it should be read overall as a single, simple, warranty of process that reasonable care had been taken in arriving at the projected warranty statement. The facts found by the judge were said to 'plainly show a radical departure from acceptable methods of forecasting'.[1] So the warranty of process was breached.

1 [1996] 1 WLR 1438 at 1443H.

8.39 Lord Hoffmann then set out his understanding of the meaning of a forecast of this nature:

> 'A forecaster who predicts that profits in a given period will be, say, $2,223,000, is not doing anything so silly as to say that in his opinion the profits will be precisely that figure. He is saying that $2,223,000 is in his opinion the most probable outcome, but that figures slightly higher or lower are almost equally probable and that on either side of them there is a range of possible figures which become increasingly less probable as they deviate from the mean. … As has been said, a forecast is always the forecaster's estimate of the most probable outcome, the mean figure within the range of foreseeable deviation.'[1]

At this stage of the judgment Lord Hoffmann thus understood a profit forecast to be like the mean value of a normal probability distribution, with values either side of the mean becoming less likely as they deviate further from it. This may be true in many forecasts, but it is not always so (as Lord Hoffmann acknowledged later in the same judgment – see below). If, for example, the principal uncertainty is as to the occurrence of a discrete event, such as whether a particular major contract will be gained in the relevant period, then the forecaster might properly include such a contract in the projection, even though that will result in a projection some way above the mean average of all likely outcomes. If the only warranty or representation that is relevant is that the projection has been prepared with reasonable care, then this might be hard for a buyer to challenge. But there may come a point where the effect of the major contract is so big in comparison to the profits that it is misleading to provide just the projection without further explanation.

1 [1996] 1 WLR 1438 at 1444E–F, 1445B.

8.40 Lord Hoffmann then explained that whether or not a particular forecast was negligent did not depend upon whether it fell within the range of possible non-negligent forecasts, but instead depended upon whether it was prepared with reasonable care. In other words, what counts for the issue of breach is process, not the absolute result. This makes a warranty of process fundamentally different from a warranty of quality. In terms of risk allocation, Lord Hoffmann said:

> 'The purchaser has accepted the risk of any deviation attributable to factors which were unforeseeable, unknown or incalculable at the time of the forecast. He has accepted the risk of such deviation whether its true extent would have been foreseeable at the time of the forecast or not. But he has not accepted the risk of any deviation which is attributable to lack of proper care in the preparation of the forecast.'[1]

1 [1996] 1 WLR 1438 at 1445G.

8.41 The consequence of this approach is that the measure of damage is highly fact sensitive. As Lord Hoffmann explained: 'In a case in which it is possible to isolate the negligent error from the rest of the forecast, as in the example [given earlier] of the single $25,000 mistake, it would be reasonable to say that in other respects the forecast would have been the same. All that is necessary is to adjust the figure by $25,000. But in this case, the breach of warranty went to the whole methodology of the forecast. It is not possible to say that in any particular respect, this vendor would, if he had taken proper care, have produced elements of the same forecast. It is therefore necessary to approach the question objectively and ask what a reasonable forecast would have been.'[1]

1 [1996] 1 WLR 1438 at 1446B–C.

8.42 Lord Hoffmann then rejected an argument based on cases like *Lavarack v Woods of Colchester Ltd*[1] that the assumption should be made that the defendant would have performed the contract in the way least onerous to itself. The argument was rejected because the contractual requirement was not to choose from a range of options the one that best suited the vendor, but instead to perform a forecast reasonably and in good faith.[2] 'In those circumstances, the only rational course open to a court is to choose the figure which it considers that a forecast made with reasonable care was most likely to have produced.'[3]

1 [1967] 1 QB 278.
2 [1996] 1 WLR 1438 at 1446G.
3 [1996] 1 WLR 1438 at 1446H–1447A.

8.43 In considering what that figure was, Lord Hoffmann described the approach in a way that shows that his earlier description of a forecast as inevitably being the mean in an evenly distributed probability distribution was only a starting point, saying (emphasis added):

> 'Their Lordships think that in considering this matter, one may start with a prima facie assumption that the range of reasonable possible

forecasts will be distributed around the figure which was the actual outcome. The uncertainty inherent in the process of forecasting may have led to reasonable forecasts both higher and lower than the actual outcome. But since those uncertainties tend in both directions, the only way in which a court, required to find a particular figure, can deal with the matter is to regard the unpredictable factors as cancelling each other out. The actual outcome is therefore prima facie likely to have represented the mean and therefore the figure most likely to have been put forward. *This prima facie assumption may however be displaced by evidence that the outcome was affected, in one particular direction, by a factor which could not have been reasonably foreseen.*'[1]

It is submitted that the words 'which could not have been reasonably foreseen' were not necessary here, because the assumption that the actual outcome represents the mean forecast could also be displaced by evidence of a *foreseeable* but uncertain event which skewed the distribution of outcomes in a particular direction. If the event happened, then it might not be the case that the actual outcome represented the figure most likely to have been put forward by a reasonable forecast. On the basis that the facts in *Lion Nathan* itself did not justify any departure from the prima facie assumption, the Privy Council reached the same conclusion as the Court of Appeal of New Zealand, albeit by a different route.

1 [1996] 1 WLR 1438 at 1447D–F.

8.44 The approach in *Lion Nathan* means that a warranty of process – if interpreted as a warranty of reasonable care – will have the same consequences as to damages as the breach of the equivalent duty of care in contract or in tort. This is a point which does not emerge from *Lion Nathan* itself, but from considering in principle the dictum: 'One must therefore return to the general principle of which that rule is only one example, namely that damages for breach of contract are intended to put the plaintiff in the position in which he would have been if the defendant had complied with the terms of the contract.'

8.45 Applying that principle, causation re-enters the analysis. If a purchaser can show that had the warranted forecast been prepared with proper care, the outcome would have been that the purchaser would not have bought the shares at all, then the starting point for damages ought to be the same as in a tort claim: the loss of the purchase price, less the gain of the value of the shares acquired. Conversely, if the purchaser cannot show that it would have acted differently had the forecast been prepared with proper care, then the vendor can assert that no loss was caused by the breach of warranty. In this respect, the approach to assessing the loss caused by breach of a warranty of process is fundamentally different from that of a warranty of quality.[1]

1 This paragraph was approved by Kerr J in *Equitix Eeef Biomas 2 Ltd v Michael Fox* [2021] EWHC 2531 (TCC) at [392].

8.46 That result is surprising because parties are taken to understand the fundamental legal distinctions set out above and would generally expect a warranty if breached to sound in damages assessed by reference to the difference in value, not by reference to what the claimant would have done. However, this different analysis must result from the approach in *Lion Nathan*. But the potential for tort-like damages to follow is mitigated by another principle which may be borrowed from cases concerning the breach of a duty to take reasonable care: the scope of duty principle derived from *SAAMCO*[1] and re-cast by the Supreme Court in *Manchester Building Society v Grant Thornton*.[2] This is not the place for a detailed exegesis of the scope of duty principle, but in short it limits the recoverable loss from a breach of a duty of care (whether in contract or in tort) to that which has a sufficient nexus with the duty to take care.

1 *Banque Bruxelles Lambert v Eagle Star*, ('*SAAMCO*') [1997] AC 191.
2 [2022] AC 783.

8.47 The result of applying both the *Lion Nathan* approach and the scope of duty principle to a warranty of process in a business sale case has yet to be explored in the authorities. In principle, at least in most cases, it should mean that the recoverable loss for breach of such a warranty should be limited to the loss that would have been recovered if the result of the forecast had been warranted rather than the process. Thus, the end result may well be the same in most cases, which may be one reason why these issues have not been much explored in the cases.

Valuation issues

8.48 When it comes to valuation, it is important to recall that it generally arises as part of the assessment of loss and, when it does, it is not subject to any balance of probabilities requirement, but instead is a question of pure assessment, with the court doing the best it can on the available evidence: see **8.05** above.

8.49 In many cases, the value as warranted will be equal to the purchase price. There is no principle of law to this effect, nor any formally recognised presumption of fact or law. It arises purely because of the obvious evidential point that the price agreed between the parties may be taken to have been the result of an arm's length negotiation between willing buyer and willing seller and therefore to represent the best evidence of the market value for the asset as described in the SPA. Many authorities evidence the acceptableness of this assumption where it is not displaced.[1] That said, there is no doubt that the assumption can be challenged if one of the parties wishes to do so.[2] If challenged, the valuation will be assessed through expert evidence.

1 See, eg, *Senate Electrical v Alcatel* at [24]; *Sycamore Bidco v Breslin* at [391]; *Ageas v Kwik-Fit* at [14]; *Bir v Mehta* at [55]–[56]; *Triumph Controls v Primus International* [2019] EWHC 565 (TCC) at [488].

2 See, eg, *Cardamon v MacAlister* [2019] EWHC 1200 (Comm) at [131]–[134]. For an especially striking example, see *Ivy Technology v Martin* [2022] EWHC 1218 (Comm) at [571] where the warranty true value was held to be zero with the result that no damages were recoverable for breach of warranty (though the claimant did still recover in fraudulent misrepresentation.) In *MDW Holdings Ltd v Norvill* [2021] EWHC 1135 (Ch), at first instance it was common ground that the warranty true value was the purchase price, but the judge assessed it at a lower figure on the basis of the expert valuation evidence. His decision in that respect was not challenged on appeal, but the rejection of the common ground led to unsatisfactory findings on other points and to the remission of the issue of the quantum of the deceit claim to a further trial.

8.50 Whether or not value as warranted can be determined relatively shortly, the determination of true value (ie, value in the light of the breaches of the warranties) is often more involved. It may be simpler in a case where the breach of warranty results in an adjustment to figures which were demonstrably the basis upon which the original price was calculated. As discussed above, in *Lion Nathan*, there was no doubt that the price was fixed as a particular multiple of the profits for a particular period. As Stuart-Smith LJ said in *Senate v Alcatel*[1] 'if this is how the original price is calculated, it is the obvious way to calculate the damages by applying the same multiplier to the shortfall in maintainable earnings/profits'. This approach would be based on the theory that the actual transaction is the best evidence of value and the pricing mechanism in the actual transaction is sufficiently transparent that a conclusion can be drawn as to what would have been the price if the true facts had been warranted. Although this may look like a tort measure, it is not, because the actual price and the mechanism used to produce it are being used only as evidential indicators of value: they are capable of being displaced by other evidence of value. Indeed, in *Senate v Alcatel* itself this approach was not adopted both because the buyer failed to show it had used the multiplier approach and because the approach could not have been used in a sale where the price was fixed by reference to a valuation of assets at £70 million and goodwill of £20 million.[2] Since the price was primarily fixed by reference to net asset value rather than the earning potential of the business, it made no sense to adjust it by reference to a multiple.

1 [1999] 2 Lloyd's Rep 423 at [33]. For the view that this approach is usually 'a first order approximation' and 'at least as a guide to the uppermost figure for damages', see *Witter Ltd v TBP Industries* [1996] 2 All ER 573 at 607b.

2 Goodwill is usually defined in accounting terms as the value of a business over and above the value of its separable net assets. Current accounting standards do not permit the recognition of goodwill unless it is purchased with an acquired business, when it becomes necessary to recognise it in order to avoid taking an accounting loss on the acquisition. On that definition, it makes little sense to value the assets and goodwill separately, because the only way to arrive at goodwill is to value the whole business as a going concern (see below) and subtract the value of the net assets. However, goodwill is sometimes understood as the value of an ability possessed by a particular business to earn returns above the normal returns attributable to its assets, because of factors like a strong brand or reputation, and in cases like *Senate* and *Levison v Farin*, it was valued separately in order to arrive at the purchase price. This approach may still be used for a more straightforward business: see, eg, *Wemyss v Karim* [2016] EWCA Civ 27 at [3] for an agreement which placed a value on the goodwill of a solicitor's practice. An even simpler concept of goodwill as 'business reputation' was also applied as a matter of construction of an exclusion of claims for lost goodwill in *Triumph Controls v Primus International* [2019] EWHC 565 (TCC) at [496].

8.51 A subtler statement of the relevance or otherwise of the approach of the actual buyer was set out by Mann J in *Sycamore Bidco v Breslin*:

> 'This accords with principle. The exercise is a valuation. The purpose of the valuation is to find what a willing purchaser would pay to a willing seller. There are various ways of conducting this investigation. In the absence of an apparent market from which a price can be derived, other techniques have to be used. Assuming a purchaser who would use a model like Dunedin's is one technique (to which I will come later). But the views of the actual purchaser and of another potential purchaser are not irrelevant. If the purchaser would have paid the same sum anyway, then that goes to value. If another purchaser is in the wind, so that that purchaser's price has to be beaten to secure the transaction, then that goes to value too.[1]

Consistently with this approach, Mann J based his assessment of value on the buyer's model, but then injected what he called a 'haggle factor' to arrive at a rounded price that a willing buyer would have paid for the company as it truly was.[2] This is plainly a highly fact sensitive exercise which is likely to be strongly influenced by expert evidence and, to some extent, by factual evidence about the negotiation process in the actual transaction.

1 [2012] EWHC 3443 (Ch) at [405].
2 Ibid at [464].

8.52 Valuation itself is the subject of valuation expertise rather than law. It has been said that 'valuation of businesses is not an exact science … there is a large element of judgment involved as to what "feels" right …'.[1] This is not of much assistance save that it permits a judge considerable margin in deciding which expert evidence to prefer. There are several texts on the theory and practice of valuation from the perspective of corporate finance. *Practical Share Valuation*[2] takes a more legally focussed approach and refers to the main cases. The principal issues which arise are summarised below.

1 Per HHJ David Cooke in *Bir Holdings Ltd v Mehta* at [56].
2 N Eastaway, D Elliott, C Blundell, C Cook (eds) *Practical Share Valuation* (7th edn, Bloomsbury Professional, 2019).

8.53 A helpful statement of the principles, as agreed by the parties before him, was set out by Blair J in *The Hut Group v Nobahar-Cookson*:

> 'As to the principles to be applied, it is common ground that:
>
> (1) The measure of loss for breach of warranty in a share sale agreement is the difference between the value of the shares as warranted and the true value of the shares, or as put shortly, "warranty true" vs. "warranty false", assessed as at the date of the share sale agreement since that is the date when the breach of warranty occurs.

(2) This involves a valuation, and as with any valuation the process involves establishing (as the defendants' expert put it), "The estimated amount for which an asset or liability should exchange on the valuation date between a willing buyer and a willing seller in arm's length transaction, after proper marketing where the parties had each acted knowledgeably, prudently, and without compulsion".

(3) However, there is no one methodology to be applied in a valuation (*Sycamore Bidco Ltd v Breslin* [2012] EWHC 3443 (Ch) at [405], Mann J).

(4) As with any valuation it is necessary, as both experts agreed, to appraise the number in question in the light of the circumstances. As THG's expert aptly put it, "… you always have to stand back and say, does the answer give you a sensible result and not get too worked up in the model itself".'[1]

1 [2014] EWHC 3842 (QB) at [180].

8.54 There are two fundamental perspectives from which it is possible to view the value of a business.[1] First, and most importantly, a business may be seen as a going concern, meaning that it is a vehicle for generating cash flows into the future. From this perspective, the intrinsic value of a business is the value of the net cash flows which it will generate into the future. Secondly, there is the break up or liquidation value, which means the price at which the separate assets of the business could be sold less the sums that would be have to be paid to satisfy its liabilities. Valuations of net assets are generally straightforward to assess. The complexities arise when trying to value a going concern.

1 See per Lord Millett in *CVC/Opportunity Equity Partners Ltd v Demarco Almeida* [2002] BCLC 108 at [37].

8.55 Since businesses are rarely bought and sold for the purpose of breaking them up into individual assets, net asset value is rarely the most relevant perspective.[1] However, it may be relevant if, for example, there is such a serious breach of warranty that the value of future net cash flows is zero or less; the break-up value of net assets could then be relevant to put a floor on the valuation of the business. Another situation in which it may be relevant is if the warranty breached was a warranty of asset (or liability) values. In that situation a difficult question may arise as to whether the loss attributable to the breach of warranty can be anything other than the difference in asset value. In *Levison v Farin* a reduction in net asset value was the only loss claimed, and awarded. In *Cypher v Bertram*,[2] the defendant argued that it was impossible for breach of a net asset warranty to give rise to any other form of loss, an issue which the judge on a summary judgment application declined to resolve. However, it was relevant that there was no warranty of profit and there was an express adjustment mechanism if the assets turned out not to have been accurately reflected in the warranted accounts.

1 See per O'Farrell J in *Triumph Controls v Primus International* [2019] EWHC 565 (TCC) at [493], rejecting the use of asset valuation where a business was sold as a going concern.
2 *Cypher v Bertram* (14 June 2001, unreported, Chancery Division) per Owen J at [26]–[27] and [32].

8.56 The two perspectives are reflected in the nature of shares, which are usually described as bundles of rights and obligations as defined by the Companies Act 2006 and the memorandum and articles of association. In most cases, the economic rights conferred by ordinary shares include a right to share in distributions of profits as and when declared and a right to share *pari passu* in a distribution of assets (after the payment of liabilities) on a liquidation.[1] If it is necessary to value other types of shares (such as preference shares) separately, that may give rise to other considerations depending on the rights attached to the shares in question. In a standard business sale case, where what is transferred is 100% of the ordinary shares in a corporation, the buyer receives the rights to share in future distributions of profit if the enterprise is a going concern, or in the net assets if it is to be broken up in the short term. The former is much more usual.

1 See per Lord Millett in *Commissioners of the Inland Revenue v Laird Group* [2003] 1 WLR 2476 at [35]–[36].

8.57 In many situations, if there is an available market for shares (just as with other commodities), the price in that market will be treated as good evidence of the value of those shares, unless contradicted by other evidence. However, this starting point is rarely of great assistance in business sale cases, partly because most disputes concern private companies in which there is not generally an available market and partly because the market price may not reflect either the warranties or the true state of affairs in respect of the breached warranties.

8.58 A related valuation approach is to take previous transactions in the shares concerned as a starting point and adjust for changes and any necessary assumptions relating the warranties in question. Again, this rarely applies in business sale disputes, since it is unusual that there have been previous transactions sufficiently recently to be of much probative value.

8.59 The next market-based approach is to use actual transactions in similar businesses to derive multiples of profits, assets etc and then apply the same multiplies to the enterprise in question. This is more often used, though it depends on the valuation experts having access to sufficient comparables, as well as on the assumption that the business is in a more or less steady state. This approach would be more difficult to apply to a young business which is expected to grow quickly in the future. There may well be disagreement between experts on how comparable previous transactions truly were. As HHJ David Cooke said in *Bir Holdings v Mehta*:[1] 'an attempt to identify comparable transactions, for example from databases, generally produces a large apparent range of prices which may have been influenced by particular factors not apparent to third parties'. Sometimes a short cut may be taken by experts simply asserting or estimating the appropriate multiplier, or adopting it from the actual transaction. The most common quantity to which the multiplier is applied is a profit figure, which is intended to represent sustainable net profits into the future, which may be derived from one or more recent sets of results.[2] Profits are often measured in the form of earnings before interest, taxation, depreciation and amortisation ('EBITDA'), but a more bespoke measure may also be adopted.

1 [2014] EWHC 3909 (Ch) at [56].
2 In *Sycamore Bidco v Breslin* at [453] Mann J said an hypothetical willing purchaser 'would not make a judgment on one year's accounts alone', which is generally true, but subject to the nature of the particular business in any given case.

8.60 In *Wemyss v Karim*[1] Lewison LJ, with the agreement of Longmore and Kitchen LJJ, said that 'in most cases the price paid for goodwill is a multiple of profit'. It would be dangerous to rely on that as a legal principle, but it does reflect the approach in a broad range of run of the mill valuations and the case illustrates the principle that the court will find a way to measure damage on the available evidence, even if in a rough and ready way.

1 [2016] EWCA Civ 27 at [49].

8.61 In the absence of sufficiently comparable market transactions, the standard way to value a going concern is to seek to project its net cash flows into the future and discount them to a net present value, or 'NPV'. This is known as a discounted cash flow ('DCF') analysis.[1] It seeks directly to measure the value of the future cash flows of the enterprise, and therefore the value of it as a going concern. The issues with DCF valuation arise because there is rarely agreement about the appropriate assumptions to adopt as inputs into the calculation, both in respect of future cash flows and the applicable discount rate. The forecast of cash flows is naturally an uncertain exercise and it is usually necessary to make an assumption that after a certain period profits will grow at a constant rate, so that the net cash flow at the end of that period and the assumed rate of steady growth thereafter can become very important variables. The discount rate, to which the calculation is often very sensitive, is a way of allowing for the time value of money and also the risk associated with the projection of future cash flows (ie that they may not turn out as projected). The standard Capital Asset Pricing Model ('CAPM') may be used to derive the discount rate, but that too requires inputs which are often controversial.

1 For example, DCF was applied in *The Hut Group v Nobahar-Cookson* [2014] EWHC 3842 (QB) at [187]; and *Triumph Controls v Primus International* [2019] EWHC 565 (TCC) at [493].

DAMAGES FOR DECEIT

8.62 The measure of loss in deceit was authoritatively stated by the House of Lords in *Smith New Court v Scrimgeour Vickers*, in which the two leading speeches were given by Lord Browne-Wilkinson and Lord Steyn, who both approved the statement of the law from the business sale case of *Doyle v Olby*.[1] The leading statement of the principles to be applied was set out by Lord Browne-Wilkinson as follows:

> 'In sum, in my judgment the following principles apply in assessing the damages payable where the plaintiff has been induced by a fraudulent misrepresentation to buy property: (1) the defendant is bound to make reparation for all the damage directly flowing from the transaction; (2) although such damage need not have been foreseeable, it must have been directly caused by the transaction; (3) in assessing such damage, the plaintiff is entitled to recover by way of damages the full price paid by him, but he must give credit for any benefits which he has received as a result of the transaction; (4) as a general rule, the benefits received by him include the market value of the property acquired as at the date of acquisition; but such general rule is not to be inflexibly applied where to do so would prevent him obtaining full compensation for the wrong suffered; (5) although the circumstances in which the general rule should not apply cannot be comprehensively stated, it will normally not apply where either (a) the misrepresentation has continued to operate after the date of the acquisition of the asset so as to induce the plaintiff to retain the asset or (b) the circumstances of the case are such that the plaintiff is, by reason of the fraud, locked into the property. (6) In addition, the plaintiff is entitled to recover consequential losses caused by the transaction; (7) the plaintiff must take all reasonable steps to mitigate his loss once he has discovered the fraud.'[2]

1 [1969] 2 QB 158.
2 [1997] AC 254 at 266H–267D.

8.63 The key point here is that the recoverable loss is all that flows from the transaction induced by the fraud. Losses are not limited to any difference in value attributable to the fraud or otherwise tied to the misrepresentation itself. The starting point is the claimant's entry into the transaction in reliance on the defendant's misrepresentation. From there, the damage caused is a factual inquiry, subject to the subsidiary principles also set out by Lord Browne-Wilkinson. It follows from this approach that the 'breach date rule' that applies generally to assessing damages for breach of warranty has no application in fraud cases. The claimant's loss is assessed by reference to these principles and not by reference to any particular presumptive date. This point was made in terms by Moore-Bick LJ in *MAN v Freightliner*[1] by reference to his reading of the speeches in *Smith New Court*.[2]

1 [2005] EWHC 2347 (Comm) at [305]–[306].
2 [1997] AC 254.

8.64 In *Smith New Court*, Lord Steyn made another point which is often relevant in business sale cases:

> '... it is not necessary in an action for deceit for the judge, after he had ascertained the loss directly flowing from the victim having entered into the transaction, to embark on a hypothetical reconstruction of what the parties would have agreed had the deceit not occurred.'[1]

The point made in this passage is that the court does not reconstruct a varied agreement that might have been made on a basis uncorrupted by the fraud, but instead measures the loss the transaction itself caused. That is on the basis that in most cases, if the representation had not been made at all, then the transaction would not have been concluded and 'damages for deceit ... seek to put the claimant in the position he would have been in, not if the representation had been true, but if it had never been made.'[2] But if the buyer would still have purchased, even if the representation had not been made at all, then it is relevant to inquire into the price that would have been paid on that hypothesis.[3]

1 [1997] AC 254 at 283F–G. See also per Lord Browne-Wilkinson at 267D–F. On this issue, the Court of Appeal's approach in *Downs v Chappell* [1997] 1 WLR 426 was disapproved. This was applied in *Invertec v de Mol Holding* [2009] EWHC 2471 (Ch) at [379] and *Glossop Cartons v Contact (Print and Packaging)* [2021] EWCA Civ 639. See also *OMV Petrom v Glencore International* at [59].

2 *MDW Holdings Ltd v Norvill* [2022] EWCA Civ 883 at [25].

3 *MDW Holdings Ltd v Norvill* at [78]–[79].

8.65 In reading *Smith New Court*, and especially Lord Browne-Wilkinson's principles (4) and (5), it is relevant to bear in mind that the assets acquired in *Smith New Court* were widely traded listed shares, but the buyer had purchased them with a view to holding them for some time and re-selling at a later date. At the date of the transaction, they could be sold in the market for 78p against a purchase price of 82¼p. As a result of the discovery of another fraud, quite separate from the one that induced the claimant to purchase, the price plummeted and the buyer eventually sold them for much lower prices. The House of Lords held that credit did not need to be given for the 78p, but only for the prices actually obtained on the later sales. The decision in *Smith New Court* therefore illustrates the principles that were set out. In particular, the recoverable loss is not limited to the damage caused by the fraud itself, measured at the transaction date. If it were, then the claimant would have had to give credit for the 78p per share benefit received. Instead, the question was what loss did the claimant suffer as a result of entering into the transaction. The buyer acted reasonably in selling the shares when it did so (starting from when it became suspicious concerning the fraud practiced on it) and therefore the whole loss actually suffered was the direct result of the transaction that had been induced by the fraud.

8.66 The test is thus the reasonableness of the claimant's response to the transaction and to its discovery of the fraud. That test does not require the loss to be measured at any one specific date. Fundamentally, the loss in a fraud case is measured as from the date of trial even if the true measure of the loss is held to be the purchase price less the market value of the asset at the transaction date. Even where that is the outcome, it is not because of the application of any 'breach date rule' but because the court concludes that any later losses or benefits are not the direct result of the transaction, but instead the result of the claimant's decision to retain the asset. As Lord Steyn explained in *Smith New Court*:

> 'It is right that the normal method of calculating the loss caused by the deceit is the price paid less the real value of the subject matter of the sale. To the extent that this method is adopted, the selection of a date of valuation is necessary. And generally the date of the transaction would be a practical and just date to adopt. But it is not always so. It is only prima facie the right date. It may be appropriate to select a later date. That follows from the fact that the valuation method is only a means of trying to give effect to the overriding compensatory rule: *Potts v Miller*, 64 CLR 282, 299, per *Dixon J and County Personnel (Employment Agency) Ltd v Alan R Pulver & Co* [1987] 1 WLR 916, 925–926, per Bingham LJ. Moreover, and more importantly, the date of transaction rule is simply a second order rule applicable only where the valuation method is employed. If that method is inapposite, the court is entitled simply to assess the loss flowing directly from the transaction without any reference to the date of transaction or indeed any particular date. Such a course will be appropriate whenever the overriding compensatory rule requires it. An example of such a case is to be found in *Cemp Properties (UK) Ltd v Dentsply Research & Development Corporation* [1991] 2 EGLR 197, 201, per Bingham LJ. *There is in truth only one legal measure of assessing damages in an action for deceit: the plaintiff is entitled to recover as damages a sum representing the financial loss flowing directly from his alteration of position under the inducement of the fraudulent representations of the defendants. ... In an action for deceit the price paid less the valuation at the transaction date is simply a method of measuring loss which will satisfactorily solve many cases. It is not a substitute for the single legal measure: it is an application of it.*'[1]

1 [1997] AC 254 at 284A–F, emphasis added.

8.67 In a business sale case, the starting point under this measure of loss is that the purchaser has lost the sum that it paid for the business. As Lord Browne-Wilkinson set out in principles (4) to (6), the purchaser must give credit for any benefit obtained from the transaction; the starting point for assessing such benefit will be the value of what was acquired at the transaction date;[1] but that is only a starting point as it is open to the claimant to show that further loss was incurred by retention of the asset after the initial purchase. In a business sale context, even more clearly than in *Smith New Court* itself, the purchaser will not usually act unreasonably if it holds the asset beyond the transaction date. It is normal to retain the business purchased for some time after the transaction. Until the purchaser discovers the fraud, further costs incurred on the business can be claimed as damages.[2] After the fraud is discovered, the purchaser will sometimes be able to show that they had little choice but to retain the business and incur further losses, but eventually a time will come when the decision to retain it further becomes a commercial decision for the purchaser's own account. If the claimant claims further losses over and above the simple equation of price paid less value received on the transaction date, then the key issue will be whether the claimant itself acted reasonably in response to the situation in which it was placed by the fraudulently induced transaction.

1 The benefits received are not necessarily limited to the value of the company acquired. In *MAN v Freightliner* [2005] EWHC 2347 (Comm) at [312]–[317] an additional benefit was deductible which arose from an agreement made alongside the SPA for a transfer in the opposite direction.

2 Numerous heads of consequential loss were considered and awarded in *Next Generation Holdings Ltd v Finch* [2023] EWHC 2383 (Ch).

8.68 The above approach means that several dates may be relevant to the assessment of loss in a business sale case: (i) the transaction date, which is the date upon which the buyer pays the price for the business and also receives (but does not realise) the true value of whatever is transferred; (ii) the date of discovery of the fraud, after which the buyer is required to act reasonably in response to what has been discovered; (iii) the date after which the buyer has a realistic choice whether to sell the business, wind it up or continue operating it, after which the consequences of those choices may no longer be the direct consequences of the fraudulently induced transaction; and (iv) the date of trial, which is in effect the long stop date at which damages can be assessed, subject to the court's rarely used discretion to adjourn final assessment until some later date.

8.69 In *Glossop Cartons v Contact (Print and Packaging)*,[1] HHJ Hodge QC referred to *Smith New Court* and said that the assessment of damages for fraud 'should not operate to insulate the claimants from potential commercial risks which they had appreciated and had factored into their calculation of the purchase price because to do so would over-compensate for the consequences of the defendant's fraud'. This statement is not correct, as the Court of Appeal confirmed.[2] The rule confirmed in *Smith New Court* is that once deceit is established, the defendant pays the claimant the loss suffered as a result *of the transaction*, not just the losses attributable to the fraud. In other words, the effect of fraud is to shift the ordinary commercial risks of the transaction from the buyer to the seller. That cannot be altered by inquiry as to whether any particular risks were appreciated by the purchaser before transacting.

1 [2019] EWHC 2314 (Ch) at [103].

2 [2021] EWCA Civ 639 at [36].

8.70 There is no objection to a claimant electing not to pursue consequential loss and instead seeking to fix its loss as the price paid less the value of the business at the date of acquisition. In some cases that might be the most beneficial approach for a claimant. That seems to have been the position in *Bottin International Investments v Venson Group* where Blackburn J said:

> '[Counsel for the claimant] submitted that damages should be assessed as at the date when Bottin was induced by fraud to invest in Venson, namely 22 December 1999, and that the measure of Bottin's loss is the difference between its investment of £10 million and what, at that time, Venson was truly worth. I agree. I was given no good reason why damages should be assessed at any later date or on any other basis. The only question therefore is to determine what Venson was worth at the time Bottin invested its £10 million. On this the two experts disagreed.'[1]

1 [2006] EWHC 3112 (Ch) at [410]–[411].

8.71 In such a case it should in principle be possible for a defendant to argue that in fact the claimant received benefits from the transaction over and above the true value of the company at the transaction date, for example, if trading was profitable in the period before the fraud was discovered. Such arguments are unlikely to be attractive if the claimant is content with measuring its loss at the breach date, but if a benefit can clearly be shown to have accrued before the fraud was discovered, then it should in principle be deducted from the loss. In *Great Future International v Sealand Housing Corp*, Lightman J considered and rejected just such an argument from the defendant on the following basis:

> 'The legal position is that in accordance with the general rule the Claimants (who have not crystallised their loss by a sale of shares) are entitled to limit the credit to be afforded in respect of the Subscription Shares to their value at the Closing Date unless (as the Defendants contend) justice requires that credit be afforded for the value of the shares at the date of the Inquiry. …
>
> In my view the Claimants who had purchased the Subscription Shares as an investment were fully entitled to elect to adopt the purchase transaction, retain the shares giving credit on their claim for damages for the value (if any) of those shares at the date of purchase and claim the difference between the purchase price and such value. The purchaser who adopts that course is in nowise unjustly enriched or over compensated. In valuing the property as at that date, he must, of course, have regard to its full potential. I cannot see why the foreseeable consequence of the Defendants' fraud on the value of the Subscription Shares should disentitle the Claimants to a valuation at the Closing Date or entitle the fraudsters to some anticipated advantage arising from the postponement of the date of valuation to the date of the

> Inquiry. The Claimants have proceeded for years at substantial cost in terms of money and management time and at substantial risk to salvage their investment. This has involved expensive and protracted litigation in England, the TCI and China and the financing to a tune of some $3.4 million the receivership of SLEC. They have faced in their efforts a concerted and unprincipled campaign of harassment and opposition from the Defendants. I do not see why in justice the Defendants should be entitled to claim or seek credit for any increase in the value of the Shares arising over the period that they concealed their fraud and harassed and delayed the Claimants when seeking to enforce their rights in the courts and to salvage their investment. That is the object and effect of the postponement of the date of valuation to the date of the Inquiry which they seek.'[1]

1 [2002] EWHC 2545 (Ch) at [28]–[29].

8.72 Similarly, in *MDW Holdings Ltd v Norvill* at [85], the Court of Appeal refused to countenance an argument that a claimant buyer should give credit for synergy benefits over and above the market value of the shares it received, Newey LJ saying:

> 'I can see nothing in the authorities to indicate that, when assessing the damages that would be due to MDW in respect of the Norvills' deceit, it could be appropriate to give the Norvills credit for anything more than the market value of the shares they sold. That is especially so since, as Andrews LJ noted in *Tuke v Hood* [2022] EWCA Civ 23; [2022] QB 659 at [58], the authorities demonstrate that "a deliberate wrongdoer is not to be rewarded for the fruits of his own deceit".'

8.73 More usually, it will be the claimant who asks the court to consider later events, as it claims further losses generated by the business after the acquisition. This exercise was undertaken in a broad brush way by the Court of Appeal in *Doyle v Olby*,[1] where the buyer was held to be entitled to recover: (i) the price paid for the business and the stock; less (ii) the price received on the sale three years later; less (iii) profits and benefits (accommodation) taken out of the business as living expenses; plus (iv) capital sums put into the business during the plaintiff' ownership (assessed broadly by reference to sums he borrowed).

1 [1969] 2 QB 158, per Winn LJ at 169D–170E. The legal principles established in *Doyle v Olby* are not set out here only because they have been incorporated into the statements in the House of Lords in *Smith New Court*, which are now authoritative. The case is referred to here as an illustration of the types of loss which may be recovered by a claimant who reasonably retains a business after being induced by fraud to purchase it.

8.74 A similar pattern was followed in the assessment of loss in *East v Maurer*, but with an important addition. In *East v Maurer*, the business was a hairdressing salon and the vendor fraudulently misled the purchaser as to the vendor's own intentions not to continue in business nearby. The judge awarded the purchaser the sale price less the eventual proceeds of re-sale plus trading losses and other expenses incurred during the period of reasonably attempting to make the business profitable. In addition, he awarded a sum in respect of lost profits and it was in respect of that head of loss that the defendants appealed. The appeal was dismissed as to the principle involved because, as Beldam LJ put it:

> 'If in fact the plaintiffs lost the profits which they could reasonably have expected from running a business in the area of a kind similar to the business in this case, I can see no reason why those do not fall within the words of Lord Atkin in *Clark v Urquhart* [1930] A.C. 28, 68, "actual damage directly flowing from the fraudulent inducement."'[1]

The appeal did succeed as to quantum, because the judge had wrongly based his figure on the amount that the actual business might have made if the representation had been true, which was essentially the contractual, warranty measure of loss. Instead, he should have considered the profits which the plaintiff might have made in a different business that she could have bought for a similar sum. On a broad brush assessment in the round, the figure was reduced on the basis of expert evidence.

1 [1991] 1 WLR 461 at 466H.

8.75 *East v Maurer* therefore establishes an important principle that profits foregone may be recovered as damages for deceit. If a buyer has limited capital to deploy in a business purchase and other similar businesses are available, this may be important. The principle was applied in another business sale case by David Richards J in *4 Eng v Harper*[1] where the claimant was able to show that there was a real and substantial chance that it would have purchased a particular alternative target. That led to damages on the loss of chance basis on the principles set out in *Allied Maples v Simmons & Simmons*.[2]

1 [2009] Ch 91.
2 [1995] 1 WLR 1602.

8.76 If either party seeks damages or benefits to be set off going beyond the transaction date, it is necessary to identify the date when the purchaser is to be treated as knowing the truth about the subject matter of the fraud. Thus in *Downs v Chappell*,[1] the Court of Appeal reconsidered the factual evidence and concluded that the plaintiffs knew by the end of 1989 that the figures they had been given a year and a half earlier had been false and as a result the book selling business they had purchased was not viable. They therefore found themselves with an unviable business and a shop premises with a market value. Their capital loss was the difference between the price they had paid (£120,000) and the value of the property at the end of 1989 (£76,000). As to income, small profits had been made and Hobhouse LJ recorded 'The defendants did not submit that there should be any set off against the plaintiffs' capital account loss.'[2] The plaintiffs were able to sell the property in the first quarter of 1990. Hobhouse LJ held 'It follows that any losses which the plaintiff incurred after the spring of 1990 were not caused by the defendants' torts but by the plaintiffs 'decision not to sell out at that date for a figure of about £75,000.' The plaintiffs did not claim that they had incurred further loss in an unsuccessful, but reasonable, attempt to mitigate loss, though they did argue that it was reasonable for them to reject an offer of £76,000 for the property in March 1990. Hobhouse LJ summarised his basis for finding that the recoverable loss was £120,000 – £76,000 = £44,000:

> 'Even accepting that they acted reasonably, the fact remains that it was their choice, freely made, and they cannot hold the defendants responsible if the choice has turned out to have been commercially unwise. They were no longer acting under the influence of the defendants' representations. The causative effect of the defendants' faults was exhausted; the plaintiffs' right to claim damages from them in respect of those faults had likewise crystallised. It is a matter of causation.'[3]

1 [1997] 1 WLR 426 at 437.
2 It is far from obvious that such a submission could have succeeded. The plaintiffs might have been prompted to argue that they would have made at least as great sums from whatever alternative activities they would have undertaken had they not bought the business.
3 At 437/F–G.

8.77 However, the date of discovery of the fraud is not an automatic cutoff of losses; it is only the date after which it may become arguable by a defendant that further losses are caused by the claimant's own commercial decisions, or unreasonable failures to mitigate. In some circumstances, the effect of the fraud continues well after the date of discovery of the fraud. *4 Eng v Harper*[1] provides a clear illustration, because in that case, the damages included a lost opportunity to invest elsewhere, which continued up to the date of trial on the basis that the claimant would have continued to earn profits from the lost investment. The defendant argued that the claimant was free from the consequences of the fraud on the date when the target went into administration. But David Richards J held that since the claimant did not recover any funds at that stage, it was still not able to make an alternative investment, so it continued to suffer the effects of the defendants' deceit. His decision on this point was approved by the Court of Appeal in *Parabola Investments v Browallia Cal*.[2]

1 [2009] Ch 91 at [55].
2 [2011] QB 477 at [45]–[46].

8.78 Numerous damages issues of the type that will arise in a larger business sale dispute where fraud is proved were considered by Moore-Bick LJ in *MAN v Freightliner*. In respect of the period between the transaction and the claimant's discovery of the fraud, he said:

> '... the same principles are equally applicable in cases where the defendant's fraud continued to operate on the mind of the claimant's

> mind [sic] after he has entered into the transaction. In such cases the original fraudulent statement may induce the claimant to act in ways that exacerbate the loss flowing from the transaction. It follows that the defendant will be liable for any further losses resulting from steps which the claimant was induced to take, even in part, by the original fraudulent statement and that actions taken in response to subsequent events cannot be regarded as truly independent of the fraud unless it played no significant part in inducing them.'[1]

1 [2005] EWHC 2347 (Comm) at [228].

8.79 Moore-Bick LJ applied that approach to determine the effect of several matters which the seller relied on as breaking the link between its fraudulent misrepresentations that the accounts had been honestly prepared and the loss suffered by the buyer. The first matter was that the individual financial controller who made the misrepresentations in the course of negotiations transferred across with the company when it was purchased and continued dishonestly to conceal the fact that he had falsified the target's accounting records. Moore-Bick LJ held that this factor never eclipsed the original fraud so as to justify a finding that it lost its potency or ceased to influence the way that the buyer ran the target.[1] Second, Moore-Bick LJ accepted the claimant's argument that the effect of the presence of the fraudster within the target company 'amounted to a latent defect in the company's staff of a kind that make it appropriate to regard losses flowing from his continuation in the same course of dishonesty as losses flowing from the transaction'.[2] Third, Moore-Bick LJ rejected an argument that the buyer acted with such commercial recklessness, irresponsibility and irrationality that its own conduct of the business of the target was an intervening event that broke the chain of causation from the purchase of the business in reliance on the fraud.[3] He concluded on the facts that, while there might be something to be said for the view that the buyer was negligent, it had not acted in a way that could be characterised as 'commercially irresponsible and irrational' and therefore had not broken the chain of causation from the original purchase.[4]

1 [2005] EWHC 2347 (Comm) at [237].
2 Ibid at [242].
3 For the test, see at [229] and at [244] where Moore-Bick LJ expressed it as being that the buyer 'pursued a course of conduct in relation to [the target] which could not be commercially justified on any rational basis'.
4 Ibid at [284].

8.80 The next point for consideration in *MAN v Freightliner* was whether the buyer had failed to mitigate its loss after discovering the fraud. Moore-Bick LJ emphasised the well-known claimant friendly approach to this question, which is even more strongly applied in cases of fraud:

> 'Given the nature of the argument, it may be appropriate to reiterate what has been said on many previous occasions, namely, that the

injured party is not obliged to do more than act reasonably in response to the situation in which he finds himself. Moreover, the burden of showing that he failed to do so is heavy. In a well-known passage in his speech in *Banco de Portugal v Waterlow* [1932] AC 452 Lord Macmillan said at page 506

> "It is often easy after an emergency has passed to criticise the steps which have been taken to meet it, but such criticism does not come well from those who have themselves created the emergency. The law is satisfied if the party placed in a difficult situation by reason of the breach of a duty owed to him has acted reasonably in the adoption of remedial measures and he will not be held disentitled to recover the cost of such measures merely because the party in breach can suggest that other measures less burdensome to him might have been taken."'[1]

1 [2005] EWHC 2347 (Comm) at [285].

8.81 Having dismissed these arguments raised by the defendant, Moore-Bick LJ then noted that 'the fact that [the buyer] chose to keep [the target] alive and eventually to integrate it into its own operations does make it necessary to determine with some care the point at which the transaction induced by the fraud ceased to be the cause of any further loss to [the buyer]'.[1] This is a significant point in cases where the buyer retains the target: there comes a date when the original transaction ceases to be the cause of further losses (or, indeed, gains) and is replaced by the buyer's own commercial decisions. The identification of that date may be important and requires a very fact sensitive evaluation in any case where the same issues arise.

1 [2005] EWHC 2347 (Comm) at [310].

8.82 A similar approach was followed by Arnold J in *Invertec Ltd v de Mol Holding BV*.[1] He held that if the misrepresentations had not been made then the deal would not have been concluded; and the company had no real market value at the date of the transaction, which was 7 October 2005, so the initial consideration was recoverable as damages. The buyer was also entitled to recover payments made under a related agreement entered into as part of a package with the SPA. The next question was whether the claimant could also recover loans made to the target on the basis of being 'locked in' to the transaction. Arnold J held that the 'starting point' was to consider the buyer's state of knowledge and found that by 'early-mid January 2006', the buyer knew enough to 'take a decision'. At this stage, the judge found that the buyer had two alternatives: it could have rescinded the SPA (though rather oddly he said this applied 'in particular before [a certain event] in December 2005'), or allowed the target to go into administration or liquidation. Its decision instead to continue to support the target and keep it trading 'was a commercial decision on the part of Invertec'. It followed that the losses sustained from January 2006 onwards were not caused by the misrepresentations. The same result was reached on the basis that the decision to keep the target trading 'was not a reasonable attempt at mitigation, but a commercial gamble'.

1 [2009] EWHC 2471 (Ch) at [378]–[387].

8.83 Business sale frauds generally involve the vendor obtaining and retaining the purchaser's money as a result of the vendor's fraud. In such cases, compound interest may be awarded on damages through the exercise of the court's equitable jurisdiction: *MAN v Freightliner*.[1]

1 [2005] EWHC 2347 (Comm) at [318]–[321].

DAMAGES FOR NEGLIGENT MISSTATEMENT AND DAMAGES UNDER THE MISREPRESENTATION ACT 1967

8.84 Damages for negligent misstatement follow the tort model: they are the sum required to put the claimant in the position as if the wrong had not been committed. However, there are several differences between the damages recoverable in fraud and those recoverable for negligent misstatement.

8.85 First, in the case of negligent misstatement, the counterfactual for consideration is that the defendant did take reasonable care in making any statement. The measure of loss will therefore be similar to that applicable in the case of a breach of warranty of process, discussed above in relation to *Lion Nathan v C-C Bottlers*.[1] That may lead to a very different outcome than if the same representation had been made fraudulently, because tracing causation through the counterfactual in negligence will involve examining how the claimant would have reacted to being given the information that it should have been given.

1 See above at [**8.32**]–[**8.44**].

8.86 Second, unlike the case of fraud, the scope of duty principle may apply to a claim in negligent misstatement: so the defendant will be able to argue that damages should be capped at the figure that would have applied if the misinformation carelessly supplied had been warranted.

8.87 Third, the remoteness principle which excludes loss that was not reasonably foreseeable to the tortfeasor does not apply in fraud, but does apply in negligence.

8.88 Finally, a partial defence of contributory fault can be put forward to a claim a negligent misstatement, but not in fraud.

8.89 The measure of damages for misrepresentation under the 1967 Act is a matter of considerable academic controversy. For now it is settled up to the level of the Court of Appeal that the Act provides for damages on the tort measure: *Royscot Trust v Rogerson*.[1] The correctness of *Royscot Trust* on this point has been reserved by the House of Lords in *Smith New Court*.[2] Specialist texts may be consulted for this controversy, but there is no basis on which lower courts should not follow *Royscot Trust* for the time being.

1 [1991] 2 QB 297.
2 See per Lord Browne-Wilkinson at 267F and per Lord Steyn at 283B.

Chapter 9

Other Remedies

RESCISSION

Nature of rescission

9.01 Rescission is a remedy by which a contract is unravelled *ab initio* and the parties are restored to the state they were in immediately prior to entering their agreement. Rescission extinguishes all of the parties' obligations to each other under the contract, whether past, present or future, and whether primary (eg an obligation to give performance) or secondary (eg an obligation to pay damages for breach). Rescission differs in this sense from termination of a contract for breach, which discharges the parties from their future obligations only, and preserves certain secondary obligations.[1]

1 *Johnson v Agnew* [1980] AC 367 at 392–393.

9.02 Rescission was historically available at common law as a remedy for fraudulent misrepresentation and in equity as a remedy for any form of misrepresentation, whether fraudulent or not.[1] The relationship between common law and equitable rescission, and the extent to which there remains a principled distinction between the two, following the Judicature Act 1873 (which fused the courts of common law and courts of equity) remains opaque. In theory they remain separate doctrines, and a number of post-1873 cases continue to recognise differences between common law and equitable rescission.[2] However, this does not appear to be reflected consistently in modern practice.[3] Many of the reported cases refer to rescission without specifying which variant (common law or equitable) is in issue, or as if it were a single unitary remedy; and claims are now frequently brought for 'rescission', again without clearly identifying the species.[4] As a result, it is not realistically possible to identify two clear lines of 'common law and 'equitable' authorities in the modern case law.

1 *Redgrave v Hurd* (1881) 20 Ch D 1 at 12–13 per Lord Jessel MR.

2 See, eg, *Erlanger v The New Sombrero Phosphate Co* (1878) 3 App Cas 1218 (the claim pre-dated the coming into force of the Judicature Act 1873, but the judgment of Lord Blackburn – set out below – has been cited with approval frequently since 1878); *Spence v Crawford* (1939) All ER 271 HL (Sc); *O'Sullivan v Management Agency and Music Ltd* [1985] QB 428. For a fuller treatment of this issue, see D O'Sullivan, S Elliott and R Zakrzewski *The Law of Rescission* (3rd edn, Oxford University Press, 2023); J McGhee (ed) *Snell's Equity* (34th edn, Sweet & Maxwell, 2019), ch 10.

3 See, eg, *Drake Insurance Plc v Provident Insurance Plc* at [31] per Moore-Bick J: 'Although equity recognised a right of rescission in a wider range of circumstances than did the common law, modern authorities do not suggest that a distinction is to be drawn between the principles that apply to the exercise of that right in different cases.'

4 J Cartwright (ed) *Misrepresentation, Mistake and Non-Disclosure* (6th edn, Sweet & Maxwell, 2022), 4-02.

9.03 It is true that in many cases there would be no practical difference in outcome regardless of which species of rescission is relied upon. In certain circumstances, however, the distinction between common law and equitable rescission could be significant. For example, common law rescission is generally characterised as a 'self help' remedy, in that it is exercised at the election of a contracting party and the court's role is limited to 'pronounc[ing] upon the efficacy of that election'.[1] It is much less clear whether, on a strict legal analysis, equitable rescission can be exercised by election, or whether it can only be ordered by the court: in *IGE USA Investments Ltd v Revenue and Customs Commissioners* Henderson LJ described this as 'a notoriously difficult subject, on which the authorities are in such a state of disarray that, in my judgment, only the Supreme Court can reconcile them'.[2] If exercised by way of 'self help', rescission is effected when the representee unequivocally communicates that they elect to rescind.[3] If the rescission is disputed, then of course the court may be called upon to adjudicate as to its validity, but it takes place when the representee communicates its election, not at the time judgment is given (with effect *ab initio*).[4]

1 *Conway v Eze* [2018] EWHC 29 (Ch) at [156] per HH Judge Keyser QC, citing with approval a passage from J McGhee (ed) *Snell's Equity* (33rd edn, Sweet & Maxwell, 2015) to this effect. There was no appeal against this part of the judgment ([2019] EWCA Civ 88), which was probably obiter in any event. See also *IGE USA Investments Ltd v Revenue and Customs Commissioners* [2021] Ch 423 (CA) at [20] and [83].

2 [2021] Ch 423 (CA) at [91].

3 It may also be possible to claim rescission by order of the court, thus effectively postponing the election until trial: see J McGhee (ed) *Snell's Equity* (34th edn, Sweet & Maxwell, 2019), 15-012; and see further *Peak Hotels and Resorts Ltd v Tarek Investments Ltd* [2015] EWHC 1997 (Ch) at [131] per Barling J, noting that there is still uncertainty in this regard.

4 See *TSB Bank v Camfield* [1995] 1 WLR 430 at 438H per Roch LJ: 'The right to set aside or rescind the transaction is that of the representee, not that of the court. The court's role in a disputed case will be to decide whether the representee has lawfully rescinded the transaction or is entitled to rescind it.' The same authority shows that a consequence is that the court may not impose terms, though of course it may declare precisely what transactions are required to effect the rescission. In this sense, 'the court has a degree of flexibility to ensure that practical justice is achieved', but that issue only arises 'in the context of seeking to achieve as full and fair *restitutio in integrum* as possible': *UBS v KWL* [2017] 2 Lloyd's Rep 621 at [210] and [223].

9.04 The distinction between common law and equitable rescission may also be relevant to the limitation analysis. As a 'self help' remedy, common law rescission is not subject to any limitation period (although claims arising as a result of the rescission are probably subject to a limitation period running from the date on which the rescission is effected).[1] However, in *IGE USA Investments Ltd v Revenue and Customs Commissioners*, the Court of Appeal held that a claim for equitable rescission on the basis of fraudulent misrepresentation is subject to a six-year limitation period, which is applied (pursuant to s 36 of the Limitation Act 1980) by analogy with the six-year period for claims for deceit.

1 *IGE USA Investments Ltd v Revenue and Customs Commissioners* [2021] Ch 423 (CA) at [83]. The point in parenthesis was common ground between the parties: see [19].

9.05 Rescission has been described as the 'normal remedy' for misrepresentation.[1] However, even where a party has a prima facie right to rescind a contract, certain countervailing factors (commonly referred to as 'bars to rescission') may exclude the remedy. These bars to rescission are discussed further below.

1 *Salt v Stratstone Specialist Ltd* [2015] EWCA Civ 745 at [24] per Longmore LJ.

Bars to rescission: (i) impossibility of 'restitutio in integrum'

Restitutio in integrum: general approach

9.06 As the purpose of rescission is to restore the *status quo ante* between contracting parties, rescission will not be available if it is impossible 'to put the parties into their original state before the contract' (or, as it is traditionally phrased, to make *restitutio in integrum*).[1]

1 *Clarke v Dickson* (1858) 120 ER 463 at 466 per Crompton J.

9.07 In a straightforward sale of goods transaction, this principle will be relatively easy to apply: *restitutio in integrum* will require the buyer to return the goods purchased and the seller to return the purchase price. In the business sale context, the same logic would apply to a relatively simple asset purchase agreement: the assets must be returned and the price repaid. However, where assets depreciate in value after they are sold, or where a business is sold as a going concern, the analysis becomes more complicated.

9.08 Historically, the approach to *restitutio in integrum* was said to be less strict in equity than at common law. In *Erlanger v The New Sombrero Phosphate Co,* Lord Blackburn stated:

> 'It would be obviously unjust that a person who has been in possession of property under the contract which he seeks to repudiate should be allowed to throw that back on the other party's hands without accounting for any benefit he may have derived from the use of the property, or if the property, though not destroyed, has been in the interval deteriorated, without making compensation for that deterioration. But as a Court of Law has no machinery at its command for taking an account of such matters, the defrauded party, if he sought his remedy at law, must in such cases keep the property and sue in an action for deceit

…

But a Court of Equity could not give damages, and, unless it can rescind the contract, can give no relief. And, on the other hand, it can take accounts of profits, and make allowance for deterioration. And I think the practice has always been for a Court of Equity to give this relief whenever, by the exercise of its powers, it can do what is practically just, though it cannot restore the parties precisely to the state they were in before the contract.'[1]

1 (1878) 3 App Cas 1218 at 1278–1279.

9.09 This passage has often been cited in support of the proposition that, where equitable rescission is sought, there is no strict need to return the parties to the precise position they were in prior to entering the contract provided that 'practical justice' can be done. Thus in *O'Sullivan v Management Agency and Music Ltd,* Dunn LJ observed that:

'This analysis of the cases shows that the principles [sic] of *restitutio in integrum* is not applied with its full rigour in equity in relation to transactions entered into by persons in breach of a fiduciary relationship, and that such transactions may be set aside even though it is impossible to place the parties precisely in the position in which they were before, provided that the court can achieve practical justice between the parties by obliging the wrongdoer to give up his profits and advantages, while at the same time compensating him for any work that he has actually performed pursuant to the transaction.'[1]

1 [1985] QB 428 at 458.

9.10 This more relaxed approach to *restitutio in integrum,* with its emphasis on doing practical justice, now appears to predominate in the modern case law. Whether this is because the distinction between common law and equitable rescission is no longer widely respected in practice, or because most claims are now treated as claims for equitable rescission, even if not stated explicitly,[1] or because the flexible approach has simply prevailed over the previous stricter approach,[2] is unclear but probably immaterial.

1 See J Cartwright (ed) *Misrepresentation, Mistake and Non-Disclosure* (6th edn, Sweet & Maxwell, 2022), 4-02.
2 See H Beale (ed) *Chitty on Contracts* (35th edn, Sweet & Maxwell, 2023), 10-136.

Change in the nature of the subject-matter

9.11 In *Clarke v Dickson,*[1] the claimant was induced by fraudulent misrepresentations to purchase shares in a partnership formed for the purpose of working a mine. After three years, the partnership was converted to a limited liability company and subsequently wound up. Erle J held that *restitutio in* *integrum* could not be made, and therefore (common law[2]) rescission was not available to the claimant, because: (i) he had held the shares for three years, and enjoyed the chance of making a profit from them (as counsel put it, offering to return the shares would be akin to 'an offer to return a lottery ticket after it has turned up a blank'); (ii) he had received dividends on the shares; (iii) the shares had changed from shares in a partnership to shares in a limited company; and (iv) the company was being wound up, and all chance of profit was over. Crompton J reached the same conclusion, on the basis that: (i) the claimant had become bound to the others in the partnership; and (ii) the shares had changed from shares in a partnership to shares in a company that was being wound up.

1 (1858) 120 ER 463.
2 *Clarke v Dickson* was decided in a common law court prior to the enactment of the Judicature Act 1873; there was no possibility of equitable rescission.

9.12 Similarly, in *The Western Bank of Scotland v Addie,*[1] the House of Lords held (on an appeal from Scotland) that *restitutio in integrum* was impossible in circumstances where a claimant had bought shares in an unincorporated joint stock company but, prior to rescission, the company had been wound up and the concern had been incorporated and registered as a joint stock company. Lord Cranworth noted that, even if the new shares had been more valuable than the old ones, they would still not be shares in the same company; and 'unless he was in a position to restore the very thing which he was fraudulently induced to purchase, [the claimant] cannot have relief by way of *restitutio in integrum*'.

1 (1866–69) LR 1 Sc 145.

9.13 Based on these decisions, it is possible to say that rescission of a share sale agreement will generally not be possible if the nature of the shares has been altered in some essential way.

9.14 However, it remains unclear whether the principle of *restitutio in integrum* would prevent a party who has disposed of shares from rescinding a share sale agreement even where identical shares are available on the market. In *Smith New Court Securities Ltd v Scrimgeour Vickers (Asset Management) Ltd,* no claim for rescission was pursued because the purchaser of shares had sold the shares in question prior to commencement of the litigation. In the Court of Appeal, Nourse LJ considered that, by selling the shares, the purchaser had 'lost the right to rescission', albeit he acknowledged this was a harsh rule:

> 'In the case of a fungible asset like quoted shares, the rule which requires restitution in specie is a hard one. Not every legal system would insist upon it, particularly in a case of fraud.'[1]

However, in the House of Lords, Lord Browne-Wilkinson appeared to doubt whether there was any such rule:

> '... if the current law in fact provides (as the Court of Appeal thought) that there is no right to rescind the contract for the sale of quoted shares once the specific shares purchased have been sold, the law will need to be closely looked at hereafter. Since in such a case other, identical, shares can be purchased on the market, the defrauded purchaser can offer substantial restitutio in integrum which is normally sufficient.'[2]

Both of these views were obiter, no claim for rescission having been made. However, we would suggest that, even if it is not possible for the purchaser to restore the precise shares acquired, the availability of other identical shares on the open market should mean that in many such cases it is possible for the court to do 'practical justice' between the parties (eg by ordering a payment of money sufficient to enable the seller to re-purchase the shares); and, therefore, that rescission should be available.[3]

1 [1994] 1 WLR 1271 at 1280.
2 [1997] AC 254 at 262.
3 For discussion of these possibilities, see *School Facility Management v Christ the King College* [2021] EWCA Civ 1053 at [39]–[43].

Other changes to a business

9.15 Not all changes made to an acquired business will fundamentally alter its legal nature (or the nature of the shares or assets) so as to preclude rescission under the rule articulated in *Clarke v Dickson* and *The Western Bank of Scotland.* For example, some changes may relate purely to the business's internal operations or structure. In those circumstances, the question of whether *restitutio in integrum* is still possible may be more difficult to assess.

9.16 In principle, the mere fact that the business, shares or assets have deteriorated in value should not by itself render it impossible for the parties to be restored to their original positions.[1] In *The Western Bank of Scotland,* Lord Cranworth emphasised that his conclusion (ie that rescission was not available) had not been based on the fact that the shares in question had depreciated in value subsequent to their purchase by the claimant; rather, it was the fundamental change in their nature which had led to the refusal of rescission.

1 *Salt v Stratstone Specialist Ltd* [2015] EWCA Civ 745 at [22].

9.17 Issues as to the impact of changes made to a business have arisen in a number of subsequent cases involving business sales or analogous scenarios. The cases can, broadly, be divided into two categories: cases in which changes to the business, shares or assets have been held not to prevent the restoration of the parties to their original position; and cases in which changes have been held to render *restitutio in integrum* impossible.

9.18 *Erlanger v The New Sombrero Phosphate Co* falls into the first category. *Erlanger* was not a misrepresentation case, but rather a case in which directors of a company had breached their fiduciary duties by purchasing the lease of an island in the West Indies for mining purposes and re-selling it to the company at a substantial secret profit. The company sought equitable rescission of the sale agreement. The central dispute in *Erlanger* revolved around delay and laches, discussed further below. However, there was also an issue as to whether the fact that the mine had been worked prevented *restitutio in integrum.* On this, Lord Selborne said:

> 'It was the act of the vendors to put their property, being of that character, in such a position; and, unless some equity arises against the Plaintiffs from some conduct or omission of their own, the vendors must take the consequences of that act. The shareholders were put into possession of the property as a going concern; they took over the manager and all the other agents whom they found upon it, and did not alter or interfere with the course of management until they found that the manager was not doing his duty properly, when they promptly did what was right, and appointed a new and a fit person to succeed him. There has, therefore, been nothing done, or left undone, to the injury of the property since it came into the company's hands which can now stand in the way of the Plaintiffs' right to relief … .'[1]

1 (1878) 3 App Cas 1218 at 1260–1261.

9.19 The House of Lords returned to this issue in *Adam v Newbigging,* another case in the first category. The respondent had been induced to become a partner in a business by (non-fraudulent) misrepresentations as to its financial position. The business subsequently sustained further losses, incurred additional liabilities and ultimately failed, and the respondent sought equitable rescission of the agreement by which he had become a partner. The appellants resisted on the grounds that the business was no longer a going concern and could not be restored to them in the state they had sold it. However, the House of Lords held that the respondent was entitled to rescind: the business had been insolvent all along, its position had deteriorated because of its inherent weaknesses at the time the respondent acquired an interest in it, and the deterioration was not attributable to the respondent. As Lord Herschell put it:

> 'It is certain that the condition of the concern at that date did not result from any act of the respondent personally. Its affairs appear to have been carried on after he was a partner in precisely the same way as before. I have already pointed out that the enterprise was insolvent to a large amount when the respondent was induced to take a share in it; and I do not think the fact that the extent of its insolvency afterwards increased justifies the contention that restitutio in integrum is impossible. To hold otherwise would be to say that where a losing and insolvent business is sold by means of the representation that it is solvent and profitable, rescission could never be obtained if the loss were increased prior to the discovery of the true state of affairs.'[1]

1 (1888) 13 App Cas 308 at 330.

9.20 In *Armstrong v Jackson,* the claimant bought shares in a company from the defendant, who was purporting to act as a stockbroker but was in fact selling the shares as a principal. The value of the shares fell and, seven years later, the claimant sought to rescind the sale agreement. Considering some of the earlier authorities, McCardie J held that *restitutio in integrum* was possible, notwithstanding that the assets of the company might have varied and the value of the shares had fallen: the company was the same company with the same objects, the shares were the same shares and it was possible for the claimant to hand them back. He added:

> 'Deterioration of the subject-matter does not, I think, destroy the right to rescind nor prevent a restitutio in integrum. Indeed, it is only in cases where the plaintiff has sustained loss by the inferiority of the subject-matter or a substantial fall in its value that he will desire to exert his power of rescission. … If mere deterioration of the subject-matter negatived the right to rescind, the doctrine of rescission would become a vain thing.'[1]

1 [1917] 2 KB 822 at 829.

9.21 In *Spence v Crawford,* a claim for rescission of a share sale agreement was brought by the seller (a company director), who had been induced by misrepresentations to sell his shares in the company to another director. The buyer argued that it would not be possible to restore the seller to his original position, as the share capital of the company had been increased such that the seller would have a smaller interest in the company. However, the House of Lords held that it was a matter for the claimant to decide whether he was content to take back the same number of shares sold by him (which decision he had effectively made by pursuing the claim for rescission). It also rejected arguments raised by the defendant regarding losses he had sustained as a result of the transaction, noting that these could be accounted for by requiring the claimant to make a payment to the defendant over and above the amount of the purchase price as compensation for the losses. It was therefore possible to do practical justice between the parties, and this was sufficient to satisfy the requirement of *restitutio in integrum.*

9.22 Notwithstanding the cases discussed above, it is clear that in some circumstances the deterioration of a business (or shares or assets) through substantive changes to its operations will prevent *restitutio in integrum* and therefore bar rescission. This is exemplified by a number of cases falling into the second of the two categories described above.

9.23 One such case is *The Sheffield Nickel and Silver Plating Co, Ltd v Unwin.*[1] The defendant had sold several patents and several businesses to a newly-incorporated company. He served as a director of the new company before deciding to retire, at which point he agreed to surrender his shares in the company and give up his rights in certain new patents in exchange for the company releasing him from certain payment obligations. The company subsequently sought to rescind the surrender agreement on the basis that the defendant had mis-described the new patent rights he had given up. The Court held that rescission was no longer possible, as the 'position of both parties had been materially altered': the company had continued to operate for several months following the defendant's resignation, and in that time it had disposed of one of the businesses and sold one of the original patents. While it would have been possible to return the shares and new patent rights given up by the director, 'the return of these would not have restored the defendant to, or placed the concern in, the same condition' as he or it was in prior to the surrender.

1 (1877) 2 QBD 214 at 223–224.

9.24 Rescission was also refused in *Lagunas Nitrate Co v Lagunas Syndicate,*[1] in which the shareholders in a nitrate mining enterprise sought to rescind a contract by which the company had purchased land from a syndicate formed by its directors. The company had worked the land for several years, had called upon the syndicate to make significant outlays and had received profits and dividends. By majority, the Court of Appeal held (distinguishing *Erlanger*) that it was impossible to restore the parties to their previous positions. Lord Lindley MR (in the majority) suggested that the position might have been different if, as in *Erlanger,* fraud had been proved, as then 'The defendants could not effectually set up their own wrong as a reason for not giving such relief against them.' However, it is not clear why (even in the absence of fraud) 'practical justice' could not have been achieved in *Lagunas Nitrate* by rescinding the contract and ordering the company to give an account of the profits made from the mining operations, as suggested by Rigby LJ in his dissenting judgment. In that respect the decision is difficult to square with Lord Blackburn's dicta in *Erlanger,* quoted above. However, the proposition that rescission will be more readily granted in cases of fraud even where complex terms are needed to ensure *restitutio in integrum* was approved by the House of Lords in *Spence v Crawford.*[2]

1 [1899] 2 Ch 392.
2 [1939] 3 All ER 271 per Lord Thankerton at 280D and Lord Wright at 288F, the latter using the memorable phrase: 'the Court will be more drastic in exercising its discretionary powers in a case of fraud'.

9.25 *Thomas Witter Ltd v TBP Industries Ltd*[1] further illustrates the kind of changes in a business that may bar rescission. In *Thomas Witter,* the buyer of a carpet business sought rescission on the basis of misrepresentations as to its finances. Jacob J held that it would not be possible to restore the parties to their original positions: although the buyer had kept the new business separate from his own existing carpet business, it was 'unrealistic to regard it as the same as the business conveyed': there had been numerous changes to staff and personnel (including the departure of a key salesperson), the personnel who had stayed were in different pension schemes, and there were mortgagees of the business. It appears that at least part of Jacob J's concern was that rescission would impact on the rights of third parties: this is discussed further below. Although this was a case of innocent misrepresentation, Jacob J said that he would not have granted rescission even if fraud had been proved.

1 [1996] 2 All ER 573.

9.26 Changes made to a business after its acquisition also precluded rescission in *Capcon Holdings Plc v Edwards.* The buyer had purchased a company, Argen, which had a part-owned subsidiary, GMBH. The sellers misrepresented to the buyer that the remaining shares in GMBH were beneficially owned by a third party, DC. Following acquisition, the buyer 'hived off' the business of Argen to one of its own subsidiaries for tax purposes and, after discovering the misrepresentation, sold Argen's shares in GMBH to DC. Sir Andrew Morritt C held that, in the circumstances, *restitutio in integrum* was not possible:

> '[The buyer] is unable to restore to the claimants that which it obtained under the agreement, if only because it had sold the shares in GMBH. But, in addition, the underlying business was hived off for tax reasons, its personnel has changed, and the shares in Argen, whilst still recognisably shares in the same company, as were sold, carry rights to what is now little more than a shell.'[1]

Rescission was therefore not available.

1 [2007] EWHC 2662 at [54].

9.27 Two further business sale cases are worth noting, though they do not fit neatly into either of the two categories above.

9.28 First, rescission of an SPA was sought by the buyer in *Erlson Precision Holdings Ltd v Hampson Industries plc*[1] around two weeks after purchasing the entire issued share capital of a subsidiary of a company listed on the London Stock Exchange. Field J accepted that the buyer was entitled to rescind the SPA on grounds of fraudulent misrepresentation. The case illustrates that it is possible, even in a scenario involving the acquisition of the whole of a business, to rescind a business sale transaction after completion. However, *Erlson* does not stand as authority for any particular point as, once the buyer's case of fraudulent misrepresentation was made out, the defendant seller appears to have conceded that rescission was possible.

1 [2011] EWHC 1137 (Comm).

9.29 Second, in *Gamatronic (UK) Ltd v Hamilton*, the claimant purchased shares in a company from two former directors of the company. The claimant subsequently alleged that the former directors had breached their fiduciary duties by secretly setting up a competing business, and sought to rescind the

SPA. Mr Akhlaq Choudhury QC (sitting as a judge of the High Court) suggested that any deterioration in value of the shares would not prevent rescission:

> 'I have had regard to the fact that the Defendants are in breach of their duties. If the shares have diminished in value such that they are now worth less than the purchase price obtained then that is something about which the Defendants can hardly complain.'[1]

However, *Gamatronic* was an unusual case because, even though restoration of the parties to their original positions would have been possible, the claimant was unwilling to return the shares to the defendants; instead, it wished to effect rescission by paying the defendants the value of the shares as at the date of the SPA. Mr Choudhury QC rejected this, holding that the claimant's proposed solution would not restore the parties to their original position.

1 [2017] BCC 670 at [222].

9.30 It is difficult to extract a single coherent principle from all of the authorities above. However, in relation to business sales, the position appears to be that:

(i) it is generally possible in principle to restore the parties to their original positions by returning the business, shares and/or assets to the vendor and returning the purchase price to the purchaser, with any additional profits or losses potentially to be accounted for by payment of additional sums;

(ii) *restitutio in integrum* is possible notwithstanding that the business has declined in value, even to the point where it is no longer a going concern, especially (but not only) where the deterioration is the result of matters attributable to the vendor or inherent weaknesses at the time of sale;

(iii) however, structural changes made by a purchaser after acquisition, especially to share ownership, may alter the nature of a business in such a way that it can no longer be restored to the vendor in the same state as it was sold; and

(iv) operational changes made by the purchaser which have an adverse impact on the business could also render it impossible for the courts to do 'practical justice' between the parties, with the consequence that rescission is not available.

9.31 In complex business sale transactions, the application of propositions (ii), (iii) and (iv) above may be the subject of debate. Some cases will clearly fall on one side of the line, eg where the purchaser acquires a minority interest and has no involvement in the conduct of the business (as in *Armstrong v Jackson*) or largely lets the business continue as before (as in *Erlanger*). Some cases will clearly fall on the other side of the line, eg where the business is carved up and parts of it sold off to third parties (as in *Capcon Holdings*). However, in many cases, a business will be acquired specifically with a view to making changes (eg to increase its efficiency, capitalise on perceived 'synergies' or integrate it into a larger enterprise). Difficult questions can then arise as to the extent to which those changes have altered the nature of the business such as to render it impossible to return the business in its original state.

Bars to rescission: (ii) affirmation

9.32 The right to rescind a contract may be lost if the party seeking rescission has affirmed the contract, either by express words or by unequivocal conduct.[1]

1 *Clough v The London and North Western Railway Co* (1871–72) LR 7 Ex 26.

Carrying on the business

9.33 In a business sale case, carrying on the business with knowledge of the grounds for rescission (eg the misrepresentation in question) was held to amount to affirmation of the contract in *Seddon v The North Eastern Salt Co, Ltd,*[1] in which the claimant acquired the entire share capital of the defendant company and immediately discovered that its financial position was not as represented, but continued to carry on its business at a net profit for several months before seeking rescission. However, this case is of very dubious authority as the principle that it stood for – namely that rescission was not possible where a contract had been 'executed' – was always controversial, never applied to fraud, and was abrogated by the Misrepresentation Act 1967, s 1(b).

1 [1905] 1 Ch 326 at 334. *Joseph Constantine Steamship Ltd v Imperial Smelting Corp* [1942] AC 154.

9.34 Whether the carrying on of an acquired business amounts to unequivocal affirmation of the contract of sale is a fact-sensitive enquiry.[1] In *Street v Coombes,* the buyer attempted (unsuccessfully) to keep the business running for around two months following acquisition while he investigated certain suspicions. Mr Launcelot Henderson QC (sitting as a judge of the High Court) stated:

> 'I cannot regard [the buyer's] actions in trying to keep the business going as evincing any kind of intention, let alone an unequivocal one, to affirm the Sale Agreement. It seems to me rather that he was struggling to make the best of a desperate situation whilst steps were being taken to uncover the true position and he was considering his options.'[2]

1 *Edwards v Ashik* [2014] EWHC 2454 (Ch) at [56].
2 [2005] EWHC 2290 (Ch).

9.35 In any event, neither words nor conduct will amount to affirmation unless the party seeking rescission knows of (i) the underlying facts giving rise to its claim and (ii) the existence of the right to rescind.[1] An allegation that the buyer had affirmed an SPA by exercising a right under the SPA to apply for the appointment of an independent consultant was rejected in *Bottin International Investments Limited v Venson Group plc*:[2] it was not until much later (following the making of an order for disclosure) that it acquired sufficient knowledge to know that it had been the victim of fraud. A similar conclusion was reached in *Street v Coombes,*[3] discussed above.

1 *Peyman v Lanjani* [1985] Ch 457.
2 [2006] EWHC 3112 (Ch) at [406]–[408].
3 At [115].

9.36 By contrast, a purchaser's claim for rescission of an SPA failed in *Blindley Heath Investments Limited v Bass,*[1] because: (i) the parties had agreed at a meeting that 'neither side wished to rescind the agreement and wanted to continue with efforts to register the transfer of the Sale Shares'; and (ii) the purchaser was pursuing an application under the Companies Act 2006, s 125 to be added to the company's register of members. In the circumstances, the purchaser had clearly affirmed the contract.

1 [2014] EWHC 1366 (Ch) at [142(v)].

9.37 In principle, there is a possible tension in business sale cases between, on the one hand, the need for a claimant not to take any action that could be construed as affirming the contract of sale; and, on the other hand, the need for the claimant to maintain the business in a state in which it can be restored to the vendor (so as to preserve a claim for rescission) and/or to mitigate its losses (so as to preserve a claim for damages). A claimant who finds itself in this position should promptly give notice to the defendant of its election to rescind the contract, offering to return the shares immediately, which should guard against any risk that subsequent conduct of the business will be treated as affirmation.

9.38 This is illustrated by *Edwards v Ashik,* a case relating to the sale of a nightclub business. The buyer, Mr Edwards, knew as of 7 February 2012 that fraudulent misrepresentations had been made and that he had a right to rescind the contract of sale. He continued to occupy and operate the business for several months thereafter. Mr Timothy Fancourt QC (sitting as a judge of the High Court) held that this was not an unequivocal act of affirmation, because Mr Edwards' solicitors had sent the seller a letter on 7 February 2012 notifying the seller of his intention to pursue remedies for fraudulent misrepresentation.[1]

But for the letter, 'the continued occupation and business use of the Premises by Mr Edwards probably would have amounted to affirmation of the Contract'. As it was, the judge held that:

> 'It was clear that Mr Edwards was intending to claim remedies for fraud and was only delaying for a while to see what [the seller] had to say about the allegations. In those circumstances, continuing to operate the business in the same way that he had for the previous 15 months or so, for a short further period pending clarification of the legal position, was not an unequivocal act. Had the use continued after the dismissive response [from the seller] of 21 March for a substantial further substantial period of weeks and months then a different conclusion might well have been justified … .'[2]

1 The letter did not, in fact, expressly refer to rescission, but Mr Fancourt QC noted at [58] that 'The obvious and natural remedy for fraudulent misrepresentation inducing a person to enter into a disadvantageous agreement is rescission of the agreement' and that 'There was nothing in the letters to suggest that Mr Edwards was limiting himself to claiming damages.'
2 At [61].

Asserting claims under the agreement

9.39 In *Arani v Cordic Group Ltd*,[1] it was held that any claim for rescission by the buyers would have been barred on grounds of both delay[2] and affirmation. In addition to having carried on the SPA since the date of completion, Mr Andrew Hochhauser QC (sitting as a Deputy Judge of the High Court) found that the buyers had affirmed the agreement by writing letters in which they purported to give notice of claims for breach of warranty under the SPA. (In fact, the letters were ineffective in this regard, as they failed to comply with the contractual notification clause.) This suggests that, where a party wishes to preserve the possibility of rescission in a case where the facts may give rise to both a claim for misrepresentation and a claim for breach of warranty, it may have to make its election to rescind clear in advance of (or, perhaps, at the same time as) giving notice of any alternative breach of warranty claims under the contractual notification mechanism. In *Arani v Cordic Group Ltd*, the notification letters sent by the buyers do not appear to have made any express reference to the possibility of rescission.

1 [2021] EWHC 829 (Comm) at [170].
2 See [**9.44**]–[**9.49**].

Estoppel

9.40 Finally, it bears emphasis that the rules on affirmation do not supplant the normal rules of estoppel, though there will obviously be substantial overlap between these doctrines. In *Capcon Holdings Plc v Edwards*,[1] the buyer was held to have estopped itself from rescinding an SPA (as opposed to having affirmed the SPA); however, the nature of the representation giving rise to the estoppel is unclear from the judgment, as the point was conceded by the buyer. Estoppel may have some advantages for a defendant, as the strict knowledge requirements of affirmation will not apply. Conversely, however, estoppel will require the defendant to prove detrimental reliance, which is not needed to establish affirmation.

1 [2007] EWHC 2662 at [35]–[36].

Bars to rescission: (iii) rights of third parties

9.41 Rescission may be barred where it would damage or destroy the rights of an innocent third party, eg because the third party has acquired an interest in the property that is the subject-matter of the contract.[1]

1 *Society of Lloyd's v Wilkinson (No 2)* [1997] CLC 1012.

9.42 Thus in *Thomas Witter Ltd v TBP Industries Ltd,*[1] discussed above, rescission was not available following the acquisition of a carpet business in circumstances where, inter alia, there had been changes to staff pension schemes and there were mortgagees of the business; Jacob J said that 'Time has moved on and third parties would, I think, be affected.'

1 [1996] 2 All ER 573 at 588.

9.43 Similarly, third party rights created a potential obstacle to rescission of an SPA in *Bottin,*[1] because part of the overall completion arrangements had involved the redemption of some or all of the minority shareholding of a third party bank (though this point was left open for further argument).

1 [2006] EWHC 3112 (Ch) at [409].

Bars to rescission: (iv) delay

9.44 A delay before claiming rescission makes it more likely that one of the bars to rescission identified above will manifest. For example, as time passes, circumstances may change such that *restitutio in integrum* becomes impossible.[1] Moreover, in *Clough v The London and North Western Railway Co*[2] it was said that 'when the lapse of time is great, it probably would in practice be treated as conclusive evidence' of affirmation of a contract, though this must now be read subject to the rule that affirmation requires knowledge of the underlying facts giving rise to the claim and the existence of the right to rescind.[3] Similarly, delay makes it more likely that the rights of third parties will intervene so as to prevent rescission.[4]

1 *Erlanger v The New Sombrero Phosphate Co* (1878) 3 App Cas 1218 at 1231.
2 (1871–72) LR 7 Ex 26 at 35.
3 *Armstrong v Jackson* [1917] 2 KB 822 at 830.
4 *Society of Lloyd's v Wilkinson (No 2)* [1997] CLC 1012 at 1028, citing with approval a passage from A Guest (ed), *Chitty on Contracts* (27th edn, Sweet & Maxwell, 1996).

9.45 Delay also appears to be an independent bar to rescission, at least where the lapse of time is such that it would be inequitable to grant the remedy.

In *Salt v Stratstone Specialist Ltd,* Roth J (sitting in the Court of Appeal) described the rule as follows:

> '... it is something of a misnomer to say that rescission may be barred by lapse of time. It is only the lapse of a reasonable time such that it would be inequitable in all the circumstances to grant rescission which constitutes a bar to the remedy. This is in essence the principle of laches, which accordingly requires close attention to the facts of the case.'[1]

1 [2015] EWCA Civ 745 at [43].

9.46 The defence of laches applies where, as a result of delay, it would be 'practically unjust' to grant the remedy in question. Factors relevant to laches include 'the length of the delay and the nature of the acts done during the interval, which might affect either party, and cause a balance of justice or injustice in taking the one course or the other, so far as relates to the remedy'.[1] Though not an immutable requirement, some form of detrimental reliance is also usually an essential ingredient of laches.[2]

1 *Lindsay Petroleum Co v Hurd* (1874) LR 5 PC 221 at 239–240.
2 *Fisher v Brooker* [2009] 1 WLR 1764 at [64].

9.47 Because the availability of laches as a defence depends inter alia on 'the nature of the acts done during the interval' (ie following the misrepresentation but prior to rescission), in the business sale context it will often involve consideration of the same matters as are relevant to the issue of *restitutio in integrum,* ie the buyer's behaviour and conduct of the business following acquisition.

9.48 In *Erlanger v The New Sombrero Phosphate Co,* discussed above, the House of Lords considered and (by majority) rejected a laches defence in a claim for rescission of a contract by which a newly-incorporated company had acquired mining rights. Most of the company's shareholders had no initial reason to suspect impropriety on the part of the sellers. Although a small number of shareholders had doubts from an early stage, it had taken time for them to investigate and obtain proof of the facts, and to persuade their fellow shareholders to pass a resolution for a committee of investigation. Thereafter, rather than rushing into litigation, the company had attempted to resolve matters with the sellers through negotiation. A delay of approximately 14 months was not therefore sufficient to preclude rescission.

9.49 The opposite conclusion was reached in *De Sena v Notaro.*[1] The claimant sought rescission of a demerger transaction by which she had given up her shares in a company jointly owned with the defendant, and certain properties held by that company had been transferred to a separate company which the claimant owned. The claimant's claims all failed, but in any event HHJ Paul

Matthews (sitting as a judge of the High Court) considered the defendant's defence of laches. He noted that there had been a long delay after the demerger transaction before the claimant sought rescission (six years). In that time, the properties transferred to the claimant had undergone changes, both physically and in terms of legal rights. Meanwhile, the defendant's company had pursued a successful, high-risk strategy which the claimant had eschewed, but in which the claimant was now trying (by her claim for rescission and the return of her shares) to share the benefits. In those circumstances, HHJ Matthews concluded that rescission would have been precluded by laches.

1 [2020] EWHC 1031 (Ch) at [232]–[233].

Bars to rescission: (v) Misrepresentation Act 1967

9.50 As a result of the Misrepresentation Act 1967, s 2(2), the availability of rescission for innocent or negligent misrepresentation is now subject to a judicial discretion to award damages in lieu of rescission. Section 2(2) provides: Where a person has entered into a contract after a misrepresentation has been made to him otherwise than fraudulently, and he would be entitled, by reason of the misrepresentation, to rescind the contract, then, if it is claimed, in any proceedings arising out of the contract, that the contract ought to be or has been rescinded, the court or arbitrator may declare the contract subsisting and award damages in lieu of rescission, if of opinion that it would be equitable to do so, having regard to the nature of the misrepresentation and the loss that would be caused by it if the contract were upheld, as well as to the loss that rescission would cause to the other party.

9.51 This discretion does not apply to fraudulent misrepresentation, in respect of which 'The victim always has the right to rescind unless one of the general bars to rescission has arisen.'[1]

1 *Sharland v Sharland* [2015] UKSC 60 at [31].

9.52 Section 2(2) effectively creates a separate statutory bar to rescission for (non-fraudulent) misrepresentation. On its face, it creates a broad judicial discretion to refuse rescission. However, the three factors identified in the provision itself – (i) the nature of the misrepresentation, (ii) the loss that would be caused by the misrepresentation if the contract were upheld, and (iii) the loss that rescission would cause to the misrepresenting party – have been said to be 'the ones to which most weight would be given' in all but an exceptional case: *William Sindall Plc v Cambridgeshire County Council.*[1] In *William Sindall,* the Court of Appeal suggested (obiter, but after hearing argument) that the discretion to refuse rescission was likely to be exercised where, as in that case, rescission was essentially being sought by the claimant as a way of escaping a bad bargain. On the facts, the claimant had purchased land for approximately £5 million. The value of the land subsequently declined by several million pounds due to a general fall in market prices. The claimant sought rescission on the basis of a misrepresentation that would have cost around £18,000 to put right. The Court of Appeal's view was that it would have been an appropriate case for damages to be awarded in lieu of rescission.

1 [1994] 1 WLR 1016 at 1043.

9.53 *British & Commonwealth Holdings plc v Quadrex Holdings Inc*[1] illustrates the application of s 2(2) in the business sale context. British & Commonwealth and Quadrex were both interested in acquiring a business, MH, but were primarily interested in different parts of the business. They agreed that British & Commonwealth would purchase MH and sell one of its divisions to Quadrex for approximately £280 million. British & Commonwealth duly acquired MH but, shortly afterwards, the stock market crashed and Quadrex failed to complete. Various claims were brought by both parties, including a claim for breach of contract by British & Commonwealth and a counterclaim by Quadrex for misrepresentation based on certain representations made by British & Commonwealth about MH's financial position.

1 [1995] CLC 1169.

9.54 As Quadrex had failed to establish that the misrepresentations in question had been fraudulent, it had no automatic right to rescind the agreement. One question that therefore arose was whether rescission for non-fraudulent misrepresentation was available, or whether damages should be awarded in lieu under the Misrepresentation Act 1967, s 2(2). At first instance, the judge held that damages, not rescission, would be 'the just and equitable course'. The Court of Appeal agreed. It upheld the judge's finding that, had the misrepresentation been corrected before the contract was signed, the parties would have renegotiated their agreement and arrived at a purchase price of approximately £260 million (ie £20 million less than was actually paid). Looking at the factors identified in s 2(2), the loss to Quadrex if the contract were upheld would therefore be, at most, £20 million. By contrast, the loss to British & Commonwealth if the agreement were rescinded would be 'far greater', the business having fallen significantly in value since its acquisition. Thus, the Court of Appeal held, the judge was right to refuse rescission.

9.55 Several points of general interest emerge from the Court of Appeal's judgment in *British & Commonwealth Holdings.*

9.56 First, the Court of Appeal indicated that it is for the party seeking to persuade the court to exercise the discretion to award damages in lieu of rescission to establish the case for that exercise. However, it rejected the suggestion that a 'special case' had to be shown to justify a departure from the remedy of rescission.

9.57 Second, while the Court of Appeal noted that 'There are obvious difficulties in assessing, years after the relevant time in drastically altered circumstances, what would have happened in a hypothetical situation that did not in fact occur', both the judge and the Court of Appeal embarked on a fairly detailed counterfactual analysis in an attempt to work out what would have happened had the misrepresentation been revealed prior to entry into the contract. Quadrex argued that the whole deal would have fallen apart, but the judge and the Court of Appeal took the view that it would have gone ahead with a discount being made to the purchase price. The judge regarded this as an important factor in the exercise of his discretion. It might follow that, where the evidence shows that the parties would not have gone ahead with the contract had they known the truth, rescission is more likely to be granted.

9.58 Third, while *William Sindall* was not referred to in *British & Commonwealth Holdings,* the two cases are entirely consistent. *British & Commonwealth Holdings* was, in a sense, another 'bad bargain' case: the buyer was attempting to use a relatively minor misrepresentation to escape from a commitment to purchase a business that had substantially fallen in value, inter alia due to market conditions. The judge and the Court of Appeal were unwilling to allow rescission to be used for this purpose.

Damages in lieu of rescission

Availability of damages

9.59 Following some uncertainty and inconsistency in a number of first instance decisions,[1] the Court of Appeal has now clarified that damages in lieu of rescission under the Misrepresentation Act 1967, s 2(2) are not available where rescission itself is not available as a remedy (eg because the contract has been affirmed or *restitutio in integrum* is impossible).[2] This is consistent with the wording of s 2(2), which says that damages may be awarded where a person 'would be entitled, by reason of the misrepresentation, to rescind the contract'.

1 See, eg, *Thomas Witter Ltd v TBP Industries Ltd* (damages available even where rescission was not); *Government of Zanzibar v British Aerospace (Lancaster House) Ltd* [2000] 1 WLR 2333 (damages not available where right to rescission had been lost).
2 *Salt v Stratstone Specialist Ltd* [2015] EWCA Civ 745 at [17].

9.60 Section 2(3) of the Misrepresentation Act 1967 provides: Damages may be awarded against a person under subsection (2) of this section whether or not he is liable to damages under subsection (1) thereof, but where he is so liable any award under the said subsection (2) shall be taken into account in assessing his liability under the said subsection (1).

9.61 This provision makes clear that damages in lieu of rescission may be awarded in addition to damages under s 2(1). Its wording also implies that the measure of damages under s 2(2) is different from the measure under s 2(1), but does not clarify the basis on which s 2(2) damages are to be calculated.

9.62 Substantial uncertainty therefore remains as to the proper measure of damages under s 2(2). In *William Sindall,* Hoffmann LJ and Evans LJ appeared to prefer the contractual measure of damages, though their views on this point were obiter,[1] and their approach has been trenchantly criticised.[2]

1 [1994] 1 WLR 1016, per Hoffmann LJ at 1038; per Evans LJ at 1044–1045. Russell LJ agreed with both judgments.

2 See, eg, J Edelman (ed) *McGregor on Damages* (21st edn, Sweet & Maxwell, 2020), 49-075–49-084. In *Floods of Queensferry Ltd v Shand Construction Ltd* [2000] BLR 81, HH Judge Humphrey Lloyd QC (sitting as a Judge of the High Court) indicated at [34] that he would have followed the Court of Appeal's approach, but his remarks were obiter as, on the facts, damages were not available to the claimant.

9.63 The issue arose at first instance in *British & Commonwealth Holdings.* Gatehouse J held that damages under s 2(2) were *sui generis* and stated:

> 'I agree with [counsel] that the Act gives the Court a complete discretion, not only at the stage when it is considering whether rescission or damages is the appropriate remedy but also at the stage of assessing damages. The Court's duty is to do justice in the circumstances.
>
> … the Court has a wide discretion to award these "statutory" damages and is not limited to the rules in tort or contract …
>
> … the loss suffered by Quadrex for which it is entitled to compensation under the Act is the loss that flows from the misrepresentation: it is not the loss suffered as a result of "losing the right to rescind".'[1]

On that basis, Gatehouse J awarded Quadrex damages of £20 million, which (as set out above) represented the discount it would have negotiated on the purchase price had the seller's misrepresentation been corrected prior to the date of the SPA.

1 Unreported, 18 October 1993, Commercial Court.

9.64 As the Court of Appeal's discussion of this point in *William Sindall* was obiter, we suggest that *British & Commonwealth Holdings* must be taken to indicate the correct approach as the law stands. Thus, damages under s 2(2) are *sui generis*: neither the contractual nor the standard tort measure of damages is necessarily applicable, and the Court has a wide discretion, but should generally look to award damages based on the loss flowing from the misrepresentation itself. However, the current state of the law remains somewhat unsatisfactory, as no reference was made to *William Sindall* in Gatehouse J's judgment (despite the Court of Appeal's decision having been handed down several months earlier); and the issue did not reach the Court of Appeal in *British & Commonwealth Holdings*[1] itself, because the appeal on this point fell away on other grounds.

1 [1995] CLC 1169 at 1249.

Contractual right to rescind

9.65 The parties to a business sale agreement may expressly provide for a right to rescind the contract in the event of a misrepresentation and/or breach of warranty. In practice, any such right is likely to be confined to the period before completion of the transaction.[1]

1 See, eg, *Marplace (Number 512) Ltd v Chaffe Street* [2006] EWHC 1919 (Ch).

TERMINATION

Termination for breach

9.66 In certain circumstances, a breach of contract by one party may entitle the other to treat the contract as having been terminated. Whether or not such a right arises will depend on the nature of the term breached and, potentially, the nature of the breach. In this regard, the courts distinguish between three categories of terms: (i) conditions, breach of which always gives rise to a right to terminate; (ii) intermediate or innominate terms, breach of which may or may not give rise to a right to terminate depending on the nature of the breach; and (iii) warranties in the narrow sense, breach of which does not give rise to a right to terminate.

9.67 The fact that the parties to an agreement have expressly characterised a particular term as a 'warranty' does not invariably mean that the term will be classified by the court as a warranty in the narrow sense above, ie as a term that does not give rise to a right to terminate.[1] In *HIH Casualty & General Insurance Ltd v New Hampshire Insurance Co,* Rix LJ suggested that there were three tests for determining whether a term was a warranty (in the narrow sense):

> 'It is a question of construction, and the presence or absence of the word "warranty" or "warranted" is not conclusive. One test is whether it is a term which goes to the root of the transaction; a second, whether it is descriptive of or bears materially on the risk of loss; a third, whether damages would be an unsatisfactory or inadequate remedy.'[2]

The *HIH Casualty* case was decided in the context of an insurance contract. The consequences of a breach of warranty in the insurance context are different from the normal position in contract law; at the time of the *HIH Casualty* decision, a breach of a warranty in an insurance contract completely discharged the insurer from liability for all risks covered by the policy. The second of Rix LJ's three tests (ie whether the term 'is descriptive of or bears materially on the risk of loss') is clearly specific to insurance contracts. However, it is suggested that the first and third tests are of more general application, as they are consistent with the general characterisation in contract law of warranties as 'minor'[3] or 'incidental'[4] terms of a contract.

1 *Barnard v Faber* [1893] 1 QB 340.
2 [2001] EWCA Civ 735.
3 *Grand China Logistics Holding (Group) Co Ltd v Spar Shipping AS* [2016] EWCA Civ 982 at [20].
4 *Finnegan v Allen* [1943] KB 425 at 430.

9.68 In practice, termination is unlikely to be available as a remedy for breach of warranty in business sale cases for three reasons.

9.69 First, most business sale cases involve agreements that are individually negotiated, frequently with professional assistance. In those circumstances, the express characterisation by the parties of a term as a warranty, though not determinative, is likely to be viewed as persuasive; the drafters of the contract are likely to be taken to have understood the technical meaning of such a word, and to have used it deliberately.[1]

1 See, eg, *Infiniteland Ltd v Artisan Contracting Ltd* [2005] EWCA Civ 758 at [88].

9.70 Second, applying the relevant tests of Rix LJ in the *HIH Casualty* case, a warranty in a business sale agreement (in the broad sense of a contractual promise as to a matter of fact) is not generally a term that goes to the root of the parties' transaction, or which is incapable of being remedied in damages if breached. In fact, the position is generally the opposite. A warranty in a business sale agreement is a tool used to distribute risk between the parties through the mechanism of damages; it is not something that must be true for the contract to be carried out.

9.71 Third, even if a term characterised as a warranty in a business sale agreement were to be classified by a court as an intermediate term, it would still be unlikely to give rise to a right to terminate the agreement. A right to terminate only arises where the breach of an intermediate term is such as to deprive the innocent party of substantially the whole benefit of the contract.[1] Again, for the reasons above, this will not generally be true of the breach of a contractual promise as to a matter of fact.

1 *Hongkong Fir Shipping Co Ltd v Kawasaki Kisen Kaisha Ltd* [1962] 2 QB 26 at 72 per Diplock LJ.

Termination pursuant to the terms of the agreement

9.72 A business sale agreement may also be brought to an end (generally only before completion) pursuant to its own terms. In particular, it is not unusual for such an agreement to include a 'material adverse change' or 'material adverse effect' provision entitling the buyer to walk away from the deal if certain events have a material negative impact on the operations or profitability of the target business. While it is possible to include a 'material adverse change' provision as a warranty,[1] it may be preferable to structure it as eg a condition precedent to completion if the goal is to ensure that the transaction can be stopped or unwound entirely (as opposed to just giving the buyer a remedy in damages afterwards).

1 See [**2.52**]–[**2.56**].

9.73 *Travelport Ltd v WEX Inc*[1] illustrates the importance (but also the difficulty) of defining clearly the events that will give rise to such a right. The target companies were providers of payment services, doing most of their business in the travel industry. Having initially agreed to acquire them for more than US$1 billion, the purchaser changed its mind after the COVID-19 pandemic (and the associated imposition of travel restrictions) significantly impacted the businesses. The SPA contained a material adverse effect provision, which specifically carved out 'pandemics', but which contained an exception to the carve-out if the pandemic (or other event) could be shown to have had a 'disproportionate effect' on the target companies as compared to other participants in the same industries. The central dispute between the parties therefore concerned the industry in which the target companies operated: if it was the business-to-business payments industry generally (as opposed to the *travel* payments industry), the buyers would have been better able to show a disproportionate impact on the target companies, such as to trigger the material adverse effect clause. Considering this question at a trial of a preliminary issue, Cockerill J preferred the broader approach advocated by the buyers: in particular, there was no 'travel payments industry' as such; both parties accepted that the business-to-business payments industry was one in which the target companies operated; and this was supported by the surrounding documentation.

1 [2020] EWHC 2670 (Comm).

9.74 However, the judgment was not an unqualified success for the buyers. A further point of dispute arose in relation to the interaction of the various carve-outs to the material adverse effect clause, which was not entirely clear from the wording of the SPA. In particular, the 'disproportionate impact' exception had been stated to apply to some types of event (such as pandemics) but not others (such as legal and regulatory changes). This discrepancy gave rise to difficulties in relation to the widespread travel restrictions in 2020, which in a general sense arose out of the COVID-19 pandemic but more directly resulted from laws and regulations enacted by different national governments. On this point, Cockerill J agreed with the sellers that, insofar as the worldwide collapse in travel arose from or in connection with changes in laws and regulations, the 'disproportionate impact' exception did not apply (even if the pandemic was the ultimate underlying cause). She acknowledged the practical difficulties to which this would give rise: in ascertaining whether the material adverse effect clause was triggered, the parties would need to try to strip out the effect of

COVID-19-related laws and regulations from the effect of the pandemic itself, something which might be difficult to do on a principled basis.[1]

1 [2020] EWHC 2670 (Comm), see [280]–[310].

9.75 In reality, it may therefore be that (as Cockerill J noted in *Travelport*) a material adverse effect provision is sometimes better viewed as 'providing fuel for renegotiation' rather than clearly allocating in advance all of the risks flowing from unanticipated changes in economic conditions.[1]

1 *Travelport Ltd v WEX Inc* [2020] EWHC 2670 (Comm) at [247].

FRUSTRATION AND FORCE MAJEURE

9.76 A contract may be frustrated if a particular event or change of circumstances renders performance impossible. In *National Carriers Ltd v Panalpina (Northern) Ltd,* Lord Simon summarised the rule as follows:

> 'Frustration of a contract takes place where there supervenes an event (without default of either party and for which the contract makes no sufficient provision) which so significantly changes the nature (not merely the expense or onerousness) of the outstanding contractual rights and/or obligations from what the parties could reasonably have contemplated at the time of its execution that it would be unjust to hold them to the literal sense of its stipulations in the new circumstances: in such case, the law declares both parties to be discharged from further performance.'[1]

1 [1981] 1 AC 675 at 700.

9.77 The courts have emphasised that the doctrine of frustration 'operates within narrow confines'.[1] In *Pioneer Shipping Limited v BTP Tioxide Ltd,*[2] Lord Roskill remarked that frustration is 'not likely to be invoked to relieve contracting parties of the normal consequences of imprudent commercial bargains'.

1 *Gold Group Properties Ltd v BDW Trading Ltd* at [68] per Coulson J.
2 [1982] AC 724 at 752.

9.78 In general, a party will not be able to invoke the doctrine of frustration where the impossibility of performance arises from its own fault.[1] Frustration will also generally be inapplicable where the risk that eventuates was expressly allocated to one of the parties by the terms of the contract.[2] If the unexpected event occurred prior to signature of the contract, or was foreseen or foreseeable as a real possibility at the time, the defence of frustration is unlikely to be available, the inference being that the parties did not intend the event to bring their agreement to an end.[3]

1 *Joseph Constantine Steamship Ltd v Imperial Smelting Corp* [1942] AC 154.
2 *Kuwait Supply Co v Oyster Marine Management Inc* [1994] 1 Lloyd's Rep 637.
3 *Edwinton Commercial Corp v Tsavliris Russ (Worldwide Salvage & Towage) Ltd* [2007] EWCA Civ 547 at [103]–[104].

9.79 In a claim for breach of warranty, the defence of frustration is most likely to be relevant when an unforeseen change of circumstances occurs between signature and completion, rendering the warranty untrue. (This assumes that the warranties are given as of the date of completion.) That is because, if the allegedly frustrating event occurred or was foreseen prior to signature of the agreement, it is likely to be inferred that the parties did not intend it to bring the agreement to an end.

9.80 In the specific context of a business sale, disputes are likely to centre on: (i) the extent to which the impossibility of performance can be attributed to the warrantor's conduct; and (ii) the extent to which the warranty itself can be regarded as a contractual allocation of the risk that eventuated. For example, where an external event following signature of the contract causes (for example) a company's net asset value to fall below the warranted minimum, questions will arise as to: (i) the extent to which the company could have avoided this by taking proper action; and (ii) whether the warranty as to net asset value, properly construed, was a deliberate allocation by the parties of the risk of the external event occurring and having an adverse impact on the company's finances.

9.81 If a contract is discharged by frustration, the parties may be able to recover any sums paid prior to discharge under the Law Reform (Frustrated Contracts) Act 1943, s 1(2). A party who has incurred expenses may be permitted to retain or recover an amount of money in respect of those expenses if the court considers it 'just to do so having regard to all the circumstances of the case' (s 1(2)). If one party has obtained a valuable benefit from the other before discharge, the party providing the benefit may be entitled to recover a sum of money up to the value of the benefit (s 1(3)). At common law, money paid under the contract may be recoverable if there has been a total failure of consideration.[1]

1 *Fibrosa Spolka Akcyjna v Fairbairn Lawson Combe Barbour Ltd* [1943] AC 32.

9.82 The parties to a contract may also cater for obstacles to performance by including a force majeure clause, which makes specific provision for the occurrence of certain types of events outside the parties' control (such as natural disasters). The precise events covered by a force majeure clause, and the effect on the contract of those events occurring (eg whether obligations are excluded entirely or merely suspended), will be a matter of construction of the clause in question. However, force majeure clauses are rare in business sale agreements.

Chapter 10

Sellers' Claims

INTRODUCTION TO SELLERS' CLAIMS

10.01 In addition to claims for breach and warranty and fraud that buyers may have against sellers, it is important to remember that there are also a number of claims that may be brought by sellers either against buyers or amongst themselves. These may be for breach of warranty or for fraud but may also include claims relating to incomplete payment, claims arising out of the conduct of the buyer during the transaction or claims for contribution against other sellers.

10.02 The following sections provide an overview and examples of the types of claims that sellers may bring. Many are highly fact sensitive and no doubt there are other claims that could be pursued by aggrieved sellers in appropriate circumstances.

PAYMENT OF PURCHASE CONSIDERATION

10.03 There are a number of different reasons why a seller might have a claim against the buyer in respect of part of the purchase price.

Payment in instalments

10.04 First, the SPA may provide for the purchase price to be paid in instalments, with some due at intervals after completion. The seller may have a claim against the buyer if later instalments are not paid.

10.05 Such a scenario arose in *New Hearts Ltd v Cosmopolitan Investments Ltd.*[1] New Hearts had purchased the entire share capital in 'Pentland' from Cosmopolitan. Pentland held 50.05% of the share capital of Heart of Midlothian Football Club ('Hearts'). Part of the consideration for the shares in Pentland was payable in instalments, and the SPA provided that New Hearts could set off any claim for damages for breach of warranty against any instalment of the deferred consideration.

1 [1997] 2 BCLC 249.

10.06 *Sellers' Claims*

10.06 New Hearts commenced proceedings against Cosmopolitan for breach of warranty in respect of various accounting matters, including the alleged valuation of a football stadium. New Hearts then refused to pay an instalment of the purchase price, and Cosmopolitan itself started proceedings for payment of this sum. New Hearts' only defence to this claim was to assert that it was entitled to set off its liability against the claims it had against Cosmopolitan.

10.07 In respect of Cosmopolitan's claim for payment of the instalment of deferred consideration, Lord Penrose set out the relevant clause of the agreement:

> 'The Purchaser shall be entitled to deduct by way of set-off from the Deferred Consideration any amount due to it under or by reason of any breach of the terms of this Agreement, (including, in particular, but without prejudice to the foregoing generality, any breach of the Warranties …) and any amount so applied shall pro tanto satisfy the liability concerned.'[1]

1 [1997] 2 BCLC 249 at p 262.

10.08 Lord Penrose continued by relating this clause to the Scots law principle of compensation:

> '… In my view it is plain that cl 5 of the agreement is a clause providing for compensation and, like compensation, operates where the mutual claims of parties are liquid. The clearest indication that this is so is to be found in the final two lines of the clause which provide for the extinction pro tanto of liability owed by the purchaser to the vendor upon the application by way of set-off of any sum brought within the scope of the clause as an amount 'due' to the purchaser inter alia referable to breach of warranty. There is, at present, no sum presently due as a liquid debt by Cosmopolitan to New Hearts Ltd and in my opinion no scope for the application of this provision.'

10.09 He continued:

> 'A more substantial question is whether New Hearts Ltd are entitled to retain the instalment against the claims made in the action at their instance against Cosmopolitan. I have held that there is no relevant basis for that case at present. I reserve my view as to the operation of retention if New Hearts Ltd's case is reformulated in a way that merits proof. A second instalment will fall due on the second anniversary of completion and the issues is likely to arise again at that stage. However, given the view I have formed following debate in New Hearts Ltd's action, I consider that it would be inappropriate to deprive Cosmopolitan of the benefit of payment of the sum presently due to them.'

10.10 The decision indicates that any buyer considering withholding an instalment of the purchase price must consider closely any contractual term providing or restricting a right of set-off. The key issue is likely to be the degree of certainty that the buyer must have in respect of the vendor's liability before an entitlement to withhold payment arises.[1]

1 See also *Arani v Cordic Group Ltd* [2021] EWHC 829 (Comm) in which fraud claims brought after the notification period were successful but were held at an earlier stage of the litigation not to entitle the buyer to withhold the payment of retained consideration to the seller once the notification period had expired.

Earnout or deferred consideration

10.11 Second, the SPA may contain an earnout or deferred consideration clause pursuant to which the seller considers that it is contractually entitled to a further payment which has not been made by the purchaser.

10.12 In *Damoco (Bermuda) Ltd v Atlanta BidCo Ltd*, the consideration payable pursuant to the SPA included a deferred consideration element, which provided that if the pro forma audited IFRS EBITDA as determined in the audited 'Deferred Consideration Accounts' was '*equal to or greater than €15,300,000 and equal to or less than €19 million*', the deferred consideration payable would be €20 million. As part of this process, the SPA required that:

> 'The Buyer will deliver to the Sellers a draft of the Deferred Consideration Accounts (draft Deferred Consideration Accounts) within 30 days after the date upon which the audited financial statements of the Company which relate to the Deferred Consideration Period are in such condition as could be formally signed off by the Auditors and in any case no later than 30 June 2019.'[1]

1 [2020] EWHC 501 (Comm).

10.13 The sellers claimed that in breach of the SPA, the buyer had failed to deliver Deferred Consideration Accounts by the relevant date, although oral assurances had been given that the EBITDA was above the lower limit based on the management accounts. An early draft of the Deferred Consideration Accounts had been provided but these were not based on near-final audited accounts as required. Nonetheless, the sellers purported to accept these draft accounts as the Deferred Completion Accounts and treated them as final and binding.

10.14 The sellers sought summary judgment on their claim for a declaration, inter alia, that the buyer had become liable to pay deferred consideration of €20 million. The application was, however, rejected by Moulder J, who held:[1]

> 'In my view the objective meaning of Paragraph 3 is as submitted for the defendant. The draft Deferred Consideration Accounts were only

> to be provided once the audited accounts were ready to be signed off by the Auditors and it is implicit therefore that the starting point for the draft Deferred Consideration Accounts before effecting the adjustments was the audited accounts in such condition as could be formally signed off even after the long stop date of 30 June had passed. I therefore find that pursuant to Paragraph 3 of Part 3 the obligation to provide the draft Deferred Consideration Accounts was within 30 days after the accounts were at the point at which they could be signed off by the Auditors (except where that date fell within the 30 day period immediately prior to 30 June). Accordingly I find that it was not open to the Company to provide draft accounts pursuant to Schedule 11 which were not based on the accounts which were in such condition as could formally be signed off by the Auditors. Thus the accounts provided on 5 August 2019 were not capable of being the "draft Deferred Consideration Accounts" delivered pursuant to Paragraph 3 of the SPA.'

1 [2020] EWHC 501 (Comm) at [61].

10.15 Moulder J also rejected the suggestion that the seller could have 'accepted' the draft accounts as final and binding. She held:[1]

> 'In my view, the defendant having made it clear that the draft accounts provided did not fall within the meaning of Paragraph 3, it was not open to the Sellers by their response and purported notice of 8 August to transform those draft accounts into Deferred Consideration Accounts which were capable of being accepted as final and binding on the parties and which entitled the Sellers to claim the Deferred Consideration as due and payable.'

1 [2020] EWHC 501 (Comm) at [72].

10.16 Although the summary judgment application was unsuccessful on the facts and as a matter of construction, it is clear that in certain circumstances a seller might have a good claim in respect of an earnout amount owing to it under an SPA.

10.17 In *Phoenicks Ltd v Bellrock Property & Facilities & Management Ltd*,[1] the seller of a business brought claims against the buyer for: (i) contingent payments it said were earned and not paid; and (ii) alleged breaches of the business sale agreement and transitional services agreement. The first task for HHJ Davies sitting as a High Court Judge was to construe the contingent payment provisions in the business purchase agreement. The judge described this as 'a difficult task' noting that his 'strong suspicion is that this is because it is the result of legal over-layering of a document produced by business people, where the legal and commercial terms are not always happily married up.'[2] The contingent payments were to comprise both a share of 'Relevant Profits' and 'Costs Savings' for the year in question, and provisions were included for procedures by which proposals to achieve such cost savings were to be dealt with. The parties disagreed on the meaning of both 'Relevant Profits' and 'Cost Savings', as well as the scope of an 'Overriding Principle' and other further aspects of the contingent payment provisions. The judge resolved these issues in accordance with the ordinary principles of contractual construction before turning to deal with the factual disputes.[3] After a detailed consideration of the facts, it was held that the claims asserting that particular costs savings could and should have been achieved if the buyer had acted in accordance with the business sale agreement did not succeed.[4] The claims made in respect of costs savings that the seller said had actually been achieved and were relevant for the purposes of calculating contingent payments due were, however, successful.[5]

1 [2021] EWHC 2639 (Comm).
2 [2021] EWHC 2639 (Comm) at [47].
3 See [44] and [58]–[99].
4 See [214]–[293]. The related claim that the dismissal of a central figure to the seller's business, Mr Smale, without six months' notice, which was said to have significantly hampered the implementation of any 'Cost Savings' and/or realisation of 'Relevant Profits', also failed both on the grounds that: (i) it was not a breach of the duty of good faith or breach of the duty of cooperation; and that (ii) his dismissal had not had the consequences alleged. See [318]–[331]. Further, certain limited claims for breaches of the transitional services agreement were successful. See [337]–[498].
5 See [294]–[316].

Funds in escrow

10.18 Third, a seller may have a claim in respect of part of the purchase price that was paid into escrow which it considers has been wrongly released to the buyer. An example of such a claim is *Bir Holdings Ltd v Mehta*,[1] which was considered in detail at **6.10** above.

1 [2014] EWHC 3903 (Ch).

10.19 In *Bir Holdings,* the SPA had failed to provide any protection for the seller against the buyer making unfounded claims leading to the refund of the part of the purchase price paid into escrow. There was no express or implied term that any relevant claim triggering the return of the funds held in escrow would be accurately calculated or based on factual substance.

10.20 While the facts of *Bir Holdings* are probably unusual, the decision demonstrates that an unjust enrichment claim may assist a seller that finds itself in such a predicament. HHJ Cooke held:

> '[28]. The alternative plea of unjust enrichment is however entirely appropriate to deal with the circumstances of the case. It is necessary for the claimant to show the essential elements of the claim before the court will order restitution on equitable grounds,

namely (a) that a benefit has been conferred on the defendant (b) at the expense of the claimant and (c) that it would be unjust in the circumstances for the defendant to retain it. The first two elements are incontestable; the provisions of the contract have enabled the defendants by putting forward Relevant Claims effectively to pay to themselves money from the Retention Account that would otherwise have been paid to the claimants.

[29]. As to whether retention would be unjust, the claimants in my judgment may show this if, in relation to any of the claims made, either (a) the claimants show that that claim is unjustified, or (b) the defendant withdraws or abandons that claim.'

LOSS OF EARNOUT

10.21 In addition to claims for an earnout or deferred consideration payment that a seller considers to be contractually due, a seller may also have a claim if the purchaser has failed to comply with obligations under the SPA or has breached a warranty with the result that an earnout payment threshold has not been met.

10.22 Two examples of such cases are *Porton Capital Technology Funds v 3M UK Holdings Ltd*[1] and *Kitcatt v MMS UK Holdings Ltd*,[2] which are considered in more detail at **6.30–6.50**.[3]

1 [2011] EWHC 2895 (Comm).
2 [2017] EWHC 675 (Comm).
3 See also *Phoenicks Ltd v Bellrock Property & Facilities & Management Ltd* [2021] EWHC 2639 (Comm), above.

10.23 In *Porton*, the first defendant buyer had acquired the entire share capital of a business for consideration comprising a cash sum and an earnout payment based on the net sales for the calendar year 2009. The business was not successful and was terminated in late 2008.

10.24 The claimant successfully brought a claim alleging that the first defendant had breached its obligations: (i) diligently to seek regulatory approval; and (ii) actively to market the product. In assessing the damages owed to the claimant, Hamblen J determined what the net sales for the calendar year 2009 would have been if the buyer had performed its obligations under the SPA. That figure was then used to determine the earnout payment that would have been payable to the seller.

10.25 In *Kitcatt*, the claimants had sold an advertising agency to the first defendant, which was a subsidiary of the second defendant. The SPA provided for the merger of the claimants' advertising agency with another agency (Digitas) in the second defendant's group to form a new agency. The consideration for the sale comprised an initial cash payment plus deferred consideration to be calculated according to the earnings of the new agency in 2012 and 2013.

10.26 Warranties had been given by the buyer confirming that the buyer and certain named individuals were not aware of any facts or circumstances that could reasonably be expected to have a material adverse impact on operating income and revenue for 2012 or 2013, including the resignation or expected loss of any of the clients of the agency with which the acquired agency was to be merged.

10.27 This warranty was breached by the buyer. Significant changes to the flow of work from the major client of Digitas had been known about by the named individuals at the time the SPA was signed but had not been disclosed. On the facts, a binding settlement had been entered into in respect of the seller's claim, which had been denied by the buyer. Certain adjustments were therefore made to the calculation of the deferred consideration for both 2012 and 2013, resulting in a deferred consideration payment of £2.6 million being due to the sellers.

BREACH OF WARRANTY UNRELATED TO EARNOUT

10.28 In addition to breach of warranty claims that have an impact on an earnout or deferred consideration payment, sellers may have alternative or additional breach of warranty claims.

10.29 In *The Hut Group Ltd v Nobahar-Cookson,*[1] both the seller and the buyer claimed in relation to the value of shares transferred to them as part of the consideration. Under the terms of the SPA, the defendants had transferred their shares in Cend to the claimant buyer, and the buyer had then transferred shares in the combined entity to the second defendant, as well as making a cash payment that was split between the defendants.

1 [2014] EWHC 3842 (QB).

10.30 The second defendant claimed damages for admitted breaches of warranty regarding the buyer's accounts and management accounts in respect of the part of the consideration that consisted of shares in the combined entity and also damages for deceit relating to alleged misrepresentations about the buyer's EBITDA and the state of its audit. The background to these claims was a fraud, only discovered after completion, committed by the Financial Controller who had been manipulating profitability figures and who was subsequently dismissed for gross misconduct.

10.31 In relation to the breach of warranty claim, the only issue concerned the quantification of damages. Blair J set out a clear summary of the principles applicable.[1] He then considered the question of whether the cap on liability in the SPA should apply where the breach of warranty arose from the Financial Controller's fraud. Having considered both the authorities and material facts, he held that the contractual cap did not apply as the breach of warranty did arise from the 'fraud of the buyer'.[2]

1 See [2014] EWHC 3842 (QB), at [179]–[185] and discussion at **8.22** above.
2 See [224]–[286].

10.32 The deceit claim failed on the facts. Blair J considered that one of the emails relied upon could not reasonably have had any reliance placed on it as giving rise to actionable representations in circumstances where any financial warranties agreed by the parties would be given in the SPA.[1] In respect of the second email relied upon, it was held that the representor did honestly believe the statement made.[2]

1 [2014] EWHC 3842 (QB), at [291].
2 At [301].

10.33 The decision in *Chalabi v Jaffar*[1] provides a further example of a breach of warranty claim by a seller which was not in relation to a lost earnout payment. The transaction in the case involved back to back agreements where the claimants sold shares to the defendants and the defendants then sold shares and assets on to a third party (TSYS) on the same day. This was an unusual claim by the first seller alleging that the defendant middle buyer/seller had obtained more from the ultimate buyer than had been warranted in the first SPA.

1 [2011] EWHC 203 (Comm).

10.34 Under the first agreement, the claimant had sold their shares for US$35.5 million. The defendant had sold the shares on to TSYS for US$54.5 million, and also received (along with certain of the underlying businesses) US$3.17 million pursuant to three tax deeds of indemnity in the second SPA.

10.35 The claimants contended that the receipt of the US$3.17 million pursuant to the tax deeds of indemnity amounted to breaches of warranty given by the defendants that: (i) the price of US$35.5 million would amount to three-fifths or more of the sum the defendants would receive from the ultimate third-party buyer; and (ii) the total sum which the defendants and the underlying businesses would receive from the sale of the shares and assets of the underlying businesses was to be US$54.5 million. Accordingly, they brought a claim for breach of warranty for three-fifths of US$3.17 million.

10.36 The claimants also brought an alternative claim in misrepresentation, contending that they were induced to sell their shares in reliance upon misrepresentations in similar terms to the warranties. They sought damages again amounting to 60% of the extra payment. This was on the basis that the claimants would not have sold their shares but for the misrepresentations, and would have held shares best valued by reference to the true amount TSYS paid the defendants.

10.37 Gloster J held at [69] that the payments of US$3.17 million were not shams or devices but rather 'payments made by TSYS with the genuine commercial purpose of compensating and indemnifying the Defendants and the two Card Tech companies for the estimated additional tax that was going to arise, or potentially arose, because of the changed nature of the transaction'.

10.38 She continued (at [75]):

> 'I conclude that it is impossible to characterise the sums received by the Defendants pursuant to the Tax Deeds as part of the "sum" which the Defendants were to "receive for the sale of the entire share capital" of the relevant Card Tech company, or which the Defendants and/or the relevant Card Tech company were to "receive for the sale of the business of" the relevant Card Tech company and/or "for the sale of all or any assets of" the relevant Card Tech company. The sums received pursuant to the Tax Deeds were received for an entirely different purpose – namely to indemnify the Defendants and the relevant Card Tech companies in respect of additional tax liabilities arising out of the restructuring of the deal.'

10.39 The claims therefore failed.

FRAUD CLAIMS

10.40 A seller may in certain circumstances have a fraud claim against a buyer. Such a claim is most likely to arise when the buyer is particularly well informed about the target business, as would be the case in a management buyout.

10.41 An early example of such a case is *Spence v Crawford*[1] in which the House of Lords permitted a vendor of shares to rescind the sale fraudulently misrepresented that the company was in a worse financial state than it truly was.

1 [1939] 3 All ER 271.

10.42 A more modern example with a similar, but more complex, fact pattern is *Vald. Nielsen Holding AS v Baldorino*. As explained by Jacobs J:

> 'This case, involving allegations of fraud, arises out of the sale of a business to its management and private equity investors in July 2009. The courts are familiar with claims made by buyers of businesses

> against sellers who are alleged to have given the buyers far too rosy a picture of the business being sold. The present case is unusual because it is the converse. The basis of the Claimants' claim is that the business being sold was far more successful than the sellers had been led by the management to believe, and that the sellers were misled into selling at the time when they did, and for the price which they received. The sellers contend that if the true picture had been presented to them, they would not have been willing to sell at that time at the price which was being offered.'[1]

1 [2019] EWHC 1926 (Comm).

10.43 The three defendants were the executive management of Updata UK, the target business in question, who bought the business with the backing of a private equity house, LMS. One of the claimants, which through various assignments was claiming in respect of entities which had held a 60% share of Updata UK before the sale, was paid £5.244 million on completion in July 2009 but claimed that the true value of its stake at that time was in fact £22 million. In March 2014, the entire business was again sold for the sum of £80 million.

10.44 The claimants argued that they had been misled in two central ways. Firstly, the defendants had dishonestly represented that a 'Financial Overview' was the latest budget that had been provided to the private equity house when in fact the management's real expectation was for higher figures which could be seen in a different memorandum. Jacobs J held that three relevant representations had been made in this regard:

> 'Accordingly, I conclude that the representations which are material to the case advanced by the Claimants, and which can properly be derived from the 20 April e-mail are as follows:
>
> a) That the figures in the Financial Overview represented the UK management's genuine (and current) forecast of Updata UK's financial position.
>
> b) That the UK management believed that facts existed which reasonably justified the figures included in the Financial Overview.
>
> c) That the projections in the Financial Overview were those which had been provided to LMS by Updata UK's management (just as they had been provided to Mr Homann and Mr Nielsen) and that these were the projections which had been used, in the sense of being considered or evaluated, by LMS in deciding upon their offer.'[1]

1 [2019] EWHC 1926 (Comm) at [185].

10.45 Jacobs J had 'no hesitation in saying that each of the representations made was false',[1] later noting 'it is not the projections contained in the [other documents] which are an aberration, but rather those contained in the Financial Overview'.[2] He also held that Mr Bennett, who had sent the relevant email, both intended to make representations in the terms set out above and had knowingly made the false statements.[3]

1 [2019] EWHC 1926 (Comm) at [205].
2 At [210].
3 At [213].

10.46 Second, the defendants had dishonestly misrepresented various matters in an email and attached presentation in June 2009. Jacobs J held that the following representations were contained in that email:

> 'For essentially the same reasons as set out in the context of the 20 April e-mail, I consider that Mr. Bennett thereby made factual representations that:
>
> i) This forecast in the Updated Kelso Memorandum represented the UK management's genuine (and current) forecast of Updata UK's financial position; and
>
> ii) The UK management believed that facts existed which reasonably justified the figures included in the Updated Kelso Presentation.'[1]

1 [2019] EWHC 1926 (Comm) at [286].

10.47 The figures in the 'Updated Kelso Presentation' were identical to those given in the Financial Overview. Jacobs J therefore held at [287] that 'it was implicit in this representation that there had been no change to the management's expectation since the time that the Financial Overview had been given. Nothing was therefore done to "correct" the prior representations as to management's "middle case".'

10.48 Jacobs J held that '[a]gain, I have no hesitation in saying that the representations were false'. He also held that the defendants intended to make representations in the terms alleged, and that the defendants knew that deliberately false statements were being made.[1]

1 [2019] EWHC 1926 (Comm) at [295]–[298].

10.49 Turning to intention to induce and inducement, Jacobs J held that 'I do not consider that there can be any doubt' that the representor intended that the representee should act upon the representation. He also held that the requirement of inducement was satisfied.[1]

1 [2019] EWHC 1926 (Comm) at [308]–[313].

10.50 The fraudulent misrepresentation case was therefore established, and as Jacobs J noted at [387]:

'These conclusions also mean that the claim in conspiracy also succeeds, although (as the Defendants' written opening submissions contemplated) it adds nothing to the successful claim in deceit.'[1]

1 [2019] EWHC 1926 (Comm) at [553]–[567].

10.51 In conclusion on causation, Jacobs J held at [511]:

'I consider that all of these factors would naturally have had the effect of driving the price offered for the shares towards their true market value rather than the price offered by LMS, which (for reasons discussed in Section I below) was substantially below their true value. Accordingly, I do not accept that, if there had been no misrepresentations, the best offer on the table at the end of June would have been the LMS offer. It seems to me that this is a necessary premise of the Defendants' argument on causation; namely that Updata Europe would have accepted the LMS offer in any event. The argument assumes that the effect of the misrepresentations was to change nothing in terms of how matters would have progressed. In my view, however, if the true position had been known, matters would simply not have progressed as they did. The misrepresentations themselves, for reasons already given, provide an evidentiary weapon, and in my view a powerful evidentiary weapon, in support of this conclusion. It necessarily follows that the Defendants' case on causation fails.'

10.52 In assessing damages, Jacobs J took into account his finding that Updata Europe would have to have sold Updata UK due to financial pressures it was facing. He therefore considered it appropriate to consider the chances of the sales achieving the true value of the shares, and to apply a discount of 25% to reflect the uncertainty of doing so.[1]

1 [2019] EWHC 1926 (Comm) at [553]–[567].

10.53 In addition to the fraud and conspiracy claims brought by the first claimant, both claimants also pursued claims for breach of fiduciary duties owed by the management team to the shareholders. This claim, however, failed. After a lengthy consideration of the authorities, Jacobs J held at [747] that:

'I consider that the facts of the present case are a long way from the circumstances of other cases where a fiduciary relationship has been held to exist, and that there are no special circumstances in the present case which replicate the established categories of fiduciary relationships.'

10.54 Such claims may, however, arise in principle, and should be borne in mind by sellers facing similar conduct by management buyers, especially if the circumstances are similar to those instances in which fiduciary duties between directors and shareholders can be held to exist as summarised by Nugee J in *Sharp v Blank*:

> '… But the relationship between directors and shareholders is not in general like that. A director is a fiduciary for his company: by agreeing to act as director, he necessarily agrees to act in the interests of the company. But he does not have, by virtue of his appointment as director, any direct relationship with the shareholders: no doubt the interests of the shareholders and the company are in general aligned but this does not mean that a director has agreed to act for the individual shareholders or has a direct relationship with them – his relationship is with the company. If he is to be held to owe fiduciary duties to the individual shareholders, there must be something unusual in the nature of the relationship which gives rise to it. That no doubt explains why the cases where such a duty has been held to exist mostly concern companies which are small and closely held, where there is often a family or other personal relationship between the parties, and where, in almost all cases, there is a particular transaction involved in which directors are dealing with the shareholders, from which the directors often stand to benefit personally. The imposition of a fiduciary duty in such circumstances reflects the fact that directors who have a close family or other personal relationship with shareholders, and are entering into transactions with them, may be tempted to exploit that relationship to take unfair advantage of the shareholders for their own benefit.'[1]

1 [2015] EWHC 3220 (Ch) at [13].

OTHER POTENTIAL CLAIMS AGAINST THE BUYER

10.55 While the claims considered above are likely to be the most common claims that sellers have against buyers, the specific circumstances of a given transaction could give rise to a wide range of other claims.

10.56 One example of a highly fact specific claim was the counterclaim introduced shortly before trial was due to commence in *Slater and Gordon (UK) 1 Ltd v Watchstone Group Plc*.[1] S&G claimed against Watchstone for damages for alleged deceit and breaches of warranty in relation to the purchase by it from Watchstone of all the shares in a large scale personal injury litigation business in 2015.

1 [2019] EWHC 2371 (Comm).

10.57 At or around the time of the transaction, both parties had engaged a number of third-party advisers. One of the firms advising S&G in respect of the transaction was Greenhill. Watchstone had announced to the market in

December 2014 that cash receipts were lower than expected in the final quarter and it had engaged PwC to carry out an independent review of the business.

10.58 Third party disclosure from Greenhill was provided to Watchstone in July 2019. As explained by Bryan J at [19]:

> 'In the course of reviewing Greenhill's disclosure, thus provided, Watchstone came across a series of email exchanges which Watchstone say shows that Greenhill had established, on behalf of and for the benefit of its principal, S&G, a secret back-channel with PwC ("the PwC back-channel"), by which it obtained confidential information in relation to [the target company] Quindell, not least PwC's view as to the time at which it would run out of cash. The emails in question are set out and quoted from in detail in the draft counterclaim.'

10.59 In particular, Watchstone alleged that a representative of Greenhill had arranged to meet with a contact of his at PwC who he described as the 'lead partner advising Quindell', and that the Greenhill representative then fed then information he obtained back to the Greenhill team advising S&G. Watchstone claimed both that S&G was responsible for its agent but also that there was evidence of direct knowledge and authorisation on the part of S&G's management.

10.60 The amendments Watchstone sought permission to make comprised: (i) amendments to the defence to include reference to these matters in respect of reliance and inducement and to make a plea of equitable set-off; and (ii) a counterclaim against S&G for damages for: (a) breach of confidence; (b) inducing a breach of contract; and (c) conspiracy.

10.61 Bryan J concluded that there was a real prospect of success in relation to each of the amendments sought and granted permission for those amendments to be made.

10.62 The claims pursued by both sides were settled in their entirety shortly before trial was due to start, and so no there was no determination on the merits of the claim or counterclaim.

10.63 A further example of a fact specific counterclaim brought by a seller against a buyer can be seen in *Invertec Ltd v De Mol Holdings BV*.[1] In that case, the defendants denied the claims against them for fraud and misrepresentation in respect of various warranties included in the SPA, and advanced counterclaims for sums it claimed were outstanding under a management services agreement and a consultancy agreement. The consultancy agreement was terminated as part of the acquisition, but as at the date of the SPA, the target business owed the defendant certain sums under it. Liability for those sums was said by the defendants to have been novated to Invertec by an exchange of emails.

1 [2009] EWHC 2471 (Ch).

10.64 At the end of the judgment in which Arnold J had found the defendants to be liable for fraudulent misrepresentation, he turned to the counterclaims. Dealing with these shortly, he noted that the claimant did not dispute that the relevant sum was due under the management services agreement but that the sums owed but not paid were extinguished by circularity of action. He also determined that the relevant exchange of emails did not constitute a novation agreement, and the claimant was not liable for the sum owed by the target business.

10.65 A further type of claim by a seller can be seen in the counterclaim in *Sycamore Bidco Ltd v Breslin*.[1] In that case, the SPA and related agreements referred to as 'LTIPs' provided for certain individuals to be paid a sum on the future sale of the GAS business. These payments when made by the target business entitled the GAS to tax relief in respect of them and the buyer had agreed in the SPA to pay any such tax relief to the sellers as additional consideration.[2]

1 [2012] EWHC 3443 (Ch).
2 At [470].

10.66 The sellers' case was that all the steps triggering their right to payment of this additional consideration had occurred. The individuals had been paid the LTIPs payments, the payments were included in the corporation tax returns for the relevant year and relief had been obtained.

10.67 The buyer resisted the claim on the basis that the amount of its warranty claims needed to be taken into account in determining its liability to make the LTIPs payments. It asserted that although it had made the LTIPs payments in full, its obligation to make LTIPs payments was in the following terms:

> 'In the event of any such disposal you will be entitled to a payment equal to [x] % of the net sale proceeds. Net sale proceeds for this purpose is the consideration actually received by the shareholders of the Company or the Company for the sale of the shares/assets as the case may be for the disposal less all costs. Costs will include legal and advisors fees, any compensation payments to Liberata UK Limited and any other direct transaction costs. Consideration would include all proceeds on completion (either in cash or any other form) plus any deferred consideration when achieved *less any successful claims for warranties under the legal disposal agreement*' (emphasis added).[1]

1 [2012] EWHC 3443 (Ch) at [471].

10.68 The buyer therefore claimed that it had overpaid the recipients of the LTIPs payments and that they would have to be informed of the overpayments and the position rectified before any payment should be required.

10.69 The sellers' claims, however, succeeded in full on the basis that the terms of the SPA required the payment of the sum claimed, without prejudice to possible recoupment under the general law if the tax relief obtained fell to be adjusted downwards. Mann J held:

> 'In my view the provision is tightly regulated as to obligations and dates, and it does not have built into it the sort of flexibility which would be required in order to allow a deemed unscrambling of the amount of the LTIPs payments and the amount of the relief for the purposes of determining entitlement. The key is what relief has been obtained. If relief has been obtained then the obligation to pay the LTIPs payment to the sellers arises, and it arises in that amount. [Counsel's] point, that until the warranty claims were sorted out it was not known what payments were made "pursuant to the LTIPs" does not work for her. First, one knows what payments were made pursuant to the LTIPs. What one does not know is whether and to what extent those claims fall to be repaid. Second, as I have just indicated, the key is the amount of Relief, and one knows the amount of the Relief and one knows that it was obtained.'[1]

1 [2012] EWHC 3443 (Ch) at [483].

10.70 Further, the SPA had expressly excluded any right of set-off that the buyer may have had and Mann J could '*see no reason why that should not operate strictly in accordance with its terms*'. The provisions of the SPA and other transaction agreements will therefore guide the application of set-off principles and any claims that the seller may have to payment under that agreement.

10.71 In addition to claims against the buyer, sellers may also have claims against each other for contribution. Contribution claims are governed by the Civil Liability (Contribution) Act 1978, which provides:

> 1(1). Subject to the following provisions of this section, any person liable in respect of any damage suffered by another person may recover contribution from any other person liable in respect of the same damage (whether jointly with him or otherwise).
>
> …
>
> 1(3). A person shall be liable to make contribution by virtue of subsection (1) above notwithstanding that he has ceased to be liable in respect of the damage in question since the time when the damage occurred, unless he ceased to be liable by virtue of the expiry of a period of limitation or prescription which extinguished the right on which the claim against him in respect of the damage was based.
>
> 1(4). A person who has made or agreed to make any payment in bona fide settlement or compromise of any claim made against him in

respect of any damage … shall be entitled to recover a contribution in accordance with this section …

…

2(1). … the amount of the contribution [under section 1] recoverable from any person shall be such as may be found by the court to be just and equitable having regard to that person's responsibility for the damage in question.

…

2(3). Where the amount of the damages which have or might have been awarded in respect of the damage in question in any action brought in England and Wales by or on behalf of the person who suffered it against the person from whom the contribution is sought was or would have been subject to — (a) any limit imposed … … by any agreement made before the damage occurred;

…

the person from whom the contribution is sought shall not by virtue of any contribution awarded under section 1 above be required to pay in respect of the damage a greater amount than the amount of those damages as so limited or reduced.

10.72 It is important to note s 2(1), which provides for the court to apportion liability on the basis considered by the court to be 'just and equitable', and any claim will therefore turn on its own facts.

10.73 Where claims are brought against multiple sellers, it will usually be prudent for the sellers to claim contribution from the other under the Civil Liability (Contribution) Act 1978. An example of this approach can be seen in *Downs v Chappell*.[1] The first instance judge dismissed the claimant's claim but nonetheless expressed a view on apportionment. This was then upheld by the Court of Appeal, which had found that the defendants were liable to the claimants.

1 [1997] 1 WLR 426 at 445B.

10.74 SPAs should usually make clear whether the liability of multiple sellers is joint and several or only several (and whether there are any caps on the individual liability of a seller) but that does not resolve questions concerning apportionment as between sellers.

10.75 By way of example, in *Demco Investment and Commercial SA v Interamerican Life Assurance (International) Ltd*,[1] the third defendant, GDH, sought contribution from the other defendants in respect of sums which it had paid out in respect of claims for breaches of warranties contained in an SPA for the sale of shares in Interlife.

1 [2012] EWHC 2053 (Comm).

10.76 *Sellers' Claims*

10.76 The SPA had contained a number of clauses relevant to the potential liabilities of the individual seller, which were explained in the judgment as follows:

> 'There were other key provisions of the Purchase Agreement:
>
> a) various representations and warranties were given by the Sellers (as defined in the Purchase Agreement) in Article 7;
>
> b) Article 10.03(b) contained the following limitation of liability provision:
>
> "The liability of each Seller shall be limited to the higher of an amount equal to (A) one-third (1/3) of the Purchase Price and (B) the product of the Purchase Price multiplied by a fraction, the numerator of which shall be the number of Shares sold by the Seller and the denominator shall be the total number of all Shares sold hereunder; provided, however, that with respect to each Seller who is not a corporate entity, the liability shall be limited as provided in paragraph (B) hereof.
>
> For the purposes of this paragraph 10.03(b), the Purchase Price shall include the Additional Price I and the Additional Price II to the extent any amount with respect thereto shall have been paid, become payable or been deposited to the First Account at the time of the discharge by the Seller of any claim hereunder."
>
> c) Article 10.04 narrowed the scope of the limitation provision as follows:
>
> "The provisions of Section 10.03 hereof shall not apply and the breaching party shall be fully liable with regard to any Claim arising from fraud, wilful misconduct or gross negligence by the breaching party, or by the Company as regards the Sellers' liability".
>
> d) Article 10.05 stated that:
>
> "The Sellers shall, subject to the limitation provided for in Section 10.03(b) hereof, have joint and several liability with regard to any Claim by the Buyer under this Agreement … ."'

10.77 An arbitration was commenced by the sellers in respect of unpaid elements of the purchase price, and a counterclaim was brought by the buyer in relation to pensions mis-selling claims that had only come to light after completion.

10.78 GDH reached a bilateral settlement with the buyer, which included a total liability figure of £21 million plus interest, plus costs. The £21 million figure was broken down to include a 'gross negligence' and a 'non-gross negligence' component. GDH paid a total sum of over £26 million to settle the claims, and no other party had made any contribution.

10.79 The arbitration continued against the other parties, and an interim award was produced which provided for further liabilities on part of the remaining defendant sellers (deductions having been made to reflect the sums already paid by GDH).

10.80 GDH brought a claim seeking declarations in respect of the liability for other defendants to contribute to the sum it had paid by way of settlement. Christopher Clarke J held that he was 'quite satisfied' that the GDH settlement was reasonable in amount, applying the approach in *Biggin & Co v Permanite,*[1] but a number of issues remained, including as to: (i) the proportion in which the sellers should contribute; and (ii) whether GDH was liable to contribute to the other parties in respect of their liability to SEB arising from the arbitration award.[2]

1 [1951] 2 KB 314.
2 For a full list of issues see [49].

10.81 In relation to the sharing of the gross negligence liabilities, Christopher Clarke J was clear at [59] that this should be done in proportion to shareholdings. This was the basis on which the sellers stood to gain from the sale, and had been agreed by all by one of the sellers.

10.82 In relation to the sharing of non-gross negligence liabilities, Christopher Clarke J held at [62]:

> 'In relation to these liabilities the position is more complicated. Liability for these is capped. The cap is not in proportion to percentage shareholding. For the corporate parties it is 1/3 of the Purchase Price and their shareholdings range from 9.62% to 30.68%. The cap is a limit on the liability of the sellers to SEB. It should not necessarily determine the just and equitable method of contribution as between the Sellers themselves. The sum of the caps is £6,550,756. If the amount recovered by the Sellers in respect of principal is less than that figure it seems to me that the Sellers should, as between themselves, contribute, as the order contemplates, in proportion to their shareholdings provided that no Seller ends up paying more than his cap. It would not be just and equitable, as between the Sellers, for Demco (9.62%) and Trygg-Hansa (14.89%), say, to end up paying the same amount as Interamerican (30.68%). If the amount recovered equals the aggregate of the caps there is no room for reallocation because Section 2 (3) requires that the Sellers shall not by way of contribution be required to pay more than their cap in respect of principal liability.'

10.83 Christopher Clarke J also noted that the consent order among many of the parties reflected the general principle that '[w]here a contributing party is, or may be, unable to contribute his full share of the liability, the Court should take this into account when considering how to allocate liability between the parties, and may allocate that party's unpaid liability amongst the others',[1] reflecting the statement of Lord Millett in *Dubai Aluminium Co Ltd v Salaam*.[2]

1 At [63].
2 [2002] UKHL 48.

10.84 Turning to the question of whether GBH was liable to contribute to the further liabilities to SEB owed by the other sellers, Christopher Clarke J held at [68]:

> 'But it seems to me neither just nor equitable that GDH, having made all the running in promoting and paying for a settlement in which all the other parties could have joined, should now have to contribute to the excess sum, together with further interest and costs which are going to have to be paid under the Award. The effect of not settling is that SEB will have been awarded compensation in relation to over £2.8 million extra in respect of gross negligence liabilities and an additional sum for other liabilities. Further liabilities have arisen in respect of interest and costs. These could have been avoided if those who have now in effect settled by the joint submission and/or are the subject of the Award had joined in the earlier settlement. No sound reason for holding out has been proffered.'

Chapter 11

Litigation Issues

INTRODUCTION

11.01 The litigation issues that arise in relation to claims for fraud and breach of warranty arising from business sales share a lot in common with other commercial disputes. This chapter aims to identify particular issues relevant to fraud and breach of warranty claims but does not endeavour to provide a comprehensive overview of commercial litigation procedure and strategy.

DISPUTE FORUM

Contractual provisions may impose restrictions

11.02 When disputes arise relating to a business sale, the first step will be to consider whether the contract itself imposes any restriction on the proper mechanism for redress. Different mechanisms may be agreed depending on the subject matter of the dispute. Such provisions may include jurisdiction or arbitration clauses, the detail of which is outside the scope of this work, but may also include the referral of matters to professional experts.

11.03 For example, in *Edward Campbell v Océ (UK) Ltd*,[1] the court upheld a provision requiring disputes regarding the completion balance statement to be referred to an accountancy firm in London appointed by the President of the Institute of Chartered Accountants of England and Wales within two months of the notification of such a dispute. The mechanism agreed had been intended to ensure a 'quick and fairly reliable way of resolving disputes as to the [completion balance statement]' and accordingly, this aspect of the sellers' claim relating to the completion balance was struck out.

1 [2005] EWHC 458 (Ch). See also [**2.59**].

11.04 In *General Electric Company v Al Alpine US Bidco Inc*,[1] the court stayed Part 8 proceedings that had been commenced by the seller relating to an expert determination process concerning a completion statement and payment. The SPA had set out a process by which disputes relating to the completion statement were to be referred to an accountancy firm if agreement could not be reached within 30 days. Certain of the disputes relating to the completion statement also raised issues concerning the historic accounting decisions and judgments of the target company. The claimant's position was that disputes concerning such historic accounting decisions could not properly be raised as part of the closing statement process but only through warranty claims. Through Part 8 proceedings, it sought declarations to this effect. Miles J held, however, that these proceedings should be stayed pending the conclusion of the expert determination process. Drawing heavily on the principles set out in *Mercury Communications Ltd v Director General of Telecommunications*,[2] he held that the issue of whether the accountants could scrutinise the historical accounting treatments formed part of the accountant's decision-making authority (rather than its jurisdiction). While the parties agreed that the accountant's approach in this regard could be scrutinised by the court, the issues between the parties were hypothetical pending the decision of the accountants (and certain input they had sought concerning legal questions from independent counsel). This was an important factor in his finding that the proceedings should be stayed pending the expert determination.[3]

1 [2021] EWHC 45 (Ch). See also [**2.60**].
2 [1994] CLC 1125.
3 See [34]–[46], with five further factors relating to the 'interests of justice' that supported a stay found at [48]–[56].

PLEADING CLAIMS

A deceit claim should be the primary claim

11.05 Where claims are to be brought in deceit as well as other causes of actions such as breach of warranty or negligent or innocent misrepresentation, the deceit claim should normally be the primary claim, and should therefore be pleaded first.[1]

1 Although the analogy is not exact when it comes to breach of warranty, at least in relation to fraudulent and negligent misrepresentation, the dictum of May LJ from *Lipkin Gorman v Karpnale* [1989] 1 WLR 1340 at 1352 applies: 'If it is desired to allege and plead fraud and, in the alternative, negligence based on similar contentions, then the former must be pleaded first and clearly and the relevant part of the plea confined to the fraud. The allegation in negligence can then be pleaded separately and as a true alternative contention.'

11.06 An example of a primary deceit claim taking precedence over other causes of action can be seen in *Invertec Ltd v De Mol Holding BV*.[1] Invertec's primary claim was that it had been induced to acquire the entire share capital of the target business by a number of fraudulent representations made by the defendants which had become warranties in the SPA. In the alternative, Invertec advanced claims for negligent misstatement and under the Misrepresentation Act 1967, s 2(1). Invertec also pursued a separate claim under a side agreement forming part of the transaction, referred to as the Tax Deed.

1 [2009] EWHC 2471 (Ch).

11.07 The fraud claim was established. In respect of the Tax Deed claim, Arnold J held that:

> 'I conclude that, subject to the effect of the fraud claim, DMH would be liable to Invertec under the Tax Deed in the sum of £37,000. For the reasons given below, however, Invertec would not have entered into the Tax Deed if the fraudulent misrepresentations had not been made. Accordingly, Invertec has no, or at any rate no separate, claim under the Tax Deed.'[1]

1 At [352].

11.08 Similarly, in respect of the misrepresentation and misstatement claims, Arnold J held that he did not need to consider these alternative claims given that the fraud claim was made out.[1]

1 At [388].

11.09 An unusual example of a claim where deceit was alleged as a secondary claim to breach of warranty was the seller's claim in *The Hut Group v Nobahar-Cookson*.[1] The background to the seller's claims was a fraud, undiscovered at the time of completion, committed by the Financial Controller who had been manipulating profitability figures and who was subsequently dismissed. In light of this, liability for the breach of warranty claim was admitted. The deceit claim, however, reduced in scope over the course of the trial and was ultimately limited to two alleged representations. The claim was unsuccessful on both counts. Given the fraudulent backdrop, however, Blair J disapplied a cap on liability for breach of warranty given the breach had arisen from the 'fraud of the buyer' and so the financial outcome was unaffected.

1 [2014] EWHC 3842 (QB) at [178]. See further at [**10.28**].

11.10 In general, however, a deceit claim should be the primary claim.

Adequate particularisation required

11.11 Parties pleading claims for breach of warranty and, particularly, fraud must ensure that their case is adequately particularised, and should endeavour to do so in the particulars of claim rather than by reference to one or more separate schedules which require the defendant and court to consider different documents in order to understand the claim.[1] The principles regarding the pleading of fraud are found in speech of Lord Millett in *Three Rivers DC v Bank of England*.[2]

1 See for example the criticisms of HHJ Eyre QC in *Scott v Singh* [2020] EWHC 1714 (Comm), in particular at [27].
2 [2001] UKHL 16 at [183]–[189].

Blaming the buyer

11.12 A defendant seller will often deny that there has been any breach of warranty and look to blame the buyer for the poor performance of the target business after acquisition. Even in a case of fraudulent misrepresentation, such arguments are often run to try to stem the recoverability of loss. See for example the discussion of *MAN v Freightliner* at **8.78** above.

A clear summary of a classic argument to this effect was summarised by Arnold J in *Invertec,* who explained that:

> 'The Defendants contend that Volante's financial difficulties after its acquisition by Invertec were not due its having a cash hole at the date of acquisition, but rather due to losses sustained as a result of the integration of ITS with Volante. The Defendants say that almost immediately after acquisition resources were diverted from Volante's business to that of ITS, in particular to deal with a contract to supply a bus interior to Singapore. Furthermore, they point out that Volante's sales in the final quarter were well below budget, and suggest that this was attributable to the same cause. Finally, they say that under Invertec's management good staff were lost and replaced by unsuitable ones.'[1]

1 At [306]. For a further example, see *Triumph Controls – UK Ltd v Primus International Holding Company* [2019] EWHC 565 (TCC) at [237].

11.13 Whether such an argument will succeed will depend on the facts but particular factors likely to be considered include: (i) how quickly after completion matters seem to have started to deteriorate; and (ii) the trends of the business.[1] If the seller is able to attribute the poor performance of the business to the buyer's conduct this may have an impact on issues such as causation, mitigation of loss and the availability of rescission as a remedy.

1 See, eg, the discussion in *Invertec* [2009] EWHC 2471 (Ch) at [307]–[322].

FREEZING INJUNCTIONS

11.14 A particular issue arises in the context of the sale of a business because the parties to the sale may well restructure post-transaction or make distributions to its shareholders. The key question here is whether an intention to make distributions will amount to a 'real risk of dissipation' so as to justify a freezing order. It should be recalled that for this purpose, dissipation means something unjustified, not amounting to conduct in the ordinary course of business.

11.15 In the absence of direct authority, an analogy can be drawn with a decision from the Court of Appeal of the Cayman Islands in the context of applications for freezing injunctions pending the outcome of statutory fair value appraisal proceedings brought by 'dissenting shareholders' following a merger.[1]

1 *In the matter of Trina Solar Ltd,* Court of Appeal of the Cayman Islands CICA 26 of 2017, 9 February 2018.

11.16 The dissenting shareholders alleged that the company had entered into post-merger transactions which had the effect of transferring away all of its valuable assets and that it also intended to transfer away the proceeds of the merger with the result that insufficient assets would be left to satisfy any judgment obtained by the dissenting shareholders.

11.17 The first instance judge considered that the restructuring and distribution issues went both to whether there was a real risk of dissipation and whether it would be just and convenient to grant the injunction. He went on to hold that the company could justifiably complete the post-merger restructuring and distribute the proceeds so long as any restructuring transactions were on terms that meant the company received fair value for its assets and proper provision was made against the dissenting shareholders' claims.

11.18 This decision was upheld by the Court of Appeal of the Cayman Islands. Martin JA stressed that the provision to be made in respect of the outstanding claim by the dissenting shareholders had to be 'proper'. It was explained that:

> '... That means that the risk that the fair value ultimately awarded to the Dissenting Shareholders will substantially exceed the merger price must be fully taken into account, and the general approach must be balanced and cautious and formulated after taking full financial and legal advice ….'

11.19 This decision strikes an appropriate balance between permitting restructuring and distribution in the normal course and protecting a claimant. If the claimant can show a real risk that the relevant assets will be distributed or otherwise moved out of the defendant company, then the defendant will need to reassure the court that any distribution will be made only on an appropriate basis as to providing for the potential liability. This may not offer the claimant full security, but it recognises that the proper function of the freezing injunction jurisdiction is not to provide security, but to restrain unjustified dissipation.

SPLIT TRIAL

11.20 Breach of warranty and related fraud claims often lend themselves to consideration of the possibility of a split trial.

11.21 If there is a dispute about notification, it will often be appropriate for that to be considered as a preliminary issue given it may provide a complete answer to the claim. Examples of cases where claims were foreclosed by findings against a claimant on a preliminary issue include *ROK Plc v S Harrison Group Ltd*[1] and *Ener-G Holdings v Hormell.*[2] Similarly, notification issues may also be addressed early on by way of a strike out application.[3]

1 [2011] EWHC 270 (Comm).
2 [2012] EWCA Civ 1059. See further at [**5.100**] ff.
3 See, eg, *Zayo Group International Ltd v Ainger* [2017] EWHC 2542 (Comm) and *Ipsos SA v Dentsu Aegis Network Ltd* [2015] EWHC 1171 (Comm).

11.22 A further natural split will often fall between liability and quantum.[1]

1 See, eg, *Belfairs Management Ltd v Sutherland* [2010] EWHC (Ch) 2276.

11.23 The utility of considering splitting the questions of liability and quantum can be seen in the decision of HHJ Hodge QC (sitting as a High Court Judge) in *Glossop Cartons and Print Ltd v Contact (Print & Packaging) Ltd.*[1] Although the expert evidence had been finalised in that case, the trial window appears to have been inadequate and therefore the defendant suggested that the expert evidence on quantum should be deferred to a later hearing. HHJ Hodge QC noted:

> 'On the morning of Day 1 of the trial, at the invitation of Mr Lander (and without opposition from Mr Dagnall, who declared his stance to be neutral on the issue) I ruled that consideration of the expert evidence should be deferred to a future hearing after the court had made its findings of fact on liability and causation. During his closing submissions, Mr Dagnall acknowledged that, in the circumstances (and not least because it would have been impossible to shoe-horn the expert evidence into the time allotted for the trial), it had been immensely helpful to have split the trial in this way. He submitted (and I accept) that at this stage I should deal with issues of principle and the correct approach to damages so that the expert accountants will know what more is required of them but not with individual items of damage. I made it clear during closing speeches that I would regard any findings in this judgment on matters touched upon in the expert accountancy evidence as provisional only and open to re-consideration in the light of that evidence (and any further expert accountancy evidence that may be appropriate in the light of my findings).'[2]

1 [2019] EWHC 2314 (Ch).
2 At [26].

11.24 It is obviously preferable, however, for a sensible split of issues to be considered in advance of trial, and it may be that the costs of the later stages can be avoided if settlement could be reached once questions of liability are determined. The need for a further hearing may also be avoided if the experts cooperate on an ongoing basis.[1] However, in some cases, issues about post acquisition management of the business can be said to be relevant to both liability and quantum so as to make a split trial harder to achieve efficiently.

1 See, eg, *The Hut Group Ltd v Nobahar-Cookson* [2014] EWHC 3842 (QB) at [10].

11.25 The parties should also consider whether a pragmatic approach would be to defer particular aspects of the quantum issues which are likely to require costly expert evidence. For example, in *Next Generation Holdings v Finch*,[1] Zacaroli J had ordered at the PTR that the specific issue of the actual value of the relevant shares be dealt with only following the main trial on liability and other quantum issues.

1 [2023] EWHC 2383 (Ch) at [135]–[139].

11.26 A party considering whether to seek a split trial would be well advised to consider the thorough analysis of the considerations a court will bear in mind when determining whether a split trial should be ordered given by Peter MacDonald Eggers KC sitting as a Deputy High Court Judge in *Jinxin Inc v Aser Media Pte Ltd*.[1] The nine factors identified in particular were:

> '(1) Whether the prospective advantage of saving the costs of an investigation of the issues to be determined at a second trial if the determination of the first trial renders it unnecessary to determine such issues outweighs the likelihood of increased aggregate costs if a further trial is necessary.
>
> (2) What are likely to be the advantages and disadvantages in terms of trial preparation and management?
>
> (3) Whether a split trial will impose unnecessary inconvenience and strain on witnesses who may be required in both trials.
>
> (4) Whether a single trial to deal with all issues will lead to excessive complexity and diffusion of issues, or place an undue burden on the Judge hearing the case.
>
> (5) Whether a split may cause particular prejudice to one or more of the parties (for example by delaying any ultimate award of compensation or damages).
>
> (6) Whether there are difficulties of defining an appropriate split or whether a clean split is possible.
>
> (7) What weight is to be given to the risk of duplication, delay and the disadvantage of a bifurcated appellate process?
>
> (8) Generally, what is perceived to offer the best course to ensure that the whole matter is adjudicated as fairly, quickly and efficiently as possible?

(9) Whether a split trial would assist or discourage mediation and/or settlement.'

1 [2022] EWHC 2431 (Comm) at [18]–[26]. The nine factors are identified at [22].

11.27 In that case, the application proposed a three stage trial. It was proposed the issues would be dealt with in the following stages: (i) the identification of the representations made, their meaning, the buyer's awareness of the representations and the buyer's reliance on the representations; (ii) the falsity of the representations, the knowledge and intention of the defendants and the defendants' responsibility for the representations; and (iii) remedies and quantum. On balance, having weighed up the considerations on the specific facts of the case, the split trial application was dismissed.[1] The judge did, however, invite the parties to consider whether a more traditional split between liability and quantum might be appropriate.

1 [2022] EWHC 2431 (Comm) at [30]–[54].

DISCLOSURE

Post-acquisition documents

11.28 Sellers will usually seek to ensure that post-acquisition documents form part of disclosure. Documents from after the completion date may assist a seller in several ways.

11.29 First, statutory accounts of the buyer post-dating completion might be useful in contradicting the claimant buyer's quantum claim. An argument of this sort can be seen in the *Senate* case.[1] Considering the treatment of goodwill in the buyer's accounts, the claimant buyer's 'massive claim' was said by the defendants to be 'quite inconsistent with the treatment in the accounts'.

1 [1999] 2 Lloyds Rep 423.

11.30 Reliance on the buyer's accounts can be a useful argument as it is difficult for a buyer to disclaim their accounts which may have been signed by directors and audited. As Stuart-Smith LJ held at [72]:

> 'We do not think that the accounts create any statutory estoppel, though it hardly lies in the mouths of the directors or auditors of Senate to say that their accounts were wrong having regard to their statutory duties. And indeed they did not say so. We think the treatment in the accounts can be reconciled with a modest difference in the price for the goodwill. But it is very questionable whether a 25 per cent reduction was modest.'

11.31 Second, as noted above, sellers may want to blame the buyer for the fact that the acquired business has not been a success. In advance of having strong evidence for this, sellers may plead a fairly weak case on causation in order to obtain access to this material in the hope that they may yield useful material in defending the claim.

Advisers' documents

11.32 In addition to post-completion disclosure, it may also be helpful for sellers to seek disclosure of documents from the buyer's advisers. If agreement cannot be reached between the parties, the party seeking third party disclosure may have to bear the costs of that disclosure exercise.

11.33 In some cases, this may be necessary because of the apparent sparsity of documents retained by the buyer itself.[1]

1 See, eg, *Belfairs Management Ltd v Sutherland* [2010] EWHC (Ch) at [17].

11.34 Adviser documents may also be necessary where misrepresentations are alleged to have been made to the buyer through its advisers, or relevant matters are said to have been disclosed to the buyer's advisers. Records of what material was provided to the advisers or meetings held between the sellers and the advisers may provide important evidence of the true factual position.

11.35 Advisers' documents may assist either party. For example, they may show that advisers were aware from disclosure of risks concerning the matters complained of by sellers. In more unusual circumstances, they may reveal matters that give rise to counterclaims by sellers.[1]

1 See above at [**10.55**] for an example.

Investigation documents

11.36 A further source of documents that may be sought are documents relating to regulatory investigations into either the buyer, the seller or the acquired business that relate to the claims being advanced. Parties may want to obtain documents from regulators where there have been related investigations into the business, for example by the company itself, the Financial Reporting Council or the Serious Fraud Office.

11.37 While certain documents such as decisions may be available in the public domain, others may be privileged or subject to statutory restrictions, and the party that they concern may be unwilling to waive privilege unless their contents are considered advantageous to the disclosing party. This is, however, a potential source of useful material that should be borne in mind.

WITNESS EVIDENCE

11.38 Many of the normal considerations of witness evidence will apply equally in the context of a claim for breach of warranty and/or fraud. For example, the dicta of Leggatt J in *Gestmin SGPS SA v Credit Suisse (UK) Ltd*[1] regarding the reliability of witnesses' memories are as applicable to such claims as to any other commercial case.

1 [2013] EWHC 3560 (Comm) at [15]–[23].

11.39 Although some breach of warranty disputes may benefit from notification periods which are shorter than the usual limitation periods, a significant amount of time may well have elapsed before trial. Accordingly, as Leggatt J explained at [22]:

> 'In the light of these considerations, the best approach for a judge to adopt in the trial of a commercial case is, in my view, to place little if any reliance at all on witnesses' recollections of what was said in meetings and conversations, and to base factual findings on inferences drawn from the documentary evidence and known or probable facts. This does not mean that oral testimony serves no useful purpose – though its utility is often disproportionate to its length. But its value lies largely, as I see it, in the opportunity which cross-examination affords to subject the documentary record to critical scrutiny and to gauge the personality, motivations and working practices of a witness, rather than in testimony of what the witness recalls of particular conversations and events. Above all, it is important to avoid the fallacy of supposing that, because a witness has confidence in his or her recollection and is honest, evidence based on that recollection provides any reliable guide to the truth.'

11.40 A further difficulty with witness evidence in SPA disputes is that, as a result of both the passage of time and the common restructuring of businesses after sale, relevant personnel may have moved on and may be unwilling to become embroiled in litigation unrelated to their current situation.

11.41 The flip side of this is that some factual witnesses who are engaged with the proceedings may have a personal interest in the outcome of the litigation. For example, in a dispute concerning entitlement to an earnout or escrow payment, former shareholders of the target will have a direct financial interest in the outcome but may also be the individuals who were involved in negotiating the sale or who remain in management roles following the transaction.[1]

1 See by way of example the discussion of the witness evidence in *Phoenicks Ltd v Bellrock Property & Management Facilities Ltd* [2021] EWHC 2639 (Comm) at [8]–[25].

11.42 A further point that should be borne in mind in relation to witness evidence is the effect on a witness's credibility of any statements made by the same individual that were less than candid in the course of the transaction, even if not giving rise to a claim. An example of this can be seen in the *Belfairs* case, where Norris J held at [22]:

> 'That is not to say that I accept that his direct answers were invariably true. It was amply demonstrated to my satisfaction that at times when Waveform faced cash flow difficulties Mr Sutherland lied to creditors about the reasons they were not paid. In the witness box he was resistant to the idea that there were cash flow problems: and his evidence about a series of arrangements with individual creditors to my mind entirely lacked conviction (save in respect of key senior active employees). So that refusal to face and to admit the truth did him no credit. Further, [counsel] succeeded in establishing that in seeking the NHS contract Mr Sutherland put a rosy gloss on his company's financial position in order to demonstrate in the pre-qualification questionnaire an adequate financial standing, exaggerating and confusing resources that were available to Waveform with his personal resources: see paragraphs B7 and B11 of the Expression of Interest of 13 March 2007. His reluctance in the witness box to accept that he had done so (and his suggestion that there were "off the record" assurances to qualify the statements in the procurement documents) did him no credit. But fending off creditors or not being punctiliously truthful in order to secure a large contract on the one hand, and giving evidence under oath on the other, are different things: what is of significance is an unwillingness under oath to accept the true position and a willingness to advance justifications under oath which the witness cannot believe represent the whole truth. Of this, Mr Sutherland was undoubtedly guilty, and it causes me to approach his evidence with very considerable caution. But it does not mean that I simply disbelieve every word he uttered. People tell lies about some issues for a variety of reasons; and much of what he said rang true when he said it, was manifestly true when compared with the documents and was in accordance with the inherent probabilities as I saw them to be.'

EXPERT EVIDENCE

11.43 Breach of warranty claims will usually require expert evidence in at least one field, and commonly more.

11.44 Experts to address quantum, usually forensic accountants, are almost invariably required.[1] Even if the trial is split, early and cooperative input from forensic accountants may assist in avoiding the need for a second hearing.[2]

1 Other expert fields may also be required in relation to quantum but valuation evidence is likely to be the most significant. For example, in *Care Tree Invest 2 Ltd v Bell* [2023] EWHC 1151

(Comm), a trial concerning quantum alone, expert evidence was given both as to the Care Quality Commission regime for assessing care homes and also valuation evidence. It was noted that the valuation evidence was the 'most significant' evidence before the judge (see [41]).

2 See, eg, *The Hut Group Ltd v Nobahar-Cookson* [2014] EWHC 3842 (QB) at [10].

11.45 In addition, expert evidence may be necessary in respect of alleged breaches of warranty. For example, accountancy evidence will often be required for alleged breaches of accounting warranties if they turn on contested issues relating to accounting standards. Industry-specific expertise may also be required in relation to causation arguments concerning post-acquisition conduct and losses.[1]

1 See, eg, *MAN Nutzfahrzeuge AG v Freightliner Ltd* [2005] EWHC 2347 (Comm), in which expert evidence from a motor manufacturing industry expert was called to support the defendant's argument that the buyer had acted in a commercially irrational manner. See in particular [244]–[245].

LIMITATION

11.46 In claims for breach of warranty, the SPA itself will almost invariably provide for a contractual limitation period, usually accompanied by notification requirements to which a putative claimant must adhere. The contractual limitation period for any warranty claims may also apply to misrepresentation claims pursued on a related basis.[1] Notification requirements and contractual time-limits are considered in Chapter 5.

1 See *Bottin v Venson* [2004] EWCA Civ 1368 at [64]–[65], considered at [**5.34**].

11.47 For fraud claims, the Limitation Act 1980, s 32 provides that time only starts to run once the claimant has discovered the fraud or could with reasonable diligence have discovered it. The limitation period is therefore six years from the commencement of the running of time. Proving fraud or deliberate concealment can therefore assist a claimant who has failed to bring a contractual or negligent misrepresentation claim in time.

PARTIES

Joining individual defendants as well as the seller

11.48 In certain circumstances, it may be advantageous for a claimant to join individual defendants as well as the seller. As set out in more detail in Chapter 7 above, an individual is liable in deceit regardless of whether they were acting as a servant or agent.[1] An individual representor will not, however, be liable in negligence in the course of acting for a corporate seller.[2]

1 See [**7.89**], *Standard Chartered Bank v Pakistan Shipping* [2003] 1 AC 959 at [22]–[23].

2 See [**7.07**], *Invertec v de Mol Holdings BV.*

11.49 While it may not be possible credibly to join an individual who is not a party to the SPA in the absence of a proper basis for pleading fraud,[1] joining an individual defendant may be attractive to a claimant who properly considers it has been the victim of a fraud and that the former assets of the selling company are to be found in the hands of the fraudulent individual.

1 Although note it may well be possible to join a disclosed principal who was not a party to the SPA. See, for example, *Bell v Ivy Technology Ltd* [2020] EWCA Civ 1563, which upheld a decision permitting a disclosed principal to be joined as a defendant to claims for breach of warranty and deceit. In considering whether such an individual is liable, it will be necessary to consider the terms of the SPA and any exclusion clauses carefully as these may seek to limit the liability of individuals and entities beyond the named parties. At trial ([2022] EWHC 1218 (Comm)), the disclosed principal, Mr Bell, was held liable on the basis that he made certain representations directly and/or by manifestly approving the making of those representations by Mr Martin but not on the basis that Mr Martin concluded the SPA as agent for Mr Bell (see [488]–[504]).

11.50 A seller may also seek to join individuals as Part 20 defendants so long as such claims are not barred by the terms of the SPA. An interesting example of this can be seen in *Macquarie v Glencore*.[1] The claimant had purchased from the defendant and two other companies the entire share capital of a holding company engaged in the business of supplying gas in the UK. The buyer issued proceedings against the seller for the breach of a number of warranties.

1 [2008] EWHC 1716 (Comm).

11.51 The defendant obtained permission to bring claims against the finance and managing directors of the acquired company, claiming damages for losses suffered as a result of entering into the sale agreement as sole warrantor. It alleged that the individuals were liable for breaches of common law duties of care and fiduciary duties owed to the seller to take reasonable care in the preparation of the company's accounts and the provision of information to the sellers for the purpose of preparing a disclosure letter under the SPA. The basis for the claims was that the individuals had detailed knowledge of the true financial position of the company and knew that the sellers would be required to give warranties in relation to the accounts and were reliant on the accuracy of the information provided to them.

11.52 The finance and managing directors had, however, refused to give personal warranties in the sale agreement and had agreed instead to reduced bonuses under a management incentive agreement. The eventual sale agreement provided that in the event of a claim being made against any of the sellers in connection with the sale, the sellers should not make any claim against the company or any director, employee, agent or officer thereof on whom any of the sellers might have relied before agreeing to any term of the agreement. The agreement also provided that the sellers would not be liable in respect any representation or warranty unless it was made fraudulently.

11.53 Walker J rejected the submission that the clause excluding claims against the target company or directors only related to claims against the directors for acts or omissions carried out in the scope of their employment. The relevant clause was included to ensure the buyer could stop any claim against the seller 'boomeranging' back.[1] He also rejected the suggestion that the clause did not exclude liability for negligence, which he described as 'the obvious claim against the additional defendants, which everyone must have had in mind when cl 6.8 was drafted'.[2] He also held that the Unfair Contract Terms Act 1977, if applicable, could not assist the seller.[3] Accordingly, he held that the seller was not entitled to bring the additional claims.

1 [2008] EWHC 1716 (Comm) at [60].
2 At [70].
3 At [84]–[90].

Claims involving guarantors

11.54 In addition to claims against sellers and fraudulent representors, a buyer may have a claim against individuals or entities which guaranteed obligations given by the seller. Such claims are likely to prove particularly valuable if the seller lacks assets against which any judgment could easily be enforced.

11.55 Guarantors of the buyer may also have claims against the seller if misrepresentations by the seller induced them to guarantee the buyer's obligations in circumstances where that guarantee was called upon.[1]

1 See, eg, *Mellor v Partridge* [2013] EWCA Civ 477.

OTHER RECOURSE

Suing professional advisers

11.56 In addition to any claim for breach of warranty, a buyer may look to professional advisers involved either in the transaction or in preparing or auditing relevant accounts in order to recover losses suffered.[1]

1 See, eg, *Marplace (Number 512) Ltd v Chaffe Street* [2006] EWHC 1919 (Ch), a claim by the buyers of a business alleging professional negligence by their solicitors in, inter alia, the drafting of the SPA. See also *Reichhold Norway ASA v Goldman Sachs International* [2000] 1 WLR 173, a claim by a buyer against the seller's agents for negligent misstatement in relation to information supplied by the agent to the buyer regarding the profitability of the business being sold. The proceedings were, however, stayed pending the resolution of arbitral proceedings in Norway between the buyer and seller.

11.57 It is perhaps an oddity that there are very few reported examples of buyers bringing claims against their own due diligence advisers. It may be that such advisers are often protected by a combination of the seller being the primary target and contractual limitations of liability. A more common target is the accountant or auditor of the acquired business, who had signed off on the target company's accounts.

11.58 It is clear that an auditor does not generally owe any actionable duty of care to any potential or actual stakeholders in the company but only a contractual, and co-extensive tortious, duty to the company itself.

11.59 In *Caparo v Dickman,*[1] the claimant had purchased further shares in the target company and completed a corporate takeover in reliance on the published accounts. The claimant brought an action against the company's auditors alleging that they had been negligent in carrying out the audit and making their report, and claiming that the auditors owed the claimant a duty of care both in their capacity as shareholders and as potential investors. Claims were also brought against the directors of the target company alleging that the accounts had been misleading and inaccurate in a number of respects. The claimant alleged that it would not have acquired the shares at the price paid or at all had the true facts been known.

1 [1990] 2 AC 605.

11.60 In the seminal speech of Lord Bridge, he held that auditors of company accounts do not owe a duty of care to members of the public at large who rely upon the accounts in deciding to buy shares.[1] He also went on to hold that the duty owed by auditors to shareholders concerned the shareholders' interest in the company's proper management of the company. The scope of the duty owed to a shareholder could not extend beyond the protection from losses in the value of the shares that it holds.[2]

1 [1990] 2 AC 605 at 623.
2 At 627.

11.61 In *MAN v Freightliner Ltd,*[1] the buyer brought claims against the seller in deceit and for breaches of warranty. The seller brought Part 20 claims against its auditors for breaches of common law duties of care in carrying out the audits of the target company, breaches of contractual and common law duties of care owed to the seller in connection with the due diligence exercise and for contribution in respect of the buyer's claim against the seller.

1 [2005] EWHC 2347 (Comm), upheld on appeal at [2007] EWCA Civ 910.

11.62 Drawing on *Caparo,* Moore-Bick LJ held at first instance at [326]:

> 'The duty of care owed by the auditors to the shareholders is unusual in a number of respects. It is not owed to shareholders as individuals, but to the shareholders as a body, and is a duty which has as its object the protection of their interest in the proper management of

the company. The damage from which the auditors must take care to protect the shareholders is a diminution in the value of their interest in the company, that is, in the value of their shares, but as Lord Bridge pointed out at page 626D–E, the interest of the shareholders in the proper management of the company is indistinguishable from the interest of the company itself and therefore any loss falling within the scope of this duty that is suffered by the shareholders will be recouped by a claim against the auditors in the name of the company. It follows that neither individual shareholders, nor for that matter the shareholders as a body, can bring an action in their own names to recover that loss. This was one of the points made by the House of Lords in *Johnson v Gore Wood & Co* [2002] 2 AC 1 and may explain why there appears to be no reported case in which shareholders individually or as a body have succeeded in recovering damages for a breach of this duty.'

11.63 He continued at [327]:

'Moreover, it is difficult to see how the loss which Freightliner seeks to recover in this case can be brought within the scope of a general audit duty of this kind. The loss is not one which arises out of the mismanagement of ERF but one which was caused by dishonest statements made by Mr. Ellis on behalf of Western Star in the course of negotiations for the sale of the company. It may be that if E&Y (UK) had carried out its audits of ERF's 1998 and 1999 statutory accounts with proper skill and care his actions would have come to the attention of Western Star, but it does not follow that the loss suffered by Western Star in this case was within the scope of the general audit duty. In my view it was not.'

11.64 Moore-Bick LJ then went on to consider whether a 'special audit duty' was owed, concluding that it was not. In relation to the later set of accounts, he held at [347] that:

'It must have been obvious to Mrs Sinderson, however, both from her knowledge of the fact that it was the parent company of ERF and from her knowledge of the negotiations, that copies of the accounts would be sent by ERF to Western Star as soon as possible, as indeed they were. She could certainly foresee, therefore, and in my view must be taken to have known, that Western Star would itself rely on the accounts in the negotiations with MN as presenting a true and fair view of ERF's financial position. Mere foreseeability is not enough to give rise to a duty of care, however. It is also necessary for there to have been a relationship between the parties of such proximity as to support the conclusion that there was an assumption of responsibility. In this case, therefore, Western Star must show that E&Y (UK) assumed responsibility to it for the accuracy of its audit statement so as to be under a duty to take care to protect it from the kind of loss which Freightliner seeks to recover.'

11.65 On the facts, he held that Western Star could not do so. He also went further and held that the loss the seller was seeking to recover from the auditor was not a consequence of the inaccuracy of the accounts but rather the fraudulent statements made by the relevant individual during the negotiations. Reflecting the *SAAMCO* principle, he held at [351] that:

> '… In neither case could it be said that the loss was of a kind that might be expected to flow from the existence of inaccuracies in the accounts and it is difficult, therefore, to accept that E&Y (UK) assumed a responsibility to protect Western Star from it. Only in the case of the misrepresentation relating to ERF's tax position could it be said that liability was the direct result of a failure to carry out the audit carefully.'

11.66 Upholding the decision on appeal (shortly after the decision of the House of Lords in *Customs and Excise Commissioners v Barclays Bank plc)*, Chadwick LJ held:

> '[55]. In my view the judge was correct to answer that question in the negative. I reach that conclusion for two reasons. First, as it seems to me, there is no factual basis for a challenge to the judge's finding that it was not foreseeable by E&Y that Western Star – and, in particular, Mr Ellis on behalf of Western Star – would make any representations as to the accuracy of ERF's accounts which went beyond, or were outside, those contained in the share purchase agreement. It was foreseeable, as the judge held, that the share purchase agreement would contain representations and warranties. But it would also have been expected, as it seems to me, that Western Star, as seller, would be concerned to limit its exposure to those representations and warranties which were contained in the share purchase agreement. Mr Ellis was an employee of ERF: he was not an officer or employee of Western Star. There was no reason for E&Y to think that Western Star would allow a position to arise in which it was exposed to liability for extra contractual representations made by Mr Ellis.
>
> [56]. Second, mere foresight is not enough, as Freightliner accepts. If authority be needed, it may be found in *Caparo ([1990] 2 AC 605,* 617G– 618B, 628H– 629A, 633F, 655C). Something more is required. In this case (as Freightliner accepts) that additional element is identified by Lord Hoffmann's guidance in relation to assumption of responsibility. Even if (contrary to the judge's finding) E&Y could have foreseen that Western Star might allow a position to arise in which it was exposed to liability for extra-contractual representations

made by Mr Ellis, it is impossible to conclude that the judge was wrong to hold that (viewed objectively) E&Y did not provide their audit statement with the intention that the accounts to which that statement related would be used in that context. To hold that the auditors assumed responsibility for the use which a dishonest employee of the audited company might make of the accounts in the context of the parent company's negotiations for the sale of the company would, I think, be to impose on them a liability greater than they could reasonably have thought they were undertaking. To adapt and apply the test posed by Lord Hoffmann in the Barclays Bank case, it is impossible to hold that E&Y (rather than Western Star) assumed responsibility for the use by Mr Ellis, on behalf of Western Star, of the information which E&Y had provided to Western Star.'[1]

1 [2007] AC 181. See also Chadwick LJ's obiter dictum at [54] to the effect that it was within a special audit duty owed by the auditor to the seller to protect it from the consequences of representations and warranties made in the SPA, which is criticised in S Salzedo and T Singla (eds) *Accountants' Negligence & Liability* (2nd edn, Bloomsbury Publishing, 2021), at 6.33.

11.67 It is clear, however, that there may be circumstances in which an accountant or auditor does owe a duty of care either to the shareholders for purposes other than the management of the company or to a third party because responsibility has been assumed. Such a duty arises most commonly in cases concerning the purchase of companies, usually where the auditor or accountant agrees to communicate directly with the purchaser in order to assist the target company in finding new funding or the target company's shareholder in selling its shares.

11.68 For example, in *Downs v Chappell,*[1] the claimants had acquired a business as a going concern from the first defendant seller. The second defendant was the first defendant's accountant who had verified the figures provided by the seller concerning the turnover and profits generated by the business for the preceding year. The figures were, however, inaccurate and the buyer suffered loss when the business was not as profitable as it had been led to expect. At first instance, the judge had held both defendants liable but found that the claimants had failed to prove their loss. The defendants did not challenge the finding on liability on appeal.[2]

1 [1997] 1 WLR 426.
2 For further examples, see *JEB Fasteners v Marks Bloom & Co* [1983] All ER 583 (the question of duty of care not in issue on the appeal although note the reasoning was questioned by the House of Lords in *Caparo)*; the dissenting judgment of Denning LJ in *Candler v Christmas & Co* [1951] 2 KB 164, endorsed in *Hedley Byrne & Co Ltd v Heller & Partners Ltd* [1964] AC 465 at 506–510, *ADT Ltd v BDO Binder Hamlyn* [1996] BCC 808 (in which the auditor had confirmed at a meeting with the purchaser that it stood by the accounts); and *Yorkshire Enterprise v Robson Rhodes* (unreported, 17 June 1998, Queen's Bench Division).

11.69 Similarly, a further claim against an auditor can be seen in *Galoo Ltd v Bright Grahame Murray.*[1] In addition to the better-known aspects of the case, the buyer of shares claimed that as a result of the auditor's negligence in overstating the company's profits, the buyer had paid more for the shares than it would otherwise have done. The basis for the duty of care was an allegation that when the auditors reported on the 2006 accounts of Galoo, they had known that the purchase price of the company was to be calculated by reference to these accounts. This aspect of the claim was not struck out by the Court of Appeal, which held that the roles of the auditors and the purchaser's own accountants with respect to the completion accounts would need to be investigated at trial.

1 [1994] 1 WLR 1360 at 1382ff.

Warranty and indemnity insurance

11.70 A buyer may have taken out warranty insurance to cover any losses incurred in the event that the warranties given by the seller turn out to be untrue. An example of a claim where warranty insurance was under consideration is *Ageas (UK) Ltd v Kwik-Fit (GB).*[1]

1 [2014] Bus LR 1338.

11.71 Under the SPA, the claimant buyer had obtained various warranties subject to a cap on liability of £5 million. In addition, the claimant had obtained a warranty and indemnity insurance policy with the second defendant for losses in excess of £5 million arising from breaches of warranty. It transpired that the warranties had been breached in relation to an accounting item concerning bad debt. The first defendant admitted liability and settled the claim against it. The second defendant insurer admitted liability but disputed the manner in which damages for breach of warranty fell to be assessed.

11.72 *Finsbury Food Group Plc v Axis Corporate Capital UK Ltd*[1] is a further example of a claim brought by a business buyer against insurers under a warranty and indemnity policy. The policy in question had been issued in connection with the sale and purchase of a specialist food manufacturer by Finsbury pursuant to an SPA. Finsbury's case was that the seller had breached the warranties given in the SPA and that these breaches were covered by the policy. The policy provided that the insurers would indemnify Finsbury for losses that it was entitled to claim against the sellers and warrantors pursuant to the transaction documents for a breach of warranty or would have been able to claim in respect of breaches if certain limitation provisions in the SPA were disregarded. The indemnity was, however, subject to exclusions, including in respect of breaches that were already known to the transaction team at Finsbury or where the breach in question had been disclosed in any of the transaction documents, disclosure letter, due diligence materials or data room.

1 [2023] EWHC 1559 (Comm).

11.73 Issues arose as to: (i) the meaning of the warranties; (ii) whether the seller had breached the warranties; (iii) whether the relevant members of the transaction team had actual knowledge of the relevant matters so as to excuse either the sellers' liability under the SPA or exclude the insurers' obligation to provide an indemnity under the policy; (iv) the warranted and actual values of the target business at the time of the sale; and (v) causation. Ultimately, however, the claim failed as the judge held that the seller had not breached the relevant warranties properly construed.[1]

1 [2023] EWHC 1559 (Comm) at [114]–[140]. The judge further held that the claim would have failed even if he was wrong on these issues as the knowledge exception applied and Finsbury would have purchased the target for £20 million in any event.

COSTS

General costs principles

11.74 The usual costs principles are applicable to claims for fraud and breach of warranty. Thus the court has discretion as to whether costs are payable by one party to another, the amount of those costs and when they are to be paid.[1] The general rule is that the unsuccessful party will be ordered to pay the costs of the successful party, although the court may make a different order.[2]

1 CPR 44.2(1).
2 CPR 44.2(2). For identification of the successful party, see *Kupeli v Kibris Turk Hava Yollari Sirketi* [2019] 1 WLR 1235 at [8]–[15].

11.75 In deciding what, if any, order to make about costs, the court will have regard to all the circumstances including: (i) the conduct of the parties; (ii) whether a party has succeeded on part of its case, even if that party has not been wholly successful; and (iii) any admissible offer to settle made by a party which is drawn to the court's attention, and which is not an offer to which the costs consequences under Part 36 apply.[1]

1 CPR 44.2(4).

11.76 The relevant '*conduct of the parties*' includes: (i) conduct before as well as during the proceedings and in particular the extent to which the parties followed the relevant pre-action conduct practice direction or protocol; (ii) whether it was reasonable for a party to raise, pursue or contest a particular allegation or issue; (iii) the manner in which a party has pursued or defended its case or a particular allegation or issue; and (iv) whether a claimant who has succeeded in the claim in whole or in part exaggerated its claim.[1]

1 CPR 44.2(5).

11.77 The court may also make issue-based costs orders but, before doing so, will consider whether it is practicable to make an order limiting the costs payable to a proportion of the overall costs.[1]

1 CPR 44.2(6) and (7).

11.78 The nature of claims for fraud and breach of warranty arising from share purchase agreements is such that it is common for one party to succeed on some but not all issues. In particular, a claimant may make good its case on some but not all of the breaches of warranty alleged, or may make good its breach of warranty claim but not its deceit claim.

11.79 There are a number of judicial statements on the award of costs in a commercial context where a party has won on some but not all of the issues. The leading decision is that of Jackson J in *Multiplex Constructions (UK) Ltd v Cleveland Bridge UK Ltd (No 7)*, in particular his summary of the principles at [72]:

> '(i) In commercial litigation where each party has claims and asserts that a balance is owing in its own favour, the party which ends up receiving payment should generally be characterised as the overall winner of the entire action.
>
> (ii) In considering how to exercise its discretion the court should take as its starting point the general rule that the successful party is entitled to an order for costs.
>
> (iii) The judge must then consider what departures are required from that starting point, having regard to all the circumstances of the case.
>
> (iv) Where the circumstances of the case require an issue- based costs order, that is what the judge should make. However, the judge should hesitate before doing so, because of the practical difficulties which this causes and because of the steer given by rule 44.3(7).
>
> (v) In many cases the judge can and should reflect the relative success of the parties on different issues by making a proportionate costs order.
>
> (vi) In considering the circumstances of the case the judge will have regard not only to any part 36 offers made but also to each party's approach to negotiations (insofar as admissible) and general conduct of the litigation.
>
> (vii) If (a) one party makes an order offer under part 36 or an admissible offer within rule 44.3(4)(c) which is nearly but not quite sufficient, and (b) the other party rejects that offer outright without any attempt to negotiate, then it might be appropriate to penalise the second party in costs.
>
> (viii) In assessing a proportionate costs order the judge should consider what costs are referable to each issue and what costs are common to several issues. It will often be reasonable for the

overall winner to recover not only the costs specific to the issues which he has won but also common costs.'[1]

1 [2008] EWHC 2280 (TCC).

11.80 Further guidance was provided by Sales J in *F&C Investments (Holdings) Ltd v Barthelemy*:

> '[16] It is frequently a feature of litigation (particularly of complex, hard fought commercial litigation such as in this case) that arguments or factual disputes may be relevant to a number of underlying issues which have to be addressed in the proceedings. It is also frequently the case that a party may rely on a number of grounds to support his claim that he was entitled to take some particular action, and succeed in showing his entitlement so to act (i.e. on one or more of the grounds advanced as justification for the action) while at the same time losing the argument that certain other grounds relied on by him provided a proper basis to justify the action taken …
>
> …
>
> [19] In exercising its discretion as to costs, a court will be cautious before concluding that an award of costs in favour of the party who has won overall should be limited in either of these cases. This is a function of the general approach that courts should avoid an unduly finely detailed division of issues and subissues when deciding what costs orders to make.
>
> [20] The general rule is that the unsuccessful party will be ordered to pay the costs of the successful party: CPR Part 44.3(2)(a). Often it will be appropriate that the winner should get an order that the loser should pay his costs even where there have been issues on which the overall winner has lost [citations omitted]. In commercial litigation, the starting point in working out who the winner is for the purposes of making costs orders will usually be to look at what money has been ordered to be paid: see *Fiona Trust & Holding Corporation v Privalov* [2011] EWHC 664 (Comm) at [36] per Andrew Smith J ("At least in commercial litigation, the party 'who ends up receiving payment' is generally characterised as 'the overall winner of the entire action', citing *Multiplex Constructions (UK) v Cleveland Bridge* [2008] EWHC 2280 (TCC); [2009] 1 Costs LR 55 at [72] per Jackson J).
>
> [21] Parties should be afforded a reasonable degree of latitude in formulating claims, including pleading alternative bases for the same basic claim. That is a normal and reasonable way to conduct litigation (where the parties are operating under conditions of uncertainty about how the court might ultimately react to the arguments and evidence to be heard in support of the claim) and may be a good way of ensuring

that the court has before it the full circumstances of the case so that it is in a position to get to the true heart of the dispute and arrive at what it regards as the just outcome. Therefore, where that is done and the party proceeding in that way has won on his claim and has acted reasonably, it will often be appropriate for a simple costs order to be made in his favour.'[1]

1 [2011] EWHC 2807 (Ch).

11.81 An example of a case with a split result is *Triumph v Primus*.[1] Triumph obtained a substantial damages award in its favour, and it was therefore common ground that Triumph was to be regarded as the 'successful party'. Triumph had, however, advanced a claim for multiple breaches of warranty, as well as a claim for a failure to serve a breach notice prior to completion. It had only succeeded on one of its claims for breach of warranty, although it was entitled to a substantial award of damages as a result.[2]

1 The trial judgment is to be found at [2019] EWHC 565 (TCC). The costs judgment is to be found at [2019] EWHC 2722 (TCC).
2 See summary at [498] of the trial judgment.

11.82 O'Farrell J held at [20] that the circumstances did not require the court to make an issue-based costs order but that a proportional costs order would be appropriate for these reasons:

> '[21] Firstly, the central issue in the case was whether Primus was in breach of the warranties in the SPA, entitling Triumph to damages. Triumph won on that central issue.
>
> [22] Secondly, both parties deployed a number of arguments in respect of each warranty claim and quantum. Every point was fought. Some points were stronger than others but none of the points argued was unreasonable or unarguable. Each party won and lost sub-issues in respect of each part of the case. But Triumph emerged as the victor with an award of substantial damages.
>
> [23] Thirdly, the length and costs of the trial would not have been significantly different had the claim been limited to the FLP Claim. I accept Triumph's submission that there was much common background and the scope of the investigation at trial largely would not have changed. The experts would still have been required to produce their reports and give evidence on the same valuation issues. Most of the key witnesses covered more than one issue or claim. Most of the Operational Warranty Claim evidence was relevant to the FLP Claim.
>
> [24] However, there were discrete areas of evidence arising out of the Nadcap Warranty Claim that took up time in court and would have caused Primus to incur costs in successfully defending the claim that would not have been otherwise incurred. That can be reflected in a proportional costs order.'

11.83 O'Farrell J concluded that Triumph should be awarded 85% of its costs. The decision illustrates that a party that wins on many issues but which is ultimately unsuccessful may well be required to pay a significant proportion of the 'successful' party's costs.

Indemnities may be relevant

11.84 It is worth considering in any given case whether the terms of any indemnities given may be relevant to the question of costs. This will be fact specific but an example can be seen in *Kelly v Baker*,[1] in which the sellers had agreed to waive any claims against any of the target companies, which was defined to include their directors and officers, and to indemnify them in respect of all losses incurred in connection with any such claims. The sellers brought unsuccessful claims against certain of the officers and employees of the target company. Cockerill J noted that given the claim had failed there was limited scope for the indemnity to operate but that 'it may have teeth as regards any shortfall in recovery on assessment of legal costs'.[2]

1 [2022] EWHC 1879 (Comm).
2 See [278]–[280].

Index

[all references are to paragraph number]